GW00417599

International Political Economy Series

General Editor: **Timothy M. Shaw**, Professor of Commonwealth Governance and Development, and Director of the Institute of Commonwealth Studies, School of Advanced Study, University of London

Titles include:

Hans Abrahamsson
UNDERSTANDING WORLD ORDER AND STRUCTURAL CHANGE
Poverty, Conflict and the Global Arena

Morten Bøås, Marianne H. Marchand and Timothy Shaw (*editors*)
THE POLITICAL ECONOMY OF REGIONS AND REGIONALISM

Sandra Braman (*editor*)
THE EMERGENT GLOBAL INFORMATION POLICY REGIME

James Busumtwi-Sam and Laurent Dobuzinskis
TURBULENCE AND NEW DIRECTIONS IN GLOBAL POLITICAL ECONOMY

Elizabeth De Boer-Ashworth
THE GLOBAL POLITICAL ECONOMY AND POST-1989 CHANGE
The Place of the Central European Transition

Bill Dunn
GLOBAL RESTRUCTURING AND THE POWER OF LABOUR

Myron J. Frankman
WORLD DEMOCRATIC FEDERALISM
Peace and Justice Indivisible

Helen A. Garten
US FINANCIAL REGULATION AND THE LEVEL PLAYING FIELD

Barry K. Gills (*editor*)
GLOBALIZATION AND THE POLITICS OF RESISTANCE

Richard Grant and John Rennie Short (*editors*)
GLOBALIZATION AND THE MARGINS

Graham Harrison (*editor*)
GLOBAL ENCOUNTERS
International Political Economy, Development and Globalization

Patrick Hayden and Chamsy el-Ojeili (*editors*)
CONFRONTING GLOBALIZATION
Humanity, Justice and the Renewal of Politics

Axel Hülsemeyer (*editor*)
GLOBALIZATION IN THE TWENTY-FIRST CENTURY
Convergence or Divergence?

Helge Hveem and Kristen Nordhaug (*editors*)
PUBLIC POLICY IN THE AGE OF GLOBALIZATION
Responses to Environmental and Economic Crises

Takashi Inoguchi
GLOBAL CHANGE
A Japanese Perspective

Jomo K.S. and Shyamala Nagaraj (*editors*)
GLOBALIZATION VERSUS DEVELOPMENT

Dominic Kelly and Wyn Grant (*editors*)
THE POLITICS OF INTERNATIONAL TRADE IN THE 21st CENTURY
Actors, Issues and Regional Dynamics

Craig N. Murphy (*editor*)
EGALITARIAN POLITICS IN THE AGE OF GLOBALIZATION

George Myconos
THE GLOBALIZATION OF ORGANIZED LABOUR
1945–2004

John Nauright and Kimberly S. Schimmel (*editors*)
THE POLITICAL ECONOMY OF SPORT

Morten Ougaard
THE GLOBALIZATION OF POLITICS
Power, Social Forces and Governance

Markus Perkmann and Ngai-Ling Sum
GLOBALIZATION, REGIONALIZATION AND CROSS–BORDER REGIONS

Leonard Seabrooke
US POWER IN INTERNATIONAL FINANCE
The Victory of Dividends

Timothy J. Sinclair and Kenneth P. Thomas (*editors*)
STRUCTURE AND AGENCY IN INTERNATIONAL CAPITAL MOBILITY

Fredrik Söderbaum and Timothy M. Shaw (*editors*)
THEORIES OF NEW REGIONALISM

Susanne Soederberg, Georg Menz and Philip G. Cerny (*editors*)
INTERNALIZING GLOBALIZATION
The Rise of Neoliberalism and the Decline of National Varieties of Capitalism

International Political Economy Series
Series Standing Order ISBN 0–333–71708–2 hardcover
Series Standing Order ISBN 0–333–71110–6 paperback
(*outside North America only*)

You can receive future titles in this series as they are published by placing a standing order. Please contact your bookseller or, in case of difficulty, write to us at the address below with your name and address, the title of the series and one of the ISBNs quoted above.

Customer Services Department, Macmillan Distribution Ltd, Houndmills, Basingstoke, Hampshire RG21 6XS, England

Internalizing Globalization

The Rise of Neoliberalism and the Decline of National Varieties of Capitalism

Edited by

Susanne Soederberg
Queens University, Canada

Georg Menz
Goldsmiths College, University of London, UK

and

Philip G. Cerny
Rutgers University, Newark, USA

First published in 2005 by
PALGRAVE MACMILLAN
Houndmills, Basingstoke, Hampshire RG21 6XS and
175 Fifth Avenue, New York, N.Y. 10010
Companies and representatives throughout the world.

PALGRAVE MACMILLAN is the global academic imprint of the Palgrave
Macmillan division of St. Martin's Press, LLC and of Palgrave Macmillan Ltd.
Macmillan® is a registered trademark in the United States, United Kingdom
and other countries. Palgrave is a registered trademark in the European
Union and other countries.

ISBN-13: 978–1–4039–4803–8 hardback
ISBN-10: 1–4039–4803–8   hardback

This book is printed on paper suitable for recycling and made from fully
managed and sustained forest sources.

A catalogue record for this book is available from the British Library.

Library of Congress Cataloging-in-Publication Data

Internalizing globalization : the rise of neoliberalism and the decline of
national varieties of capitalism / edited by Susanne Soederberg, Georg Menz,
and Philip G. Cerny.
    p. cm. —(International political economy series)
Includes bibliographical references and index.
ISBN 1–4039–4803–8 (cloth)
  1. Globalization. 2. Neoliberalism. 3. Capitalism. 4. Economic policy.
I. Soederberg, Susanne, 1966– II. Menz, Georg, 1973– III. Cerny, Philip G., 1946–
IV. International political economy series (Palgrave Macmillan (Firm))

JZ1318.I558 2005
327.1′7′09051—dc22   2005049674

10   9   8   7   6   5   4   3   2   1
14 13 12 11 10 09 08 07 06 05

Printed and bound in Great Britain by
Antony Rowe Ltd, Chippenham and Eastbourne

Contents

List of Tables

Notes on Contributors

Philip G. Cerny   is Professor of Global Political Economy in the Division of Global Affairs and the Department of Political Science at Rutgers University Newark, New Jersey, USA. He studied at Kenyon College (Ohio), the Institut d'Etudes Politiques (Paris) and the University of Manchester (UK) and has previously taught at the Universities of York, Leeds and Manchester in the UK. He is the author of *The Politics of Grandeur: Ideological Aspects of de Gaulle's Foreign Policy* (1980); and *The Changing Architecture of Politics: Structure, Agency and the Future of the State* (1990), and editor or co-editor of six books, including *Finance and World Politics: Markets, Regimes and States in the Post-Hegemonic Era* (1993). He has published articles in *International Organization, International Journal, Government and Opposition, Civil Wars, New Political Economy*, the *European Journal of Political Research*, the *Review of International Studies*, the *European Journal of International Relations* and *Global Governance*. He is co-editor of *Power in Contemporary Politics: Theories, Practices, Globalisations* (2000).

Mark Evans   Professor of Public Policy, Head of the Department of Politics and Provost of Halifax College at the University of York. He is the author of *Constitution-making and the Labour Party* (2003), *Policy-making and Policy Processes* (2003), *Understanding the Europeanisation of British Public Policy* (2002) and *Policy Transfer in Global Perspective* (2004), among others. He is also editor of the international journal *Policy Studies* and Director of the World-wide Universities Public Policy Network.

Bui Duc Hai   is Head of the Department for International Co-operation of the Institute of Social Sciences in Hochiminh City, Vietnam. He is the author of 'The Social Impact of Economic Integration on Farmers in Rural Areas' (*Social Sciences Review*, November 1999), 'Female Workers' Working and Living Conditions in Vietnam–Korean Joint Ventures in the Textile Industry' (2001); the 'Social Integration of Agent Orange (dioxin) War Victims of the Second Generation in Vietnam' (March 2000, HOCP), and *International Donors – Overseas Development Aid and Structural Reform in Vietnam* (2002), among others.

Stephen McBride   is Professor in the Department of Political Science and Director of the Centre for Global Political Economy, Simon Fraser University, Vancouver, Canada. He has published widely on political economy and public policy. His research interests include the impact of neoliberalism and globalization on nation states and the role of labour in the global era. His most recent book is *Paradigm Shift: Globalisation and the Canadian State* (2nd edn 2005).

Paul McVeigh lectures in International Political Economy and European Studies at the University of Portsmouth, UK. He is currently researching Spanish labour market reform and European integration. Publications include: *Economic and Industrial Performance and Policy in Europe since the Oil Crisis* (1995), with David Coates; 'Globalization and national economic strategy: the case of Spain' (*Journal of European Area Studies*, 1999) and (forthcoming) with Peter Starie 'Europe and the United States: Trade, Finance and Development' in Fergus Carr and Andrew Massey (eds) *Public Policy and the Agendas of the New Europe*, 2006.

Georg Menz is Lecturer in Political Economy at Goldsmiths College, University of London. His research interests include international political economy, industrial relations, social and labour market policies, and migration, especially in the European Union. His research has led to publications in the *Journal of European Social Policy, Journal of Ethnic and Migration Studies, Journal of European Public Policy,* and *Politique européenne*. He is the author of *Varieties of Capitalism and Europeanization: National Response Strategies to the Single European Market*, 2005 and *The Future of European Migration and Asylum Policy*, 2006.

Anastasia Nesvetailova is currently a Lecturer in the Department of International Relations and Politics, University of Sussex. Her research interests include the global political economy of credit, international financial crisis, and the process of capitalist evolution in Eastern Europe and the CIS.

Guillermo Ruiz Torres is a doctoral candidate at the Freie Universität in Berlin, and researcher at the Berlin Institute for Comparative Social Research, Germany, where he is currently coordinating a project on 'Roma and the Labour Markets'. He is author of *Democracy and Authoritarism in Peru of the Nineties* (forthcoming). Research interests include state and political system, democratization processes, civil–military relations, and human rights in Latin America.

Susanne Soederberg is a Canada Research Chair of Global Political Economy of Development and Associate Professor in the Development Studies Programme at Queen's University, Kingston, Canada. Research interests include global political economy, international corporate governance, global finance, development theory, and the securitization and privatization of the global aid architecture. She is author of *The Politics of the New International Financial Architecture: Imposed Leadership and the Global South* (2004), and *Global Governance in Question: Empire and the New Common Sense in Managing North–South Relations* (forthcoming 2006).

Sven Steinmo is Professor of Political Science at the University of Colorado at Boulder, USA. Steinmo's research, writing and teaching range broadly in the fields of political economy, comparative politics and policy, and American government. His books include *Structuring Politics* (co-editor) (1992), *Taxation and Democracy* (1993), *Tax Policy* (ed.) (1998) and *Restructuring the*

Welfare State (co-edited with Bo Rothstein) (2002). His current projects include: 'The Land of Milk and Honey: A Short History of America and the People it Created' and 'The Evolution of the Modern State'.

Marcus Taylor   is an Assistant Professor in the Department of Anthropology and Sociology at Concordia University in Montreal. His research interests are development theory, the international division of labour and the political economy of Latin America. Recent publications, appear in *Historical Materialism, Global Social Policy, Latin American Perspectives,* and *Research in Political Economy.* He is author of *From Pinochet to the Third Way? Neoliberalism and Social Transformation in Chile, 1973–2003* (forthcoming 2006).

Abbreviations

ADEX	Asociación de Exportadores (Exporters' Association) (Peru)
AFTA	Asian Free Trade Area
AICs	Advanced Industrialized Countries
AP	People's Action (Peru)
AP	Popular Alliance (Spain)
APRA	Alianza Popular Revolucionaria Americana (American People's Revolutionary Alliance)
BCNI	Business Council on National Issues (Canada)
BDA	Bundesvereinigung Deutscher Arbeitgeberverbände (Federal Association of German Employers)
BDI	Bundesverband der Deutschen Industrie (Federal Association of German Industry)
BIS	Bank for International Settlements
BoJ	Bank of Japan
CDC	Democratic Convergence of Catalonia
CDU	Christliche Demokratische Partei (Christian Democratic Party)
CEMRB	Central Enterprise Management Reform Board (Vietnam)
CETES	Mexican government Treasury bonds
CONFIEP	Confederación Institucional de Empresarios Privados (Institutional Confederation of Private Entrepreneurs) (Peru)
CSB	Central and Southern Europe and the Baltic States
CTM	Industrial workers' union (Mexico)
DETR	Department of the Environment, Trade and the Regions (UK)
DFAIT	Department of Foreign Affairs and International Trade (Canada)
DfEE	Department for Education and Employment (UK)
DGB	Deutscher Gewerkschaftsbund (German Union Federation)
DSS	Department of Social Security (UK)
EMU	European Monetary Union
EPI	Export Promotion Industrialization
ESN	Unified social tax (Russia)
EU	European Union
FDI	Foreign Direct Investment
FDIC	Federal Deposit Insurance Corporation (US)
FDP	Free Democrats (Germany)
FIRA	Foreign Investment Review Agency
FOM	Public Opinion Foundation (Russia)
FONCODES	Fondo Nacional de Cooperación y Desarrollo (National Funds for Cooperation and Development) (Peru)

FPS	Federation of Socialist Parties (Spain)
FRC	Financial Reconstruction Commission (Japan)
FSA	Financial Services Agency (Japan)
G-7	Group of Seven
GATS	General Agreement on Trade in Services
GATT	General Agreement on Tariffs and Trade
GDP	Gross Domestic Product
GKOs	Government short-term bonds (Russia)
ICT	Information and Communications Technology
IDB	Inter-American Development Bank
IEA	International Economic Agreement
IFIs	International Financial Institutions
IMF	International Monetary Fund
IPE	International Political Economy
IPOs	Initial Public Offerings (Japan)
IPRSP	Interim Poverty Reduction Strategy Paper (Vietnam)
ISI	Import Substitution Industrialization
IU	Izquierda Unida (United Left) (Peru)
IWS	Industrial Welfare State
LDP	The Liberal Democratic Party (Japan)
LO	Landsorganisationen (Swedish Trade Union Confederation)
MAI	Multinational Agreement on Investment
MERCOSUR	Mercado Común del Sur (Southern Cone Common Market)
MoF	Ministry of Finance (Japan)
MRTA	Revolutionary Movement Túpac Amaru (Peru)
NAFTA	North American Free Trade Agreement
NEP	National Energy Program (Canada)
OAS	Organization of American States
OFZs	Long-term bonds of the Russian government
PAN	National Action Party (Mexico)
PCE	Spanish Communist Party
PCP	Partido Comunista del Peru (Communist Party of Peru)
PECE	Pact for Economic Stability and Growth
PFI	Private Finance Initiative
PMC	Private Military Contractor
PNV	Basque Nationalist Party
PP	People's Party (Spain)
PPP	Public–Private Partnership
PRD	Party of Democratic Revolution (Mexico)
PRI	Institutional Revolutionary Party
PROGRESA	Program of Education, Health and Nutrition (Mexico)
PRONASOL	Mexican anti-poverty program
PSE	Economic Solidarity Pact (Mexico)
PSOE	Spanish Socialist Workers Party

PSP	People's Socialist Party (Spain)
SAF	Swedish Employer Federation
SAP	Structural Adjustment Program
SEA	Single European Act
SEC	Securities and Exchange Commission (US)
SEM	Single European Market
SIN	Servicio de Inteligencia Nacional (National Intelligence Service) (Peru)
SMEs	Small and Medium-sized Enterprises
SNI	Sociedad Nacional de Industrias (National Society of Industrialists) (Peru)
SOEs	State-Owned Enterprises
SPD	Sozialdemokratische Partei Deutschlands (Social Democratic Party of Germany)
SUNAT	Superintendencia Nacional Tributaria (Peruvian national tax office)
TEA	Trade Enhancement Agreement (Canada)
TINA	'There Is No Alternative'
TNCs	Transnational Corporations
TPRM	Trade Policy Review Mechanism
TRIPs	Trade Related Intellectual Property Rights
UCD	Union of Democratic Centre (Spain)
UDC	Democratic Union of Catalonia (later CiU, Convergence and Union)
UGT	General Workers' Union (Spain)
VCP	Vietnamese Communist Party
WTO	World Trade Organization

1

Different Roads to Globalization: Neoliberalism, the Competition State, and Politics in a More Open World

Philip G. Cerny, Georg Menz, and Susanne Soederberg

1. Globalization and political action

Internalizing globalization is about how people are changing their domestic political worlds in the context of growing complex interactions – economic, social, and political – across national borders. Globalization itself is in turn reshaped by and through local conditions and domestic political objectives; it is not just imposed from outside. It starts from the competing goals of people in everyday politics and economics – especially over the meaning and character of the 'general welfare', as the Preamble to the United States Constitution terms it – and seeps into the deepest nooks and crannies of everyday life. International and domestic politics are therefore *not* two separate arenas, but parts of an interpenetrated set of webs of politics and governance that increasingly cut across and entangle the nations of the world, summoning forth and molding the actions of ordinary people. Globalization affects how giant corporations and small firms alike go about their business; how politicians and bureaucrats build (and rebuild) coalitions and generate public policies; how people work and get paid; how consumers decide what to buy, or whether they have the resources to participate in consumer society at all; and how people in general get to know and understand a rapidly changing world.

Globalization as a highly contested concept

Globalization is itself a highly contested concept. It is most often viewed as primarily concerning external economic changes and how these constrain domestic actors, undermine the state's capacity to make economic and social

1

policy, and put international capital in the driving seat. It is therefore seen as being imposed both from the 'top down' and from the 'outside in'. In this book, by way of contrast, we argue that globalization is also 'bottom up' and 'inside out'. People increasingly act both individually and collectively – in personal life and in social life, in interest groups, ethnic and value groups, classes and 'fractions' of classes, in both public and private sectors – by attempting to manage, manipulate, and 'own' diverse processes of globalization in order to defend their interests and pursue their goals. Thus they seek to *internalize* globalization, and in doing so they accelerate it and embed it further in their own institutions and practices. This process in turn propels, magnifies and, indeed, reshapes and reorganizes how technology, trading patterns, production systems, financial markets, and the like, impact on politics and society.

Growing interdependence and the transgressing of boundaries between local, domestic, transnational, and international playing fields increasingly enmesh individuals, classes, interest groups, ethnicities, nations, and institutions of all kinds in social, political, and economic processes that are both unfamiliar and yet at the same time intimately entangled in everyday life. Actors seek not merely to avoid losses and consolidate gains in the short term, but also to alter those playing fields themselves – political processes and institutions – within and upon which they act in the longer term. They seek to capture the benefits of globalization, both for the economy and society in general, and also for their more local and personal constituencies and coalition-building activities. They do this through politics, that is, through the gaining, maintaining, exercising – and restructuring – of political power.

Complexity, convergence, and diversity

One theme that keeps recurring in this book is *complexity*. In order to internalize globalization people must face a growing diversity of playing fields and a widening repertoire of potential proactive responses and strategic possibilities – even while the world is 'shrinking' in terms of communications, ideas, social and economic interactions, and politics. This book, like other contributions to this debate, sees convergence and divergence as happening together, locked in an intimate embrace or dialectic (cf. Huelsemeyer, 2003). The difference between this book and most other work focused on already contrasting national models – the 'path dependency' approach, emphasizing continuities – is that the authors here, however, argue that what is going on is a process of diversity *within* convergence.

In contrast to what is called the 'varieties of capitalism' literature (e.g., Zysman, 1983; Berger and Dore, 1996; Crouch and Streeck, 1997; Hall and Soskice, 2001), we attempt to demonstrate that globalization is essentially a *political process* of convergence. The core of that convergence is increasingly found in the discourse and practice of neoliberalism and in the restructuring of domestic political institutions and practices around the competition state – both defined later in this chapter. At one level, the economic dimensions of globalization constitute *necessary but not sufficient conditions* for change. More than that, however, they actually create a range of 'permissive conditions' for change where alternative outcomes – 'multiple equilibria' – are possible. Nevertheless, within this diversity, neoliberalism is not only becoming hegemonic, but is itself evolving too – from raw market orthodoxy in the 1980s to various attempts to innovate new forms of what we call 'social neoliberalism' in the twenty-first century.

Most discussions of globalization as such focus on economic changes at the international level. This includes the globalization of financial markets; the expansion of world trade at rates several times faster than growth in output; the internationalization of production chains, especially around the activities of multinational corporations; the expansion of foreign direct and portfolio investment; the development of new technologies that create direct linkages and networks of communication and information across and below borders; and the increasing salience of international regimes and so-called 'global governance' to deal with consequent dislocations and to promote 'structural adjustment' to these more strictly economic and material trends.

In this context, political institutions, processes and actors at the regional, national and sub-national levels have been seen as more or less directly constrained by such economic trends to converge on neoliberal economic policies. Neoliberal policies therefore are normally viewed as including the freeing up and deregulation of markets; the shrinking and hollowing out of the state in terms of industrial and welfare policies; privatization; financial orthodoxy and the fight against inflation; and a shift from government accountability to domestic electorates towards various kinds of less formal 'governance' that give internationally competitive businesses a privileged position (Lindblom, 1977) in shaping the role of the state and of interstate processes and institutions.

Of course, not all outcomes are possible. Real material constraints – and opportunities – may make it possible for political actors to pursue different roads to globalization and to manipulate a range of growing divergences in order to manage and shape change in line with their political projects – but those different roads still constitute roads to globalization. Although there may be room for maneuver, there is nevertheless no going back to insulated, autonomous, abstractly sovereign nation-states able to craft their own national models according to wholly domestic conceptions of social justice, natural hierarchies, corporatist social pacts, eternal values, or whatever.

From sovereignty to webs of politics

Indeed, this latter myth of the nation-state and of sovereignty, however important in the past in shaping modernity, is becoming increasingly counter-productive. The concept of sovereignty is usually thought of as having two interlocking dimensions. In the first place, whoever is – or whatever institutions are – sovereign are those that constitute the highest overarching level of both *legitimate* and *effective* rule, power, or control within a particular state (see Thomas Hobbes's *Leviathan*). The 'sovereign' was at first indeed the monarch as a person, although at the time of the French Revolution it was thought to pass to the people as a whole – 'popular sovereignty'. This dimension of sovereignty is therefore *endogenous* to the particular state. The second dimension is *exogenous*, that is, the effective situation when different sovereign rulers or institutionalized actors *recognize each other's sovereignty*. These two dimensions of sovereignty are mutually dependent and reinforcing, giving the state *per se* an exclusive and solidaristic kind of supreme power unmatched in any other part of the domestic or international political system.

But whatever its formal-legal status, sovereignty can never be taken for granted. It is a political project, characterized by conflict and compromise, and is never finally achieved (James, 1986; Krasner, 1999). Indeed, sovereignty today is usually viewed as much more complex – less externally exclusive and internally hierarchical, and more shared, 'pooled', and divided among different levels of governance and nodes of political activity and authority. Exclusive sovereignty is losing its effectiveness as a political tool today. In terms of security, territorial stalemate and multilateralism constrain it from above, while pressures form transnationally linked business and other interest groups, ethnic and religious conflict, civil wars, terrorism, and demands for local and regional autonomy, undermine it from below (Cerny, 2000d).

In particular, crises and collapses in postcolonial states are undermining claims that national sovereignty creates political stability, democratization and welfare; indeed, in weak or divided states, it can lead to just the opposite and become a site of endemic conflict and even a tool of oppression. International economic interdependence, too, means that endogenous national development strategies and welfare priorities are being discarded by today's modernizing elites for integration into a more open, post-Fordist, 'flexibilized' world. Indeed, the fastest growing areas of the world today are those that have become most dependent on their links with the world economy to drive that growth.

In this context, the state is not simply 'retreating' (Strange, 1996); indeed, in many ways the state is continuing to develop and to extend its authority. What is different, as we will argue below, is that its *mode* of authority is changing. Rather than giving priority to the direct provision of domestic welfare, direct support for and ownership of key strategic industries and infrastructural services, maintenance of full employment, and the redistribution of resources among individuals and social groups, the state is becoming a 'competition state'. While this process of change challenges many of the ways the nation-state developed in the nineteenth and twentieth centuries and seeks to draw back and hollow out the state at some levels, at others it can significantly expand and deepen various old and new roles of the state – substituting regulation for redistribution (Cerny, 1990; Moran, 2003), attracting rather than shunning foreign capital, marketizing and privatizing (commodifying) economic and social activities, and enmeshing the state in cross-border and extraterritorial economic and legal institutions and practices.

This kind of change is not monolithic but often fragmenting, pluralizing, and experimental – necessarily driven by short-term as well as medium- and long-term political priorities, often flying blind with only untested theories and hunches to go by, and characterized by attempts to reconcile perceived global 'realities' with the real constraints of domestic pressures, interests, and values. Thus political actors, to paraphrase Marx, are making history, but not in conditions of their own choosing.

2. What is globalization?

Definitions

There are almost as many definitions as there are scholars and actors writing and thinking about globalization. However, we will focus here on three basic categories: essentialist or teleological definitions; narrow economic definitions; and 'additive' or 'interactive' definitions of globalization as a political process.

In the first place, we find extremely broad, macro-social definitions derived from images of some sort of 'end state' of a truly globalized world, and which contend that globalization is a process of moving towards that condition. In particular, the concept of the world as becoming a single social, economic, and political space is a powerful metaphor. Probably the best known of these definitions in academic terms are those of Kenichi Ohmae, Jan Aart Scholte, and Roland Robertson. Ohmae (1990) argues that we are moving towards a 'borderless world'. Trade, finance, production, consumption, regulation, and the like will eventually operate within a seamless playing field. National governments, in this context, will simply progressively lose their capacity to adapt and shape economic activities to national or local conditions.

Scholte (2000) argues that globalization means 'deterritorialization'. Territorial forms of governance and politics are in ongoing tension with economic, political, and social activities that are increasingly deterritorialized; however, more and more activities come into the second category. Roland Robertson writes: '[W]e may best consider contemporary globalization in its most general sense as a form of institutionalization of the two-fold process involving the universalization of particularism and the particularization of universalism' (Robertson, 1992: 102). In all three cases, the process is a teleological one that encompasses and incorporates the world in general in an immanent transformation of its very economic and sociological essence.

At the other end of the spectrum lies a range of narrow definitions that identify quite specific economic processes and attempt to evaluate their impact on key features of the international and domestic political economy. Given their methodological congruence with economic statistics, these definitions have the advantage that they can more easily be operationalized in terms of formal economic theory and quantitative data. As noted earlier, these definitions usually attempt to evaluate globalization by testing hypotheses about the direct effect of the growth of international trade interdependence, the integration and expansion of international financial markets, the expansion and interlinking of international production chains and multinational firms, and the rapid development of new technologies. However, the authors in this book argue, globalization is not a process that can be logically or empirically derived from particular economic data or trends; indeed, political decisions (and non-decisions: Strange, 1986) are themselves the source of such trends. They also shape these trends as they develop, and determine what sort of complex multiple equilibria result from them.

The third category, 'additive' or 'interactive' definitions, sees globalization as the complex interaction of a range of uneven – sometimes even incompatible – trends that, lumped together, lead to the growth of new multidimensional and multilayered forms of politics, above, cutting across, and below the nation-state, enmeshing states in uneven global political webs. These webs involve both a newer and wider range of political playing fields – often called 'multi-level governance' – and of cross-cutting processes of politicking – which we call 'multi-nodal politics' – that together constitute globalization *as a political process* (Cerny, 2003a).

Globalization in this context is the sum total of the wide range of political, economic, and social processes of 'transnationalization' and 'internationalization' taking place in the world today – and their dynamic interaction over time. By *internationalization* we mean the development of formal and informal mechanisms of cooperation and integration *among states*, whether rooted in treaties, formal institutions, international regimes, common norms, cultural responses, or regularized 'practices' among state actors – sometimes referred to as the development of 'international society'. By *transnationalization*, we mean the development of a wide range of formal and informal structures and processes among so-called '*behind-the-border actors*', including 'private' economic institutions and market structures such as firms, trade associations, private regimes, and so on; socio-political organizations and associations such as pressure groups, non-governmental organizations (NGOs), transnational advocacy networks, and so on; and socio-cultural linkages, from the mass media's 'global village' from above to the intensification of various forms of cross-border ethnic, religious and other social identity structures from below.

Multi-nodal politics

Globalization therefore gives rise to multi-nodal politics. Multi-nodal politics is, in effect, an extension of an old idea in Political Science – that of pluralism, or, more recently, 'neopluralism' (Lindblom, 1977). To understand the politics of globalization, therefore, involves examining the way that coalition-building processes and other forms of *politicking* adapt in order to pursue those interests and values on a globalizing set of inextricably intertwined playing fields. A significant premium therefore attaches to flexibility – and flexibilization – of strategy, tactics, and organization. Groups and political entrepreneurs must be able to operate – and effectively to coordinate the actions of themselves and others – at all the levels of multi-level governance, *navigating* effectively back and forth among them. They must be able to organize locally, regionally, nationally, and globally. They must be in a position to negotiate cooperative arrangements both domestically and transnationally. And they must be able to operate horizontally, vertically, diagonally, and so on, across and around those playing fields.

At the same time, this also means that institutional actors – bureaucrats and policymakers at various levels of governance – must be able to negotiate flexibly too if they are effectively to plan, coordinate, and manage the processes of policy-making and policy implementation. The ability of decision-makers to shift back and forth, up and down, among various levels of 'plurilateral' negotiations, to coordinate myriad diverse actions, to negotiate ever more complex bargains, and to bring wider and more disparate coalitions into potentially tenuous forms of collective action, will be at the highest premium (Slaughter, 2004).

This, of course, does not simply mean organizing top-down authority in new ways. Indeed, it means moving away from hierarchical modes of decision-making and implementation. It means experimenting with systematic networking, the diffusion and delegation of authority, self-regulation, the use of performance indicators rather than the direct provision of public services, contracting out, redefining 'public goods' in ways that permit more quasi-public or mixed goods to be provided through mixed public–private mechanisms, and so on. To some analysts, this also means building in self-regulating or cybernetic, autopilot-like mechanisms to lighten the load and keep the show on the road. More broadly, it means that groups have to be co-opted rather than coerced, that a wider range of 'stakeholders' – people who see themselves as having a stake in the success of a particular process or institution – has to emerge, and that decentralized processes like markets, *ex post* litigation, and democratization have to be built in and regulated (a theme to which we will return later).

When did 'globalization' take off?

Finally, we cannot leave the issue of globalization without speaking about its periodization. Can we identify when it started and what phases it has gone through? We suggest that four phases can be identified in each of which international and domestic trends intertwine in distinct ways: the 'Long Boom' from the late 1940s to the late 1960s; the recession of the 1970s;

early neoliberal revival of the 1980s; and the more complex forms of neoliberal hegemony since the early 1990s.

The Long Boom after the Second World War followed half a century in which the international political economy had been dominated by the politics of national capitalism and the prioritization of domestic and autarchic (self-sufficiency-oriented) approaches to 'late industrialization' and economic development – from the autarchic empires of Nazism, Fascism, Japan's Greater East Asian Co-Prosperity Sphere, Stalinism, and so on. Indeed, the early stages of the New Deal in the United States, as well the beginnings of import substitution industrialization (ISI) in Latin America, involved versions of such 'domesticist' approaches. Trade closure, 'beggar-thy-neighbor' policies, and imperial expansionism to bring raw materials and markets under the same bureaucratic umbrella became the rule. However, the liberal, pro-free trade – so-called 'internationalist' – forces within the Roosevelt Administration developed a strategy in the mid-1930s that they carried through America's Economic War Aims and the Bretton Woods Conference of 1944 to reshape the Postwar Era in a more open, liberal fashion (Gardner, 1964; Penrose, 1953).

The postwar period, dubbed the 'embedded liberal compromise' by John Ruggie (1982), involved combining domestic Keynesianism and the welfare state – especially 'fine tuning' of the economy, macroeconomic demand management, indicative planning, and full employment – with the reduction of tariff protectionism and eventually the convertibility of major currencies in a much more open international, but not yet global, political economy. Embedding, in this context, mainly meant (a) closely involving both producer and consumer interest groups and building coalitions to support continued international economic opening rather than returning to protectionism (in effect, internalizing embedded liberalism), and (b) establishing a set of rules, institutions, and practices in both domestic governance and international regimes that would counteract any tendencies to return to closure. By the 1960s a far more interdependent international political economy had emerged, rooted in these domestic coalitions and practices.

However, this interdependence was to be sorely tested by crucial events and trends from the mid-1960s to the early 1980s. American support for the Bretton Woods dollar-based 'adjustable peg' exchange rate regime proved to be fragile as the US developed a chronic balance-of-payments deficit and eventually a trade deficit. The resulting 'dollar glut' or 'dollar overhang' led to a decade of international challenges to the role and value of the dollar, exacerbated by spending on the Vietnam War, and eventuating in the removal of the dollar's link with gold in 1971 – 'closing the gold window' (Gowa, 1983). The subsequent move to floating exchange rates, initiated a massive increase in already growing international capital flows. The United States was accused of abandoning its internationalist role and becoming a 'predatory hegemon', provoking new 'beggar-thy-neighbor' responses elsewhere too.

The oil crises of 1973–74 and 1979–80, along with instability in other inter-national commodities markets, only exacerbated the sense of international economic destabilization. Although the word 'globalization' was rarely used at this stage, observers began to write about 'complex interdependence' (Keohane and Nye, 1977) and called the United States an 'Eagle Entangled' (Oye and Rothchild, 1979) in webs of international political economy.

At the same time, the postwar consensus was unraveling domestically in Europe and the US as economic stagnation and eventually recession set in alongside a growth in inflation – called 'stagflation'. A 'New Protectionism' was called for, using quotas, voluntary export limitation agreements, domes-tic content rules, infant industry protection, subsidies for declining industries threatened by imports, and so on – rather than tariffs – while 'overloaded governments' at first sought to counteract the recession through more neo-corporatism and reflationary spending. Industrial policies emphasized sup-port for 'national champion' industries, copying Japan's state-led form of development. Many Third World countries increased their international indebtedness in a rush to develop along the lines of state-led import substi-tution industrialization (ISI), and the Soviet Union and Eastern Europe mainly abandoned their experiments at liberalization under Leonid Brezhnev's stag-nating bureaucratic rule. 'Domesticism' rather than internationalism was back in fashion for a time.

As the recession spread in the mid-1970s, however, crisis and instability grew. As inflation increased, interest rates went up dramatically but became negative in real terms; wage increases – often negotiated in bitter disputes that undermined the postwar mood of consensus – could not keep up with inflation; government reflationary spending had less and less impact on growth (what Sir Keith Joseph called the 'ratchet effect', as reflation simply led to more inflation); world trade continued to stagnate; and 'hot money' sought refuge in speculation rather than unprofitable investment. Advanced capitalist countries were seized by a new 'malaise', while many Third World countries became mired in hyperinflation, debt, bureaucratic expansion, crony capitalism, and military coups. Some of them sought to further ISI, while others prefigured some aspects of economic neoliberalism mixed with dictatorship, as in the 11 September 1973 coup in Chile.

In this context, academic commentators and policymakers alike, along with sections of the mass public and a range of interest groups and political party factions, began to look for solutions that would *both* reinvigorate the world economy and counteract stagflation at home. In the United Kingdom and the United States, what we now think of as early neoliberalism (called 'conservatism', but actually a radical form of economic liberalism) combined financial orthodoxy – especially the priority given to beating inflation – with deregulation and attempts to reduce the role of the state interventionism and spending, on the one hand, with the lifting of capital controls and a move away from the new protectionism and towards trade expansion, on the other. As Eric Helleiner has argued, the 're-emergence of global finance' (Helleiner, 1994) was not the result of a spontaneous market expansion but rather of specific decisions taken by governments attempting to kick off a virtuous cycle of investment by freeing up international finance; Susan Strange also attributed the resurgence of 'casino capitalism' (Strange, 1986) to both decisions and 'non-decisions' by governments, especially the United States.

With regard to the Third World, the World Bank and the International Monetary Fund adopted a neoliberal perspective using the conditions attached to their loans ('conditionality') to impose Structural Adjustment Policies (SAPs) that prescribed severe anti-inflationary measures, deregulation, privatization, and the like, on borrowing countries. In the trade issue area, moves were begun that led to the opening of the Uruguay Round trade talks in 1986 and eventually to the establishment of the World Trade Organization in 1994. Individual countries like New Zealand went farther in their neoliberal zeal (see Chapter 3), and even the European Community (later the European Union) got on the bandwagon with the Single Market Act in 1986.

Thus globalization as we know it was an evolving political dialectic at several increasingly intertwined levels:

- international and domestic crises that undermined the postwar embedded liberal consensus;
- domestic and transnational interests, pressures, and shifting coalitions, caught in the vise of the 'ratchet effect', 'stagflation', and 'overloaded governments';
- the resurgence of the belief that domestic economic problems could only be addressed in the longer term through international – global – economic expansion;
- specific state policy decisions to liberalize both domestic and international policy regimes;
- a move away from redistributive state interventionism to arm's-length regulation (see below);
- the growth, dynamism, and integration of newly prioritized international markets; and
- the emergence of multi-level global governance and a new multi-nodal global politics.

The result, as we shall argue below, was the spread of a hegemonic 'embedded neoliberalism'.

3. What is neoliberalism?

From liberalism to neoliberalism

Neoliberalism is a recent concept and is open to several often conflicting interpretations. It has primarily taken on two distinct and partly contradictory definitions, to a large extent reflecting the historical ambiguity of its main precursor, 'liberalism'. Liberalism is itself a complex mixture of meanings, reflecting the ambiguity of its central referent, the notion of liberty and, in particular, the centrality of the individual, rather than of a more holistic conception of society. In continental Europe, the notion of liberalism has tended to retain much of this fundamental anti-statist meaning, and is seen to a large extent as a political philosophy of the capitalist right. American 'liberalism', in contrast, is a label for the moderate centre-left; in Australia, this latter version of liberalism has long been referred to as 'social liberalism'.

In international relations and international political economy liberalism – and, today, neoliberalism – can also be seen as having two distinct meanings. The first of these originally derives from the quasi-idealist tradition of 'liberal internationalism' that was associated with the legacy of Woodrow Wilson and the League of Nations. Liberal internationalism involved the construction of international – intergovernmental – institutions made up of sovereign states, the provision of 'collective security', and the expansion of international law along relatively liberal lines. The United Nations' Universal Declaration of Human Rights is seen as a key document in this tradition, along with UN sponsorship of development, health, food and housing programs, and the like.

The establishment of the Bretton Woods system of international economic institutions at the end of the Second World War is also seen to represent international economic liberalism – what John Gerard Ruggie called the postwar system of 'embedded liberalism'. However, Ruggie's analysis went much further, linking international economic liberalism with American-style domestic liberalism (or European-style social democracy) through Keynesian macroeconomic policies, the welfare state, German-style neocorporatism, French-style indicative planning, the Bretton Woods system, and elements of the postwar consensus (Ruggie, 1982). It is this latter sort of domestic, interventionist liberalism that today's neoliberalism opposes.

Neoliberalism *versus* neoliberal institutionalism

It is worth making a brief detour here, to deal with a different use of the term neoliberalism in the study of international relations. Robert O. Keohane, in particular, has referred to 'neoliberal institutionalism'. Neoliberal institutionalism was a concept developed out of 'regime theory' and posited that the development of the international system since the Second World War was characterized primarily by a general but rather *ad hoc* proliferation of international regimes, whether broad (Ruggie's the 'regime of embedded liberalism') or narrow, dealing with particular issue areas – the International Monetary Fund, the General Agreement on Tariffs and Trade, the International Labor Organization, specialized organizations for the law of the sea, shipping, intellectual property, and so on. Indeed, by the 1980s, according to Keohane, the hegemony of a leading power or national economy was in the process of being replaced by system or regimes (Keohane, 1984) – a sort of more pragmatic, economically-oriented liberal internationalism.

In contrast, the second use of the term 'neoliberal' – as it is increasingly used in the study of political economy today – is quite different, being derived from the continental European conception of liberalism, that is, 'nineteenth century' or 'classical' liberalism. The key to understanding this way of thinking about neoliberalism is the assertion that the *market* is the core institution of modern – capitalist – societies and that both domestic and international politics and policy-making are (and *should be*) primarily concerned with making markets work well.

Neoliberalism and marketization

This overriding policy goal has several component parts. In the first place, it is said to be necessary to design and to establish institutions and practices that are market-based and market-led. This objective is important not only with regard to more developed capitalist countries, but also for so-called 'transition' (ex-Communist) states and for the developing world. Secondly, it is thought to be crucial to instil a culture of individualistic, market-orientated behavior in people of all social classes, counteracting the 'dependency culture' of the Keynesian welfare state – blamed for the slump of the 1970s – by 'ending welfare as we know it' (Bill Clinton) and deregulating the labor market, what Jessop calls the 'Schumpeterian workfare state' (1994).

Thirdly, governments themselves and international institutions too should be imbued with market-friendly attitudes and practices – whether 'reinventing government' (Osborne and Gaebler, 1992), privatizing social and public services, promoting international competitiveness, deregulating and liberalizing specific markets or sectors, and/or using international aid and regulation to promote marketization through 'conditionality'. The concept of rule-based 'good governance' would replace top-down state authority. Fourthly, barriers to international trade and capital flows should be progressively dismantled. The most efficient markets, in theory, are those with the largest numbers of buyers and sellers, so that an 'efficiency price' can be established that will 'clear the market'. The latter means that all the goods offered for sale will be purchased at a mutually acceptable price. Therefore the most efficient markets, according to neoliberals, ought to be world markets because they include the largest numbers of market actors.

4. From 'embedded liberalism' to 'embedded neoliberalism'?

This second type of neoliberalism developed from the domestic conservative – neoliberal – programs of successful political actors in the 1970s and 1980s such as Margaret Thatcher and Ronald Reagan, and from the return to fashion in academic economics of the theories of free market economists such as Milton Friedman in the United States or more intellectual policymakers like

Sir Keith Joseph in the United Kingdom. But the real springboard for their newfound intellectual hegemony was the experience of crisis in the post-Second World War economic order, both domestic and international.

Policy shifts in the 1970s and 1980s

The crisis of the 1970s (actually from the late 1960s to the early 1980s), briefly discussed earlier, had several dimensions. The first was the 'fiscal crisis of the state' (O'Connor, 1973), in which the budgetary costs of social policies, public services, nationalized industries and bureaucracies were seen to grow faster than the tax base. This dimension, after contrasting twists and turns by successive governments in different countries, led neoliberals to propose the reduction of tax rates and government services with the aim of producing additional economic growth that would result in higher tax payments despite lower rates ('supply side policy'). Second was the issue of 'social partnership' or 'neocorporatist' arrangements – usually tripartite, state supported institutions or negotiating fora, bringing together management, labor and bureaucrats – that had become increasingly important in the 1960s for negotiating wages, working conditions, hiring and firing of workers, and so on. The 'stickiness' of wages in an inflationary context – leading to wage-price spirals – and the slowdown in investment were blamed for economic stagnation, leading to proposals to deregulate labor markets and end the postwar political emphasis on full employment.

International and domestic economic conditions changed dramatically too from the reduction in the growth rate of world trade in the 1970s and an alarming rise in the new protectionism to increasing stagflation. There was a fear of a return to the vicious circle of the sort of protectionist economic policies that were seen to have deepened the Great Depression of the 1930s. Most salient, was the breakdown of the 'adjustable peg' system of managed exchange rates. Endemic exchange rate crises that had first led to the end of the dollar's link to gold (1971–73) were dramatically exacerbated by the Yom Kippur War of 1973–74 and the fourfold rise of oil prices that resulted. In particular, the recycling of the 'petrodollars' earned by oil-producing countries, especially through the Euromarkets in London, fuelled inflationary pressures, leading to interest rate rises and the explosion of Third World debt, entrenching the deepest recession since the 1930s.

The ideological and cultural glue that the 'long boom' from the early 1950s to the early 1970s had reinforced – accepted even by most conservative parties in the 1950s, 1960s, and early 1970s – dissolved. Various middle class groups and, indeed, fractions of the working class began to vote for parties and leaders promoting the new brand of economically neoliberal 'conservatism'. Forty two per cent of trade unionists in Britain voted Conservative in the key election of 1979 that brought Margaret Thatcher to power, while in the United States the working-class 'Reagan Democrats' also became part of the new neoliberal consensus.

The British Labour Party and the Democratic Party in the United States subsequently moved distinctly to the right in order to recapture the center ground, with labels like 'New Labour', the 'New Democrats', and the 'Third Way'. The failure of much of the 'socialist' (i.e., state capitalist) program of French President François Mitterrand, elected in 1981, to pull France out of the slump led to his administration partly reversing, although much of French statism has remained in watered-down form (Schmidt, 2000). Germany and Japan are still in the midst of this transformation. The European Union has been seen as a driving force of neoliberalization too, especially in terms of competition policy and the development of the single market after 1985.

This process was of course not limited to the developed world. Much worse stagnation in the 1970s and 1980s in Soviet Bloc countries alienated many of the same groups – leading to the protests that brought down the Berlin Wall in 1989 and ended the Cold War, and thereafter to a wide variety of neoliberal experiments throughout the so-called 'transition countries'. And bureaucratic authoritarian governments in the developing world, especially those mired in the debt crisis of the early 1980s, found their quasi-nationalist, quasi-socialist coalitions dissolving in hyperinflation and crony capitalism. The rapid industrialization taking place in many transition and developing countries, fuelled by globalization, created a demand for neoliberal policy innovations, broke up old socio-political coalitions, and laid the ground-work for new coalitions to emerge seeking to mobilize both existing and potential new supporters.

Severe social disruptions resulted, especially when particular socio-economic groups became unemployed and impoverished, whether in developed countries or, more sweepingly, in those developing countries that suffered most from overextended and/or collapsed states, deteriorating terms of trade (especially the 'commodity trap' whereby raw materials declined in relative value), political divisions along communal or class lines, and so on. Endemic financial and economic crises from the Latin American debt crisis of 1982 to the Asian and Russian crises of 1997–98 and the Argentine crisis of 2001–02 demonstrate that adjustment to neoliberal policies and structural reforms can be a very painful and politically divisive experience. At the same time, attempts to articulate and construct alternatives to neoliberalism have also been ineffectual and often incoherent, at least in practice. Mrs Thatcher famously said that 'there is no alternative' and that 'you can't buck the markets'.

5. Dimensions of the neoliberal consensus

So what are the core dimensions of neoliberalism? At least four can be identified. However, as the following chapters reveal, the precise combination of policy measures and the degree of convergence along each dimension in different geographical areas (especially national political systems) depends upon the configuration of (a) existing domestic institutions and practices, (b) the stance of interest groups both national and international (and the linkages between groups across borders), and (c) the impact and interpenetration of the growing international and transnational public and mixed private/public sectors.

Toward a more open world economy

The first dimension, the one most directly related to the development of the post-Second World War international political economy, involves reducing barriers to trade and capital flows. Negotiations under the aegis of the General Agreement on Tariffs and Trade in 1947 led to several rounds of tariff reductions and, from the 1970s onward, attempts to tackle non-tariff barriers too. The transformation of the GATT into the World Trade Organization in 1994, along with the negotiation of a range of regional and bilateral trade agreements, have indicated that despite great unevenness and some backward steps, free trade is in many ways the core building block of both embedded liberalism and later neoliberalism. This transformation has been accompanied by a growing consensus that new trade barriers lead to a vicious circle of retaliation, leaving all participants worse off, whereas free trade, so long as it does not lead to serious short-term structural disruption, is a long-term public good benefiting poor as well as rich countries by creating a virtuous circle of economic development and growth.

Furthermore, since the collapse of the adjustable peg exchange rate regime in 1971–73, several factors have led to a multiplication of cross-border capital flows. In particular, the combination of floating exchange rates, the globalization of financial markets, and the failure of import substitution industrialization and international aid regimes to foster effective development has led to the widespread reduction of capital controls. Developed countries, led by both government deregulation and the increasing clout of internationally linked market actors in both banks and securities markets, began seriously to reform their financial systems in the 1970s, while the International Monetary Fund, the Bank for International Settlements and other international regimes pushed for liberalization and established a range of standards and benchmarks for doing so, such as the 1988 Basel capital adequacy standards.

Meanwhile, formerly 'Third World' countries, some of which are today called 'emerging markets', now look primarily to foreign sources – both foreign direct investment and international portfolio investment – for otherwise scarce capital. Despite frequent financial crises and the acceptance that some capital controls may be useful for encouraging longer term investment (Chile) and for preventing capital flight in a crisis (Malaysia), the debate on international capital mobility today focuses chiefly on how to institute effective financial regulatory systems at national, regional (European, North American, and Asian) and international levels (the concept of a 'global financial architecture') in order to smooth adjustment to an open global capital markets regime (Armijo, 2001; Soederberg, 2004).

Another aspect of economic globalization, the internationalization of production, linked to both trade and financial liberalization, concerns the increasing acceptance of a leading role for multinational corporations. Developed and developing states alike, along with the major international economic institutions, have come to see MNCs, despite widespread (and partly justifiable) fears of exploitation and market distortion, as desirable partners in the search for economic growth. All in all, freer trade, financial liberalization, and the internationalization of production are increasingly taken for granted as core drivers of both domestic and international economies in the twenty-first century and form the cornerstone of the neoliberal project at both national and international levels.

Embedded financial orthodoxy and the neoliberal state

The second key dimension of neoliberalism is the reform of national finances. The central feature of this process has been the attempt to control inflation, linked with a shift away from Keynesian macroeconomic demand management to a more structural approach to fiscal and monetary policy. With regard to fiscal policy, both personal taxation – especially at higher rates – and, increasingly, corporate taxation rates have been widely lowered with the express intention of freeing up private capital for investment ('supply side' policy). Balanced budgets are in theory another central tenet of embedded financial orthodoxy, although in the United States deep tax cuts under the Reagan Administration (1981–89) and the George W. Bush Administration (2001–09) have led to historically unprecedented budget deficits. The European Union's Stability and Growth Pact limits national budget deficits to 3 per cent of Gross Domestic Product, although this has been coming under strain recently. International Monetary Fund and World Bank aid has increasingly become subject to conditionality that requires recipient countries to run budget surpluses, and political leaderships of both left and right in many developing countries, for example Brazil, have adopted tight budgetary discipline.

Other aspects of embedded financial orthodoxy have been reforming state ministries and agencies in order to reduce waste and make them operate according to the same sort of efficiency standards used in successful businesses; subjecting the mechanisms by which governments and state agencies manage the money supply to supposedly non-political disciplines, including the manipulation of the money supply through open market operations and the trend towards making central banks independent of political control; and carrying out macroeconomic management through monetary rather than fiscal policy. Embedded financial orthodoxy is a key component of what Paul Krugman and others have called the 'financialization' of both business and public policy.

From outcome orientated interventionism to the competition state and the regulatory state

The third dimension of neoliberalism is a sea change in the character of state intervention in the domestic economy. In the postwar period the key objectives of public policy were economic growth, the promotion of industrialization, full employment, and a certain amount of redistribution of wealth and income through the tax system and the welfare state. With this package came a broad commitment to greater equality, especially with regard to social policy. Even center-right and right-wing parties once paid lip service to this objective, especially in the wake of the Great Depression and the Second World War.

The concept of 'regulation', in this context, was a general one, which mixed together two distinct modes. The traditional mode involved direct or indirect public control of sectors of the economy and of social and public services that left to themselves were seen to operate in ways that might potentially run counter to the public interest. The second mode, developed mainly in the United States, has been called 'arm's-length regulation' – that is, that the role of 'regulators' by definition was not to intervene in order to produce particular outcomes, but rather to establish and enforce general rules for a particular sector, industry or service – to produce a 'level playing field' for market actors. It is the latter of these two conceptions of regulation that is at the core of the neoliberal project. As the authors who coined the phrase 'reinventing government' have written: 'Governments should steer but not row' (Osborne and Gaebler, 1992). Ideally, they say, governments ought not to run industries themselves or to supply services directly, but instead should provide a working framework of rules and performance indicators or targets for market actors to follow.

Indeed, in this context, neoliberals are rather divided on one major aspect of this process. Neoliberals in the 1970s and 1980s used to argue that government should stop intervening in the economy more or less entirely. The concept of 'deregulation' originally meant just what it said – repealing whatever rules that caused market participants to behave in any other way than their own self-interest and that thereby distorted markets and made them inefficient. Markets would be automatically efficient – the so-called 'efficient market hypothesis'. However, other neoliberals argued that it was the *type* of regulation that mattered and that arm's-length 'prudential' regulations, the second type outlined above, were increasingly necessary in order to promote efficient market behavior.

The new burdens of pro-market regulation

Deregulation was never really deregulation; it increasingly became the replacement of outcome-orientated and discretionary interventionism with new market friendly regulations – a form of *pro-market re-regulation*. Indeed, in many cases the new regulations were more complex and onerous than the old type (Cerny, 1991; Moran, 2003). A well-known example is that of insider trading regulation in financial markets, almost unknown (except in the US) before the 1980s. And, despite the rhetoric of deregulation, neocorporatism in labor markets has been replaced not so much by the abolition of regulations – although employers' freedom to hire and fire has generally been increased – as by a wide range of new regulations and programs designed to 'enable', or actually compel, the poor and unemployed to enter the labor market through a combination of carrots (training, education, temporary employment subsidies) and sticks (reduced and time-limited welfare benefits).

The core of the regulatory approach is contractualization and '*ex post*' regulation – that is, that behavior should not be constrained *a priori* but should be both organized by contractual agreements and subject to later litigation, including judicial and quasi-judicial procedures, to enforce those contracts, especially through independent regulatory agencies (sometimes called 'agencification'). Such rules-based systems, however, also require extensive monitoring, surveillance, and audit (Power, 1997) in order to determine whether agreed targets have been met, rather than the exercise of discretionary '*ex ante*' control. Ever more aspects of economic life are today subject to extensive regulation of this sort imposed by governments of both left and right in both developed and developing worlds. Indeed, one of the main roles of the IMF, the WTO and the World Bank today is to proselytize the regulatory creed and spread 'best practices' and 'good governance' throughout the world.

Reinventing governance

The fourth core dimension of neoliberalism concerns the role of the private sector. However, the emphasis has shifted from the direct sale of government-controlled industries, as in the United Kingdom under the Thatcher Government, to 'contracting out' services, the development of public–private partnerships (PPPs), and the use of private sources of finance for public purposes, for example the UK's Private Finance Initiative (PFI) for the construction and sometimes operation of schools, hospitals, prisons, and so on. The 'New Public Management' school has developed sophisticated prescriptions along these lines (Dunleavy, 1994).

Proponents argue that structural changes in the economy, especially the development of information and communications technology (ICT), have fundamentally transformed how firms work and shifted the boundaries between public and private sectors, that is, skewing governance towards private sector models of control. Opponents argue that such services necessarily have a public character that is undermined by privatization; a key example cited is the privatization of aspects of military and defence provision, from suppliers of materiel at home to the use of private military contractors (PMCs) to support military activities in the field. Another objection is that cost savings have not materialized and that governments have assumed private contractors' financial risks where cost overruns and quality deficiencies have occurred, as with the PFI in the UK. This dimension is closely linked with the shift to the regulatory approach discussed earlier, insofar as contractualization, the use of financial performance indicators, and *ex post* enforcement are at the heart of the system.

6. Who's driving change? Neoliberalization from top down, bottom up, inside out and outside in

The overdetermination of neoliberal politics: actors, institutions, discourses

The emerging embedded neoliberal consensus is therefore not simply developing 'from outside' or 'from above'; it is also a political construction promoted by political entrepreneurs who must design projects, convince others, build coalitions and ultimately win some sort of political legitimacy 'from inside' and 'from below'. In this process, neoliberalism, like embedded liberalism before it, would actually appear to be 'overdetermined' – in other words there are several interests, pressures and structural trends pushing in the same direction:

- the role of *state actors* (politicians, bureaucrats, political parties, etc.) in formulating new public policies designed to overcome the legacy of the 'overloaded state', 'stagflation', and so on, and in breaking up old and building new political coalitions at both elite and mass levels to win elections or control and reshape bureaucracies in order to promote marketization, competitiveness and the like;
- the role of *'global governance' institutions* – the World Bank, the IMF, the WTO, the Bank for International Settlements, the G7/8, the (new) G22, the International Labor Office and many more – in spreading the neoliberal message;
- political and economic *power differentials among states* – especially the role of the United States and the American model with its inbuilt 'globalization premium' (neoliberal political culture; multi-level federal institutions; marketized economy; regulatory culture; etc.);
- the growing role of private or *quasi-private sector institutions, groups, and networks* such as think tanks (Stone, 1996), non-governmental organizations (NGOs), 'epistemic communities' (Haas, 1992), transnational and transgovernmental policy networks, and the like in setting the global agenda;
- the changing balance of *interests and pressures* as more and more businesses, political actors, voters and consumers alike (not to mention scholars)

become aware that insulated national political solutions are increasingly difficult to support in an open, interdependent world; and

- the increasing dominance of the *'discourse'* of neoliberalism, entrenching, through socialization, *a priori* anticipated reactions that internalize neoliberalism in the way people frame political and economic issues.

Reinventing the social and the emergence of social neoliberalism

Neoliberal public policies, however, do not merely constrain but also bring opportunities. Contemporary politics entails both a process of choosing between different versions of neoliberalism and the attempt to innovate creatively *within* the new neoliberal playing field. Several kinds of socially significant policy innovations are being experimented with in different issue areas and at different levels:

- a shift to microeconomic industrial policy with an international dimension – an obsession with the *promotion of competitiveness* – especially significant for small- and medium-sized enterprises in an open world economy;
- linking trade opening to *environmental and labor standards*;
- a range of *welfare reforms* that has in some instances expanded certain welfare services while cutting back and privatizing others;
- demands for stricter and more accountable *international rules and procedures* for corporate governance, accounting standards, bond rating agencies, private mediation and arbitration procedures, antitrust regulation and so on;
- a change in the *discourse of global governance* towards more socially oriented goals, including the World Bank's shift in the mid-1990s to giving priority to poverty reduction goals;
- increasing emphasis by the major international economic institutions, the leading developed states, and many non-governmental organizations (NGOs) on *'good governance' and democratization* as key objectives necessary for stability and growth;
- the new prominence of *advocacy group debate* through the World Social Forum and various non-governmental organizations, shifting the focus from anti-globalization to alternative approaches to globalization;
- a growing focus on the *reinvention of domestic social policies* in the context of globalization by political leaders like Presidents Fernando Henrique Cardoso and Luiz Ignácio Lula da Silva of Brazil;
- Kofi Annan's *Global Compact*, which seeks to develop a kind of transnational neocorporatism through collaboration with business to promote social goals;
- and, despite US withdrawal, the Kyoto Protocol, the International Criminal Court, the Ottawa Convention on Landmines and a range of

other international agreements, prefiguring a new kind of incremental *public legal internationalism.*

The combination of the embedded neoliberal consensus, on the one hand, and a political imperative to reinvent the social dimensions of politics in a complex, multi-level world, on the other, is at the heart of political debate, conflict, competition and coalition-building today. Thus we may be witnessing the emergence of a new, multidimensional *social neoliberalism* that a few years ago would have seemed like a contradiction in terms.

7. Globalization, neoliberalism and the erosion of national models of capitalism

Different roads to globalization

What we are seeing, therefore, is not so much the continuity or maintenance of older 'varieties of capitalism', but rather the emergence of *varieties of neoliberalism* – of diversity within convergence, of the forging of different 'roads to globalization'. In all of the countries studied in this book, there is no turning back to bureaucratic, neocorporatist, or insulated national models of capitalism – 'organized', 'co-ordinated', or 'concerted' capitalism, as earlier writers have called it. Rather there is a process of the internalization of neoliberal globalization, of complex adaptation, of policy experimentation, of the break-up and rebuilding of political coalitions, of the increasing salience of transnational linkages and networks in a more open world, and of changing public attitudes towards the new disciplines of competitiveness and change.

In many cases, of course, these changes have been wrenching, and are hardly complete. Governments and entrenched coalitions have sometimes been able to maintain their hold on power and partially to resist internalization, but their positions are increasingly precarious. At times, too, governments have acted in a relatively authoritarian fashion – paradoxically – to impose neoliberal disciplines on their own citizens. In yet other cases, previous experiences of stagnation, corruption, bloated bureaucracies, hyperinflation, and the like have enabled surprising coalitions of popular forces and neoliberal globalizing elites to form. Where resistance to neoliberalism has been most effective, it has emerged less from strongly entrenched national states than from a mix of transnational and sub-national social forces such as religious fundamentalism, ethnic identities, transnational mafia and criminal networks, and tribal, warlord or clan-type factions in collapsed or 'failed' states (Cerny, 2005a). And finally, some countries have embraced neoliberalism but also attempted to inject reinvented social norms into that process.

Commencing with the so-called 'Anglo-American' countries represented in this volume – the United Kingdom, the United States, Canada, and

New Zealand – the lowering of barriers to international trade and capital flows, courting of foreign direct and portfolio investment, radical public sector restructuring, extensive privatization, anti-trade union legislation and monetarist anti-inflationary policies have represented the concrete implementation of the neoliberal agenda. A belief in the superiority of 'government by market' (Self, 1987) came to penetrate international financial institutions (IFIs) such as the World Bank and the International Monetary Fund (IMF), which modeled the conditions they imposed on those developing countries seeking aid accordingly. Meanwhile, in the European context, the European Monetary System (EMS), despite a rocky start in the mid-1970s, was based on the German Bundesbank's monetary policy with its emphasis on anti-inflationary policy and monetary stability, while the more recent completion of Economic and Monetary Union (EMU) and the introduction of a single currency with its concomitant Stability Pact, has 'locked in' a policy based on limited state budgets, low inflation, and constrained public spending.

This paradigmatic shift is still more pronounced in Latin America and Southeast Asia, where national governments were made to accept the externally imposed obligations of the IMF's structural adjustment programs (SAPs), or what some refer to as the 'Washington Consensus' (Williamson, 1990). Over the past two decades, SAPs have helped make the South more dependent on foreign portfolio and direct investment. This has translated into greater discipline of transnational market actors in the South than previously. Similarly, in East Asia, even the highly organized Japanese variety of capitalism, once celebrated as a successful counter model to the US version, is showing signs of convergence and disintegration (cf. Cerny, 2004, 2005b). States are increasingly becoming 'competition states' (Cerny, 1990 and 2000b; Sassen, 1996; Hirsch, 1998).

Changing political coalitions

The 'first wave' of globalization literature of the late 1990s lacked sufficient micro-level studies; this is the first empirical gap in the literature we seek to fill here. Second, we challenge the empirical basis of the recent 'second wave' literature on comparative political economy (Kitschelt *et al.*, 1999; Scharpf and Schmidt, 2000; Hall and Soskice, 2001; Schmidt, 2002) that stresses the continued resilience of national models or varieties of capitalism, despite common external and internal challenges. In doing so, we highlight the fact that the character of *policy output* has changed dramatically even in former bastions of neocorporatist, 'co-ordinated' capitalism such as Sweden and Germany. In particular, contributors seek to identify channels of policy diffusion through which neoliberalism has entered the political sphere.

Although neoliberal 'reforms' have been almost without exception elite-driven, they require wider coalitions for their effective adoption and implementation. They emerged based on sustained support from converted academics, policy advisers and consultants both within and outside the public sector, government officials, and firms and other economic actors, especially representatives of employer and business associations, and, especially consumers and many taxpayers – often ready allies against high-price import substitution economies, bloated bureaucracies, and hyperinflation.

Nevertheless, because of the detrimental social, economic, and political ramifications of neoliberal restructuring on the poorer sections of the community and on many traditional domestic industries, these reforms have often proven relatively unpopular. This backlash against those neoliberal policies, commonly enacted by the right in the 1980s and early 1990s, later led to the electoral successes of the center-left in Europe, North America, and the Antipodes in the mid-to-late 1990s, and Latin America in the early twenty-first century – the rightward shift undertaken by the 'New Democrats' in the US, 'New Labour' in Britain and New Zealand, the *Neue Mitte* in Germany, and the Socialist Party in France representing a fundamental realignment of the Left around various versions of social neoliberalism.

At the same time, we have witnessed the emergence of a global protest movement against what are perceived as the excesses of a globalization 'run amok' (Klein, 2000), demanding the global re-regulation of capitalism, and of global trade and international finance in particular. This protest movement has emerged partly due to the embrace of neoliberalism and competition state imperatives by those center-left parties, and partly due to a growing number of financial and political crises, as in Mexico in 1994, much of East and Southeast Asia in 1997–98, Russia and Brazil in 1998, Turkey in 2001, Argentina in 2001–02 and elsewhere in less spectacular forms.

8. The outline of the book

The changing nature of macroeconomic policy-making and power dynamics between capital and labor in the three European cases of Germany, Sweden and Spain are analysed in chapters by Georg Menz, Sven Steinmo, and Paul McVeigh. Germany and Sweden have often been considered bastions of co-ordinated market capitalism, in which, to varying degrees, strong labor movements and powerful Social Democratic parties had succeeded in securing consensual co-ordinated macroeconomic policymaking. Steinmo describes how, even in Sweden, this bastion of neocorporatism and 'democratic socialism', neoliberal rhetoric and policy have gained a stronghold and have led to a dramatic reconfiguration of macroeconomic and monetary policy, paradoxically alongside the maintenance of the welfare state. Georg Menz similarly sketches the decline of commitment in Germany to the postwar 'German Model' both by the political parties, including Chancellor Schröder's Social Democrats, and by business.

Paul McVeigh emphasizes the role of the European Union considerably more than the previous two authors in accounting for Spain's shift to neoliberal policies under the purportedly socialist government of Felipe Gonzalez in the 1980s, reinforced by the association of state interventionism with the completely discredited and loathed authoritarian Franco regime and its brand of fascism. Mark Evans's chapter on Britain traces the dynamics of policy transfer in welfare and social policy, especially since the late 1990s when Britain's 'New Labour' government has been keen to adopt the disciplinary 'welfare to work' approach pioneered by Clinton's New Democrats as opposed to any European models closer to home. In this context, a major facet of competition state policy has been the transfer and cross-over of policy among states.

The shift towards neoliberal policy has been even more pronounced in Latin American countries that moved to authoritarian rule *cum* neoliberalism in the 1970s and 1980s, often under political and economic pressure from the IMF, the World Bank, and the US. In Chile, Mexico, and Peru authoritarian governance has been not only compatible with but necessary for the adoption and implementation of neoliberal policy. The Latin American cases thus cast some doubt on the promise to transition countries that more liberal capitalism would necessarily lead to Western-style liberal democracy. They also demonstrate that while neoliberal policy reform may in some ways entail the 'retreat of the state' (Strange, 1996), it is better described not as a retreat but a redefinition of the role of the state towards stabilizing and enforcing a more pro-market order.

Guillermo Ruiz demonstrates in his chapter how the neoliberal policies of Peru's President Alberto Fujimori, partly imposed by the IMF, went hand in hand with increasing, not decreasing, authoritarianism, while the re-establishment of democracy following Fujimori's removal has suffered from trying to balance popular expectations with neoliberal imperatives. Marcus Taylor underlines how authoritarian neoliberalism in Chile led to ambiguous and even disastrous results, despite the shift to liberal democracy and the victory of the Social Democrats in recent years. Susanne Soederberg finds that the overall results of the Mexican reforms leave the country dangerously exposed to the demands of foreign investors, experiencing the massive rapid withdrawal of foreign capital while *maquiladora*-style investment along the US border has had little lasting positive effect.

Concerns over falling behind in international competitiveness have likewise motivated other Anglo-American countries to follow Thatcherism and Reaganomics. Stephen McBride and Georg Menz analyse Canada and New Zealand. As McBride shows, the introduction of neoliberalism by the Mulroney government in the 1980s was greatly enhanced by international trade negotiations and further 'locked in' through the Canada–US Free Trade Agreement (later to include Mexico as the North American Free Trade Agreement, NAFTA). New Zealand, which in the 1980s 'made Thatcher look timid', according to Menz, has been likewise influenced by developments abroad, but the zealously and rigorously implemented 'blitzkrieg-style' reform programs of the Lange government in the 1980s presented New Zealand with a decade of sluggish growth, high unemployment, rising crime, growing income disparity, greater exposure to foreign portfolio investment, and the virtually complete handover of state assets into foreign ownership.

In her chapter on Russia, Anastasia Nesvetailova examines the politics of transition to market capitalism in what was once its key systemic rival. In Russia, as in many other East European countries, former elites have secured key positions in the once state-owned enterprises, now privatized, and pervasive corruption prevails. Neoliberal policies once again failed to provide fertile ground for a shift towards bourgeois democracy and a *Rechtsstaat* or rule-based state, but instead go comfortably hand in hand with neo-feudal societal power dynamics. The current Putin Administration is trying to ride both horses and it is not yet clear which will predominate in the future. Mark Evans and Bub Duc Hai explore the transition from old-style Communist rule in one of the last bastions of state-led socialism, Vietnam, to neoliberalism, an extreme volte-face for a system that only recently represented an idealistic form of socialist revolution.

Finally, Phil Cerny compares the neoliberalization of the United States and Japan by examining their respective processes of financial market liberalization. From very different starting points, they are converging on highly regulated – not deregulated – market systems, reflecting the significance of financial globalization for forging alliances between rapidly internationalizing financial elites and modernizing regulatory bureaucracies.

9. The research agenda

Broadly speaking, there are three sets of questions shared by all contributors that comprise our collective research agenda. First, we examine the dynamics of the dissemination of neoliberal ideology and policy programs. Secondly, we attempt to explain how globalization has become embedded and internalized world-wide. Why and how does this process seem to lead to functional convergence on a competition state model? And, thirdly, we ask whether globalization is irreversible. Are we moving beyond globalization, or merely adapting to and coping with it?

Discourses of neoliberalism

The mantra of open economic borders, liberalization, privatization and deregulation has assumed ubiquitous status. But how did this Washington Consensus indeed become a consensus at all, and among whom? In attempting to account for the global transfusion of neoliberal tenets, it is useful to conceive of cohorts of decision-makers as epistemic communities (Haas, 1992) that often employ similar language and concepts, deploy a similar pattern of education and socialization, and share a common core of values, norms and ideas. The pivotal role of ideas has also been recently highlighted by the 'constructivist' turn in international relations (Katzenstein, 1996; Wendt, 1999), while scholars in the tradition of comparative politics too have underscored the importance of 'ideas' as mental maps or guideposts guiding and directing decision-makers (Hall, 1989; Goldstein and Keohane, 1993). The 'neo-Gramscian' approach to political economy also emphasizes the role of ideas in historical materialism (Gramsci, 1992; Cox, 1987, 1993; Gill, 1990; Rupert, 2001; van Apeldoorn, 1999; van der Pijl, 1998; Soederberg, 2004, 2005). In particular, one factor behind the elevation of neoliberalism from a previously obscure strand in economic thinking to the status of dominant paradigm was the extent to which it dovetailed with the views of key actors in the ranks of the US government. Nevertheless, the key to the implementation of such policies lies in their internalization by domestic actors in *other* countries, both state and non-state, in what Cerny and Endo (2004) call 'infrastructural hegemony' – that is, hegemony from below, the crucial concomitant of both coercive and structural hegemony from above and/or outside.

Functional convergence

This leads us to our second set of concerns. How has globalization – understood here as a historical era – helped usher in such *functional convergence* on a competition state model (Cerny, 1990; Hirsch, 1998) of politico-economic governance? The authors in this book focus on the role and strategies of state and non-state actors, organized interest groups, and civil society groups in advocating, supporting, or seeking to obstruct or impede implementation of neoliberal policies. In the former 'Third World', the role of local elites in advocating, lobbying for, implementing, and continuous monitoring of neoliberal policies deserves special mention. Despite the rhetoric, the introduction of so-called 'turbo-capitalist' policies in countries like Chile, Peru, or Russia has helped sustain and stabilize quasi-feudal societal structures. Whether more effective democratization and a new focus on social goals will come 'later', as neoliberalism evolves, is still an open question in many cases.

International institutions and regimes have likewise played a key role. International free trade agreements, notably NAFTA, ASEAN (the Association of Southeast Asian Nations), the WTO, and the EU have explicitly banned a range of modes of state economic interventionism that are seen as an obstacle to free trade. The Single European Act, adopted in 1985 and ratified in 1986, was explicitly aimed at reducing the size and scope of state intervention in the regulation and especially management of the economy in order to create a single economic space with a free flow of capital and trade across borders, with minimal constraints from national government interventions and regulations. Since then the EU has promoted and even imposed privatization of once-formidable public sector enterprises in transportation, telecommunications, electricity, water, gas and other areas of public service provision (not to mention a range of other manufacturing and service industries), helping to usher in policies anticipated by the Thatcher Government in the UK in the early 1980s. Likewise, the so-called Maastricht 'stability' criteria impose a tight monetarist corset on public deficits and inflation levels among members of the single currency. With regard to particular European states, margins of maneuver have been curtailed substantially, and while existing institutions of politico-economic governance may not appear to have changed radically, their internal balance of power has been affected dramatically, especially with regard to the changing role of labor – either marginalized and ejected from neocorporatist arrangements, or absorbed into the neoliberal consensus through the discourse of growth and competitiveness.

A 'weak' or 'retreating' state in macroeconomic, labor, social, trade and environmental policy thus need not be contradictory to augmenting the role and capacity of the state in enforcement and control. Growing pro-market state regulation of financial and business activities, as exemplified by the legislative reaction to the failure of Enron and the abuse of their role by major accounting firms and brokerages, as well as increasing health and safety regulations and the like, indicate that whereas the state may intervene less in determining market outcomes such as prices, states intervene increasingly in trying to impose market forms of production and exchange in order to enhance their competitiveness and supposed market efficiency.

Institutionalization

Our third set of questions concerns the extent to which what we call the erosion of national models of capitalism is irreversible. Many of the architects of neoliberal implementation have attempted to secure and safeguard their policies through processes of institutionalization. Independent central banks are a key building block in this process, especially the European Central Bank, which lies at the heart of the neoliberal discipline of EMU. Furthermore, the international financial institutions have adopted a new rhetoric and style that blends neoliberalism and ostensibly social objectives. Analysts now refer to the 'Post-Washington Consensus', although its meaning and content are still debated (Fine *et al.*, 2001; Pincus and Winters, 2002; Soederberg, 2004). The shift of the World Bank from structural adjustment to 'poverty reduction' as its main institutional goal and the refocusing of the International Monetary Fund away from simple removal of capital controls to the establishment of strong domestic regulatory systems in the financial issue-area are totems of this change.

10. The new politics of neoliberalism

Opposition to neoliberalism

Despite the continued intellectual hegemony of the neoliberal paradigm in academies and government ministries around the world, however, the late

1990s witnessed growing public dissent and protest against the unmitigated implementation of free trade agreements, the opaque and distinctly unde-mocratic decision-making structure of international institutions such as the IMF and the World Bank, the apparent reduction of national sovereignty, and the numerous more extreme social and political ramifications of liberal-ization, privatization and deregulation. The most important success of this new international counter-movement was the derailment of the proposed Multinational Agreement on Investment (MAI) in 1997, and in 1999 envir-onmental groups, trade unions, and left-wing groups demonstrated against the WTO at its 1999 Seattle meeting.

But rather than just opposing globalization, critics of neoliberal globaliza-tion have been increasingly moving towards presenting proposals and projects for forms of globalization more responsive to social needs and values – what we earlier tentatively called 'social neoliberalism' – as put forward at a now reg-ular annual gathering of the World Social Forum in Porto Alegre, Brazil, explicitly designed as a counter-event to the long-standing gathering of cor-porate executives, politicians and representatives of international institu-tions, or World Economic Forum, held annually in Davos, Switzerland. New transnational advocacy groups have emerged, some rooted in particular issue areas, some in developing broad public policy proposals. But a pressing problem for the anti- or alter-globalization movement has been the formu-lation of concrete alternatives to the neoliberal globalization process they criticize (Starr, 2000). The movement's success is based on a relatively modest core catalogue of demands, primarily revolving around a small tax on inter-national currency transactions, the so-called 'Tobin tax'; to demand a more comprehensive and/or radical array of reform measures could conceivably undermine a fundamentally divergent and colorful coalition.

Even among top officials of the WTO and the World Bank (Stiglitz, 2002; Gilbert and Vines, 2003; Vreeland, 2003) there has been increasing criticism of their role and the conviction is growing that globalization may require some form of more socially responsive and responsible re-regulation (Held and Koenig-Archibugi, 2003). Taking into account purely standard macro-economic indicators, such as growth in GDP, inflation rates, and unemploy-ment rates, the evidence of neoliberal reform measures in the long-term is at best mixed. In the short term, the record would appear to be negative in several respects. Neoliberal reforms often result in tumultuous 'adjustment periods' with little growth and sometimes prolonged spasms of recession. This is especially true for countries that do not have the kinds of resources, skills, or stable political-economic coalitions that are necessary in order to restructure their economies to take advantage of international markets, technological change, and productivity growth.

Maximizing the role of cheap labor alone as a competitive advantage, often a policy goal in the Global South, may not suffice if several countries pursue this strategy at once. Indeed, even in the developed world, low productivity continues to weigh on the British and New Zealand economies.

Those seeking to use countries like Chile or New Zealand as 'models' typically focus on the short term or on spatially or sectorally selective periods. Thus for some critics even the US 'job machine' of the 1990s relied on the abolition of the rudimentary US welfare state in 1995 and the imposition of work requirements to force individuals to take up employment that barely permits survival (Ehrenreich, 2002). In the 2004 presidential election campaign, it was noted that although employment was moving up off its lowest levels of two years previously, the George W. Bush Administration was the first since the Hoover Administration in the Great Depression to see a fall in jobs over a whole presidential term of office.

Nevertheless, earlier models of development, especially those rooted in import substitution, the state–bank–industry 'finance capital' nexus, state promotion of industrialization, and cross-class neocorporatist coalitions have been disadvantaged in the more open world economy of the late twentieth and twenty-first centuries. Bureaucratic authoritarianism, entrenched hyper-inflation, embedded quasi-feudal special interest coalitions, distributive populist politics often interspersed with military rule (including recurring bouts of torture, the brutal repression of ethnic minorities and tribal rivals, etc.), economic periphery status and dependency on First World aid and loans, among other things, have made adjustment to globalizing pressures extremely difficult. Crises are endemic under such conditions. It is not so much a case of getting on an upward trajectory to a more prosperous world, but rather one of not getting left further and further behind as technological change, investment opportunities, trade outlets and so on, move the goalposts.

Facilitating access by foreign capital, increasing reliance on such foreign capital, and the privatization of state-owned enterprises not only raise pressing questions of national sovereignty, but they also make a country more susceptible to the preferences of international capital investors and impose the dictate of credit rating agencies, themselves heavily biased towards a certain brand of monetary policy. Increasing the linkage with the global economy thus can result in more not fewer potential sources of instability, as the recent financial crises in East Asia, Russia, Turkey, and Argentina dramatically illustrate. The break-up and privatization of state-owned enterprises followed by the liberalization of such sectors leads to the replacement of stable and secure jobs with fewer, more precarious, less well-paid, and commonly non-unionized jobs.

Antisocial behavior and rising crime are commonly associated with the trend towards increasing income inequalities. The marketization of areas formerly thought of as key areas of public provision, including health and education, has commonly impeded access to such services by members of lower social strata. The pauperization of segments of society also tends to affect ethnic minorities disproportionately. Thus the main downside to neoliberal policies is that they have led to an increasing relative gulf between rich and poor. Income disparity is on the rise in all countries that have experimented with neoliberalism. This outcome can have extremely serious social effects related to the dissolution of the social contract of society: crime, desperate poverty, and ill health. In this environment, the rhetoric of the far right seeks to address popular anxieties and worries, in particular portraying immigration as one such undesirable consequence of globalization.

Simultaneously, neoliberalism has helped perpetuate and even aggravate the gulf between a rich, highly developed Triad and a poor, largely underdeveloped rest of the world. While a few countries joined the elusive Triad club in the 1970s and 1980s – hence the 'Asian tigers', South Korea, Singapore, Taiwan, Hong Kong – it is remarkable that the state-led developmental approach embodied by South Korea at that time was diametrically opposed to the policies currently advocated, prescribed, and administered by the IMF on developing countries around the world – including South Korea itself since 1997. Central and Eastern European countries have notably not been able to emulate Tiger-style policies, but as a condition of admission have had to copy the neoliberal policies enforced by the European Union on its present members. Of course, post-Communist elites in these countries are themselves overwhelmingly converts to neoliberalism of one sort or another, although many of them are moving from radical 'first wave' neoliberalism, as practiced in Poland and the Czech Republic in the early 1990s, to a less radical form.

In sum, globalization and neoliberalism are not merely structural trends but constitute a new terrain for political (and scholarly) debate. Normative projects abound: some calling for the regeneration of the state and the revival of older forms of social democracy; some involving the reinforcement of European and other regional-level institutions; some looking to develop more comprehensive forms of 'global governance' through the expansion of international regimes and the strengthening of their social dimension; and some seeking to bring NGOs, popular movements and other actors together in some form of 'global civil society' – and, of course, some seeking to resist globalization *tout court.*

Cutting across all of these alternatives except the last, however, two conclusions stand out and run through each of the chapters of this book. The first is that, for better or worse, neoliberalism in one form or another is now hegemonic, whether from above or below, inside out or outside in. The second, therefore, is that effective political action and coalition-building in the twenty-first century will inevitably involve political, social and economic actors attempting to develop alternative normative projects – ones that do not simply take neoliberalism as given in its starker 1980s manifestation, but that attempt to manage, reshape, transcend and/or reform it – emphasizing in the latter case not only Washington Consensus-style priorities of economic efficiency but also goals like social inclusion. Politics in the future may well be about the competition and interaction of competing mixes of these two core goals, difficult though they are to reconcile.

Part I

Developed Countries' Experiences with Globalization

2
Auf Wiedersehen, Rhineland Model: Embedding Neoliberalism in Germany

Georg Menz

> *You see, we have taken the slogan from the 1980s – we only borrowed this planet from our children – and brought it up to date. Being responsible for the future of our children today means not racking up unsustainable public debt and thus implies budget austerity.*
>
> German Green Party MP (Author's interview, Berlin 2001)

1. Introduction: toward functional convergence in Germany

A Thatcherite revolution never occurred in Germany. Indeed, notwithstanding considerable pressures toward convergence on the liberal Anglo-American model (Harding and Patterson 2000), emanating from economic liberalization induced by the European Union (EU) and the global dissemination of neoliberal ideology and policies, the relative institutional stability of Rhineland capitalism has been interpreted as evidence of its continuing resilience. The highly organized neocorporatist Rhineland political economy of Germany has commonly been considered a distinct coordinated or 'nonliberal' variety of capitalism (Albert, 1991; Streeck, 1996; Coates, 2000; Schmidt, 2002; Streeck and Yamamura 2002).

The purpose of this chapter is threefold. First, it introduces the reader to the key pillars of the Rhineland model, both in institutional and ideological terms. Second, it argues that despite some institutional resilience, ideological changes and the elite's embrace of neoliberalism imply that since the 1990s the model's policy output has changed considerably. In this context, I argue that a process of functional convergence has occurred, meaning that despite institutional stability in certain aspects of the model, the functional output is very different. The academic debate over convergence is often static and obscures the view of significant changes in policy *outcome*. Despite *relative institutional* stability of the established Rhineland model, at least in some

33

areas, any assumption of resilience is inaccurate, for established institutions may well serve differently defined goals and produce a very liberal policy outcome. Not all Rhineland-style institutions have simply collapsed, as the more pessimistic literature of the early 1990s predicted, but many have, and where they persist they serve an internalized neoliberal agenda shared by German policy-makers, political parties, employers, the media, and other decision-makers in public policy.

Third, it supports this claim by an in-depth empirical study of developments in macroeconomic, labour and social policy. The role of agency by political actors is thus not denied, but actually emphatically underlined; functional convergence requires the active embrace, dissemination, and implementation of neoliberal policy.

2. The Rhineland model: what is it and why is it under threat?

Following earlier work on divergent systems of capitalism (Polanyi, 1957; Shonfield, 1969; Zysman, 1983; Katzenstein, 1985; Scharpf, 1991), a vivid debate about the future of European capitalism unfolded in the 1990s (Albert, 1991; Crouch and Streeck, 1997; Kitschelt *et al.*, 1999; Coates, 2000; Menz, 2005a). At the heart of the rapidly unfolding literature on comparative political economy, there were two central assumptions, shared at first by many, but later questioned and even heavily criticized: First, that the demise of Eastern European state socialism would shift the focus of systemic competition to the different varieties of capitalism and second, that globalization and an ever more intensified, accelerated, and deregulated global capitalism would undermine organized Rhineland-style capitalism.

With his influential piece on German capitalism, Wolfgang Streeck (1996) came to be principally associated with the 'declinist' approach. Despite its superior performance in sustaining low inflation and unemployment during the turbulent 1970s and early 1980s (Katzenstein, 1985; Scharpf, 1991; Calmfors and Driffill, 1988), the prospects of Rhineland-style capitalism in the 1990s and 2000s were regarded as fairly dire. Streeck highlighted (West) Germany's growing unemployment problem, constituting a serious drain on a welfare state system presupposing high employment rates, major problems in maintaining market share in light of sustained Japanese and US competition, and an extremely costly transfer of the West German welfare state eastwards during unification. Albert (1991) had pointed out that despite higher social cohesion and an impressive macroeconomic performance at least during its heyday, the Rhineland model rested on institutional foundations that would be extremely difficult to 'export' or copy by others and that would experience grave challenges. Indeed, the high value added high price production model of (West) Germany encountered serious East Asian competition from the late 1970s onwards. The strong yet docile trade unions faced industrial relocation to Southeast Asia, slowly declining membership rates and internal dissent. The welfare state, based on stable labor market participation, was challenged to cope with rising unemployment and mass early retirement.

Other authors have examined different pillars of the German model, including features such as a system of industrial relations based on 'co-determination' and relatively consensual wage bargaining (Hassel, 1999; Thelen, 2001; Hassel and Streeck, 2004) along with a long-term oriented finance system involving cross share-holdings by major banks that served both as lenders and partial stakeholders of businesses (*Hausbanken*) (Lütz, 2000).

This evolving network of institutions was a direct reflection of the respective balance of power between organized labor and capital, and the Social Democratic (SPD) and Christian Democratic (CDU/CSU) parties. Since the Christian Democrats governed alone or in coalition with the liberal Free Democrats (FDP) until 1967, it is not surprising that postwar West Germany was firmly committed to a market economy, free trade and abolition of intra-European trade barriers through membership of the European Economic Community in 1957. Fervent anti-Communism both in light of the systemic competition with East Germany and the Western allies' influence prevented the Social Democrats from becoming serious electoral competitors until the late 1960s. However, the trade union DGB (German Union Federation) played a significant role in securing early pro-labor legislation. Part of the West German success story was based on a steady labor supply from Eastern Germany and Central Europe, keeping wages low. After the Berlin Wall sealed off this pool, employers turned to Southern Europe to recruit cheap labor.

The heyday of German neocorporatism were short-lived. The tripartite *Konzertierte Aktion*, initiated by the SPD in 1967, collapsed in 1977. In the meantime, Germany had decided to float its currency in 1970. The *Bundesbank* switched to a monetarist policy in 1974, forcing trade unions to accept wage restraints to avoid further rises in unemployment. Nevertheless, by comparison with other European countries, Germany emerged from the 1970s relatively well, with low inflation and unemployment (Scharpf, 1991; Scharpf and Schmidt, 2000).

While much of the literature focuses on the institutional pillars of the Rhineland model, with its Bismarckian welfare state, its high quality 'Mercedes Benz model' of production, its particular neocorporatist framework of industrial relations, and the *Hausbanken*-style finance model, two ideological aspects merit attention.

In terms of *ideology*, there was some common ground between Catholic tenets of social equality and Social Democratic values of egalitarianism and redistribution. Both the Christian Democrats (CDU/CSU) and the Social Democrats (SPD) were popular catch-all parties (*Volksparteien*) and could ill afford alienating a clientele of farmers and small business owners on the right and industrial workers on the left.

However, these conditions have changed. Both mainstream parties and the smaller liberal FDP and the center-left Greens have accepted the *pensée unique* of neoliberalism (interview B). Responding to the decline of working class identity, the Social Democrats have embraced permanent austerity, monetarism, and 'Third Way' rhetoric (Giddens, 2001), emphasizing the need for competitiveness (interview C). In the process of secularization, the Christian Democrats have shed their commitment to Christian social values and have become more heavily influenced by their business clientele. At the level of the political parties, the commitment toward a social market economy has thus waned. Across the political spectrum, the rhetoric and policy stance has shifted toward a much more 'pro market' direction.

Until 1989 West Germany was a frontline state in the systemic competition between state socialism and Western capitalism. Much of the growth of the welfare state and the development of co-determination in industrial relations needs to be regarded as a concession made to the political left in light of this competition from the East. Importantly, systemic competition also developed across *historical* lines. In Germany, the rise of Nazism is regarded not least as a consequence of letting the class struggle unfold openly in the 1920s and 1930s. Consensual institutions and decision-making, which incorporate the class struggle and deflate its radicalism through concessions, were thus chosen to avoid a renewed rise of fascism.

However, state socialism is no longer a serious ideological competitor and Nazism is diminishing as a historical category of comparison. Questioning welfare state spending and attacking the institutions of consensual economic policy-making have thus become acceptable, as these institutions are no longer perceived as a bulwark against either fascism or state socialism. Given the history of forced labor and concentration camp internment for so-called 'antisocial elements' during the Third Reich, the recent polemic against welfare cheats by mainstream politicians deliberately breaks a taboo. Similarly, the introduction of 'workfare programs' into the welfare state debate should be reason for concern, but does not seem to raise substantial opposition.

In terms of the institutional structure, at least two of the Rhineland model's pillars are in the process of unravelling, owing to a combination of external challenges and conscious internal changes. For reasons of space constraint, these shall be examined only very briefly.

The emblematic long-term oriented finance system involved the three major banks serving as lenders and partial shareholders in businesses, permitting less emphasis on equity culture, and a long-term profit orientation often superior to precarious Anglo-American 'short-termism'. Meanwhile, communal and regional savings banks (*Sparkassen/Landesbanken*) played a similar role in nurturing small- and medium-sized business (SME) (Lütz, 2000). This finance system seemed to offer the best of all worlds: stability and long-term orientation comparable to Japanese *keiretsu*, while avoiding heavy handed state interventionism as in France or accepting the neglect of SMEs as in the UK.

The *Hausbanken* model is disintegrating. Encouraged by a 1999 change in the tax regulations, permitting tax-free sales of cross-share holdings, major banks are dissociating from their portfolios. In the late 1990s, the three major German banks focused their strategic efforts on lucrative investment banking; while this strategic shift has been partly reversed in light of the stock market decline of the early 2000s, there is little indication that they will be complacent with their historical role of providing 'patient capital'. In a bid to attract foreign institutional investors, especially from the US, and often secure listing in New York as well, Germany's listed companies have long adopted quarterly reporting, and are actively seeking equity finance. In fact, car manufacturer Porsche was denied inclusion in the index of medium-sized listed companies, MDAX, precisely because it refused to embrace this change. Meanwhile, the EU Commission is scrutinizing the communal and regional savings bank system, portraying it as profiting from improper state aid. While these efforts have so far only reined in the more ambitious foreign adventures of the regional savings associations, epitomized by the spree of foreign acquisitions by WestLB, the future of the local savings association looks uncertain. The strategic shift of the major players in the early 2000s includes challenging the local savings associations' dominant position in retail banking.

Rhineland capitalism depended not on power parity between business and labor, but on a commitment by both to the ideology and institutions of industrial relations involving mutually binding collective bargaining. Ironically, the forced integration of the union movement by the Nazis served as a source of strength after the war.

There is now a plethora of literature chronicling the decline and erosion of organized industrial relations in Germany (Hassel, 1999; Hassel and Streeck, 2004; Menz, 2005b). There are a number of factors underpinning this trend, first and foremost related to the declining employer commitment to the institutions (interview A). German employer associations are losing members, dramatically so in the East. According to recent studies, the percentage of employees covered by a sectoral agreement based on organizational membership of their employer stood at 70.1 per cent in the West, but only 55.4 per cent in the East in 2000. A combination of variables of political culture (distrust) and hard-nosed economics (a dismal economic situation, high unemployment leading to employers having leverage) is responsible for low coverage in new sectors, but also in traditional sectors such as construction, basic material processing and trade, where 60.9, 72.4, and 77.6 per cent respectively of all companies are not covered. The East is also experiencing a greater growth of company level agreements. These are often 'wildcat' agreements without approval from above. Illegal undercutting of standard wage levels is common, though obviously statistics on this trend are difficult to assemble. Companies exit these associations to avoid the obligation to pay standard wages. According to surveys conducted by economic research institute DIW, 79 per cent of East German employers were no longer members of an employer association in 1998, up from 64 per cent in 1994. Companies founded after 1989 are even less likely to be members. Since membership implies obligation to pay standard wages, exiting the associa-tion (*Verbandsflucht*) is a way to avoid doing so. More disconcertingly, even among members only 67 per cent actually adhere to these standard wages, down from 83 per cent in 1994 (DIW 1999).

Even union strength is declining. The union movement is challenged to integrate non-traditional, female, and ethnic workers, and to expand into the service sector. Where traditional institutions of industrial relations still exist, they very strongly reflect the shifting power balance in favor of business.

3. How much variation is there among the varieties of capitalism?

While I stress not only institutional erosion in some areas, but also a shifting ideological stance on the part of political elites, a recent strand in the compar-ative political economy stresses the institutional resilience of the Rhineland model. Despite the external challenges identified by the Streeckian strand and self-imposed changes, including increasing global competition, the privati-zation programs of the 1980s, EU-induced market liberalization, the transfer of control over crucial policy domains, such as monetary policy, to the EU, and significantly weaker trade unions facing more aggressive employers, the rejection of the earlier convergence thesis (Kitschelt *et al.*, 1999; Scharpf and Schmidt, 2000; Schmidt, 2002) led to the prediction that divergent 'varieties of capitalism' continue to prosper and prove resilient. This neo-Ricardian argument emphasizes that business actors may well remain committed to established high-wage, high-quality production patterns that are embedded in institutionalized coordinated mechanisms of interaction. In these coor-dinated market economies where 'considerable nonmarket coordination directly and indirectly between companies [exists], with the state playing a framework-setting role, and in all these economies ... labor remains "incorporated" ' (Soskice, 1999: 103). Companies profit from the 'produc-tion regimes' of coordinated Rhineland market economies. These entail cooperative industrial relations, educational and vocational systems jointly organized with the trade unions, and long-term oriented finance systems in cooperation with banks extending loans. Far from seeking low wages and low regulation environments, companies find it advantageous to remain embedded in the high-wage, high-regulation and high-trust environment of Rhineland-style industrial relations (Thelen, 2001: 75ff).

While laudably bringing actors back in, the problem with this line of argument is that the empirical evidence does not support it strongly. Recent studies of the massive abandonment of German industrial relations institutions (DIW, 1999; Hassel and Streeck, 2004; Menz, 2005b) and the increasing importance of equity financing to the detriment of the traditional *Hausbanken* model (Lütz, 2000) casts serious doubts on two pillars of Soskice's (1999) coordinated market economies.

However, possibly more seriously, to infer general resilience derived from institutional stability is inaccurate and misleading. Despite prevailing institutional stability, these said institutions serve in the implementation of neoliberal policy. Conservation of traditional Rhineland institutions is not the same as continued 'divergence'. In terms of the policy output produced that these institutions serve, there is convergence on a more market-oriented consensus among key policy actors, with the partial exception of some, but not all, trade union leaders. The functional purpose of the traditional institutions, their brief, aims, and targets henceforth reflect the internalization of neoliberal policy. Commencing in the late 1970s, but gathering pace since the late 1980s, an embrace of neoliberal policy by the leading political parties, the business community, the media, and parts of public opinion have helped usher in policies that clearly have moved beyond the era of 'embedded liberalism'.

The key factors underpinning the postwar Rhineland compromise have disappeared, partially because of global developments, but more importantly because of domestic trends. Although one influential analyst within the comparative political economy literature recognizes the importance of 'discourse' and emphasizes how such 'normative content of arguments proposed to justify unpopular policy initiatives' (Schmidt, 2000: 231; Schmidt, 2002) plays an important role in the neoliberal restructuring programs, she surprisingly fails to unearth such discourse in her somewhat cursive analysis of Germany. If we take seriously the increasingly aggressive rhetoric from German business association BDI and consider the ideological re-orientation of all political parties, it is difficult not to assess a trend toward functional convergence.

But it is not just the major business organizations that are espousing labor market deregulation and cutbacks in welfare provision (interview A). Nor are German employers' associations isolated when they use the threat to re-locate production to East European low-wage countries as a powerful bargaining chip vis-à-vis trade unions. The mainstream political parties and even more so coalition partners Greens are embracing neoliberal economic policy (interviews B, C) and have accepted the logic of the 'competition state', whose 'predominant goal is the optimization of the capital investment process at the national level in regard to the globalized accumulation process and [in doing so finds itself] in permanent competition with other national "locales for investment" ' (Hirsch, 1998: 33). While Germany has always been export-dependent and a strong supporter of free trade, the postwar ideology embedded in the 'social market economy' was a *quid pro quo* compromise solution. This compromise between strong unions and their Social Democratic allies on the one hand, and business in coalition with the Christian Democrats on the other, ensured that while unions accepted only small, but steady wage increases and thus some participation in corporate profits, employers accepted the 'social' component of the social market economy, in the form of co-determination, protective labor and social regulation, and relatively generous welfare state provisions, particularly insuring workers against the risk of unemployment, sickness and old age. Business now seems no longer willing to accept its part of the compromise and is captivated by the notion of rendering the country more attractive as a locale for investment (*Wirtschaftsstandort*), by cutting taxes, and social and labor regulations. Given the pervasiveness of this ideology among business and employers' organizations and political parties, and feeble trade union resistance, one might speak of 'embedded neoliberalism' (van Apeldoorn, 1999), reflecting the shift in normative goals.

The discussion about whether or not Germanic neocorporatism was or is disintegrating (Streeck, 1993, 1996), though initially helpful, often obscured the view of the underlying distribution of power. Of course, Germanic neocorporatism has *always* helped secure labor acquiescence, wage moderation, absence of industrial action, and thus rendered these countries attractive locales for investment. However, what sets German neocorporatism of the 2000s apart from its 1970s predecessor is that is no longer 'negotiating a secure status for workers and unions, insulating these from economic fluctuations ...' a priority, but rather 'adjusting the governance of the employment relationship to the imperatives of joint economic success' (Streeck, 1998: 15). 'Joint success' appears as somewhat of a euphemism. 'The trade unions ... accept a policy of wage restraint in return for an undertaking ... to preserve existing employment levels, *and preferably, whenever possible*, to create new jobs' (Fajertag and Pochet, 1997: 11, my emphasis). *There is no obligation whatsoever for employers and the state to live up to this vague promise.* While there has therefore not been a wholesale convergence toward liberal capitalism, particularly in institutional terms, the persistence, or re-emergence, of neocorporatist institutions does not serve as an accurate indicator of a distinct variety of capitalism, since such institutions serve the new priorities and reflect the underlying shift in balance of power between business and labor.

4. Varieties of neoliberalism? The changing nature of the Rhineland model

Upon close inspection, changes to the Rhineland model commenced in the 1980s, though unification proved a particularly pivotal watershed. In 1983, Helmut Kohl became chancellor, leading a CDU/CSU/FDP coalition that was to survive until 1998. While Kohl had campaigned with the slogan of 'more market, less state' in 1983, the 1987 slogan 'Carry on, Germany' (*Weiter so, Deutschland*) was more indicative of macroeconomic policy in the 1980s. Helmut Kohl's much touted turn-around (*Wende*) came nowhere close to the radical tempest of Thatcherism, as Kohl was hemmed in by powerful unions, an influential labor-friendly wing of his own party, and pervasive Catholic social values among his smaller coalition partner. The ideological commitment to the Rhineland model was still fairly vibrant within the political establishment. When Kohl confronted the unions by ending the payment of unemployment compensation to striking workers, he was successful in the end, but encountered major resistance (Zohnlhoefer, 2001: 237). This was a far cry from the Thatcher government tackling the union movement head-on.

Since the domestic arena was replete with veto points, a more fruitful path toward economic liberalization lay in promoting the completion of the Single Market. Kohl was a fervent supporter of the 1986 Single European Act (SEA). The SEA, comprising the completion of the Single Market by 1992 and conceiving a common monetary policy and eventually a common currency, was very much colored by the neoliberal belief in 'more market, less state' that had come to influence European decision-makers in the early 1980s. The liberalization, privatization, and deregulation of sectors such as air and rail transport, telecommunications, energy provision, and financial services were all entailed in this document. Tellingly, a close adviser of the Thatcher government Lord Cockfield had been the author of the White Paper on the Single Market.

This retreat of the state through the European backdoor was easier to secure, since the passage of the SEA depended on like-minded heads of government in the European Council. Fortunately for Kohl, the SEA was not subject to a popular referendum back home. He skillfully exploited the country's collective memory of the Nazi past by framing the question of the Single Market in terms of 'war and peace'. Opposition to the SEA and later Maastricht was thus portrayed as unacceptably nationalist. Indeed, the lone sceptical voice came from the head of the central bank Karl Otto Pöhl. He was placated by Kohl's insisting on strict monetarist stability criteria as a condition for EMU participation (Beuter, 1994).

Since alternatives to European integration were portrayed as a relapse into German nationalism, economic liberalization could be marketed as *the price to pay for Europe*. The Maastricht project served as a useful tool and excuse to push through changes in economic policy, which would have been difficult or even impossible to secure at the domestic level. The European Commission became a formidable player in breaking up Europe's once powerful state monopolies in railroads, telecommunication, air transportation, and, more recently, gas and electricity provision (Heritier *et al.*, 2000). The partial privatization of Deutsche Telekom, following the break-up of state-owned post, telecommunication, and banking giant Deutsche Bundespost in 1989, and the issuing of shares on 18 November 1996 and 28 June 1999 (*Frankfurter Rundschau*, 13 July 2002) were used to create a culture of equity holdings in a risk-aware country wedded to traditional bank deposits.

German unification served as a launching pad for a more aggressively neoliberal macroeconomic policy and experimenting with shock therapy. Having discredited opponents to European integration as latter-day nationalists, during the 1990 general election Kohl attacked Social Democrat candidate Oskar Lafontaine for not sharing nationalist exuberance over the prospect of reunification and pointing miserly to the costs instead.

Unification proved very dear. Between 1991 and 1998, a total of DM 1.370 billion were transferred to the East for social security, state aids, investment, and infrastructure programs (DIW, 1999). Wholesale institution transfer abolished the more progressive East German welfare state. Kohl accepted a conversion rate of parity between the two currencies. This priced East German products out of their markets everywhere. The privatization of the formerly state-owned enterprises, involving some 8490 companies in 1990, 23 300 companies in 1994, and still 23 610 in 1998 (DIW, 1999), enabled Western companies to skim off the cream of the crop among Eastern companies, often only to close them down eventually anyway and rid themselves of unwanted competition. As Eastern industry collapsed, unemployment skyrocketed (Czada, 1998). Between 1989 and 1998, the registered number of employers in the East decreased from 9.858 million to 7.757 million, while unemployment increased accordingly (DIW, 1999). The subsequent drain on the welfare systems was enormous. According to *Bundesbank* figures, between 1991 and 1998, social security payments in the East increased from DM 56 million to DM 84 million annually (DIW, 1999).

The recession of the early 1990s and the rapid rise of unemployment were portrayed by economic liberals as products of the German model's structural deficiencies (*Berliner Zeitung*, 15 July 1996, 15 April 1997; Siebert, 1997, 1999; Funk, 2001) rather than the ramifications of a poorly engineered economic unification process. Indeed, the persistent differences in unemployment rates between the East and the prosperous South question such systemic crisis. The national unemployment rate of 10.4 per cent masks the persistent differences between unemployment in Western states Bavaria (5.3) and Baden-Württemberg (4.9) and Eastern states Saxony-Anhaltine (19.7) and Mecklenburg-Pomerania (18.3). In absolute figures, there are 1.373 million unemployed in the East with roughly 17 million inhabitants, yet only 2.478 million unemployed in the West out of a general population of 60 million (Destatis, 2005).

Despite persistent unemployment and union weakness in the East that allow for more 'flexible' wage levels and working hours there, investment has been lackluster. Economic liberals did not reflect upon this challenge to their claims that lower wages and complacent employees would lead to more investment. Instead, the association of major businesses, BDI, drummed up a vociferous debate on the need to deregulate the labor market, cut taxes, and abandon the system of standard wage contracts to secure the future of Germany as an attractive site for investment and production (*Standortdebatte*) (*Berliner Zeitung*, 15 July 1996, 20 September 1997). This debate was mainly conducted and supported by the economically liberal dailies (*Die Welt, Die Zeit, FAZ*) and the business press (*Handelsblatt, Wirtschaftswoche, Capital*) and supported by economic liberals in academia (Dornbusch, 1993; Siebert, 1997, 1999). The key assertion was that presumably inflated wage levels and employer contributions to unemployment compensation schemes presented an intolerable burden on business and kept both domestic and foreign companies from investing in Germany. In 1997 President Herzog famously demanded a fundamental shift (*Ruck*). The head of the major business organization BDI Hundt encapsulated this sentiment when he quipped: 'Societal consensus has cost us millions of jobs.' The threat to 'exit' and relocate production was often mentioned; relocation not necessarily to Southeast Asia, but to low-wage high-skill locales nearby, such as Portugal or Ireland within the EU, and Poland and the Czech Republic (at the time) outside the EU, but in close geographic proximity. A second important strand of this debate was the search for models, from which Germany could presumably learn lessons to reform its labor market and welfare state. The attention turned from neoliberal 'models' like New Zealand and the US to the 'Dutch miracle' and more lately to Denmark, even though none of these countries is truly comparable to Germany in terms of size or economic structure. The BDI along with employer association BDA has lost its faith in the Rhineland model (interview A).

Latter-day corporatist alliances have proved very useful in Europe to assure labor acquiescence to unpopular measures, such as austerity measures, cuts in welfare spending, and the deregulation of the labor market. The Kohl government united employers and unions in the 'Alliance for Employment' in 1996. As an indication of things to come, the government sought to reduce wage payment during periods of illness to 50 per cent. If this measure was supposed to test the water, it only proved that the unions were not yet prepared to go down without a fight. They left the alliance and refused to usher in further 'reform'.

The SPD had failed to win the national elections with a leftist candidate in 1990 and a centrist in 1994. In 1998 a representative of the right was nominated. As prime minister of the *Land* of Lower Saxony, Schröder had been on the board of directors of partially *Land*-owned car company VW. His fit with the business community was accordingly close. Though representing a clear shift to the right, the SPD re-branded itself as the *Neue Mitte* (New Center) and offered 'not to make everything differently, but a lot of things better'. This involves internalizing the competition state logic of rendering Germany attractive to international investors. Indicative of this policy paradigm shift is the Schröder–Blair paper of June 1999, enthusiastically welcomed by the BDI. This joint policy paper emphasizes that 'competitiveness' is best secured by reducing taxes on corporations and high-income earners and capping public expenditure, while reducing labor and social protection and forcing welfare recipients to accept employment. While in the past 'the path towards social justice has always been one of higher public expenditure, without regard for results or the effects of a high tax burden on competitiveness, employment or private expenditure' and 'the belief that the state should address damaging market failure all too often led to a disproportionate expansion of the government's reach and the bureaucracy that went with it' this path is to be abandoned in favor of 'competition in the product markets and free trade [which] are of pivotal importance for the stimulation of productivity and growth' (Schröder /Blair, 1999: 2). Government's role is to do 'all it can to support enterprise but never believes it is a substitute for enterprise' since 'the essential function of markets must be complemented and improved by political action, not hampered by it.' Similarly, 'corporate taxes should be simplified and the income tax reduced' while to 'make the European economy more dynamic, we have to make it more flexible as well', involving making the supply-side 'adaptive' (Schröder/Blair, 1999: 4). This involves not only avoiding deficit spending since it is 'an unfair burden on future generations', but also that 'we expect, however, that everyone accepts the [job] opportunities afforded to him'. In rhetoric plainly reminiscent of the US New Democrats, the authors go on to posit that 'part-time work and seasonal work is better than no work' and thus it is only logical that 'all recipients of transfer payments ... are to be examined regarding the extent to which they can earn their own income' (Schröder/Blair, 1999: 6). Finally, 'the labour market needs a sector with low wages to afford low qualified with jobs' (Schröder/Blair, 1999: 7).

The SPD's left wing had not been silenced yet. Its vocal representative, Schröder's first Minister of Finance Lafontaine, was encouraged to resign on 11 March 1999 over Schröder's rejection of his neo-Keynesian budget proposal. The unions were placated by nominating former union official Walter Riester to the post of Minister of Labor and Social Affairs and by minor policy concessions that undid some of the last minute labor market liberalization efforts of the Kohl government, but proved more of a tactical concession than a divergence from the path outlined in the policy paper.

Schröder's new and current Minister of Finance Hans Eichel adhered to 'permanent austerity' policies. Notwithstanding the extended recession since 2000/2001, the Schröder government insisted on budget consolidation and has aimed at reducing the deficit to zero by 2006. In fiscal policy, the tax reform of 14 July 2000 exempts companies selling shares from tax liability, thus encouraging banks to sell off their cross-holdings, underpinning the Rhineland-style system of finance. Corporate tax rates were reduced to 25 per cent (*Frankfurter Rundschau*, 25 June 2002).

If the Social Democrats described a turn to the right, the Greens were even better for surprises. At the very moment that it could have left its imprint, the party's economic policy was dominated by staunchly neoliberally oriented MPs, predominently Oswald Metzger. For the Greens in power, an anti-statist tradition could easily translate into neoliberal advocacy of a lean state. Its support base of now well-established former student protesters accept this policy. Consequently, the Greens' initiatives of introducing a substandard wage sector and merging unemployment compensation with the minimal welfare benefits to a new 'basic subsidence' (*Financial Times Deutschland*, 29 May 2002) resemble those of the liberal Free Democrats.

Unemployment might have been the straw that broke Kohl's back; Schröder's campaign pledge was to reduce it. He wasted no time in reviving the Alliance for Jobs and Education in the fall of 1998. Thematic working committees were set up. A group of *Neue Mitte* social scientists, partially funded by media conglomerate Bertelsmann, was commissioned to draw up reform proposals. Its findings advocate New Democrat-style active labor market policy (Bertelsmann Stiftung, 2002). One such initiative was the proposed establishment of a low-wage sector for which the state would cover employers' social contributions.

In 2002 a commission led by VW personnel manager Peter Hartz proposed similar measures aimed at labor market deregulation. These proposals seek to increase the individual's burden in the job search. In rhetorically setting the stage for further cuts in social expenditure and higher demands on job seekers, Schröder announced that there is 'no such thing as a right to sloth'. This discourse is embodied in the 'Job Aktiv' Law of 19 September 2001 (*Frankfurter Rundschau*, 27 June 2002). In the autumn of 2002, Schröder pledged to implement further Hartz proposals. Strengthened by having won the elections, he merged the 'red' Ministry of Labor with the staunchly economically liberal Ministry of Economic Affairs, replacing ex-union official Riester with Wolfgang Clement, a proclaimed admirer of Thatcher's reforms.

On 14 March 2003, Schröder launched a wide-ranging legislative proposal that seeks to deregulate the labor market, decrease welfare spending, and partially privatize health insurance. Known as 'Agenda 2010', this package is based on the Hartz proposals, but also contains significant cuts in personal tax for both the highest income earners and more modest reductions at the bottom end. Although accepted both by the Social Democrats and the Greens, as well as the opposition Christian Democrats and initially approved in the *Bundestag* on 17 October 2003, the opposition briefly blocked the passage of this law in the *Bundesrat*, successfully demanding that certain limits on 'acceptability' (*Zumutbarkeit*) of jobs for the unemployed be abolished. Agenda 2010 is a clear indication of the extent to which business and employers' associations have been successful in colouring the political agenda with their *Standortdebatte*. Indeed, the BDI enthusiastically welcomed this package, while the unions were unable to formulate a coherent policy position (*Berliner Zeitung* 30 May 2003, 2 June 2003b).

The four Hartz measures implemented so far are a drastic illustration of choosing US-style workfare policy over traditional Social Democracy and preferring punitive supply side policy to constructive demand side stimulus. Their actual performance record is mixed. The first part of Hartz, implemented in January 2003, permitted private labor agencies temporarily to hire unemployed individuals and despatch them to third parties. Only one-third of the 44 732 individuals involved have found permanent employment as a result. The second part, effective as of April 2003, created a tax-exempt status for low-income earners and promoted entrepreneurism. Critics highlight the conversion of standard jobs into multiple 'mini jobs' and question just how sustainable the 142 000 newly created one-man companies will turn out to be. The third section of Hartz has renamed and sought to restructure the unemployment offices, starting in January 2004. The fourth component has caused the most controversy and opposition. It abolishes the second tier of German unemployment assistance and limits eligibility for the more generous upper tier of unemployment benefits to 12 months. Critics point out that the new level of the lower tier in many cases lies below the official poverty line. Mass demonstrations, especially in the East, have highlighted the danger in imposing workfare policies on regions where the labor market cannot accommodate most job seekers. Individuals refusing 'reasonable job offers', 'employability' training measures, and constant efforts to actively seek employment face punitive measures in the form of benefit cuts by up to 100 per cent in the case of youngsters under 25. Most menacing from the perspective of unions is the imposed duty for recipients to accept jobs that are remunerated at up to 30 per cent below standard wage clauses. Regional and communal governments are exempted from this requirement and may remunerate their employees at even lower rates.

5. Conclusion

This chapter contributes to one of the key debates in comparative political economy on 'varieties of capitalism', influenced by the challenges of greater economic internationalization. I argue that *both* the early predictions of convergence on an Anglo-Saxon model (Albert, 1991; Streeck, 1996) *and* more recent studies emphasizing continued divergence of distinct 'organized variety of capitalism' (Hall and Soskice, 2001; Scharpf and Schmidt, 2000) need to be amended. While the politico-economic governance institutions in Germany continue to diverge from the liberal Anglo-Saxon model, functional convergence is occurring as policy and rhetoric endorses standard neoliberal measures. Thus, while no neoliberal 'revolution' has occurred as in Britain and New Zealand, actual policy output has assumed a distinctly neoliberally tinted direction.

Numerous veto points have helped impede the rapid policy implementation characteristic of the neoliberal reforms aided by Westminster-style political systems. The federal system of Germany and its bicameral parliament presents numerous opportunities to curtail rapid and comprehensive reform. In addition, historically relatively strong and united trade unions can act as extra-parliamentary veto players.

However, a more gradual move toward neoliberal policies commenced in the 1980s nevertheless. Crucial to this was the ideological shift first of the conservative parties and later the Social Democrats. Catering to a changing electorate that is less Catholic, less rural, or less overtly self-identified working class might provide part of the explanation. Certainly, the advocacy of organized business is another powerful factor. The smaller coalition partners such as the Free Democrats, and curiously later the Greens, have further sustained and supported the endorsement of a more liberal policy agenda. I have highlighted the decline of systemic competition posed by state socialist East Germany and Nazism.

Realizing the difficulties implied by a multiple veto point political system, policy-makers have employed three tactics to implement economic liberalization: first, seek to circumvent the national arena by supporting economic liberalization through the backdoor of the EU; second, attempt to secure union compliance or even support of unpopular economic measures by unions; third, rhetorically present economic liberalization as the only possible path, thus applying the Thatcherite slogan of 'there is no alternative'.

While not having experienced wholesale convergence and despite the resilience of distinct Rhineland-style institutions, it is essential not to overestimate the importance of such continued institutional divergence and misleadingly insist on organized capitalism as a distinct variety. Functional convergence implies that in terms of both policy and discourse, Germany has accepted the neoliberal logic of the competition state. It has accepted the constraints of the Maastricht criteria and even helped create them. With neoliberalism having engulfed a country traditionally considered a stalwart of Rhineland resistance in the Anglo-American world, there is relatively little competition or challenge left for ideological hegemony currently enjoyed by this paradigm.

Interviews

A – Representative of German Employer Federation BDA, Berlin, March 2001.
B – Green MP, Berlin, April 2001.
C – Representative of SPD, Berlin, April 2001.

Further reading

Harding, Rebecca and William E. Paterson (eds) (2000) *The Future of the German Economy: An End to the Miracle?*, Manchester, UK: Manchester University Press. An excellent edited volume, comprising a number of important contributions on the debate about the future of the German political economy.

Bischoff, Joachim, Frank Deppe, and Klaus Peter Kisker (eds) (1998) *Das Ende des Neoliberalismus? Wie die Republik verändert wurde*, Hamburg: VSA Verlag. An interesting collection of essays that reflect on the Kohl era and its impact on the political-economic culture, economy, and society in Germany.

Dümcke, Wolfgang and Fritz Vilmar (eds) (1996) *Kolonialisierung der DDR: Kritische Analysen und Alternativen des Einigungsprozesses*, Münster, Germany: Agenda. A thought-provoking edited collection on Kohl's approach to German unification, in many ways contributing to the current political and economic malaise.

Useful websites

<www.diw.de>   Website of the German Institute for Economic Research in Berlin.

<www.bmwa.bund.de>   Website of the German government's newly created joint ministry for economic and labor affairs.

<www.iab.de>   Website of the governmental Institute for Labor and Employment Research.

3

Making Thatcher Look Timid: the Rise and Fall of the New Zealand Model

Georg Menz

> *Social – we had quite enough of that. What we needed was the market, was liberalization.*
>
> Roger Kerr, former New Zealand Treasury official, quoted in *Der Spiegel*, 2 September 1996: 36

> *Do not try to advance a step at a time. Define your objectives clearly and move towards them in quantum leaps. ... Once the programme begins to be implemented, do not stop until you have completed it. The fire of opponents is much less accurate if they have to shoot at a rapidly moving target.*
>
> Roger Douglas, former New Zealand Minister of Finance, in Douglas 1993: 67

1. Introduction

Over the course of the past 20 years, the remote South Pacific nation of New Zealand has attracted a great amount of interest from policy-makers, journalists, and academic analysts alike. Formerly renowned as the home of a paternalistic comprehensive welfare state, green politics, and its pioneering role in granting females the right to vote, the Lange Labour government and ambitious Minister of Finance, Roger Douglas, commenced a comprehensive and radical program of economic liberalization, deregulation and privatization in 1984. This remarkable comprehensive package of neoliberal macro-economic reform measures was implemented at breakneck speed. Despite the absence of pressure from international financial institutions, the nature and even the sequencing of this new 'New Zealand Model' very closely resembled Washington Consensus-style structural adjustment programs. Obvious parallels to the United Kingdom appear as well, though New Zealand policy-makers were 'out-Thatchering Mrs. Thatcher' (*The Economist*, 1991). Within less than four years, the country's economy changed from being one of the most regulated in the OECD to being among the least deregulated (*The Economist*, 1996; Goldschmitt, 1996), receiving high marks by the right-wing Fraser's Institute in its index of economic freedom. The 'Kiwi School of Economics' impressed international press, foreign policy-makers, and academics. In the 1990s, 'Model New Zealand' was warmly endorsed and recommended by economic liberals in Europe and North America alike as a successful exercise of embracing the best way 'to get fit for the tough economic competition out there' through a policy of 'reduced ... Government's deficit, lowered taxes, deregulated industry and opened ... markets' (US Senate Hearings, 19 April 1994). Although the architect of 'Rogernomics' himself stepped down in the wake of the popular backlash against his policies, the conservative National Party continued his legacy after having ousted Labour from power in the 1990 elections. Under the stewardship of the new Minister of Finance, Ruth Richardson, both the formal structures of New Zealand's welfare state were dramatically cut back and its informal structures in the form of statist industrial relations and industrial policy were radically transformed.

However, despite creating much excitement among economic liberals for making Thatcher and arguably even Pinochet look timid, by the early 2000s it appeared as though the wheels were coming off the 'New Zealand model'. Even staunch defenders had to concede that the reforms were 'far from optimally executed' and that 'nobody can argue that New Zealand is now a world-beater' (Wolf, 2004). Fifteen years of painful economic and social adjustment had failed to deliver sustainable economic growth. The reforms had done little to address two persistent structural weaknesses of the New Zealand economy: its pronounced dependence on foreign direct investment and its heavy reliance on exporting primary commodities. The Labour government returned to power in 1999 may have embraced Blairite 'Third Way' rhetoric, but, unlike its British counterpart it felt compelled to implement a number of social and labor market policies that marked clear departures from Rogernomics, reflecting both pressure from the smaller coalition partner and the tremendous unpopularity of the New Zealand model among the electorate.

This chapter has three objectives: first, to analyse the neoliberal reforms; second, to trace the ideological origins of the New Zealand reform program and highlight the domestic institutional parameters or receptors that facilitated the speedy and comprehensive implementation, offering Douglas and his cohort in the Treasury the opportunity to turn the country into a 'test tube of neoliberalism' (Halimi, 1997); and third, to explore to what extent New Zealand is congruent with an international trend toward functional convergence on the competition state model. I advance the claim that many of the economic ideas influencing policy-makers were imported from international financial institutions, think tanks, and universities in the US;

'policy learning' from the former colonial power influenced New Zealand greatly, and the Treasury's 'competency monopoly' in combination with the unique powers afforded to governments in Westminster-style systems permitted rapid implementation and stifled opposition.

2. Introducing New Zealand's economic reform program

While other Anglo-Saxon countries, such as the US and the UK, preceded the paradigmatic movement from Keynesianism to New Right monetarism and indeed served as models for New Zealand, no other OECD country underwent a policy shift as radical, thorough or as quickly. From being one of the most regulated countries in the OECD the pendulum swung to the opposite extreme.

Perhaps surprisingly, it was a Labour government which jump-started a radical program of deregulation, market liberalization and privatization of state-owned enterprises. Both the OECD and *The Economist* were most impressed with the rapidly implemented economic reform program,[1] which radically altered the role and scope of government in New Zealand within a few years.

The reform program bears a striking resemblance to Washington Consensus-style structural adjustment programs (Lattimore, 1987), leading one analyst to study New Zealand as a 'critical case', and demonstrating its shortcomings, pitfalls, and the prolonged period for any positive macroeconomic performance to emerge, even under amiable conditions (Schwartz, 1991). Indeed despite the absence of IMF or World Bank pressure, a highly developed infrastructure, and an educated workforce, the immediate results of neoliberal adjustment were nearly 10 years of stagnation in terms of real GDP growth and rapidly increasing unemployment (from 4.6 per cent in September 1984 to 10.9 per cent in 1991, still at 7.7 in 1998, commencing decline only in 2000). Not only was the economic track record of Rogernomics highly mixed even on its own terms, and at close inspection very far removed from the success story portrayed in the media, these reforms created serious social problems commonly associated with neoliberal structural adjustment, including rapidly rising crime rates (Kelsey, 1997) and the replacement of an egalitarian social culture with the celebration of income and social inequality. Macroeconomic growth in the mid-1990s once again came to a standstill in 1997, when short-term portfolio and real estate investment fled New Zealand during the Asian financial crisis and export to that region was heavily affected. Almost 20 years after reforms commenced, New Zealand is worse off in terms of macroeconomic growth, unemployment, and income distribution than it was in 1984.

Tables 3.1 and 3.2 provide a comprehensive overview of the key reforms enacted in the 1980s and 1990s.[2] The sequencing of the reforms appeared to shadow the classic pattern of structural adjustment programs, but also

52

Table 3.1 The New Zealand reform program in terms of international trade, monetary and fiscal policies

International Trade

8 November 1984	Export-oriented subsidies and incentives removed completely or announced to be phased out – affected areas included manufacturing, agriculture, fishing, forestry, and tourism.
21 November 1984	Package of measures aimed at the liberalization of the financial sector.
6 March 1985	Limits on foreign ownership of New Zealand financial institutions removed.
1985	Deregulation of foreign direct investment; very liberal regime for portfolio investment and repatriation of profits.
9 September 1985	Treasury announces schedule to phase out import licensing by 1992 and reduce tariff protection.
18 August 1988	Prime Minister signs protocol for free trade agreements with Australia, removing most trade barriers by 1 July 1990.
18 April 1989	Manufacturing trade barriers between NZ and Australia to be removed as of July 1989.
December 1991	Government announces further streamlining of approval of foreign direct investment.

Monetary Policy

18 July 1984	New Zealand dollar devalued by 20 per cent.
30 August 1984	Interest rate control removed.
21 December 1984	Reserve Bank effectively abolishes restrictions on foreign currency exchange.
14 February 1985	Minimum public sector security and reserve asset ratios removed.
4 March 1985	New Zealand dollar floated – abandonment of 'crawling peg' and fixed exchange rates.
Since 1987	Tight monetary policy (private savings growth below rate of inflation).
15 December 1989	Reserve Bank of NZ Bill passed. 'Bundesbankization': Bank is now more independent from government, but overall more accountable: government defines objectives, while Bank designs policies. The sole aim for monetary policy is now defined as 'achieving and maintaining stability in the general level of prices'. Target of 0–2.5 per cent price increase by 1992–93.

Fiscal Policy

8 November 1984	As part of 1984–85 budget, government announces first tax reform: removal of some tax exemptions, fringe benefits tax,

Continued

Table 3.1 Continued

	lower marginal income tax rate, announcement of the introduction of a general goods and services tax (GST) as of 1 April 1986.
20 August 1985	Government announces details of further tax reforms, effective as of 1 October 1986: GST tax is to replace most other indirect taxes, its level is set at 10 per cent; a simplified income tax which entails huge cuts at the top end from 66 per cent to 48 per cent and much smaller cuts at the bottom end from 20 to 15 per cent; small adjustments to Social Welfare payments to compensate for the effects of the GST.
18 June 1987	Two months before general elections, the Minister of Finance announces $379 million government surplus and repayment of $600 million overseas debt. This was calculated on a cash flow basis, thus incorporating the gains from the first wave of privatization and the revenue from state-owned enterprises (SOEs), now placed under an obligation to make profit.
17 December 1987	Government announces increase of GST to 12.5 percent as of 1 October 1988 (later postponed to 1 July 1989), an increase in the company tax rate from 28 to 33 per cent as of 1 April 1989, and a flat personal income tax (later withdrawn; instead, income tax at top end reduced to 33 per cent as of 1 October 1988).
10 February 1988	Company tax rate reduced to 28 per cent, personal income tax brackets reduced to three: 33 per cent for income over $30 875 and 24 per cent below, this amounts to another tax cut at the top and a tax increase at the bottom. An exception was made for income below $9500, which was now taxed at 15 per cent. Both changes effective as of 1 October 1988.
19 December 1990	Government announces Economic and Social Initiative, marking the beginning of the end of the welfare state in NZ. Government cuts income support entitlements by between 2.9 and 24.7 per cent as of 1 April 1991. It tightens the benefit eligibility criteria. It establishes reviews to reduce expenditure in housing, education and health.
June 1994	Fiscal Responsibility Act is passed, safeguarding the reforms and curtailing the room for maneuver for future governments. Section 4 mandates that total debt must be reduced to 'prudent levels', operating expenses must not exceed operating revenue on average over a reasonable amount of time, a positive value for government net worth must be maintained, fiscal risks must be managed prudently, and the level and stability of tax rates should be reasonably predictable for future years.

Source: See note 2.

Table 3.2 The New Zealand reform program in terms of industrial and labor policies

Industrial Policy

December 1985	Government announces new guidelines for its commercial activities sector, essentially turning it into profit-making corporations, imposing performance objectives on their managers, non-commercial functions (e.g. employment policy) are cast off.
20 May 1986	The Electricity Division, State Coal Mines, Post Office and Civil Aviation are removed from their respective departments and turned into entities resembling private sector corporations ('corporatization'), which are now subject to taxes and dividends and stripped of any special privileges.
1986	Commerce Act is passed, stating in its preamble that it is 'an Act to promote competition in markets within New Zealand', including such fields as banking, air travel and taxi cabs.
1 April 1987	The State-Owned Enterprises Act goes into effect, providing a legislative framework to these aims. This mandates the newly created state-owned enterprises (SOEs) to operate 'as profitable and efficient as comparable businesses that are not owned by the Crown'. Government corporatizes its trading sector, by turning it into SOEs. 24 SOEs are established, among them the Government Property Services, the Airways Corporation, Forestcorp, Landcorp, NZ Post, Post Office Bank, Electricorp, Telecom, Railways Corporation and Coalcorp.
3 March 1988	Government sells 70 per cent of shares of Petrocorp to Fletcher Challenge.
27 July 1988	Government announces its intention to sell Government Property Services.
28 July 1988	As part of the 1988 budget, government announces its intention to sell off $2000 million worth in assets that year.
18 August 1989	Government sells Rural Banking and Finance Corporation to Fletcher Challenge.
12 December 1989	Government sells Government Printing Office to Rank Group.
3 May 1990	Government sells State Insurance Office to Norwich Insurance.
14 June 1990	Government sells Telecom to Ameritech and Bell Atlantic and NZ companies Fay Richwhite and Freightways.
15 June 1990	Government sells Tourist Hotel Corporation of NZ to Southern Pacific Hotel Corporation Ltd.
May 1992	Government announces studies for further privatization programs.
July 1992	Government sells 57.3 per cent share in Bank of NZ to National Australia Bank.

Continued

Table 3.2   Continued

Labor Policy

Labour Relations Act: regulates size of unions, abolishes practice of using agreements in second-tier bargaining as yardsticks for next round of wage bargaining, Arbitration Court is abolished and replaced by Mediation Service, Arbitration Commission, and a Labour Court.

1 April 1988	State Sector Act extends provisions of Labour Relations Act to the state sector.
3 December 1988	In light of high unemployment, government announces job-subsidy scheme, paying employers for hiring long-term unemployed to perform community work.
19 December 1990	Government abandons tripartitism. Employment Contracts Bill is introduced as part of the government's Economic and Social Initiative. It becomes effective as of 15 May 1991. It repeals the Labour Relations Act of 1987 and combines the Mediation Service Court into an Employment Tribunal and renames the Labour Court into Employment Court. It liberalizes the labor market, by abolishing mandatory union membership and allows employees and employers to choose between collective and individual employment contracts. Since employment contracts can be negotiated with or without the aid of an intervening agent, union power is severely undermined.

Source: See note 2.

displays remarkable similarities to early 1980s Thatcherism. Essentially, neoliberal restructuring in New Zealand proceeded in two major phases. The Labour Party, in power between 1984 and 1990, implemented textbook-style monetarist policy. The government committed itself to a strictly monetarist anti-inflationary regime by means of sustaining high interest rates and exchange rates, just as Thatcher had done during her first term (Riddell, 1983: 61). Price stability was enshrined as the overarching goal in the Reserve Bank Act of 1989, leading to what can be described as the 'Bundesbankization' of the institution. The first steps of deregulation affected the financial sector, and included the removal of exchange rates and a floating of the New Zealand dollar. In international trade, tariffs and currency controls were removed, export subsidies and incentives abolished, regulations on foreign direct investment eased and a free trade area with Australia was created. Fiscal policy was also radically reconfigured, cutting top tier income tax and embracing indirect taxation. A goods and services tax (GST) was introduced, following equivalent measures by the UK Conservatives (Riddell, 1983: 62). In industrial policy, government activity and the public sector as a whole were fundamentally restructured. Government departments were reorganized into so-called state-owned enterprises (SOEs), resembling the structures of the corporate sector. In most cases these transformed entities were consequently privatized, transferring ownership predominatly to Australian or American companies. This two-step process of 'corporatiza-tion' imitated that of the UK (Riddel, 1983: 170–83; Kavanagh, 1990: 222), but went much further, including not only telecommunications, transporta-tion services, oil, banking, insurance, postal services and government-owned forests, but extending to government research facilities, hospitals, public housing, and universities. The changed industrial policy also entailed dras-tic reductions of state subsidies for farmers, a traditional clientele of the National Party. Farming subsidies were reduced from NZ$1.2 billion in 1983 to NZ$206 million in 1990. While National promised the return to a 'Decent Society' in its 1990 campaign, once in power, it continued the reforms, tar-geting the lower socioeconomic strata and Labour's milieu with its cuts in social and welfare spending and legislation aimed at drastically curbing union influence. Collective bargaining was completely abolished in the 1990 Employment Contracts Act and essentially ended the influence of trade unions overnight. Both political parties shared the same underlying neolib-eral philosophy (for useful overviews of the reform program see Easton, 1989; Boston, 1991; Sharp, 1994; Bollard *et al.*, 1996; Kelsey, 1997).

This 'big bang' reform program is all the more remarkable as it constitutes a radical departure from the past. New Zealand has a long history of heavy state interventionism and extensive government regulation. Government intervention, traditionally regarded as beneficial and a cautiously modernizing force, included measures more commonly associated with state socialism, such as tight controls on the import and export of currency, high tariffs, import quotas, and a central government agency coordinating export policy. Barry Gustafson notes that:

> Manufacturers and wage-earners were protected by import controls, and farmers were encouraged to produce and were protected from fluctuations in overseas markets by subsidies, tax incentives, and producer boards [responsible for the co-ordination of marketing of products]. The banking system and value of the currency were tightly controlled. (Gustafson, 1997, my addition in square brackets)

New Zealand had previously attracted international attention for a very different reason; a world-wide pioneer in creating a universal health care system during Labour's first term in office (1935–49), the government also endeavored to attain full employment as the core pillar of its employment-based welfare state. Through sheltering domestic production, limiting immi-gration, and directly intervening into wage settlement through juridical settlement of wage claims, the government aimed at providing 'fair wages', while the welfare net created in the 1940s supported the minute number of unemployed. The patriarchic 'male breadwinner' aspect of social policy was partly addressed through legislative bans on gender discrimination in wage policy in the 1970s and the establishment of a domestic purposes benefit (DPB). Unemployment reached an annual average of 10.7 per cent between 1960 and 1974 (Roper, 1977) and in the early 1970s government ministers could still credibly claim to know all the unemployed of Wellington on a first-name basis.

The structure of antipodean social policy was thus quite different from other regimes, but it also critically hinged on near full employment. With its heavy reliance on the export of primary commodities and an industrial policy aimed at sheltering its manufacturing sector from world markets, a form of import substitution policy, the New Zealand economy bore curious resemblance to Latin American structures. Indeed, just like many developing countries, the country weathered the 1970s very poorly. The world market prices for the key export goods – wool, meat, and dairy products – comprising 40 per cent of total exports as recently as 1981 had deteriorated by over 20 per cent from the early 1970s to the end of the decade. Since oil prices had increased dramatically, the terms of trade had suffered accordingly. The key export market Britain had dramatically reduced its agricultural imports following European Community entry in 1973 (Gould, 1985: 43; Schwartz, 1991: 235; Dalziel and Lattimore, 1996: 30–46). The center-right Muldoon government responded by raising public expenditure and creating major industrial plants and infrastructure facilities. Vaguely Keynesian-inspired, these measures were marketed as 'think big' industrial policy, but were ridiculed by opponents as 'sink big'. Social policy expenditures rose steadily, as National had managed to take over power from Labour in 1975 partly by promising a generous pension scheme that offered retirees a 70 per cent rate of their final salary.

3. Ideological origin and the role of domestic receptors

Serious economic problems discussed above notwithstanding, the complete ideological turnaround and the radical departure from Muldoon's 'paternalistic Keynesianism' in the early 1980s is puzzling. Obviously, the end of *les trente glorieuses*, stagflation, the oil crises, and the emergence of low-price, high-quantity competitors in manufactured goods in Southeast Asia were global phenomena that challenged the Keynesian postwar consensus throughout the West. In addition, New Zealand's 'Third World problem' of possessing a distorted economic structure as part of its colonial heritage was shared by many parts of the Global South. What makes New Zealand remarkable is that despite the absence of pressure from international financial institutions, or indeed a military junta as in Chile, comprehensive neoliberal reform measures were implemented that were not only more radical than Thatcherism but also much more alien to New Zealand's political-economic culture, which had embraced state interventionism and had thus split company with the much more limited state activity and liberal concepts of residual or minimal state activity of the former colonial power. How and why did New Zealand elites embrace neoliberalism so comprehensively and why were alternative trajectories disregarded? Even the process (as opposed to the content) of the reforms was unique, pursued in a deliberately rapid, confrontational, and aggressive fashion that stunned and outmaneuvered opponents both within and outside of Labour. Juxtaposed with Australia, which adopted a much more gradual and cautious reform program (Easton and Gerritsen, 1995), incorporating unions rather than antagonizing them, resulting in much lower rates of unemployment and higher macroeconomic growth, Douglas's blitzkrieg-style approach, epitomized in the epigraph to the chapter becomes apparent.

The simplest answer (and indeed rhetorical defense) is the mantra of 'there is no alternative'. Douglas himself (1993) and fellow ideological travelers (Massey, 1995: 176) claim that given the structural economic problems, coupled with growing public debt and unfavorable productivity trends, the harsh neoliberal medicine administered was precisely what was needed to jumpstart economic growth and curtail worrying economic developments. Yet this would appear more of an ideologically inspired dictum then an accurate analysis. On its own terms, the reforms have not had the desired success. The macroeconomic performance is mixed at best. Major structural problems have not been addressed sufficiently. If the strategy was to turn New Zealand into a competition state, ensuring the 'optimization of the capital investment process at the national level in regard to the globalized accumulation process and in permanent competition with other national "locales for investment" ' (Hirsch, 1998: 33), then the results are lackluster, given the lack of success in attracting foreign direct investment.

Yet it is unclear why there was no alternative. Numerous European countries successfully finetuned macroeconomic policy-making in the 1980s and only later, and less radically, began to implement neoliberal policies.

Analysing the intellectual sources and channels of influence can provide a more sophisticated answer to the question why this particular type of reform was pursued. Three factors played a crucial role. First, *channels* through which largely foreign ideas could travel, secondly, the *structural configuration* of the political system and a perceived *competency monopoly* benefited the reformers, and thirdly, *opportunity space* for actors existed. In the rapidly expanding literature, policy learning (Sabatier, 1988), that is, conflict of actors, is set apart from policy transfer (Dolowitz et al., 2000; Evans, 2004).

New Zealand in 1984 had several alternatives to pursuing an economic policy that marked a clear break from its previous history of paternalistic state interventionism. A clear break from any path dependency, the ideas and intellectual constructs embraced by Douglas and his fellow travelers at the Treasury, Reserve Bank and the right-wing think tank, New Zealand Business Roundtable, were imported from abroad. Key actors had received training or education in the US. The reformers benefited from the qualities of the 'elected dictatorship' of a Westminster-style system that left little room for parliamentary opposition. Maybe equally importantly was the perceived *competency monopoly* that Treasury officials enjoyed on economic issues. Their comprehensive reform package was successfully portrayed as both scientifically competent, relevant to the context, and as the only possible solution. Other societal actors were unable to voice alternative approaches. Finally, *opportunity space* existed, as Muldoon's policies had become thoroughly de-legitimized. Somewhat ironically, left-wing discontent over Muldoon's patriarchical heavy-handed policy-making style, including not least his permission for apartheid-era South Africa's Springbok rugby team to tour the country, led to his government's downfall in the 1984 elections. Serving both as prime minister and minister of finance, his vulgar Keynesianism seemed to have exacerbated the structural problems, while contributing to the balance of payment problems experienced in the early 1980s. While the seriousness of this crisis is debatable, the climate fostered facilitated opportunity space for new radical approaches. Far from having convinced the elite, or even the entire Labour Party, a small circle of influential government bureaucrats, along with business lobbyists and academic economists united in a common vision of policy proposals, supported by the political pro-business think tank Roundtable of Industrialists and led by the strong-minded minister of Finance, Roger Douglas, radically overhauled the nature of economic policy-making in New Zealand.

4. Ideational sources of the economic reform program

Where did these ideas originate, since they are so alien to tradition? A brief analysis of the two major documents prepared by Treasury officials before the 1984 (*Economic Management*) and 1987 elections (*Government Management*) is highly revealing. Goldfinch (1997) correctly assesses that these 'papers show the influence of a range of New Right neoclassical theory and prescriptions ... Often these writings are borrowed almost verbatim and with questionable relevance to New Zealand's historical and social context'. *Economic Management* was compiled within a mere six weeks and provided the blueprint for the economic policies, which were to be enacted over the course of the following six years.[3] The spirit and letter of these documents betray their heavy indebtedness to the Thatcherite belief in the superiority of market over state, the monetarist Chicago School ideology (Goldfinch and Roper, 1993: 58), and the Public Choice writings, all of which came to dominate the New Zealand reform process (Bollard, 1988; Easton, 1988; Boston, 1991). In that sense, they parallel 'Monetarism is not enough' published by Thatcher ally Keith Joseph in 1978 and the Downing Street Policy Unit's Conservative Manifesto of 18 May 1983 (Kavanagh, 1990).

While there is no room to discuss the normative ideals of Milton Friedman,[4] Friedrich Hayek,[5] and James Buchanan,[6] a fundamental distrust in the state and a reliance on the market for the efficient allocation of resources and the promotion of the greater good can be identified as a common thread.

Referring to the Keynesian policies of the 1970s, the authors of *Economic Management* contest:

> The account of recent history illustrates how the Government has responded to the consequences of unbalanced policies by increasing reliance on interventions designed to suppress the symptoms rather than address the underlying causes of our economic malaise. Other policies are an overhang from past policies and have ceased to promote – or have even come to undermine – the objectives they once had ... [such as] unwarranted state monopolies in the communications and energy sectors ... the protected position of the public service and wider areas of the state sector such as education and health systems ... the protected position of the unions under existing registration procedures ... the under-pricing of state-supplied goods and services. ... There are many explanations for the continuing patterns of unbalanced policy but at the core has been an unwillingness to accept realistic limits as to what the government can deliver to various interests and what it can protect them from. ... There is no room to further stimulate domestic activity in an attempt to raise employment and past experience shows this ineffective beyond the very short term. ... monetary control is going to be essential. This requires the removal of interest rate controls and a substantial program of debt sales. (New Zealand Treasury, *Economic Management*, Part 2, ch. 1: 5–14)

The 1987 document *Government Management* contains similarly spirited advice:

> The more rapidly inflation can be reduced the sooner growth will return. ... Current levels of public expenditure represent a significant burden on the economy. The cost of financing this expenditure is acting to discourage effort and saving ... High debt levels represent a burden on the economy. They also imply a risk of a break in confidence. ... We also believe that wage regulations in a number of areas affecting the labour market are acting to restrict employment opportunities ... We consider that a basis now exists for sustained improvements in New Zealand's overall economic performance. To secure this, though, it seems vital that the disinflation process is maintained; that it be supported by further fiscal consolidation, a further evening out of assistance structures across the economy and an ongoing process of regulatory reform. (New Zealand Treasury, *Government Management*, ch. 4: 4–7)

This brief presentation of key passages from the Treasury's two pivotal policy documents reveals both their intellectual indebtedness to New Right ideology and a tendency to apply textbook-style 'one-size-fits-all' adjustment policies, without reflecting on some of New Zealand's structural particularities. While containing a sweeping indictment of Keynesian-style demand management and government interventionism, even these points of criticism are couched in extremely general language and do not reflect much analysis of how these policies failed in this specific context. The abstract nature of the arguments made is significant because it is indicative of both the highly dogmatic, ideological approach recommended by Treasury officials, while the lack of concrete reference to the New Zealand context reflects the foreign origins of these ideas. In the following sections, the origin and implementation process of these ideas will be examined in close detail.

5. Network channels

There are two network channels of influence worth highlighting. The first major intellectual source was Britain. The former colonial power still holds a considerable amount of influence over the intellectual climate, culture, and educational system of New Zealand. We have noted the remarkable similarities between the two countries' neoliberal reform programs throughout, an observation underpinned by Boston's (1987, 1989) more in-depth comparison. Owing to space constraints, only two will be highlighted in addition to parallels alluded to before. First, the extensive restructuring of the public sector commencing with 'corporatization' of government ministries into SOEs and their consequent privatization (Riddell, 1983), the notion of introducing competition into the public sector and 'managing government' like a private enterprise (Boston, 1991) were concepts used by the Thatcher government in the early 1980s to remodel the British public service radically. Second, Thatcher's key ambition – not unrelated to the privatization of public enterprises – was to curtail the power of a key veto player, trade unions, remove their grip on collective bargaining, atomize it, and render union membership less attractive by encouraging individuals to negotiate on the terms of their work and pay conditions by themselves. Though New Zealand unions were nowhere near as powerful, the country followed this path by adopting the Labour Relations Act of 1987, extended to the rapidly shrinking public sector on 1 April 1988 through the State Sector Act. This legislation sought to curtail union power by regulating their size and abolishing the practice of using agreements in second-tier bargaining as yardsticks for the next round of wage bargaining. It was informed by pure ideology, namely the conviction that excessive wage demands by trade unions constituted the root cause of inflation. Couching the retreat of the state from traditional tripartism into rather euphemistic terms, the Treasury observed in 1987:

> The last three years have seen some significant changes in the labour market and the role of the Government in this market. The Government has moved away from a centralised approach to industrial relations, and wage-fixing in particular. Instead the people directly involved have been encouraged to assume a greater degree of responsibility for finding solutions for their own specific problems. (New Zealand Treasury, *Government Management*, ch. 4: 83)

The National Party added insult to injury with the 19 December 1990 Employment Contracts Bill as part of the so-called Economic and Social Initiative, which repealed the Labour Relations Act, abolished mandatory union membership and allowed employees and employers to choose between collective and individual employment contracts. Since employment contracts can be negotiated with or without the aid of an intervening agent, union power is severely undermined.

While the intellectual influence of Thatcherism is palpable, there was ultimately no frank acknowledgment of British influence by New Zealand policy-makers and Douglas himself (with Callen, 1987, 1993) made scant reference to the UK. Indeed, more tangible and concrete evidence on the import of ideas can be obtained from analysing the careers and educational background of key Treasury personnel.

A second important network channel was educational exchange with the United States. A substantial number of Treasury officials had either received their graduate degrees in the US, had been sponsored by the Treasury to do so, were US economic consultants seconded to New Zealand (Kelsey, 1997: 54), or had spent time at US-based international financial institutions IMF and World Bank. Key personnel, including many of the authors of *Economic Management* and *Government Management*, had therefore received academic training or accumulated job experience abroad, and were keen to implement ideas acquired there in their home country. Grant Spencer worked for the IMF between 1981 and 1984. Rod Deane had worked for the IMF for four years before becoming chief economist and then deputy governor at the Reserve Bank, guiding policy formation (Kelsey, 1997: 47–54). Indeed, former treasury official and current director of the New Zealand Business Roundtable, Roger Kerr admitted: 'We were taught the criticism of Keynesianism and the desire to initiate structural adjustment at international conferences organized by the OECD, World Bank and IMF. We were also always up-to-date on the publications of think tanks, such as the Cato Institute, the Heritage Foundation and the Institute for Economic Affairs in London' (cited in Halimi, 1997). Out of the four Treasury officials who had authored *Economic Management*, two had spent stints at Harvard

(Bryce Wilkinson and Rob Cameron) and one (Graham Scott) had obtained his PhD from Duke University and received additional training at Harvard Business School in 1985 before serving as an adviser and later chief executive of the Treasury between 1980 and 1993 (Kelsey, 1997: 47). This IMF training may help account for the striking similarities of New Zealand's neoliberal reform program to classic IMF structural adjustment programs. Not unlike Chile's 'Chicago Boys' (Valdes, 1995), graduates returning from extensive stints abroad were eager to put neoliberal theory into practice.

Finally, an important domestic source of neoliberal and monetarist ideas that should be mentioned briefly was the department of economics at the University of Canterbury, Christchurch, which many Treasury bureaucrats had attended for their undergraduate education. Whereas Keynesianism was still a dominant paradigm in New Zealand's academic economics department, Canterbury stood at the forefront of embracing neoliberalism, especially faculty member Richard Manning.[7]

6. Domestic receptors

In order to examine a polity's susceptibility to the influx of imported ideas the particular domestic institutional structures merit attention. Two particularities of the domestic system enabled the swift and rapid enactment of comprehensive economic reforms. The *receptors*, or the domestic constellation of political institutions and structures relevant for policy-making in the field of economic policy, responded favorably to the actual implementation.

First, as part of its colonial heritage, New Zealand possessed a Westminster-style 'first past the post' political system, composed of a one-chamber parliament and only two major political parties. In fact, the absence of an Upper House notwithstanding, the country is considered by one analyst to have constituted a more perfect example of the Westminster model than Britain (Lijphart, 1984). The adoption of so-called mixed member proportional (MMP) representation that followed a 1993 referendum has since meant a modification of the previous 'elected dictatorship', creating a need to form continental European-style coalition governments and empowering parliamentary opposition parties. Some analysts have argued that the success of this referendum not only reflected concerns over this 'untamed power' of an 'elected dictatorship' (Kelsey, 1997: 44–5; Schellenberger, 1998), but was also a vote against a political system that facilitated the swift implementation of Douglas' 'blitzkrieg-style' policy-making, 'involving a policy goal radically different from the existing configuration, to be implemented in a short period, following a surprise announcement and a very rapid implementation' (Easton, 1994: 215). Once Labour had won the elections in 1984 and National in 1990, they commanded a comfortable absolute majority of seats. The opposition party could hardly bear any influence on the course of events. Douglas and his allies were notorious for keeping both the public and the

Cabinet uninformed of their next steps. In fact, he himself later acknowledged and even recommended this strategy, as cited in the epigraph. If New Zealand's Westminster-style political system neutered the parliamentary opposition, and aided in a rapid, yet opaque and often even secretive policy-making process, opponents of the hugely unpopular reforms neglected to consider that coalition governments are hard pressed to *reverse* them. Indeed, in rendering the political system more accountable and closer to liberal democratic ideals, a blitzkrieg-style campaign aimed at undoing the reforms became nigh on impossible.

An important second domestic receptor was the unquestioned *competency monopoly* on all questions of economic policy (Goldfinch and Roper, 1993; Boston, 1989) that the Treasury enjoyed. During the Labour government of 1984–90, the Treasury prepared the blueprint documents for the great contours of the reform and generated new policy proposals at rapid speed. Its competency was neither questioned nor challenged from within the government or indeed the party. In fact, it 'became the principal initiator' and formed a 'consistent, cohesive, intellectually convicted group' as Prime Minister Lange later recalled in an interview. In his view, it was able to do so owing to its 'near-monopoly position ... with respect to economic policy advice' within the 'unitary, centralized structure' of the political system in New Zealand (Nagel, 1998: 242). The pivotal role of the Treasury and its Minister continued after the 1990 elections and Ruth Richardson continued the pathway charted by her predecessor. Opposition outside of the government and parliament was slow to form, found it difficult to make its voice heard and even more difficult to challenge the claims of scientific neutrality and value that underpinned the Treasury's approach. The institutional power of the Treasury within the government was not only based on other departments being slow in proposing alternative legislative proposals, it was enhanced through the gatekeeper function the department enjoyed following the 1985 establishment of a Cabinet Policy Committee (Kelsey, 1997: 49), henceforth being able to strike down any challenges to the pathway it helped draft and implement.

Though hardly a unique feature of New Zealand, the role of the influential right-wing think tank, New Zealand Business Roundtable, deserves mention as it played an important role in receiving and disseminating neoliberal ideas, sustaining the Treasury's reform program intellectually, helping propagate Rogernomics as being without alternative, while also serving as a source of inspiration and a gathering forum for like-minded government officials, businessmen, consultants, and academics. Given its ideological proximity to Douglas and later Richardson, the Roundtable's influence on government policy formation was formidable and much more pronounced then that of the somewhat more academic Center for Independent Studies, a New Zealand offshoot of an Australian New Right think tank.

7. Opportunity space for implementation

In addition to a favorable domestic institutional context, the reformers benefited from successfully commanding *opportunity space*. This concept can help account for the fact that certain policies are being received and, more importantly, become implemented at certain moments in time and neither before nor after. Such opportunity space will arise, I suggest, in a situation characterized by a given set of exceptional circumstances or in a crisis, in which a newly arriving leadership confronts a serious economic or political challenge, unusually unfavorable circumstances, poor macroeconomic performance, coupled with an ideological de-legitimation of its predecessor. Such ideological de-legitimation might simply arise from the predecessors' inability to address this crisis effectively, which can then be exploited politically by attributing this failure to the underlying ideological orientation of this government, that is, its ends, not its means.

In 1984, New Zealand found itself in a severe economic crisis, just as Britain did in the late 1970s. The former Muldoon government, its heavy-handed authoritarian state interventionism, and paternalistic Keynesianism had been discredited ideologically. A similar ideological de-legitimation had occurred in the UK. Under these circumstances, Douglas and his collaborators at the Treasury had a formidable opportunity to imprint the ideas they favored upon the economic agenda. A surprisingly frank statement made by Prime Minister Lange in an interview illustrates this point vividly:

> When the crisis hit in July 1984 it was Roger Douglas who, above all, had thought through the economic issues – so when the Cabinet needed to fall back on an economic philosophy, it was Douglas who had one. (*National Business Review*, 11 July 1986)

Opportunity space is therefore an important component in the implementation of New Zealand's reforms. The concept is slightly more encompassing than 'windows of opportunity' and 'punctured equilibria', concepts used in the literature to account for changes in otherwise stable and path-dependent trajectories. An important and interesting question to consider is to what extent interested parties can portray situations as crises specifically for the purpose of broadening the availability of opportunity space. Critics of the New Zealand reforms accused Douglas of exaggerating the extent of the country's balance of payment difficulties in 1984.

8. Embracing the competition state Kiwi-style

A seemingly remote and obscure island nation, New Zealand captured international attention for enacting the most ambitious and thorough neoliberal economic reform program of the 1980s and early 1990s. It has since adopted a more conciliatory policy stance, which, in the words of Michael Cullen, current Minister of Finance, does not, however, question fiscal conservatism and monetary orthodoxy.

New Zealand is a paradigmatic or 'textbook' example of adopting the policies of the New Right, restructuring and fundamentally reshaping the structure, function, and aims of the state. Whereas the previous paternalistic welfare state sought to guarantee an income level through high minimum wages, agricultural subsidies, and a policy aimed a securing high employment, and helped New Zealand enjoy the second highest per capita income in the OECD throughout the 1950s and 1960s, this statist model was challenged by the external shocks of the 1970s as well as by problems adjusting its primary agricultural export products to a changed and often tariff-protected global marketplace. The shock therapy administered by the neoliberal reforms of the 1980s entailed a radical departure from the 'institutionalization of comprehensive class compromises through the incorporation of Social Democratic parties and unions into the political regulation process' (Hirsch, 1998: 29) and an abandonment of the postwar compromise. The goal of this commercialization of New Zealand has been to turn the country effectively into a 'competition state' (Cerny, 1990; Hirsch, 1998), to secure the country's long-term international competitiveness, and to establish it as an attractive locale for international investment. In so doing, the welfare state has been drastically curtailed, the state's functions have been redefined and limited, organized labor has been effectively circumvented, the public sector privatized and sold off to foreign corporations, and society has been thoroughly commodified and marketized. Unsurprisingly, income disparity and social exclusion, particularly among the native Maori, and crime have all risen over the past 20 years.

While neither the economic nor the social ramifications produced by this conversion support any notion of a 'Model New Zealand', as the country was heralded in the late 1990s, the extent to which such attempts were made demonstrate the role of media, along with international institutions, universities, and think tanks to help export ideas globally and provide intellectual support to the process of *internalizing globalization*. The intellectual support of the paradigmatic ideational shift provided by these institutions is of pivotal importance (cf. Gramsci, 1971). Thus, liberal pundits continue to insist that there was no alternative to the textbook conversion of New Zealand to monetarism (e.g. Massey, 1995).

The analysis provided highlights the importance of economic 'ideas' developed at US universities, and applied by the Conservative government of Margaret Thatcher in Britain, have played in New Zealand. Such ideas had to be imported through clearly identifiable *network channels*, namely the role of the UK as a model and New Zealand Treasury officials who had either received graduate training in the US or had served as officials at international institutions such as the IMF. Thatcherite reforms served as a source of inspiration upon which the reform of the public sector and an assault on union power were modeled. Finally, the importance of *receptors* is highlighted, that is, the *domestic political structures and institutions*. In the New Zealand case the Westminster-style political system, ensuring an absolute majority for one party, and the strong influence that the Treasury could exert, both facilitated the policy transfer.

'Rogernomics' has deeply changed the fabric and contours of the New Zealand political economy. Many of the reform measures have been solidified by being turned into legislation that is difficult or even impossible to amend or repeal under the new electoral rules necessitating coalition governments. One example for this is the new independence of the central bank. The privatization of the public sector is similarly difficult to reverse. Thus, even if desired by its citizens, a return to the Keynesian postwar model is impossible.

The Labour–Alliance/Progressives coalition government that took power in 1998 has realized the unpopularity of Rogernomics and made some modest adjustments. These include notably paid parental leave, more generous terms for tertiary education loans and grants, the establishment of a public bank, the partial renationalization of national carrier Air New Zealand, moderate personal tax increases at the top end and, possibly most audaciously, the 2000 Employment Relations Act, repealing previous legislation. Yet despite a shift away from the confrontational policy style and radical content of the 1980/90s reforms, the fundamental architecture has not been affected and the government has avoided revising both the framework and most of the content of its predecessors. Certain similarities with Britain's New Labour Party are obvious, not least given the rhetorical commitment to 'getting the fundamentals right' and emphasizing supply side measures to raise labor market participation rates as the guiding approach to social policy.

The erosion of the old New Zealand model and its replacement by textbook neoliberalism is an example of pursuing the internalization of globalization through the very radical implementaition of a dogma with very controversial practical implications. On closer inspection, New Zealand appears far from being an enviable model. Its policy-makers have learned certain lessons and have abandoned the undiluted neoliberalism of the 1980s. However, recent modest reforms must not be misinterpreted as a sign of radical departure from the framework set in place during the years of Rogernomics. The model may have lost its shine, but the latest wave of reformers not so much seeks to overhaul it completely as adjust it very modestly. New Zealand in the 2000s is still a neoliberal competition state, but it has turned toward 'neoliberalism with a human face'.

Further reading

Kelsey, Jane (1996) *Economic Fundamentalism: A World Model for Structural Adjustment?*, London: Pluto Press. Accessibly written, critical, and based on meticulous research, this comprehensive and authoritative study of the New Zealand neoliberal reforms is probably the best available single monograph on the subject.

Easton, Brian (1997) *The Commercialisation of New Zealand*, Auckland: Auckland University Press. Based on case studies of various policy domains, this detailed and thorough examination of 'Rogernomics' merits attention.

Douglas, Roger (1993) *Unfinished Business*, Auckland: Random House New Zealand. Though self-congratulatory and tirelessly smug, the reflections of the chief architect of New Zealand's economic reform process and his policy advice are worth exploring.

Useful websites

<www.treasury.govt.nz>   Website of the New Zealand Treasury with links to useful statistics and policy papers.

<www.beehive.govt.nz>   Website of the New Zealand Government with many interesting links, named after the curiously shaped parliament building.

<www.nzbr.org.nz>   Website of right-wing think tank, New Zealand Business Roundtable.

<http://www.vuw.ac.nz/ips/index.aspx>   Website of Victoria University's Institute for Policy Studies.

4
Neoliberalism and Policy Transfer in the British Competition State: the Case of Welfare Reform

Mark Evans

1. Introduction

My main submission in this chapter is twofold. First, the British Labour government has adopted a policy agenda, which in its most crucial aspects reflects the continuing transformation of the British State into a competition state. Secondly, within a competition state policy actors and institutions increasingly promote new forms of complex globalization through processes of policy transfer in an attempt to adapt state action to cope more effectively with what they see as global 'realities'. Complex globalization in this context refers to the way in which public policy-making in a globalizing world is increasingly internally and externally complex due to the sheer range of state and non-state actors involved in the delivery of public goods through multi-level governance.

The purpose of this chapter is to consider the significance of these two developments for our understanding of the politics of coping, adapting and internalizing globalization. However, given the sheer size of this task I must begin by limiting the scope of my field somewhat. It will be argued in this chapter that the adoption of contracting post-welfarism in Britain is a key feature of the competition state and a rich source of hybrid policy transfer from the United States and elsewhere. Hence, it is claimed that the study of policy transfer in the welfare policy arena provides fertile ground for investigating the significance of the competition state as a lens for observing both the changing nature of the nation state and the role of state actors and institutions in promoting new forms of complex globalization.

The argument is developed cumulatively and organized into four parts. The first part presents a brief account of the rise and fall of the Industrial Welfare State (IWS), and its replacement with forms of the competition state under neoliberal and centre-left governments in Britain and the United States. It then moves on in the second part to outline the key features of the competition state and generates a series of propositions that are subject to a brief empirical investigation. In the fourth section of the chapter an overview of welfare reform under the current Labour government is presented together with an assessment of the philosophical foundations to Labour's new thinking, and an evaluation of the sources of its ideas. The final substantive section presents data from a case study of policy transfer in the welfare policy arena – the New Deal. The chapter concludes with some general observations about what this case study of the emergence and development of a policy transfer network tells us about the impact of the competition state project on welfare policy development in Britain.

2. The rise of the competition state

The key to understanding the partial victory of the neoliberal approach, whether Thatcherism in the United Kingdom, Reaganomics in the United States, or a range of other fully-fledged or partial experiments, lies in its focus on the priority of controlling inflation. Indeed, the most important single step involved the collapse of the exchange rate system, which had been set up at the end of the Second World War as the core of the Bretton Woods system of international economic cooperation. Differential rates of inflation in different countries were making the system of government-set exchange rates unworkable and it was eventually agreed, if mainly by default, to let exchange rates float (Strange, 1986). In other words, countries with high inflation would see capital flee to countries where the value of the currency was 'sounder'.

Governments responded to this in three main ways. The first was to give priority in macroeconomic policy to fighting inflation over employment and welfare policies, and, in particular, to privilege monetary policy over fiscal policy. The second was to remove capital controls and deregulate financial markets (in addition to other forms of deregulation). And the third was to adopt more rigorous financial management systems and financially led programmes of privatization in the public sector. From the beginning, then, the impetus behind the emergence of the competition state was to adjust the economic policies, practices, and institutions of the state to conform to the anti-inflationary norms of the international financial markets.

In other words, neoliberal states moved away from the 'embedded liberalism' of the postwar period towards an 'embedded financial orthodoxy' in order to root out inflation. On the left, the response was twofold. The first response, especially in Britain, was to revive a belief in increased state intervention, as exemplified by the Labour Party's Alternative Economic Strategy in 1983. However, the second response, after the failure of the first, was to accept the bottom-line of an anti-inflation strategy and to shift the boundaries of the left in order to support rather than undermine such a strategy.

The changes, which occurred to New Labour's policy agenda, must also be understood within the context of internal Labour Party revisionism in response to electoral despair. The revisionism of former leader Neil Kinnock, which developed incrementally after 1983, dealt with the modernization of internal party machinery and the removal of obstacles within to policy innovation. This included a period of consolidation after the defeat of the Bennite-left and the strengthening of the power base of the Parliamentary Labour Party to make policy through the National Executive Committee. These changes permitted the emergence of a new policy agenda crystallized around pro-Europeanization, pro-nuclear defence, the rejection of a general commitment to nationalization and a commitment to a market-oriented economy.

However, it was not until Labour leader John Smith's untimely death in May 1994 and the election of Tony Blair to the Labour leadership in July of that year that Labour revisionism took on an almost evangelical zeal. New Labour's electoral project refocused its attention on supplanting the Conservatives as the natural party of government and represented a historic compromise between social democracy and the market orientation of neoliberalism. New Labour's ability to be perceived as the party of the economy was crucial to the achievement of this aim (Panitch and Leys, 1997). It also meant forging a coalition dedicated to putting the competition state strategy into practice. This was led by Blair but crucially backed up by his closest ally Peter Mandelson, and his main rival Gordon Brown and thus combining 'les enfants terribles' of both 'Old' and 'New' Labour.

By the mid-1990s, the Thatcherite project of a more undiluted neoliberal version of the competition state had lost both its economic edge and its political cohesion, and with the victory of Bill Clinton – who was pursuing much the same project as Blair and Brown (although in a more complex and constraining institutional context) in the 1992 American presidential election – the political tide that saw centre-left governments returned to power across Europe had turned. By this time the New Labour project had become clearly focused on accepting the propositions of the competition state. When considered in the context of Britain having suffered two of the five worst recessions among G7 countries in postwar economic history (1979–81 and 1990–92) it is not surprising that Conservative and Labour governments looked to the epithets of the competition state for answers to the UK's economic problems. Although they have clearly deployed different strategic devices and policy instruments for coping with the impact of varying forms of globalization the degree of coherence across both economic projects has been striking. Policy initiatives such as: the rejection of Keynesian demand management; the emphasis on promoting economic growth through the introduction of supply side policies aimed at freeing up markets and expanding choice; close attention to financial management and control of public expenditure; the defeat of inflation; and, ensuring the conditions for stability in the private sector's planning environment, have all represented common themes in contemporary British economic discourse. Indeed, it is only in Gordon Brown's promissory note to develop an economic package, which achieves 'Globalization with a human face' that certain, contrasts can be found.

After the 1997 general election, the government refocused its programme on reinforcing and extending the neoliberal marketizing trends of the Thatcher period. Brown has launched five main initiatives: greater independence for the Bank of England; the adoption of a code for fiscal stability; a new fiscal framework; the creation of a new finance watchdog; and measures to streamline the Bank of England's operations in currency markets to make them more transparent. Much of this was already under way under the Tories; indeed, it was John Major who first established the counter-inflationary anchor for economic policy between 1990 and 1994. As one might expect from a reform programme of this magnitude, Brown attracted considerable praise and criticism. Will Hutton captures the nature of this reception with some insight with the observation that 'to his right, there is general acclaim; to his left, general dismay' (*The Guardian*, 7 February 1998).

Blair and Mandelson took it as a given that globalization imposes limits on all social and economic policies, and thus the only ones worth promoting are those that are acceptable to 'the market'. Former US President Bill Clinton, Blair and their advisers may view this acceptance of the need to marketize the state as a key element of an emerging policy agenda for the centre-left. On 6 February 1998 Blair and Clinton joined teams of British and US advisers and intellectuals in Washington for a 'wonkathon' (after 'wonk', a US slang term for a policy expert) with the aim of forging an international consensus on the goals of the centre-left for the twenty-first century. Earlier the same day Blair had addressed the US State Department outlining what he termed the 'five clear principles of the centre-left', which he argued were common to both New Labour and the Democrats:

> stable management and economic prudence because of the global economy; a change in the emphasis of government intervention so that it dealt with education, training and infrastructure and not things like industrial intervention or tax and spend;
> reform of the welfare state ('otherwise the right will dismantle it') through Welfare to Work and managed welfarism;
> reinventing government, decentralization, opening-up government ('so that what counts is what works'); and,
> internationalism in opposition to the right's isolationism. (*Ibid.*)

The influence of the New Democrats' 'Progressive Declaration', which was published by the Democratic Leadership Council in 1996, was evident in Blair's statement, particularly the three pillars of the declaration – equal opportunity, personal responsibility and the mobilization of citizens and communities through rights and responsibilities. The main difference between the two projects lay in Brown's emphasis on the importance of long-term organic growth and investment, which is a reflection of Britain's inferior economic position. However, an ever-lengthening list of common policy initiatives developed between the two states providing significant evidence of lesson drawing between Blair and Clinton's advisers. Prominent examples include welfare reform (welfare to work, redirecting welfare to the most needy, creation of work incentives such as working family tax credit), and central bank reform. Certain of these reforms reflect what the New Labour and Democrat spin doctors have subsequently spun as the Third Way, further defined by Blair's favourite political theorist Anthony Giddens (1998, p. viii) as 'social democratic renewal', or similarly by Charles Leadbeater (2000) as 'the core beliefs and values which will sustain the centre-left's hegemony in Britain and beyond'.

The debate over a credible Third Way in British politics between the traditional positions of the Old Right (anti-state and pro-market), and the Old Left (pro-public ownership and state intervention and anti-market), emerged within the context of trying to establish a more coherent future for social democratic politics. There is, of course, nothing new about the use of the term in Labour Party history, although it has been given different meanings. For example, in 1912, Labour Party leader Ramsay Macdonald's claim that Labourism was 'a Third Way between State Socialism and Syndicalism', was greeted with equal derision. However, this particular debate was brought about by three main developments. The first, we have already discussed, the decline of the consensus underpinning the rise and consolidation of the industrial welfare state. The second is related to the fall of the Soviet Empire and the misguided view that this marked the 'final discrediting of Marxism' (Giddens, 1998). The third is a reflection of the emergence of a British Labour government with a large majority but accused of lacking a distinctive political philosophy. The New Labour project emerged as a pragmatic response to electoral failure but grew in coherence as the government matured. Initially, the Labour Party was purely interested in instrumental 'win–win' policies, but once electoral success was achieved the luxury of developing a political philosophy could be explored. Giddens would provide the most comprehensive, though flawed, polemic on the Third Way. Indeed, his thesis would inspire the creation of a virtual industry on the subject (see Giddens, 1998, 2000, 2001, 2002 and Callinicos, 2001, for the finest critique). His argument proceeds from the assumption that '[s]ocial democracy can not only survive, but prosper on an ideological as well as a practical level' (1998, p. vii).

Giddens may justly be criticized for overestimating the impact of processes of globalization on the nation-state. The degree to which globalization conditions state, economy, society and politics differs from state to state, from level of governance to level of governance and from place to place. He may also be accused of underestimating competing strategies for achieving equality such as the role of social or new social movements. It is also far from evident that the knowledge economy can serve as a key instrument for emancipating citizens from the contradictions of capitalism, for the knowledge economy both empowers and disempowers citizens depending on their access to knowledge resources. However, the most serious sins of omission lie in the absence of any detailed consideration of praxis: of how to effectively bond rights and responsibilities in a way that makes sense to the ordinary citizen; of how to create the incentive for citizens to exercise their rights and forge an active citizenry; and, of how to remove barriers to political participation. What we require is specific practical recommendations and not a set of declamatory statements. The devil is in the detail. At the same time he must be praised for offering a center-left vision of future society that has facilitated a progressive war of ideas on the left throughout Britain, Europe and beyond. It is as controversial as it is intellectually provocative.

However, the extent of his influence on Blair remains far from clear. The vagaries surrounding the influence of the Third Way on practical New Labour policy-making is broadly reflective of a working compromise at the heart of the New Labour government between the last shackles of Brown's Old Labour idealism and Blair's pragmatism. The remnants of Brown's 'Old Labour' ideology makes him uncomfortable with fashionable ideologies, while Blair's lack of an ideological center makes him prone to flirtations with in vogue ideas from communitarianism to Christian socialism, from stake-holding to the Third Way. The real influence of the Third Way can be seen in Blair's terms as taking 'the hard edges off capitalism without losing its essential wealth creating drive' (*The Times*, 8 February 1998). In practical terms this means fostering job market flexibility, but at the same time ensuring that those displaced by it are continually retrained so that they remain employable. As Brown (*ibid.*) argues, '[i]t shies away from stiflingly big government, while rejecting the minimalist state favoured by some British Tories and the Republican right'. In sum, the embracing of the ephemeral concept of the Third Way by the Blair government may be viewed as a clumsy attempt to provide a pragmatic political project with some belated ideological coherence in the face of mounting criticism of its social democratic credentials from the Old Left.

3. The theory of the competition state

The main challenge facing governments all over the world is their capacity to adapt to the exogenous constraints and opportunities brought about by different processes of globalization while maintaining a relatively effective domestic policy programme. Within this context, the challenges faced by centre-left parties and governments are particularly problematic. For most of the twentieth century these parties have believed in expanding the boundaries of the state to provide public goods for working peoples, minorities, and other socially valued groups and causes. These interventionary strategies have depended historically upon the capacity of states to make domestic policy in ways that preserve key spheres of autonomy for policy-makers vis-à-vis international capital. However, such autonomy is increasingly being constrained by processes of globalization. Some theorists of globalization suggest that all states are losing power and coherence (for example, compare McKenzie and Lee, 1991, with Reich, 1991), while others maintain that governments are able to adapt and to transform state structures in ways that alter, but do not fundamentally reduce or undermine, state capacity, not only for neoliberal governments of the right but also for social democratic governments of the centre-left (for example, compare Hirst and Thompson, 1999, with Garrett, 1998).

The theory of the competition state provides an alternative conception of this problematic which, while accepting that the state is losing power and coherence because of processes of globalization and transnationalization, argues that the competition state will increasingly become the engine room and the steering mechanism of a political globalization process that will further drive and shape economic, social and cultural globalization (see Cerny and Evans, 2000a, Evans and Cerny, 2003). It should be noted from the outset that the theory of the competition state stands in contrast to the 'Post-Fordist State' of Regulation Theory, which asserts that the restructuring of the state as a consequence of globalization effectively permits the state to maintain its 'generic function' of stabilizing the national polity and promoting the domestic economy in the public interest. It presents six main propositions about how states and state actors adapt and respond to the imperatives of globalization that can be used to explain the trajectory of the British State under the Blair government in Britain.

Proposition 1: the Changing Form and Functions of the State

The competition state involves both a restructuring and a qualitative disempowering of the state in the face of processes of globalization and transnationalization. It may also lead to the empowering of the state in certain areas.

By prioritizing the promotion of international competitiveness, the state over time loses its capacity to act, in Oakeshott's (1976) term, as a 'civil association' and comes more and more to act merely as a promoter of various 'enterprise associations'. In addition, an endogenous process often referred to as the 'hollowing-out' of the state leads to the loss not just of its previous interventionist role, but also of much of its traditional raison d'être. Rhodes (1994, 1997) has argued that there are four key interrelated trends that illustrate the scope of this process: privatization and limits on the scope and forms of public intervention; the loss of functions by central government departments to alternative service delivery systems, such as 'next step' agencies and through market testing; the loss of functions to European Community Institutions and national assemblies through devolution; and the emergence of limits to the discretion of public servants through the New Public Management.

Policy networks are central to understanding internal 'hollowing-out' while globalization is central to understanding a concomitant process of external 'hollowing-out' in a world of complex interdependencies. Hence the policy focus of the state shifts from the macro-level of the Industrial Welfare State (IWS) to a micro-level analogous to the space traditionally occupied by local, provincial, regional or US 'state' governments. Indeed the competition state itself becomes a pivotal agent in the erosion of many of those social and economic functions that capitalist states had taken on in the first two-thirds of the twentieth century. This outcome stems from the interaction of two main variables. In the first place, we can identify an exogenous independent variable – the horizontal restructuring of the global economy and polity, and, perhaps must crucially, the formation of transnational networks and discourses of power and governance.

This exogenous, cross-cutting process of restructuring sets up a series of fundamental challenges to the vertically organized national state and political economy. More specifically it places less emphasis on the physical forces of production per se and more on other factors of capital, especially globally mobile finance capital, and the emergence of relatively autonomous transnational elites who adopt the discourses and practices of globalization in order to pursue their own goals and values on a wider field of action. In other words, the impact of globalization on the policies and policy-making processes of states increasingly involves attempts by governments to capture the perceived benefits of internationally mobile capital. The competition state is thus itself an authoritative agent of globalization, embedding that process in its domestic practices as well as its international and transnational linkages.

The competition state will also seek to enhance its capacity to steer the nation-state. Indeed, Labour's constitutional reform project – the incorporation of the European Convention on Human Rights into British law, the introduction of a Scottish parliament and a Northern Ireland and Wales assembly, the abolition of hereditary peers and reform of the second chamber, the introduction of proportional representation for European elections, and, a Freedom of Information Act – represents a good example of this. For it constitutes a strategy of integration; a process through which new and old political communities are either defined or redefined, created or discarded in both institutional and attitudinal terms. Indeed, historically, devolution has been used as a policy instrument by British governments to assimilate the demands of nationalist movements within the 'nations' seeking greater autonomy (see Evans, 2003). Its main aim is to secure elite attachment to the UK system of governance through the forging of a consensus on national policy goals.

Proposition 2: the Nature of Political Agency

Rather than attempting to insulate states from key international market pressures, as state actors in the National Industrial Welfare State sought to do, political actors in competition states embrace openness and marketization.

State actors and institutions promote new forms of complex globalization in the attempt to adapt state action to cope more effectively with what they see and portray as global 'realities'. Hence they seek to make the domestic economy more competitive while accepting the loss of key traditional social and economic state functions, which were central to the development of the IWS. However, in attempting to meet the challenges of globalization, domestic political and bureaucratic actors increasingly transform the domestic political system into a terrain of conflict underpinned with profound policy debates around alternative responses to globalization (e.g. in Britain the issue of the single European currency). Out of this process of domestic rearticulation, a particular range of policy options comes to represent a restructured, loosely knit consensus: first on the right (many of whose 'neoliberal' members have always believed deeply in the disarming of the economic state) and then on the left, as traditional alternatives are incrementally eroded. This increasingly familiar consensus involves both an extensive process of deregulation, liberalization, and flexibilization not only of public policy but of the state apparatus itself and a refocusing of the state on supporting, maintaining and even promoting transnational and international market processes and governance structures at home. The latter manifests itself in a moral emphasis on personal responsibility, an economic and political acceptance of the correctness of market outcomes, and, paradoxically, an increase in pro-market regulation and intervention (Cerny, 1990; Vogel, 1996). Thus the rationale for state intervention is aimed not only at sustaining the domestic economy but also at promoting its further integration into an increasingly open global economy in the acceptance that the imperatives of international competitiveness and consumer choice have a higher ideological status than issues of domestic social solidarity.

Proposition 3: the Diminishing Role of Ideology

As a result of these changes, some consensual, some coercive, the ideological divide between left and right comes to lose many of its traditional landmarks.

Social democratic and other centre-left parties begin to search for policies, which, while adapting to the new constraints, are intended to promote a diluted form of neoliberalism, or what has been termed the 'Third Way'. In Britain this represents the outcome of the war of ideas between the forces of social democracy and neoliberalism.

Proposition 4: the Internationalization of the Policy Agenda

The creation of a competition state involves a policy agenda, which seeks to provide the conditions that will help the state to adapt state action to cope more effectively with what they perceive as global 'realities'.

In terms of the key elements of economic policy transformation, transnational factors have interacted with domestic politics to bring five specific types of policy change to the top of the political agenda. First, there has been an emphasis on the control of inflation and general neoliberal monetarism – hopefully translating into non-inflationary growth. This has become the touchstone of state economic management and interventionism, reflected in a wider embedded financial orthodoxy. Secondly, a shift from macroeconomic to microeconomic interventionism has occurred, as reflected in both deregulation and industrial policy and in new social initiatives such as 'welfare-to-work' schemes. Thirdly, a shift in the focus of interventionism has also occurred at the international level away from maintaining a range of 'strategic' economic activities in order to retain minimal economic self-sufficiency in key sectors to a policy of flexible response to competitive conditions in a range of diversified and rapidly evolving international market places. Fourthly, new regulatory structures have been established to enforce global market-rational economic and political behaviour on rigid and inflexible private sector actors as well as on state actors and agencies. Finally, a shift in the focal point of party and governmental politics away from the general maximization of welfare within a nation (full employment, redistributive transfer payments and social service provision) to the promotion of enterprise, innovation and profitability in both private and public sectors has been initiated.

Proposition 5: the Proliferation of Policy Transfer

Policy transfer has become a key mechanism for delivering the policy agenda of the competition state through elite structures of governance.

This policy agenda is spreading primarily as a consequence of four key developments. First, as a consequence of processes of globalization both external to the nation-state and the 'hollowing-out' of the nation-state itself have created new opportunity structures for policy transfer. Secondly, a process of Americanization has helped to reinforce key features of the competition state in the UK through bilateral forms of policy transfer (see Deacon, 2000). Thirdly, policy transfer is more likely to occur in an era that R. Rhodes (1996: 652) has termed 'the New Governance: Governing without Government', in which in times of uncertainty policy-makers look to 'quick fix' solutions to public policy problems that policy transfer can sometimes provide. Fourthly, key agents and agencies within the state have also moved up the institutional pecking order in highly significant ways to enforce such changes in emphasis directly. Probably the most important of these are central banks, whose power has increased not only because of their location at the crossroads of the national financial economy and the global financial marketplace, but also because governments of both centre-left and right have come more and more to accept that such agencies should be independent and free of sup- posedly 'short-termist' political pressures in making key decisions on the setting of interest rates, control of the money supply and regulation of increasingly transnationalized financial institutions and markets.

Proposition 6: the Decline of Social Solidarity

These developments challenge the capacity of state institutions to embody the kind of communal solidarity, which gave the modern nation-state its deeper legitimacy, institutionalized power, and social embeddedness.

The cumulative effect of these various pressures and processes is a redefini- tion of the boundaries of the political. The restructuring of the political arena forces parties and governments of the left to redefine their conception of the 'social' and the 'public' away from the traditional confines of the 'modern' state. In Britain this has been reflected in two main developments. First, the residual rights approach to citizenship that underpinned Britain's unwritten constitution has been replaced with the introduction of legally enforceable individual rights through the incorporation of the European Convention on Human and Political Rights into British law. Secondly, there has been a paradigm shift in British welfarism that has been manifested in an attack on welfare dependency and the bonding of welfare rights and obliga- tions. This latter process of reform is the subject of the next section of this chapter.

4. The post-welfare contracting state

> We understand that economic stability is the prerequisite for radicalism in social policy rather than an alternative to it. We must be the parties of fiscal and economic prudence. Combined with it must be reform of the welfare state ... Welfare has become passive; a way of leaving people doing nothing, rather than helping them become active. (Tony Blair, speech to the Party of European Socialists' Congress, June 1997)

There are two key features of this crucial dimension of the competition state. First, the ideology of welfare from which subsequent welfare reform has flowed has changed and lessons have directly been incorporated from the United States. The ideological sea change underpinning the philosophy of British welfarism began in earnest with Sir Keith Joseph's (1972, 1974) attack on the post-war settlement in the mid-1970s which proved particularly influential in shaping Margaret Thatcher's thinking on the welfare state. However, it was the American conservatives, especially Charles Murray, Lawrence Mead and the *New Consensus on family and welfare* (AEI, 1987) that gave the critique of welfare dependency greater policy and programmatic expression. Indeed it is also possible to trace a change to the discursive construction of British welfarism from this conjuncture.

The work of the American conservatives also had a profound impact on New Labour's thinking especially in relation to their argument that rights and responsibilities were mutually reinforcing elements of sustainable welfarism. This, of course, challenged the key premises of Labour's postwar conception of welfare entitlements as the key policy instruments for achieving social equality and solidarity. The importance of bonding welfare rights and obligations won the war of ideas in the mind of Blair and 'no rights without obligations' became 'a prime motto for the new politics' under New Labour (Giddens, 1998, p. 65).

The second feature of the post-welfare contracting state can be identified in the shift in welfare policy itself in favour of integrating people into the private sector workforce through active labour market inclusion largely based on the American model. However, it is important to note that once again the development of the post-welfare contracting state, pre-dates the Blair government. As Anne Gray (1998, p. 6) argues, 'New Labour has explicitly chosen to continue the Tories' "workfarist" approach to labour market policy and to encourage adoption of its new labour discipline in other EU states by pressing for a minimalist social chapter and promoting the "New Deal" as a model policy'. This focus on the need to produce incentives in the welfare state constitutes an appropriation of a key New Right concept – the need to destroy the welfare dependency culture through getting people back to work rather than keeping them on benefits. This emphasis on the virtues of work was central to Blair and Clinton's assault on what Thatcher termed the 'evils of welfare dependency' and despite the considerable differences that exist between the two welfare systems, not to mention political traditions, Blair and Clinton argued that the two countries share a common problem of welfare dependency, which can be tackled through welfare-to-work.

5. The case of the New Deal

This chapter now moves on to explore a case study of policy transfer in the welfare reform arena – the New Deal. The case study is evaluated using the policy transfer network approach as presented in the previous chapter. Table 4.1 illustrates how, for analytical purposes, the voluntary policy transfer process can be broken down into 12 stages. Stages one to three involve the identification of a public policy problem and the search for ideas.

Table 4.1 The emergence and development of a voluntary policy transfer network

1	2	3
Problem recognition	**The search for ideas**	**Contact with potential agents**
economic crisis	regime	of transfer
globalization	international	
modernization	transnational	
policy failure	national	
electoral change	regional	
conflict	local	
legitimation	cross-sectoral	
⇒	⇒	⇒
4	**5**	**6**
The emergence of an information feeder network	**Cognition and reception** (identification of agents of transfer)	**The emergence of a policy transfer network**
⇒	⇒	⇒
7	**8**	**9**
Elite and cognitive mobilization (agenda-setting)	**Interaction**	**Evaluation of options**
⇒	⇒	⇒
10	**11**	**12**
Decision enters formal policy stream	**Formal policy processes**	**Implementation to outcome**
⇒	⇒	⇒

Stages four to nine and twelve represent potential periods of policy-oriented learning. Stages ten and eleven signify periods in which the policy enters formal policy processes. Each of these putative stages within the process of voluntary policy transfer will be analysed in detail within the ensuing case study. It must be noted that I am making no claims here about the rationality or otherwise of the policy transfer process. The capacity for a policy to pass through these stages is contingent on environmental factors (e.g., prevailing economic conditions, changes in government) and the type of agent of transfer involved. Moreover, processes of policy transfer can break off at any point past 'search' and still result in a form of transfer (e.g. the drawing of a lesson or the transfer of rhetoric). The scheme that I present in the following sections is thus wholly illustrative and provides a frame for organizing empirical research.

Problem recognition

The emergence of a policy transfer network begins with the recognition by a decision-making elite, politicians or bureaucrats, of the existence of a decision problem, which requires, due to environmental factors, pressing attention. This illustrates the rationale behind Blair's aim of increasing the aggregate skill levels of British peoples in order to compete in the international economy. As Chris Holden (1999: 437) illustrates, 'New Labour's conceptions of social exclusion and globalization thus fit together to produce a labour market policy geared toward increasing labour market participation ... in order to increase labour market efficiency within what is perceived to be an ever more competitive world market'. This quotation further illustrates the marriage between the imperatives of a competition state and the government's attitude towards work and by implication welfare-to-work. In sum, since coming to power New Labour has expanded the scope of the post-welfare contracting state through the ending of free higher education and the introduction of 'Workfare' (an American concept from the 1960s and 1970s) and 'Learningfare' as part of what is called the New Deal for unemployed 18 to 24-year-olds. The Blair government has placed welfare reform at the heart of the competition state project. £5 billion has been spent on the welfare-to-work programme representing by a considerable margin the new government's largest single public spending commitment. In addition, in successive budgets, Gordon Brown has introduced a raft of financial incentives in an attempt to lift people out of the poverty trap. These measures have included the introduction of the Working Families Tax Credit, and the lowering of national insurance contributions and tax levels for lower paid workers.

The Treasury has played the key co-ordinating role in the development of the New Deal proposals as the centre-piece of the government's welfare-to-work strategy. The official reason for why the Treasury led the project rather than the Department for Education and Employment (DfEE), although it was represented in deliberations, was that it symbolized the broader movement of employment policy away from training. However, it may also be argued that it reflected Brown's desire to maintain control over welfare reform in order to steer the competition state. As a senior Treasury official put it, '[e]verybody knows that this is about the marketization of the state, that's why Brown's so involved: what we don't know is whether he really thinks that it can have some redistributive effects'. It was also argued that it was evident from similar programmes in the US that the delivery of the New Deal would require a co-ordinating body to ensure joined-up delivery across departments at the national, regional and local levels. It was Brown's view that the Treasury was best equipped to perform this role as it had the necessary expertise to take advantage of evidence-based learning from the United States and elsewhere.

The search for solutions

The absence of acceptable policy responses or solutions may lead an agent to engage in a search for policy ideas. This is quite often an ad hoc process characterized by trial and error. Search activity is a key feature of the process of policy transfer. For as we shall see it is within this process of search activity that the nature of information gathering enters new arenas and forms of collaborative governance emerge.

The rationale for why ideas and developments in the US have been so influential on the British welfare reform debate has already been discussed in the previous sections of this chapter and have also been well documented elsewhere (see Deacon, 2000). Suffice to say that history, language, ideology, and a shared belief in the competition state project (in particular, macroeconomic analysis) have all played a role. Although to term this 'Americanization' of the British welfare debate (see Walker, 1998) would be a slight exaggeration. As a senior Department of Social Security (DSS) official observes, '[a]part from the ability to communicate more easily (and this isn't always the case I can assure you) there is really no compelling reason why America is always our first port of call for welfare ideas. After all they have such a different welfare tradition to ours'. This tension between traditions would manifest itself in the evaluation stage of the policy transfer process. Indeed there is plenty of evidence to suggest that the Treasury has also been influenced by initiatives in Australia ('Lone Parents and Partners', 'Working Nation' and 'single gateway/one stop shops' programmes), Sweden ('Working Nation'), the Netherlands ('single gateway/one stop shop' programmes) and Canada (the 'Making Work Pay' scheme). In addition, institutional memory (for example, 'Job Seekers Allowance' and 'Restart' schemes from 1988 and 1996) has also been influential. Nonetheless, the US remains the pioneer in ideas about welfare-to-work programmes, and, in particular, issues of policy presentation.

It was therefore unsurprising that the Wefare to Work Unit should narrow their search to the United States, the Commonwealth and certain European exemplars such as the Netherlands and Sweden. In an important sense this focused enquiry on readily accessible exemplars where programme success was easily demonstrated through sophisticated forms of programme evaluation. As a senior Treasury official notes, 'the very fact that the United States could offer over 50 cases of "Welfare to Work" systems that included rigorous evaluations of strengths and weaknesses was an attraction in itself. In order to develop an effective search for ideas, the Welfare to Work Unit set up what may be described as a 'Welfare to work Treasury Nexus' that included participants from other issue-related departments of state such as the DfEE, the DSS and the Department of the Environment, Trade and the Regions (DETR). This enabled the unit to draw on the expertise of other key governmental stakeholders.

Contact with potential agents of transfer

During the search process an organization may come across a potential agent of transfer with specialist 'cognitive' and 'elite' mobilization skills (e.g. a policy entrepreneur associated with a powerful epistemic community). In this context, 'cognitive' mobilization refers to the ability of the agent of transfer to develop the necessary political and knowledge resources to satisfy successful policy development. 'Elite' mobilization refers to the ability of the agent of transfer to gain access to knowledge elites and bring their expertise into the transfer network. At this juncture the potential agent of transfer will only be interested in disseminating basic information to the potential client with the aim of seducing them into a dependency relationship. It must be noted that for some agents (e.g. a private sector consultancy such as Ernst and Young), policy transfer is a lucrative business. Hence a significant deal of strategic calculation will go into closing a lead from their part.

From its inception the Welfare to Work Unit established close relations with public organizations in the United States who were responsible for delivering and evaluating welfare-to-work programmes such as the Department of Labor and the United States Office of Personnel Management. In addition, the expertise of several high profile American academics with considerable experience in the welfare-to-work field, such as Richard Layard (1997), was also sought. Contact was also made with the architects of 'best practice models' in local experimentation such as 'GAIN' in Riverside, California, 'Florida Wages' and 'Wisconsin Works' (see House of Commons, 1998). As a Treasury official notes, '[t]hese cases were of interest and influence because of their emphasis on work and not training and because they were all demonstrably successful'.

The emergence of an information feeder network

If the curiosity of the client (in this case the Treasury 'Welfare to Work Nexus') is aroused through preliminary contact the principal agent of transfer will develop an information feeder network in order to increase both the volume and the detail of information. At this stage the agent will be intent on demonstrating the quality of their access to communication and knowledge networks and further opportunity structures for transfer.

The Welfare to Work Unit held several bilateral meetings with their American counterparts in order to develop more detailed information on delivery and evaluation issues. As one former official who played a search role in the 'Treasury Welfare to Work Nexus' recalls, '[f]or what seemed like months I spent more time with our American counterparts than with my husband. I stayed in regular contact through email and continue to do so in my new job ... [t]he main lessons that we got from the States were about how to join-up services across a devolved structure'. The British team was struck by the quality of research conducted in the United States on wefare-to-work programmes. As the same official observes, '[t]hey are really brilliant at the evidence-based evaluation stuff and to be honest we're very poor at it'. This conclusion was also reached at the 530th Wilton Park Conference in New York entitled 'Welfare and Work in Britain and America'. The conference was funded by the Rockefeller, Charles Stewart Mott and Nuffield Foundations with additional financial assistance from the DfEE, DSS and HM Treasury and was held in July 1998. It represents a classic example of the development of an information feeder network with participants from every level of governance including the transnational level, together with members of think tanks and academics. The conference report concludes that, '[i]n the UK, there is not the same tradition of non-profit research evaluation. It is dependent on the Government, which is not very good at it, and does not always like the results' (see <http://www.wiltonpark.org.uk/conferences/>).

Cognition, reception and the emergence of a transfer network

The client will evaluate the information that has been provided through the information feeder network. Cognition and reception will then usually depend on both client and agent of transfer sharing a commitment to a common value system. In this sense policy transfer networks tend to be the preserve of elite activity and involvement in the game is wholly dependent on an agents resources. Table 4.2 provides a snapshot of the key features of the policy transfer network that emerged in relation to the New Deal. An inner circle developed within the 'Treasury–Welfare to Work Nexus', which privileged the competition state's aim 'to rebuild the welfare state around work'. This meant emphasizing the bond between welfare rights and responsibilities as an anti-poverty strategy and promoting active labour market policies. For the former, certain lessons would be drawn from the United States and from British welfare traditions, and, for the latter, lessons would be drawn from Australia, Europe and local experiments in the United States.

It is here that differences between welfare traditions became evident and started to play a role. Although the United States and Britain are struggling with the same fundamental underlying challenges, four main differences can be identified. First, the UK approach to welfare-to-work forms part of a comprehensive UK framework of benefit systems, while the United States approach is far more fragmented because of the nature of the federal system. Secondly, the two approaches involve different contexts and different priority groups – in the United States the focus is on lone mothers; in the UK, a broader group is involved, including young, long-term unemployed males. Thirdly, the concept of public–private partnerships is far more developed in the United States and hence it is easier to reach small and medium sized enterprises (SMEs) through trade associations. Fourthly, and fundamentally, work is treated as an ethical issue in the United States and as an anti-poverty strategy in the UK. In sum, welfare reformers in the United States believe that the UK already does too much for the jobless and welfare support should be targeted more effectively. The final proposals would be sensitive to these cultural differences.

Table 4.2 The key characteristics of the New Deal policy transfer network

Dimension	Case study characteristics
Membership	
number of participants	Very limited, the system has a bias against certain inputs, emphasis on bureaucratic and technocratic elites. An inner circle was co-ordinated through the 'Welfare to Work' Unit in the Treasury. This included representatives from key departments, US bureaucrats, academics and knowledge institutions.
type of interest	The agents of policy transfer included affected politicians and bureaucrats.
Integration	
frequency of interaction	Within the set time scale, frequent, high quality interaction took place on all matters related to the policy transfer.
continuity	Originally the policy transfer network was an adhoc, action orientated network set up with the specific intention of engineering policy change but it still remains in place with a different membership.
consensus	All participants share the basic values of the competition state project although cultural differences exist between UK and US approaches to welfare-to-work.
Resources	
Distribution of resources (within network)	All participants hold resources in exchange relationships.
Distribution of resources (within organizations)	Policy-makers are dependent on the intelligence gathering skills and knowledge resources of the donor organization.
Power	The success of the policy transfer network rested on the ability of the agent of transfer to satisfy the objective policy problem of the client. This was achieved.

At this stage of the policy transfer process policy transfer networks can act as gatekeepers to the decision-making centre and hence the policy agenda may develop a bias against certain inputs. In the case of the New Deal there were four key determinants of the policy agenda – the new welfare ideology of rights and responsibilities; the emphasis on developing processes of market integration; the need to create incentives to keep people off benefits; and, finally, the importance of evidence-based reasoning.

Interaction

The agent of transfer will be expected to organize forums for the exchange of ideas between the client and knowledge elites with policy-relevant knowledge. These may take the form of representatives of an epistemic community who have similar professional beliefs and standards of judgement and share common policy concerns. It is through these forms of diffusion activity that agents of transfer can act as agenda setters. In the case of the New Deal the establishment of free flowing information systems through an effective information feeder network led to the creation of coherent systems of interaction at an early stage in the process of policy transfer. Hence, the organization of bilateral fact-finding missions, conferences and the exchange of programming and evaluation documents occurred quickly and were effectively co-ordinated through the 'Treasury–Welfare to Work Nexus'.

Evaluation

Once the client is satisfied with the degree of intelligence gathering that they have engaged in, a process of evaluation will commence that is critical in determining the objects, degree, and the prerequisites of transfer which will condition the nature of the policy or programme. The New Deal was to be financed through the 'windfall tax' on the privatized utilities to the tune of £4 billion. The final proposals added an element of compulsion to incentivization and were aimed primarily at the young unemployed. It offered four options including subsidized employment and education, and, in line with Labour's intention to increase overall participation in the labour market, the New Deal was also extended to disabled people, carers and single parents. The issue of compulsion, taken for granted in the United States, is now a feature of the New Deal for 18 to 24-year-olds. It is judged to be politically acceptable for this age group, but the impact of compulsion for older age groups is open to discussion, and there is an enduring political reluctance to adopt compulsion for lone mothers. Indeed the imposition of welfare time limits or other policies that might cause severe hardship have not been adequately debated in the UK. As a senior Treasury official puts it: '[e]verybody knows that this is about limiting state commitments and marketizing the state. All you have to do is look at the website for the evidence'.

The formal decision stream

In the case of the New Deal there can be little doubt that a favourable economic climate, combined with its fit with the broader competition state project, pushed it to the top of the policy agenda. As one senior Treasury official observes:

> Let's face it if we were suddenly hit with a recession, and one seems likely over the next year or so, much of this would collapse. Why? Because the left is waiting for a chance to reassert itself and Brown has been foolish in resurrecting the language of full employment in a period of economic stability. A recession would provide them with a set of opportunities to fight for more direct intervention into the economy.

This raises the important question of what happens if the economy goes into recession. Will policies conceived in good times be sustainable in times of economic crisis? It is already possible to identify some implementation problems with New Deal. First, the New Deal for young people has been generously funded for political reasons and has taken a significant proportion of the £4 billion made available from the windfall tax on privatized utilities. The allocation to other strands of the New Deal, such as the sick and disabled and lone parents, has been correspondingly far less. It remains to be seen how effective these elements of the programme can be. Secondly, attempts in the UK to reach SMEs through trade associations have not proved effective. A local approach may be more effective to reach local companies.

6. Conclusion: policy transfer, welfare reform and the competition state

What does this case study of the emergence and development of a policy transfer network in the New Deal policy arena tell us about *the politics of coping, adapting and internalizing globalization* in Britain?

Five main conclusions can be drawn from the case study. The policy transfer network approach proves useful in helping us to understand how decision-makers acquire knowledge and how they can act as agents of the competition state. Four important conclusions can be drawn here. First, the timescale which is established to search for policy ideas informs the scope of enquiry and almost inevitably draws policy-makers to accessible exemplars in either the United States, the Commonwealth or the private sector who share a similar commitment to the competition state project. Secondly, multi-level search activity creates a pathology for hybrid forms of cross-national and cross-sectoral policy transfer and consequently policy and programme copying becomes very rare. The New Deal initiative inherited much from the Thatcher and Major governments and represents a paradigm shift in the philosophy of welfarism. The front page slogan on the New York Welfare to Work website sums up this shift in thinking perfectly. Here the slogan 'Welfare to work is a programme that creates independence' is superimposed over the words 'Welfare creates dependence'! Thirdly, the quality of information improved as more sophisticated processes of information gathering developed and further opportunity structures for transfer emerged. Policy transfer thus became an inevitability and begat further policy transfer. In the case of the New Deal, new service delivery approaches have been adopted including one-stop shops on the Iowa model and the introduction of a single gateway to the benefit system.

Fourthly, an inner circle of policy-making participants emerged who shared a commitment to the common value system of the competition state and in which participation was circumscribed by knowledge resources and organizational capacity. A process of gate-keeping took place in which elite players were selected by the primary agents of policy transfer largely because of their ideological compatibility with the broader competition state project. Indeed it is here that both agents of policy transfer and Treasury officials are seen to be playing a central co-ordinating role in promoting the competition state project and new forms of complex globalization in the attempt to adapt state action to cope more effectively with what they see as global 'realities'.

Fifthly, the battle for the hearts and minds of the British people is a key problem for the competition state for many of its key reforms rest on changing norms and values and challenging the dependency culture of the post-war settlement (e.g. welfare-to-work, pensions, student loans). These reforms have dramatically symbolized a move away from the norms of labourism (from collective to individual level bargaining, from public to private ownership) and towards consumerist rather than productionist values. In particular, the policy agenda of New Labour attempts to change individual and group attitudes to entrepreneurship whether through welfare-to-work, pensions policy, student loans, or central bank reform.

Welfare policy has thus been incorporated into the new economic orthodoxy of the competition state through its emphasis on reducing dependency, removing any potential obstacles to the control of inflation and integrating the socially excluded into the labour market. In Brown's words, this calls for 'balanced budgets', 'tight control of interest rates', and the need to deal with unemployment through the marketplace and not through government intervention. Hence, new patterns of behaviour are established in order to cope with the imperatives of globalization.

Further reading

Farazmand, A. (1999) 'Globalisation and Public Administration', *Public Administration Review*, 59(6), 509–22.
Giddens, A. (1999) *Runaway World: How Globalization is Re-shaping Our Lives* (Profile).
Keohane, R.O. and Nye, J. (2000) 'Globalization: What's New? What's Not? (And So What?)', *Foreign Policy*, 118, 104–19.
Richards, D. and Smith, M. (2002), *Governance and Public Policy in the UK*, Oxford: Oxford University Press.

Useful websites

<www.worldbank.org>   World Bank

<www.sussex.ac.uk/Units/CST/for/3rdway/polecon.rtf>   D. Arnold (2003), 'Labour's Economic Policy and the Competition State: A Social Democratic Critique of the Political Economy of the Third Way'

<http://ideas.repec.org/p/wop/wispod/1223-01.html>   R. Walker and M. Wiseman (2001), 'Britain's New Deal and the Next Round of US Welfare Reform'

<http://www.newdeal.gov.uk>   New Deal

<http://www.hrmguide.co.uk/jobmarket/newdeal.htm>   An evaluation of the New Deal by the Human Resource Management Network

5
Embedding Neoliberalism in Spain: from Franquismo to Neoliberalism

Paul McVeigh

During almost four decades of dictatorship, General Franco was apt to justify his country's divergent political and economic path with reference to Spain's exceptionalism (Heywood, 1999). The notion of fundamental Spanish 'difference' was proclaimed to underpin a model of political and economic development centred on a protected internal market, wide-ranging centralized bureaucratic intervention in economy and society, and a relatively low regard for civil and democratic rights. Less than three decades after the dictator's death, Spain is a stable and modern liberal democracy, firmly embedded in European Monetary Union (EMU), and exhibiting a bipartisan consensus over the basic framework of economic governance. Indeed, Spain has become one of the most active members of the European Union (EU) in terms of labour market reform, privatization and deregulation, engaged in policy dialogue at the highest levels with the European bastion of the Anglo-Saxon model, the United Kingdom. So much for Spanish exceptionalism. What accounts for this transformation of the framework of economic governance in Spain?

For some commentators, the transformation is purely the inevitable result of a process of economic globalization in which external pressures progressively erode domestic economic sovereignty and policy choices (Bauman, 1998; Beck, 2000; Gray, 1999; Rodrik, 1997). However, sceptics within the globalization debate contest its extent and consequences for state sovereignty and/or national models arguing that the space remains for distinctive models to persist, for example the Danish model (Hirst and Thompson, 1999). Similarly, they maintain that model erosion arises as much from internal as external contradictions and pressures (Grahl, 2001; Hirst and Thompson, 1999). Following this argument, the sense of inevitability often attached to the globalization concept is highly contestable, constituting little more than a neoliberal bid for intellectual and political hegemony (Cox, 1987; Gill, 1995; Hirst and Thompson, 1999; Rupert, 2001).

This chapter argues that Spain has followed a neoliberal path over the last two decades, and seeks explanations for Spain's trajectory in the confluence of a very real domestic economic and industrial crisis in the immediate post-Franco era, and association of that crisis with the state corporatist structures of Franquismo at both elite and popular level. This neoliberal path embraces the key themes mapped out by Cerny *et al.* (cf. Chapter 1, this volume) involving a substantial opening of the Spanish market, the pursuit of financial orthodoxy, erosion of the 'decommodification' functions of welfare capitalism and state intervention and a shift towards a 'competition state' model of economic governance.

Again, the causes of this shift are complex and multiple but analysis of the Spanish case reveals the interplay of the key forces identified by Cerny *et al.* (Chapter 1 of this volume): namely, the exhaustion of a national model whose legitimacy was eroded by popular dissatisfaction, international economic crisis, fiscal pressures and ideological changes arising from the breakdown of the Bretton Woods system and the end of the postwar boom. What the Spanish case indicates is the heightened vulnerability of weaker and less institutionalized national models of capitalism to these forces given the relative lack of legitimacy of Franquismo, its much less developed institutions for social partnership, its lack of working class support and the structural economic weaknesses it failed to address.

It is argued that general dissatisfaction with the Franco regime, and in particular with its authoritarian excesses, had, by the time of the dictator's death in 1975, facilitated a widespread desire within Spanish society for democratization, modernization and an end to Spain's isolation from the main currents of European political and economic development (cf. Taylor, Chapter 10, this volume; Holman, 1996: 74; Share, 1989: 139–41). These goals were successfully presented as priorities outweighing all others; and under the PSOE (Spanish Socialist Workers Party) governments of 1982–96, the primacy of 'normalization' and European integration laid the basis for a sustained assault on the authoritarian and protectionist institutions of the Francoist political economy, and a diminishing of the perceived space for alternative strategies of economic governance (Share, 1989: 110–17). The rise of neoliberalism in Spain has enjoyed a symbiotic relationship with European integration: participation in this project being both the prize of, and the justification for, profound economic liberalization. Spanish neoliberalism must therefore be understood in the context of the political, economic and cultural inheritance of the post-Franco era and its structuring effects both on political discourse and economic policy options. If we compare Spain with the United Kingdom, for example, we see radically different elite and popular attitudes towards the European project co-existing with quite striking similarities in terms of neoliberal policy agendas and outcomes (cf. Evans, Chapter 4, this volume; Risse, 2002): all of which underlines the importance of internal forces in the construction of neoliberalisms, in line with the sceptic thesis that globalization and the external constraints it imposes should not be seen as determining outcomes nor of creating insurmountable pressures to domestic strategies. That Spain has followed such a neoliberal course is substantially a matter of internal political determination and dynamics with globalization often serving an ideological and justifying role.

This chapter is organized into four sections. In the first section, the discussion focuses on the relative deviation of Franco's Spain from the three generic models of economic governance, which dominate the literature on national capitalisms. It is argued that without a deeply embedded social-corporatist or developmental state, post-Franco Spain was uniquely ripe for, and vulnerable to, radical reform in its economic governance. In the second section, the discussion centres on the role of the PSOE governments in the construction of Spanish neoliberalism from 1982 and argues that their political hegemony and their pursuit of the European project provided the space and political capital to launch neoliberal reform. The third section outlines the external constraints arising from internationalization, and charts the PSOE's major policy responses to economic crisis, detailing how the political goals of modernization and European integration privileged certain policy options over others. This agenda was largely taken up and extended by the PP (People's Party) from 1996 onwards, culminating in Spain's participation in Monetary Union. A concluding section considers the rise of neoliberalism in Spain and the role of the Spanish state in internalizing globalization.

1. Spain and the 'models of capitalism' debate

The literature on national capitalism often asserts the existence of three main models of capitalism (Albert, 1993; Hart, 1992; Hutton, 1995) and of the possible pressures towards model 'convergence' under the pressures of globalization (cf. Cerny *et al.* Chapter 1, this volume; Crouch and Streeck, 1997). An Anglo-Saxon model is postulated as operating in the UK and the USA (Hutton, 1995); a 'social-corporatist' model is associated with Northern European economies typically Germany and the Nordic and Alpine countries (Meidner, 1992; Steinmo, Chapter 8 this volume; Streeck, 1998) and a 'developmental state' model normally associated with East Asian economies primarily Japan, South Korea and Taiwan (Wade, 1990). The literature on all three models involves a high degree of generalization. However, accepting both the validity and limitations of generalization, Southern Europe does not easily fit within any of these stylized models. The definitive industrialization of the Spanish economy took place within the context of the Franco dictatorship, a crucial factor differentiating Spain's developmental experience from these models. Superficially, the Franco regime may be held to bear resemblance to a developmental state or, given its corporatist sobriquet, a social corporatist model. But detailed comparison of its political economy reveals significant differences, which become even more significant when analysis turns to the institutional, political, economic and cultural legacies of the regime.

It is fairly obvious that Franco's corporatist state did not rest on any institutionalized or agreed compromise between capital and labour. The corporatist state was born out of Franco's triumph in the most acute class conflict of the 1930s and was imposed from above with no social dialogue between capital and labour (Holman, 1996: 53–5). Not only did this deny post-Franco Spain both the deep-rooted tradition of social accords and institutionalized collective bargaining as in Sweden or Germany (cf. Steinmo, Chapter 8, this volume; Menz, Chapter 2, this volume) it also left its imprint on the Spanish economy in an array of serious competitive weaknesses and an undeveloped welfare system (Wright, 1977: 71–7, 83–101, 121–36). At best Franquismo might be judged as 'corporatism without the social'; at worst it bequeathed a system of industrial relations and work organization lacking in flexibility, stability or even allegiance from capital or labour (Martinez-Lucio, 1992). Given its lack of support and its rigidities, this would make the system all the easier – and more necessary – to discard in the democratic era.

While the interventionist excess of Franquismo clearly disqualify it as an Anglo-Saxon system, the protectionist tendencies, state-holding companies, penchant for planning and the apparent developmental successes of the regime may make it superficially tempting to class it alongside Japan and South Korea as a developmental state. Such a classification would overlook the critical failures of the Franco model to imitate the same extent of competitive export success as its counterparts in the Far East, and for that matter, France (Hall, 1986).

First and foremost, the Spanish economy's performance was less impressive than it appeared. True, Spain's record of economic growth during the period 1958–73 outperforms all OECD economies apart from Japan (Salmon, 1995: 3–7). Likewise, official unemployment figures were highly impressive and the economy did achieve a definitive industrialization. However, the economic miracle was highly dependent upon the international postwar boom that mitigated Spain's weak current account performance. Exports did increase in the 1960s but this increase was dwarfed by the rise in imports, particularly taking into account the very low base from which exports grew (Harrison, 1985: 144–5). A systematic trade deficit existed and on Spain's visible trade account only a handful of industrial sectors displayed a trade surplus in 1975: footwear, ships and cars. In all cases this was largely due to protection of the market (Harrison, 1985: 161).

Prior to the oil crisis, several factors mitigated this deficit (Harrison, 1985: 155–7, 175; Salmon, 1995: 3–7, 254–5; Wright, 1977: 146–9). Invisible earnings – primarily those from tourism – consistently contributed to the trading accounts. By 1975, tourism earnings equalled 18 per cent of Spain's visible imports and covered 40 per cent of the visible deficit (Instituto

Nacional Estadística, 1977). In the same year, the remittances of Spanish emigrants working abroad reached a total of $700 million; another substantial boost to Spain's trading accounts (Harrison, 1985: 152). In addition foreign direct investment eased the deficit; investment flows amounted to $6.775 billion between 1970–74 (Lieberman, 1982). The cheap price of oil prior to 1973 was also significant as Spain depended entirely upon oil imports.

Even during the boom, these 'safety-valves' could not hide periodic trade imbalances, which required the application of short 'stops' to the process of domestic demand expansion. From the mid-1970s onwards Spain's trading position deteriorated substantially. In 1975, for example, the oil import bill alone absortbed some 70 per cent of Spain's visible export earnings. Ominously, the 'safety-valves' were all undermined after 1973 as international recession and political instability in Spain impacted adversely on tourism and foreign investment, the oil price leapt and emigration flows were reversed (Harrison, 1978: 175; Lieberman, 1982; Wright, 1977).

Structural weaknesses were rooted in Spain's pattern of economic development such as its over-specialization in traditional industries such as steel, shipbuilding and textiles. In contrast, Spain was under-specialized in emerging technologies and industries (Castells *et al.*, 1986). Dependence on foreign capital was strong in such sectors as machine tools, electronics and machinery. One-third of all investment during the period 1964–74 constituted the purchase of foreign equipment (Criado, 1990: 121). Few domestic players existed in these industries and there was a heavy reliance on import (Aragón, 1990: 73). Furthermore, foreign capital in these industries showed a strong preference for the importation of equipment and components adding to the structural trade deficit, feeding technological dependence and reducing the scope for domestic suppliers to break through (Aragón, 1990).

If the focus is shifted to Spain's pattern of comparative advantages, the main source of Spanish comparative advantage was in low costs and low wages: factors which were gradually undermined by developments in the labour market (Lieberman, 1982; Wright, 1977: 75–7). The typical Spanish firm was small in scale with an excessive orientation to the internal market, a correspondingly low propensity to export, producing standard consumer goods of relatively low quality, frequently on outdated machinery (Ahijado *et al.*, 1993; Viñals *et al.*, 1990). In consequence there was a lack of large internationally competitive Spanish producers; this was even clearer in dynamic sectors (Salmon, 1995: 166–9). The industrial economy displayed a continuing lack of competitiveness and diversification (Aragón, 1990; Lieberman, 1982). Investment in skills and technology bases was low in both public and private sectors despite frequent commitments by the regime to a reform of science and technology policy (Criado, 1990; Lieberman, 1982: 232). Franquismo failed to rationalize the industrial base, to build international class firms, to penetrate foreign markets or to diversify the manufacturing economy.

The bias toward a protected internal market and lack of adequate incentives to international competitiveness contrasts sharply with the strategy pursued in East Asia, and arguably, in France (Balassa, 1981; Hall, 1986; Henderson, 1993; Wade, 1990). In both the Japanese and Korean models, selective protection of the home market was conditional upon companies making visible improvements to competitiveness and this was measured in terms of demonstrable increases in exports and international market shares (Johnson, 1982; Wade, 1990). This more rigorous application of industrial support in East Asia was matched by a more rational targeting of sectors encouraging a switch out of traditional industries and into fast-growing and high technology sectors such as electronics (Henderson, 1993).

Policy failures cannot be disconnected from the nature of the regime. Franco came to power supported by an array of established economic and political interests that had increasingly relied on economic nationalism throughout the opening decades of the century (Holman, 1995: 36–9, 42–4). These interests continued to exert pressure on the regime pushing it towards policies that consolidated existing sectors and firms – the so-called 'privileged circuits' of the Spanish economy (Wright, 1977: 110–14). The Civil War* of 1936–39 entrenched the power of existing, uncompetitive and internally focused economic interests while the Second World War and its aftermath destroyed such interests in East Asia. This translated into a major contrast between the two regions in terms of state autonomy during the postwar boom, providing East Asian economic bureaucrats with greater discretion to pursue a forward- and outward-looking, but nevertheless nationalistic, development policy which was not possible in Spain.

Moreover, Spain's isolation from the international economy as exemplified by its marginalization from Marshall Aid condemned it to a decade treading water on the periphery of the postwar boom. Its economic miracle really began after 1958; Spain had less time to build up its industrial effort before the oil crisis impacted upon it and did so without the extent of US sponsorship that the more strategic East Asian area received (Deyo, 1987).

In sum, it is difficult to classify the Francoist state as a developmental state in the same mould as, say, South Korea. Its trajectory corresponds more to a model of intermediate development with significant dependence on foreign capital and technology, a relatively weak state, and major structural deficiencies (Aragón, 1990; Holman, 1996: 36–9). Franquismo may have modernized the economy but it left no viable or popular development strategy for the long-term, leaving many of its institutions vulnerable to attack (García-Díaz, 2000: 44; Wright, 1977: 158).

2. Abandoning Francoism: political transition, the rise of the PSOE and the road to neoliberalism

The political inheritance left by the Franco regime consisted of a broad, but not universal consensus that the old political and economic model was not sustainable or desirable (Alza, 2000; Holman, 1996: 73–96; Threlfall, 2000). On the left, there was no question that Spain must democratize. On the right there remained elements within the bureaucracy and the military opposed to democratization but significant sections of the political elite were ready and willing to embrace democracy (Alza, 2000). The final years of the regime had seen a radicalization of opposition against the dictatorship and increasing popular mobilization to this end. Any attempt to continue authoritarian rule would be contested by increasingly militant working class and nationalist movements, notably the unofficial trades unions (the '*comisiones obreras*') and the radical Basque nationalist terrorist grouping, ETA.

The defining characteristic of the political transition to democracy in the period up to the election of the Socialist government in 1982 was the search by political elites to ensure a smooth and negotiated political reform (the '*ruptura pactada*'), and to curtail the possibility of a violent stand-off between revolutionary forces and the remnants of Franco's support (Share, 1989: 50–8; Threlfall, 2000). The potential for instability was underlined by a rising tide of Basque nationalist violence and an attempted coup in 1981. A negotiated reform was uneasily but ultimately successfully achieved, led initially by democratizing forces within the Franco state machine (Alza, 2000; Carillo, 2000; Share, 1989; Threlfall, 2000). All political parties were formally legalized including the communists and a series of negotiations took place between political parties, newly legalized trades unions and employers' organizations establishing a democratic Constitution (see Threlfall, 2000). This gradual and inclusive process sought to marginalize and dilute those forces on the Right and Left who opposed liberal democracy. This marginalization was legitimized through elections in 1977 which concentrated electoral support and political power within the democratic forces on both the left (the PSOE and their rival socialist groups: the FPS – Federation of Socialist Parties, the PSP – the People's Socialist Party, and the PCE – the Spanish Communist Party) and the right (the UCD – Union of the Democratic Centre, and the AP – the People's Alliance), enabling them to slowly consolidate the democratic project through a decentralization of political power to democratically elected regional governments and a series of social accords aimed at macroeconomic stabilization in a context of galloping inflation. At regional level, democratic parties also participated in the consolidation process; most importantly in Catalonia (the CDC – Democratic Convergence of Catalonia, and UDC Democratic Union of Catalonia, later to fuse into Convergence and Union, CiU) and in the Basque Country, the PNV (Basque Nationalist Party).

The political transition provided the space for the PSOE to establish a political hegemony leading to its election to government in 1982 and a period of 14 years of PSOE rule (Holman, 1996; Share, 1989). Two sets of observations are especially relevant in considering the role of the PSOE in constructing neoliberalism in Spain: first, the hegemony of the PSOE within the Spanish political system and, secondly, the capacity of the PSOE to reflect and build support for a neoliberal trajectory.

The PSOE gradually achieved a hegemonic position on the left through a mixture of charismatic leadership, its historical legacy and its moderation, which cemented its democratic credentials (Share, 1989: 44). This was important against the historical antecedents of the Civil War of 1936–39. The political cleavages of the 1930s were roughly repeated in the 1977 elections with a similar left–right and class division of the electorate (Gunther *et al.*, 1986). Against this backcloth, the popular aspiration for liberal democracy advantaged the centre-left and centre-right against more extreme political forces as for much of Spanish society there was no appetite for renewed political polarization.

Despite the moderate Eurocommunist stances of the PCE, the first democratic elections of 1977 provided the PSOE with a preponderance of electoral muscle on the left with 29 per cent of the popular vote (Alza, 2000: 30). This enabled it to integrate the smaller socialist parties within itself and with further internal reform and moderation, the PSOE emerged as a modern centre-left party committed to the new democracy. In particular, the PSOE achieved a cross-class appeal way beyond that of any rival on the left or right, providing it with legitimacy (Gunther *et al.*, 1986); the defection of significant centrist political figures to its ranks consolidated this appeal. In contrast, the PCE fell into a gradual decline amid internal disunity (Carillo, 2000; Share, 1989).

Likewise, the centre-right UCD – though playing a critical role in building the basis for a functioning democracy – was divided into any number of competing strands, lacked a coherent political programme beyond democratization, and contained a number of former Francoists whose presence served to undercut its democratic credentials. Its rightward shift during the period 1979–82 hastened its decline in popularity. After the 1982 electoral defeat, the AP emerged as the main centre-right party but the prominence in its ranks of former Francoists made it 'unelectable'.

The PSOE was therefore well placed to assume the position of the natural party of government in the new democracy. The party's resistance to Francoism provided it with a residual hostility to all elements of the Francoist state. It owed no allegiance to the old model of development and in associating substantial elements of that model with both the gathering economic crisis and the authoritarian nature of Franquismo was able to create a political discourse in which most aspects of the old model were presumed guilty and in need of reform and modernization (Holman, 1996: 76–8; Share, 1989: 109–11).

In advancing the need for reform and modernization, the PSOE was able to mobilize the sentiments of much of the electorate for a desertion of the old, model. Similarly, the institutions of the Francoist political economy elicited little support from either capital or labour. With its own links to organized labour through the UGT (General Workers' Union) the PSOE's main vulnerability would come from the right. However, its orthodox economic policies, espousal of labour market reform and economic liberalization meant that it did not engender the hostility of Spanish capital; on the contrary the more dynamic and outward-looking elements of Spanish capital held no brief for the old developmental model and provided the PSOE with varying degrees of support in replacing Franquismo with a business-friendly neoliberalism (Holman, 1996).

The assault on Francoism underlined the appeal of a wider project of political and social modernization, which lay at the heart of the transition to democracy (Holman, 1996). One critical aspect here was Spain's relation with Europe. The Franco regime had crystallized Spain's isolation from the mainstream of Western Europe; both physically through protectionist and political barriers, and psychologically through the persistence of an authoritarian political system which deviated from the prevailing norms of western, liberal democracy (Holman, 1996: 46–52, 78). This had been a major barrier to Spain's participation in the European Community (Harrison, 1985: 163). Having built a nascent liberal democracy, Spain now had the credentials to join the European Community. In turn, membership would be symbolic, marking an end to Spain's isolation and embedding the gains of the political transition, making any reversion to Francoism impossible to contemplate. For the PSOE, Europe had always had an alluring quality. It had enjoyed strong links with the West German Social Democrats (the SPD) during the final years of the Franco regime and was strongly influenced by the need to establish Spain in the European mainstream (Holman, 1996). Full participation in the European project became the primary goal of the PSOE governments and this goal enjoyed considerable popular appeal. There was little organized opposition to membership among political elites and no little enthusiasm for entry among the electorate. Again, within Spanish capital the more outward looking, internationally connected and competitive sectors were keen proponents of internationalization (Holman, 1996).

But as Spain was about to enter the Community, this Community was itself changing with the move to a Single European Market (SEM) planned for 1992. As Spain entered the Community in 1986, it was committed to full participation in the SEM and hence its transition period prior to 1992 would require considerable efforts in terms of harmonizing legislation, removing trade barriers and preparing the relatively weak and uncompetitive Spanish economy for the 'shock' of intense competition in a single market (Ahijado *et al.*, 1993; Viñals *et al.*, 1990). Integration would require, and provide the platform for, an intense restructuring of the Spanish economy featuring root and branch reform of industrial and trade policy. Depending on one's view, this reform would extinguish the vestiges of the Franco developmental model or, alternatively, destroy the existing basis for a developmental state model in Spain. Equating modernization with (rapid) integration and mobilizing elite and popular opinion to this end, the PSOE governments adopted the former interpretation. They were later judged by some on the left to have thrown out the baby of the developmental state with the bath water of Franco's authoritarianism (Buesa, 1994). In any event, with social-corporatism so weakly embedded and European integration prioritized, the die was cast for a neoliberal transformation of the Spanish political economy.

3. The economic crisis, external constraints and neoliberal reforms

As the previous section outlined, internal forces contributed to the pursuit of neoliberalism by the PSOE governments. However, external forces were important in constraining policy responses and instrumental in the political discourse. The constraints were especially real in light of the competitive deficiencies and the parameters of the Francoist model that were reviewed in the first section. With the collapse of the buoyant international conditions underpinning the boom, and the political uncertainty following Franco's death, the economic miracle came to an abrupt halt. Oil price rises, industrial conflict and the rigid labour market encouraged an inflationary spiral, which was unwound only slowly and partially through successive social accords from 1977 onwards (Lieberman, 1982; Wright, 1977).

Even so, Spanish capital suffered a deep crisis of accumulation concentrated in the industrial sector (Segura et al., 1989). Investment fell and a process of de-industrialization accelerated in the early 1980s. The crisis was particularly acute in traditional industries in which Spain was overspecialized and, by now, a relatively uncompetitive producer. By the mid-1980s unemployment exceeded 20 per cent due largely to the crisis in manufacturing which had seen three-quarters of a million jobs shed in a decade (Myro Sánchez, 1993).

Although the PSOE was wary of making precise commitments prior to the election of 1982, its discourse did involve vague promises of a 're-industrialization' strategy centred on both corporatist methods and developmental economic policies aimed at reversing Spain's industrial malaise (Share, 1989: 60–73). In particular, the PSOE hinted at an expansionary policy to create 800 000 new jobs.

The retreat of the PSOE from this agenda has been documented (Royo, 2000). It is salutary to record the fate of the French socialists' strategy of 'Keynesianism in one country', and the effect this had on opinion within the PSOE (Share, 1989). It was argued that any expansionist strategy of re-industrialization would meet severe external constraints, which would manifest themselves through trade imbalances, currency instability and capital flight. In the Spanish case, the risks were greater owing to more pronounced international dependence of the economy. It was argued that this ruled out any project of autonomous expansion. In contrast, macroeconomic stability and European integration would create opportunities to modernize Spanish industry through the discipline of competition. In particular, the restraint of wage costs and 'flexibilization' of the labour market would provide incentives to investment, streamlining and technological development. The outlines of the competition state began to be drawn: the interventionism of Francoism would gradually be discarded through a liberalization process designed to transform Spain into an attractive location for investment, particularly foreign investment. This would drive the reform of labour laws, the public sector and state aids. The job creation agenda of the government would hinge upon removing obstacles to hiring, firing and deploying labour flexibly.

Neoliberals within the PSOE such as Miguel Boyer – formerly a member of the centre-right UCD – were entrusted with economic strategy and speedily dispensed with notions of re-industrialization (Share, 1989: 140; Holman, 1996). Economic strategy in Spain since 1982 has centred on a project of structural reform and market liberalization circumscribed by an orthodox macroeconomic policy emphasizing sound money, currency stability and the defeat of inflation. These core policies have been pursued vigorously and have been central to the framework of economic strategy laid out in successive official statements of government policy. The pursuit of growth, it has been argued, is heavily dependent upon attaining these objectives in a context marked by the increasing globalization of markets, intense international competition and enhanced capital mobility (MINER, 1989; MINER, 1995, Ministerio de Economía y Hacienda, 1993). What follows here is a brief summary of the neoliberal reforms of the Spanish economy since 1982 encompassing the following areas: the labour market, market liberalization, and privatization.

4. Labour market reforms

As a result of their drive to defeat inflation, restore Spain's cost competitiveness and thereby encourage profitability, the socialists began a long process of reform in the rigid Francoist labour market. Once economic expansion was considered to be impractical, the sheer scale of unemployment, which exceeded 20 per cent from the mid-1980s, demanded a response and propelled reform (Share, 1989: 71–8). The impact in terms of segmentation between insiders and outsiders has been a constant feature, opening up large inequalities within the market. The reform has embraced several fronts: the introduction of temporary, part-time and fixed term contracts with lower entitlements to social security and severance, reform (and reduction) of severance/redundancy entitlements of workers on 'permanent' contracts ('Despido'), limits on wage rates for overtime work, and the elimination of the myriad of regulations on work practice and organization (the '*Ordenanzas Laborales*') (OECD, 1994). After an initial consolidation of the Spanish welfare state, the 1990s saw the labour market reform extended to welfare arrangements with substantial cuts in benefit entitlements, rates and expenditure justified in terms of the fiscal constraints of the EMU convergence criteria and the need to reduce wage floors and raise incentives (OECD, 1994). As the reform proceeded, the PSOE was increasingly open to criticism from its union partners in the UGT for a lack of action in the fields of unemployment and social policy (Gillespie, 1990). Indeed, by 1986 the series of social accords came to an end amid no little recrimination paving the way for the renewed industrial conflicts and strikes of 1987–88.

The PP governments from 1996 followed this agenda and although social pacts have resumed sporadically in recent years, these have been primarily to agree reform measures within areas such as redundancy, training and social protection and on ensuring Spain met the criteria for membership of EMU (Durán López *et al.*, 1994; MTAS, various years; Regini, 1999) Hence the accords of the late 1990s lacked the breadth of the social-corporatist model seeking as they did to 'accommodate' the Spanish labour market to the pressures of international markets through wage restraint and financial orthodoxy. However, they have at least allowed organized labour an input into the reform process. At the same time, however, the impact on the Spanish social model has been adverse. As a whole, the Spanish workforce has rather less job security and social protection than its North European counterparts while segmentation has concentrated the worst effects of this on a relatively large peripheral workforce composed of new market entrants, young people and women (Gough, 1996; Rhodes, 1996). Social expenditure in Spain fell as a percentage of GDP throughout the decade following 1994 and stands significantly below the EU average (*The Economist*, 2004: 10). Likewise significant casualization and segmentation of the workforce has taken place with 30 per cent of the workforce on temporary contracts and therefore enjoying significantly lower social entitlements than core workers (*The Economist*, 2004: 10).

The entire process of labour market reform has been explicitly linked to the need to create jobs and to do so by converting Spain into an attractive site for multinational corporations and foreign direct investment. It dovetails closely with the reform of industrial policy in which state aids have been radically reformed to the same ends.

5. Market liberalization and the new industrial policy

Participation in the European Union (EU) has directly structured policy choices (MINER, 1989). This is nowhere more visible than in areas such as trade and competition where entry in to the Single European Market has directly removed an array of trade barriers and required reforms in competition policy and state aids (MINER, 1989). It is worth adding that against common perceptions, the EU's own foreign trade policies nave seen a substantial liberalization in recent years (Hanson, 1998).

The Spanish market has been opened up rapidly over the last decade and a half (González Romero and Myro Sáchez, 1989; Myro Sánchez and Martínez Serrano, 1992). While this has directly contributed to inflows of FDI, it also intensified the restructuring processes of the 1980s, exposing a weak industrial base to the discipline of market competition while imposing strict limits on the role of the state in attenuating these forces. The European Commission monitors national industrial policies to ensure that principles of fair competition are met. Industrial subsidies must not be used to shield domestic firms from, or distort, competition: yet this was their raison d'être in the developmental state model (Wade, 1990).

Although there are many regional and sectoral exceptions to the provisions on state aids, it is clear that Spanish industrial policy has been oriented to meeting the criteria of fair competition. In the promotion of new industries, there is no question of protective measures, subsidies of loss-making firms, nor of discrimination against foreign firms located in Spain (MINER, 1989, 1995). On the contrary, and like other countries discussed in this volume, Spain's competition state actively seeks to attract foreign capital through increased labour market flexibility, a relatively low tax take, and progressive deregulation of the market.

In Spain, as across the EU, there has generally been both a decline and a reorienting of state aids (Petitbò, 1993). A new industrial policy designed to promote competitiveness and internationalization has been instituted and deepened since the late 1980s and has been articulated in successive policy documents (see, for example, MINER, 1989, 1995). The strategy seeks to provide support only to 'horizontal' initiatives to deepen infrastructures in communications, science and technology, risk and seed capital and the promotion of exports and foreign investment (both inward and outward).

A strong element in the policy discourse has been the necessity to compete and engage in a global market. The foreign trade institute ('ICEX') has strongly supported an export drive and internationalization of Spanish capital through foreign investment (MICYT, 1992). This is the reverse side of the courting of extensive inward investment, and appears to see Spain as much as a 'globalizer' as the 'globalized' reversing Spain's historical legacy of technological dependence, particularly in the banking and telecommunications sectors and especially in Latin America. Likewise, Spanish governments have been able to point to considerable support from EU structural funds over the last decade. These have facilitated a large number of regeneration and development projects. Major new transport and communication infrastructures stand out as testaments to the opportunities provided by Europe; not the constraints. In political discourse therefore, both PSOE and its successor in power, the PP, have been successful in demonstrating clear benefits to integration, and have maintained a broad consensus over the necessity and desirability of the integration process.

6. Privatization

European integration has created further constraints on policy choices. The long process of convergence towards monetary unions locked Spain into a macroeconomic strategy governed by the need to reduce public debts and thereby lower pressure on real interest rates (Motamen-Scobie, 1998). This in turn produced fiscal and resource constraints on the state, which have rebounded on industrial and labour market policy; again providing a rationale and a space for radical reforms. These pressures have not only squeezed spending per se, but have also provided further impetus to the process of privatization (Bilbao Ubillos, 1995; Navarro, 1990). Restructuring of the public sector and privatization of the state's industrial holdings have been common threads in the strategies of both PSOE and PP governments (Motamen-Scobie, 1998). Since the 1980s most of the state-holding company's major industrial holdings have been privatized by both PSOE and PP administrations including those in 'strategic' industries such as electronics, cars, energy and telecommunications (Myro Sánchez, 1993; *The Economist,* 2004: 10).

Alongside and overlapping this policy has been the restructuring of traditional industries that were in crisis by the late 1970s. This restructuring programme arose after the nationalization of 'lame duck' firms in sectors such as textiles, shipbuilding and steel in the 1970s and the earlier creation of public firms in these sectors (Navarro, 1990). The Spanish socialists inherited a large public sector concentrated in declining industries and loss making firms. The subsidization of these firms and the payment of their outstanding debts was a severe drain on government resources. In the longer term their modernization and restructuring was also overseen by the state involving large financial commitments in areas such as redundancy packages for workers affected by plant closures, rationalization of capacity, investment in new plant and machinery, retraining packages and aids to the worst affected regions such as Galicia (El Ferrol and Vigo), the Basque Country (Bilbao and the Vizcaya region in general), Asturias, Cadiz and Barcelona (Navarro, 1990).

Critics of the new Spanish strategy point to the combination of resource constraints and excessive liberalization and argue that, given Spain's history of technological dependence on foreign capital, the headlong rush to neoliberalism has been premature (Royo, 2000). Spain has opened up too much too quickly without first taking the opportunity to address structural weaknesses through more traditional, state interventionist means (Buesa and Molero, 1987; Buesa, 1994). In effect they argue that a developmental state strategy could have been pursued but was sacrificed on the altar of rapid European integration. This view underlines the existence of 'alternatives' during the post-Franco period, and points to the capacity of the PSOE to mobilize public and elite dissatisfaction with the Franco model in order to steer Spain toward a neoliberal agenda. In this context, the capacity of the PSOE to use iesuuice and regulatory constraints arising from integration as tools with which to embed a neoliberal consensus and drive reforms forward faster demonstrates the limitations of approaches that overlook domestic forces in the globalization debate.

7. Conclusion

The Spanish economy has performed rather well in recent years. Macroeconomic stabilization enabled participation in European Monetary Union and labour market reforms enabled unemployment to fall to below 11 per cent in 2001 (and to stay below 12 per cent since then), the lowest level since before the 'industrial crisis' (*The Economist*, 2004: 10). These successes have been achieved at a cost, namely a high degree of labour market segmentation and a relatively underdeveloped welfare model. Nevertheless, public attitudes to the EU have remained rather positive and democratization has produced a stable liberal democracy. It has been the argument of this chapter that these political goals have been key forces, weighing heavily in political discourse and permitting the consolidation of neoliberalism in Spain. International forces and domestic economic weakness were real constraints on the post-Franco governments; autonomous expansion would have entailed risks of capital flight, trade crisis and currency instability. However, what propelled the political goals of European integration and ultimately the neoliberal project was not a genuine external crisis. Neoliberalism was not imposed by any external force but adopted by important currents within the PSOE and later the PP. In both cases, pragmatism combined with the balance of social forces pertaining after Franco, were key forces in the transformation. The 'autarchic' Franco model was clearly problematic both in its economic performance and its lack of popular support making it vulnerable to attack and with international economic forces providing a highly plausible prism within which to argue for its radical reform. But the pace and extent of that reform have been conditioned by domestic social, cultural and political forces. After all, the pace of Spain's integration in the European Union was clearly the result of internal factors among which the political culture of the democratic transition was crucial. Having joined the European project so rapidly, radical reforms were legitimized with reference to making this project successful, so buying political elites the space and opportunity to fundamentally transform the Spanish political economy and marginalize alternative strategies.

Note

* The Civil War of 1936–39 was precipitated by Franco's 'Nationalist' coup against the existing Republican government. The long-term causes of the Civil War lay in the extreme polarization and class conflict of Spanish society in which assorted

anarchist, regionalist and communist movements had emerged to create a 'revolutionary situation' of land seizures and strikes which met fierce resistance from the right and through the Civil Guard, with the Republican government increasingly incapable of maintaining control. Franco's attempted coup led to one of the most bitter and defining conflicts of the twentieth century in which the Fascist powers intervened in support of Franco – most infamously in the German aerial assault on the Basque town of Guernika. Stalin supported the Republican side. However, the efforts of pro-Stalinists to centralize and control the Republican cause alienated Spanish communist and anarchist groupings undermining the Republican cause. Franco emerged victorious from the civil war and established a repressive state machine executing thousands of republican, socialist, Basque and Catalan nationalist, and communist opponents while forcing many more into exile. Nevertheless, throughout the Franco period socialist, regionalist and communist movements survived underground and as the 1960s progressed posed an increasing threat to the regime, culminating in the Basque Nationalist group ETA's assassination of Franco's chosen successor, Carrero Blanco in 1973.

Further reading

Farrell, M. (2001) *Spain in the EU: the Road to Economic Convergence*, Basingstoke: Macmillan. An account of the 'hard road' to convergence.

Harrison, J. and Corkhill, D. (2004) *Spain: A Modern European Economy*, Aldershot: Ashgate. A snapshot of the state of the Spanish economy after its integration into the European Union covering the strengths, weaknesses and structural challenges facing the Spanish economy.

Martin, C. (2000) *The Spanish Economy in the New Europe*, translated from the Spanish by Phillip Hill and Sarah Nicholson, Basingstoke: Macmillan. An insider's account of the contemporary Spanish economy, its integration into Europe and the associated reform process.

Useful websites

<www.ine.es>   The Spanish National Statistical Institute

<www.la-moncloa.es>   The Spanish Government

<www.congreso.es>   The Spanish Parliament

<www.elpais.es>   El Pais

<www.elmundo.es>   El Mundo

<www.ccoo.es> and <www.ugt.es>   Trade unions

<www.ceoe.es>   Employers

<www.pp.es>   Partido Popular

<www.psoe.es>   Socialist Party

6
Exporting and Internalizing Globalization: Canada and the Global System of Power[8]

Stephen McBride

1. Introduction

Since Canada has always depended on the international economy for its prosperity the chapter opens by considering its historical strategies for actively managing its interaction with more powerful international economic actors. In the 1980s the Canadian strategy shifted to one of neoliberalism and free trade. The new strategy, explored in a subsequent section of the chapter, involved accepting constraints on aspects of national sovereignty and some reorganization of state institutions through the provisions of NAFTA and the WTO.

Although the emphasis here is on Canada's interactions with the emerging global system and, in particular, the way international economic agreements act as a 'conditioning framework' (Grinspun and Kreklewich, 1994) serving to lock in place domestically engineered neoliberal reforms, Canada's turn to neoliberalism cannot be understood simply as an externally-induced phenomenon. Following the apparent exhaustion of the Keynesian welfare state in the mid-1970s the Canadian government, dealing with a crisis of 'stagflation' (simultaneously high levels of inflation and unemployment), jettisoned its commitment to full employment policies and adopted policies of financial orthodoxy focused on control of inflation and achieving balanced budgets (McBride, 1992). Similarly the rhetoric of the competition state was used to re-engineer Canada's social programmes and coercively re-attach many former beneficiaries to the low end of the labour market (McBride and McNutt, 2004). The roots of the change of strategy are to be found in the structural characteristics and articulated preferences of Canadian business. Business preferences were reflected in the recommendations of the 1985 Macdonald Royal Commission on the Economic Union and Development Prospects for Canada (Canada, 1985), and in the programmes of the Conservative Party under Brian Mulroney and, later, the Liberal Party of Jean Chrétien. Thus the primary channel of policy diffusion stems from reorganized organizations of capital but a key mediating role is played by a royal commission, the traditional Canadian instrument for engineering a shift in policy paradigm (Bradford, 1998) and by the electoral process and political parties.

2. Coping with Canada's external constraint: a brief historical account

The international economy has always imposed constraints on the Canadian state. In dealing with these Canada relied, until the 1980s, on an active role for the state in managing its insertion in the global political economy. This 'statism' served to distinguish Canada from its southern neighbour. At both federal and provincial levels, the Canadian state was historically more likely to intervene in economic and social matters than its counterpart in the United States. Canada devised 'National Policies' for managing its domestic economy, achieving social cohesion in a sociologically fragmented context, and regulating its relations with the United States (see, for example: Bradford, 1998; Brodie, 1990; Eden and Molot, 1993; Fowke, 1952; Leslie, 1987).[9] Moreover, the state, in the sense of political system, played a major role in creating the Canadian state, in the sense of country (Smiley, 1967).[10]

The initial nineteenth century national policy involved a significant degree of state involvement in economic development, through tariffs, provision of transportation infrastructure, immigration and land settlement. A second, mid-twentieth century national policy grafted a version of Keynesian economic management onto an economy shaped by dependence on resource exports but accustomed to a relatively active state role to compensate for market deficiencies. The second national policy incorporated the construction of a social welfare state that was distinctive in North America and served also, as when public Canadian health care was contrasted favourably with privately provided health care in the United States, as source of national identity. Measures designed to enhance Canadian identity and culture and distinguish the country from its larger neighbour were integral to these strategies.

As postwar Keynesianism unravelled in the 1970s, and a crisis of simultaneously high levels of inflation and unemployment afflicted Canada, two potential successor strategies emerged. One, a continuation of traditional statism, was a nationalist-inspired industrial strategy that would use the state to stimulate the economy and promote domestically controlled capital accumulation. The other, by contrast, viewed the state as a major cause of the crisis and based its cure in free-market solutions, domestically and abroad (Brodie and Jenson, 1988: 294).

In its 1980–84 term the Trudeau Liberal government did adopt a version of the first approach. This featured an industrial strategy in which the federal government was to play a highly interventionist role. Its chief component was the National Energy Program (NEP). The strategy aimed to consolidate Canadian ownership in the energy sector and to use the sector as the cornerstone of an economic development strategy (Clarkson, 1985: ch. 4).

The fact that such policies could be launched led some to assume that a nationalist fraction of Canadian capital had become influential in shaping economic policy. Niosi (1985) considered one such possibility: that indigenous Canadian capital was pursuing a strategy of 'continental nationalism'. However, concluding that US-owned businesses and large Canadian corporations, including banks, were opposed to the policy, Niosi cautioned 'the continental dimension may take precedence over the nationalist aspect ...' (Niosi, 1985: 64). An alternative view seemed plausible; rather than being the product of a nationalist fraction of Canadian capital, this was a period in which the Canadian state enjoyed considerable autonomy and, while its efforts were firmly linked to the interests of private capital accumulation (Pratt, 1982: 40–1), it was prepared to promote indigenous over foreign-owned capital. But if this was an example of state autonomy it was to prove short-lived. Despite its attachment to private enterprise, the Liberal attempt at a third national policy encountered major opposition from the United States and from the Canadian business community which itself included a significant component of managers of US branch plants. A contemporary study of capital's attitudes on these issues provided little support for the notion that any significant portion of Canadian capital supported a nationalist strategy (Ornstein, 1985).

This new, third national policy failed for two reasons. First, it was dependent upon the fortunes of the international commodities market. To sustain the strategy and support the energy megaprojects, oil prices had to keep rising. In fact, they dropped. Second, the initiative ran into major ideological opposition from US and Canadian business. The week after the NEP was launched, Ronald Reagan was elected president of the United States. It was predictable that an interventionist and nationalist policy would attract the enmity of the new US administration. But opposition from the United States was accompanied by internal hostility from business in Canada and from provincial governments. The pressures emanating from these sources were accentuated by structural factors. Increased Canada–US trade had made the economy vulnerable to US policy and threats of retaliation (Brodie and Jenson, 1988: 318). US-based capital successfully encouraged its state to pressure Canada to abandon its new national policy. And Canadian business generally, both indigenous and foreign-owned, became increasingly nervous about the degree of state interventionism inherent in the Liberal strategy and evident in such initiatives as the earlier Anti-Inflation Program (McBride, 1983) as well as the NEP. Such concerns had prompted business to increase its representative capacity – hence the formation of the Business Council on National Issues in 1975 (Langille, 1987).

Perhaps if energy prices had remained high the attractiveness of energy self-sufficiency would have enabled the federal government's interventionist wing to build a political base that would have sustained the NEP. As it was, oil prices fell and the Canadian state was vulnerable to pressures from within and without (Laxer, 1983). The potential material basis for its autonomous and ambitious strategy diminished with falling oil prices, and the NEP was abandoned. With the election of the Mulroney government the state, reflecting the articulated demands of Canadian business (Langille, 1987), adopted a neoliberal economic strategy.

Domestically the election of a Progressive Conservative government under Brian Mulroney symbolized the triumph of neoliberal ideology in Canada. However, the precise impact of the Mulroney government on existing programmes was a matter of debate in the 1980s and early 1990s. In social policy, for example, the prevailing view was that change was incremental and consisted of erosion rather than outright dismantling (Banting, 1987: 213). In retrospect it appears that incrementalism and 'stealth' over a protracted period produced fundamental change, especially when the same direction was sustained by the Liberal governments of the 1990s. However, the means of implementing changes in social programmes indicated a cautious approach on the part of Canadian neoliberals. Common techniques included transforming universal into selective programmes, tightening eligibility requirements, and imposition of ceilings on programme costs – or, alternatively, attempting to make programmes self-financing or subject to 'clawbacks' over a certain benefit level (Houle, 1990). Stephen Phillips (2000: 5–6) notes that in 1979 universal programmes paid out 43 per cent of income security benefits, and by 1993, 0 per cent. Benefits paid in social insurance programmes increased; but the most dramatic increase, from 14.2 per cent of total income security benefits to 43 per cent, came in selective or targeted programmes.

Caution was deemed necessary because of continued public support for an active state. The Liberal Party's election campaign in 1993 seemed to recognize the deep-rooted attachment of Canadians to social programmes and widespread fears about those programmes being under threat (Liberal Party, 1993). Again, however, once the Liberals were in office, their implementation of neoliberal prescriptions proved more energetic even than that of the preceding government.

The 1995 federal budget marked a fundamental shift in the role of the federal state in Canada. Prior to the budget one prominent journalist commented: 'All manner of rhetoric will be used to mask Ottawa's decline: "reinventing government", "flexible federalism", "modernizing Canada"... The essence of the matter, however, is this: the shrinking of the federal government, attempted by the Conservatives under the guise of fiscal restraint and constitutional reform, will now be accelerated by the Liberals ...'

(Jeffrey Simpson, *Globe and Mail* 27 January 1995). Others defined the budget as the end of an era: 'It is now clear that the Minister of Reconstruction's White Paper on Employment and Income of 1945 can be regarded as one bookend on a particular period in Canadian history, and Paul Martin's February [1995] budget as the other' (Kroeger, 1996: 21).

The case for 1995 as the termination point of the Keynesian welfare state rests on the primacy of deficit reduction over maintenance of the social safety net. The determination to reduce the deficit through spending reductions in the social policy area quickly resulted in declining federal transfers to provinces, diminished conditions attached to those transfers and a fundamental redesign of the unemployment benefit system.

3. Trading sovereignty

Emerging in the mid-1980s as a priority, Canadian economic strategy was based on free-market principles and became focused on the negotiation of a bilateral free trade agreement with the United States, a policy continued by the Liberals on their return to office in 1993. Ironically, although the Canadian state had by the early 1980s reached its most advanced stage of development in history, the federal government's decision to pursue a Free Trade Agreement with the United States resulted in the abdication of most of Canada's economic and cultural sovereignty (Clarkson, 1991).

Two obvious questions arise. First, how can we delineate or measure such a loss of sovereignty? Second, why did the Canadian state, as promoter of this and subsequent free trade agreements, engineer a loss of sovereign decision-making capacity?

Some account of the characteristics of newer international economic agreements is necessary to address the first of these questions, since negotiation and ratification of such agreements are part of a process, which produced fundamental changes affecting Canadian sovereignty. To sustain this argument it should be recognized that newer international economic agreements, such as NAFTA and the WTO, are qualitatively different from earlier agreements. Previously, economic agreements like the General Agreement on Tariffs and Trade (GATT), covered certain aspects of inter-state relations, such as the duties that might be levied on goods crossing a border. But beyond that, national sovereignty was little affected. The new generation of agreements have a much broader scope. Typically they cover services, investment, and intellectual property rights, and expand the definition of trade, in some cases, to cover anything that might be 'trade-related'. They intrude much further into the internal politics and policies of signatories (Wolfe, 1996).

Some argue that sovereignty is maintained because signatories reserve the right, usually at relatively short notice, to withdraw from the agreements.

This is true but reduces sovereignty to a formal legal attribute. Amendment, or withdrawal from international economic agreements may, on paper, be relatively easy. However, in practice, changes involve the agreement of actors external to the Canadian political system; and withdrawal, though legally achievable by decision internal to Canada, may be prohibitively expensive once the integration promoted by these agreements has had time to develop.

The reach of these agreements is such that there is a growing literature depicting them as constitutional or quasi-constitutional in their effects (Clarkson, 1993; Schneiderman, 1996). Less widely noticed is the link between the constitutionalism of the agreements and their impact on sovereignty. Constitutions, whether broadly or narrowly defined (McBride, 2003), pertain to a particular society, a given people occupying, normally, a certain territory and exercising sovereignty over it. The independence implied by sovereignty serves to define the constitution's sphere of application (Hobsbawm, 2000: 22–3). As sovereignty is diminished so too is the scope for constitutional government and democratic choice.

To make this link, sovereignty needs to be broken down into its components. Krasner (1999: 9–10) has drawn a distinction between authority, the recognized right of a state to take certain actions, and control, its actual capacity or ability to engage in them. On this basis his typology helpfully distinguishes between:

> domestic sovereignty, referring to the organization of public authority within a state and to the level of effective control exercised by those holding authority; interdependence sovereignty, referring to the ability of public authorities to control transborder movements; international legal sovereignty, referring to the mutual recognition of states or other entities; and Westphalian sovereignty, referring to the exclusion of external actors from domestic authority configurations. (Krasner, 1999: 9; see also Philpott, 2001)

Of these, only international legal sovereignty remains entirely intact. Indeed, maintenance of international legal sovereignty is a precondition for states' ability to engineer the diminution of the other forms of sovereignty.[11] It is clear that the state played an active role in the erosion of the other forms of Canadian sovereignty. The fact that Canada can withdraw with minimal formal difficulty from agreements like NAFTA and the WTO signifies that its international legal sovereignty remains intact. To the extent that the agreements alter the configuration of domestic authority, or restrict the scope for exercising such authority, they represent a negotiated, by-invitation[12] infringement of other forms of other sovereignty. Table 6.1 presents a summary of these developments.

Table 6.1 NAFTA and WTO, institutional change and diminished sovereignty

Domestic sovereignty	Interdependence sovereignty	Westphalian sovereignty
(i) how public authority is organized	*(i) how public authority is organized*	*(i) how public authority is organized*
Negotiation of international economic agreements has reinforced executive domination of the Canadian political system, functioning as a sort of 'executive federalism' writ large. The agreements appear to have increased federal supervisory powers by stipulating that the federal authorities must ensure the compliance of subnational governments. Arguably the scope of the federal 'trade and commerce' power (Section 91(2) of the Constitution Act, has been enhanced.		There has been a growth in international adjudication of state actions under both NAFTA and the WTO. Already this process has removed important policy instruments from states. New forms of international scrutiny and monitoring of Canadian policy-making have been established (Trade Policy Review Mechanisms under the WTO and various provisions of NAFTA Ch. 18.)
(ii) level of effective control	*(ii) level of effective control*	*(ii) level of effective control*
Regulatory capacity in several areas must now be exercised in the 'least trade restrictive' way possible. (WTO Agreement on Technical Barriers) The Canadian state is committed, under GATS, to the progressive liberalization of service provision. Performance requirements on foreign investment are restricted or prohibited under both NAFTA and the WTO. Capacity to institute a domestic price for energy different from the export price is prohibited under NAFTA. A WTO ruling effectively dismantled the Canada-US Autopact (a production sharing agreement.)	NAFTA (Article 605) prohibits controls on the proportion of energy production that can be exported. Similarly it prohibits altering the previous mix of energy products that are exported. In the periodicals case NAFTA and WTO panel rulings have prohibited using taxes or subsidies as instruments to sustain Canadian cultural distinctiveness.	Foreign investors have new rights that permit them to take complaints against Canadian policy directly to an adjudication venue of their choice.

4. Effects of International Economic Agreements (IEAs) on how public authority is organized

The first effect is an indirect one. It stems from but further enhances the already executive dominated nature of the Canadian parliamentary system (Savoie, 1999). Intergovernmental negotiations that settle important aspects of public policy at the federal-provincial level have been criticized for leaving little room for legislatures, political parties, or the public at large to have effective input (see Dyck, 1996: 85). The same point applies to international agreements. Thus, the more things are settled in the secrecy of international trade negotiations, the more influence is concentrated in the hands of the executive and, particularly, the Prime Minister who, as Savoie (1999: 362) describes the situation, 'holds all the cards'.

Moreover, there are indications that the agreements are redrawing the federal distribution of power. Earlier international economic agreements had little effect on the balance of power between federal and provincial governments. More recent agreements extend the notion of trade to include investment and services and, as a result, potentially impinge into areas of provincial jurisdiction. Both NAFTA and the WTO require the federal government to obtain the compliance of subnational governments.

Although consultations about trade negotiations have been held with the provinces (Brown, 1991) they are not present at negotiations and their consent to any agreement is not required (Doern and Tomlin, 1992: 126–51). To the extent, therefore, that agreements bind provinces in areas of provincial jurisdiction this represents an extension of the federal power over trade and commerce. This can be regarded as altering the internal distribution of legislative power in Canada as federal power previously had been constrained by judicial decision in the *Labour Conventions* case of 1937. That judgment determined that the federal authorities lacked the power to implement international treaties if they interfered with provincial jurisdiction. Macdonald (1998) noted that until then NAFTA federal governments had been reluctant to reach international agreements that would require enforcement in provincial areas of jurisdiction. But NAFTA appeared to indicate a changed stance on Ottawa's part. This can be attributed to the broad definition of trade, which has come to include some types of investment, services as well as goods, intellectual property rights, and now includes other matters which may be 'trade related'. As this broad range of issues has been rolled under the trade and commerce power of the constitution, it has acquired greater significance than it had in the days when trade meant trade in goods.

As with many possible consequences of the new economic agreements it is difficult to be certain how far-reaching a change in federalism this represents. In a number of decisions the Supreme Court had already indicated a greater tolerance for federal use of the trade and commerce power (Richards, 1991) than formerly. Provinces so far have been unwilling to launch any challenge to federal authority. Possible reasons include shared commitment to the ideology behind the new agreements, unwillingness to appear inhospitable to potential investments, and fear of losing in the court. However, there is a considerable body of academic legal opinion that considers a significant constitutional change has been accomplished under the rubric of an international economic agreement (Howse, 1990; Luz, 2001–02; Trebilcock, 2001; Vegh, 1996). If so, this development shows the ability of global agreements to bypass domestic constitutional procedures. However, it also shows the willingness of domestic political elites to use this extra- or quasi-constitutional means to accomplish their political and economic ends.

New power relations are reflected in new forms of scrutiny and accountability. As well as parliamentary scrutiny of the executive, which, in the Westminster model, is far from effective, domestic policy is continuously monitored by the international organizations to which the country belongs. Conducted in the name of 'transparency' such scrutiny exercises a strong 'moral suasion' effect not only for compliance with the letter, but also with the neoliberal spirit of the agreements to which Canada is a signatory.

Under the WTO, a Trade Policy Review Mechanism (TPRM) operates to 'contribute to adherence by all members to rules, disciplines and commitments made ... by achieving greater transparency ...' (Laird, 1999: 742). As a member of the Quad, the inner group of trade ministers representing the United States, the European Union, Japan and Canada, which co-operate to set the WTO agenda, Canada is reviewed every two years. The period between reviews varies from four to six years for the rest of WTO members depending on members' size as a trading entity. The more important a country is in terms of trade, the more regularly it will be reviewed. A review involves questionnaires sent out by the WTO Secretariat and a site visit by a WTO team. It has been claimed that through this monitoring role the WTO 'not only contributed to the fulfilment of commitments in the multilateral trading system but has also contributed to the development of national policies'. (Laird, 1999: 760).

NAFTA Chapter 18 contains a number of transparency provisions that open up the policy process to the early intervention of NAFTA partners. The chapter provides that contact points must be established to facilitate communications and provide information regarding matters covered by the agreement and that all measures affecting the agreement must be made public in a timely manner. In particular, Articles 1802 and 1803 provide for advance notification of any measure affecting the agreement that it proposes to adopt, and guarantee a reasonable opportunity to comment. Little has so far been written on this aspect of NAFTA but on paper it provides structured opportunities for early intervention of NAFTA partners into the policy process of other members.

To some extent international trade panels have replaced the Canadian courts as final appeal mechanisms on substantive issues. Under NAFTA, for example, a binational review panel displaced judicial review of most issues concerned with dumping and anti-dumping, at least for disputes between NAFTA members. And, in NAFTA Chapter 11, foreign investors are given the option of pursuing disputes against member states directly through domestic courts or arbitration panels. Whereas under the anti-dumping and countervailing subsidies provisions the panels are applying domestic law, under the investment chapter they apply international law and are able to award damages and impose other sanctions (Lemieux and Stuhec, 1999: 146).

Disputes arising under the WTO are referred to dispute panels once attempts at consultation and mediation have failed to produce a mutually acceptable resolution. The scope of regulations under the WTO expanded dramatically as a result of the Uruguay Round. The dispute resolution mechanisms were also strengthened to eliminate delays and the right of the guilty party to eventually veto decisions. Enforcement mechanisms include elimination of the regulation or legislation found to be in breach of WTO provisions, payment of compensation or, should the offending party fail to implement panel findings, sanctioned retaliation by the injured party. The WTO has already deemed Canadian magazine legislation, promoted as defence of Canadian culture, and the Auto Pact, to be contrary to WTO provisions. These examples indicate the scope of the WTO and its extra-territorial adjudication mechanisms.

5. Effects of IEAs on the level of effective control: or, how public authority is limited by IEAs

The WTO and NAFTA seek to embed neoliberal ideology as the key reference point for state decision-makers. Even when the explicit right of government to regulate the market is recognized, it is circumscribed by privileging neoliberal values. For example, the WTO Agreement on Technical Barriers to Trade[13] permits government regulation of matters like health and safety. However, it protects market criteria by stipulating that regulations should not be more trade-restrictive than necessary, must be non-discriminatory, and respect the national treatment principle.

With the transformation of GATT into the WTO, the world's trade regime was transformed from shallow or negative integration, based on reciprocal reduction of border measures, into ' "deeper", positive or "behind the border" integration which can require analysis of almost any national policy likely to have spill over or external effects across borders' (Wolfe, 1996: 692–3). This arrangement triggered a class-based division of social forces. Business groups were supporters of deep integration; labour, social and environmental groups tended to be in opposition.

In signing the WTO agreement, countries committed to further liberalization of trade in services (Das, 1998: 110). The General Agreement on Trade in Services (GATS) is tilted toward progressive 'opting-in' and the WTO

Secretariat is very open about its capacity to intrude into national decision-making: 'The reach of the GATS rules extends to all forms of international trade in services. This means that the GATS agreement represents a major new factor for a large sector of world economic activity. It also means, because such a large share of trade in services takes place *inside* national economies, that its requirements will from the beginning necessarily influence national domestic laws and regulations in a way that has been true of the GATT only in recent years' (WTO, 1999a). The ideological roots of this are explicit: in a related document the secretariat cited as advantages the ability of bindings, once undertaken, to 'lock in a currently liberal regime or map out a future liberalization path' (WTO, 1999b: 1) while overcoming domestic resistance to change.

Critics have focused on the potential for the GATS to undermine public provision of services. Defenders point to the fact that governments must act to include particular service areas within the GATT, and can therefore choose to exclude particular service areas from much of its coverage. Similarly, services supplied 'in the exercise of government authority' (GATS Part 1 2b) are excluded. However, the definition of the 'exercise of government authority', which means 'supplied neither on a commercial basis, nor in competition with one or more service providers' (GATS Part 1 2c) appears to limit this exemption. Cohen (2001: 14–15) notes that it is not unusual for public services to levy user fees and to operate in contexts where there are other suppliers. With the exception of the national security exemption, other government services may be inadequately protected. She concludes (Cohen, 2001: 57–9) that steps to deregulate public utilities like electricity fail to anticipate the impact of the GATS and other trade agreements such that even partial and hesitant steps toward deregulation could lead to further escalation. One analysis of the impact of the GATS on Canada's publicly administered health services concludes that GATS and other trade agreements do not threaten the public health system as it currently exists. However, any attempt to expand the system could produce compensation claims from private sector health care providers using NAFTA Chapter 11 rights of foreign investors. And increasing the privately provided component could erode the protections presently built into the GATS (Johnson, 2002). Similarly, Ouellet (2002) noted that the measures taken by Canada to exclude health services from the purview of international economic agreements had, so far, worked. But it was not implausible that they would in future 'no longer be able [to] adequately protect our public health systems'. (Ouellet, 2002: vi). The system of declining to make commitments to include health care services, under the WTO's GATS is quite different from the method of exempting health care from NAFTA by means of exceptions and reservations. The interaction between the two agreements and different methods of assuring exemption for health is complex and intrinsically risky.

The pressure to further transfer public functions to the private sector comes from the world's two largest traders, the US and the EU, which are, notwithstanding other differences between them, both strong supporters of further liberalization. Indeed, the German Chancellor, Gerhard Schröder, has accused the EU Commission of being more neoliberal than the United States (*National Post*, 15 July 2002: A15). The impact of this, and scope for further liberalization of the GATS can be seen in (recent) EU proposals on the GATS, which triggered a storm of NGO denunciation for the 'extraordinarily aggressive' content of the proposals (*Bridges Weekly Trade News Digest*, 23 April 2002, http://www.ictsd.org/weekly/02-04-23/story3.htm). In the view of the *Guardian* the EU 'was demanding full-scale privatization of public monopolies across the world as its price for dismantling the common agricultural policy'. (*Ibid.*) Here we should note that the WTO is a 'single undertaking' so leveraging concessions in one area to win concessions in another is built into its fabric. While the EU document is, of course, only a negotiating position, its implications are far-reaching and thoroughly consistent with the neoliberal ethos prevalent at the WTO. One assessment of the EU's proposals for Canada to open up its services sector concluded: 'A broad range of Canadian policies at every level of government would have to be eliminated or changed ...' (Gould, 2002: 1). In Gould's view the package adds up to a generalized attack on publicly delivered services.

We must await the outcomes of these and similar initiatives. However, the general direction, unless political forces that are committed to reversing the trend achieve greater success, is one of further privileging market forces at the expense of state sovereignty.

Willingness to constrain state sovereignty can also be inferred from the creation of property rights for international investors. NAFTA Article 1116 permits investors to directly launch a claim without 'their' government acting as an intermediary and, in so doing, confers a form of property rights on foreign investors. Such provisions strengthen the position of multinational corporations vis-à-vis states and also privilege 'corporate citizens' in relation to 'natural' or human citizens. Protection of intellectual property rights is strengthened under both NAFTA and WTO. Provisions in the Canada–US Free Trade Agreement featured in the successful insurance company lobby against proposed public no-fault auto insurance in Ontario in the early 1990s (*Washington Post*, 14 August 1991; *World Insurance Report*, 30 August 1991). In essence the provisions guaranteed enjoyment of future profits, or compensation for loss thereof, to investors.

Under the WTO investors do not have the right to initiate actions (though they would have had under the MAI). But investors' rights, especially intellectual property rights, are well-protected. For example, the Trade Related Intellectual Property Rights (TRIPS) agreement covers areas such as copyrights, trademarks, and patents.

6. International Economic Agreements: an external or internal political constraint?

If the effect of these agreements is to diminish Canada's sovereignty, why did the Canadian state voluntarily pursue such a strategy? One answer is that there was nothing voluntarily about it, that Canada had little option but to pursue economic integration with the United States. This might be attributed to US pressures such as protectionism, or to more general influences promoting globalization but which, in the North American context, produced continentalism.

There is no doubt that external pressures of this sort existed. However, the fact that Canada was the *demandeur*, in the original free trade talks (Clarkson, 1991) and that the initiative was part of a comprehensive re-orientation of both domestic and international policy demanded by Canadian business points to a more domestic causation. Having helped create and fully internalized the norms of liberalized trade Canada has been an enthusiastic exporter of them. Schneiderman (2000: 761) notes that Canadian trade negotiators actively promote these principles in their own bilateral negotiations. For example, the Canada–South Africa bilateral investment agreement has constitutional implications for South Africa as its property rights provisions contravene South Africa's constitution.

Historically, Canadian business leaders were conservative nationalists who supported a degree of state activism. However, their nationalism was not altruistic. Their economic interests were served by having the state contribute to the process of capital accumulation. In the post–Second World War period, Canada's economic elite tolerated the expansion of the social functions of the state. These were activities that served to legitimate the free enterprise system at a time when it was engaged in 'cold war' with an ideological rival and when its own, then recent history, in the Great Depression of the 1930s, demonstrated that its performance was deeply problematic. However, Canadian capital's interest in 'nation building' proved, over the long-term, to be contingent. Canadian capital had promoted the establishment of a Canadian state and retained a degree of caution about the continentalist option until the 1980s. Until then, the national state continued to be seen as functional for the needs of capital. But from the 1980s capital shifted to a continentalist policy and demanded that the state orchestrate the agreements necessary to achieve continental integration.

By the early 1980s, under the leadership of the Business Council on National Issues (BCNI), all major organizations representing Canadian capital had moved to a free trade position and remained remarkably unified throughout the whole debate (McBride 2001: ch. 3; Richardson 1992).

The ratification of the Free Trade Agreement between Canada and the United States concluded a long-standing tension between continentalist and economic nationalist tendencies in Canadian history (see Merrett, 1996: ch. 2).

The FTA, and subsequently NAFTA, heralded much closer continental economic integration. The move to continental integration was domestically driven – a product of the growing maturity and strength of Canadian capital. The state complied with business pressures and negotiated agreements, ostensibly about trade, that had far-reaching consequences beyond any reasonable definition of that term. Capital's influence proved decisive in moving the state authorities in the desired direction and many of the characteristics that had shaped the Canadian polity came under sustained assault as a result of this shift (McBride and Shields, 1997).

The new strategy removed constraints on foreign investment, dismantled FIRA and the NEP, and opted for continental free trade (Leslie, 1987). The shift to a free trade strategy was much assisted by the conclusions of the Macdonald Report (Canada, 1985), a commission whose counsels appear to have been wholly influenced by orthodox free market economists (Simeon, 1987) and the representations of the business community. The adoption of this strategy showed conclusively that hopes for a nationalist fraction within Canadian capital had been exaggerated (Carroll, 1986; Layton, 1976).

Business in Canada articulated its demand for a free trade agreement before Ottawa launched the free trade initiative. Indeed, a delegation from the BCNI broached the free trade idea with US officials as early as 1982 and began to publicly promote the idea in Canada from 1983 (Merrett, 1996: 33). In early 1984 the Business Council floated the idea of a bilateral 'Trade Enhancement Agreement' (TEA) and noted in 1985 that 'A framework agreement along the lines of TEA was one of four policy options canvassed in both the consultation paper issued by the Minister for International Trade in January 1985, and then in the External Affairs discussion paper released later' (BCNI, 1985: 7–8).

Developments inside the state facilitated business pressure for free trade. In September 1982, a cabinet shuffle diminished the economic role of the nationalists in the Trudeau cabinet while enhancing the influence of those considered more business-friendly. This signalled that a change of course within the state was possible.

By 1983 the possibility of a free trade agreement had emerged into the public view. The Liberals tentatively explored a sectoral free trade agreement with the US, an initiative that was stillborn, in part because the US wanted a comprehensive agreement and in part because of a leadership transition within the governing Liberals. In September 1984 Brian Mulroney's Conservatives were elected in a landslide victory. Almost immediately the business lobby for free trade intensified its efforts to get it on the national agenda (Doern and Tomlin, 1992; McQuaig, 1992).

The decisive public intervention came from Donald Macdonald, the head of the ongoing Royal Commission on the Economic Union and Development Prospects for Canada. In November 1984 Macdonald leaked a 'leap of faith' analysis to the media: 'Although the commission had neither completed its studies nor framed its conclusions, Macdonald nevertheless announced that he favoured free trade between Canada and the United States as the principal long-term solution to Canada's economic problems' (Doern and Tomlin, 1992: 24).

When in September 1985 the Macdonald Commission report was finally released to the public, its message was unambiguous: 'Market liberalization, social adjustment, and limited government were the cornerstones of the Macdonald Commission's public philosophy' (Bradford, 1998: 113). At the centre of this analysis was the conclusion that free trade with the United States was essential to any Canadian economic strategy. But there were to be major domestic implications as well. The Commissioners argued: 'Our basic international stance complements our domestic stance. We must seek an end to those patterns of government involvement in the economy, which may generate disincentives, retard flexibility, and work against the desired allocation of resources' (cited in Bradford, 1988: 114). Clearly the domestic implications of this stance were as important as the international ones. The commission mirrored the business community sentiment that free trade really was a kind of 'tough medicine' way of making Canada more efficient (McQuaig, 1992: 26–7). Essentially the free trade agreements and associated domestic policies legitimated the notion of Canada as a 'competition state'.

The Macdonald Commission's principal public argument for free trade agreement with the United States was defensive or prudential. Canada was defined as a trade-dependent nation, particularly reliant on the US market, and the threat of rising protectionism depicted as jeopardizing that trade. Thus a free trade deal with the United States was a way to guarantee Canadian access to the US. The Commission expressed scepticism as to whether the GATT, and Canada's traditional multilateral approach to trade negotiations could serve as a vehicle for future expansions of Canada's exports. Rather, the Commission argued that bilateral negotiations promised quicker results (Canada, 1985 v.1: 293–6). The Commission concluded that Canadians were missing out on opportunities in the US (Canada, 1985 v.1: ch. 6). Thus, much like the 'leap of faith' speech, the Commission ended up with only one option. Canada must expand its exports to the United States. Thus, Canada must get a free trade agreement with the United States. In 'selling' this argument the commission placed more emphasis on the threat of losing access to the US market than upon the theoretical merits of free trade per se.

A number of factors are crucial in explaining the embrace of continentalism in Canada. Most important is the overwhelmingly consensus that emerged in the business community in the 1980s in support of this position. Fostered by a maturation of Canadian capital (Carroll, 1986) and the emergence of a powerful new political voice, the BCNI (Langille, 1987), business successfully promoted comprehensive free trade with the United States. The main public rationale was that of protecting Canadian interests from rising US protectionism. But reducing the economic power of the Canadian state was an important underlying motive.

In the postwar period Canadian capital had matured. If it exhibited some differences from capital in other countries these in no way made it exceptional. As its interest in international markets and opportunities waxed, its interest in maintaining the vestiges of 'statism' in Canada waned. The drive to (continental) free trade was accompanied by and was part of a broader ideological or paradigm shift from Keynesianism to neoliberalism. Under conditions of economic difficulty, such as occurred in the 1970s, business organizations became enthusiastic supporters of the belief that the Keynesian welfare state could no longer be afforded and that its extent was, in fact, an obstacle to competitiveness. By the 1990s, these ideas, the neoliberal paradigm, were hegemonic.

Initiatives on the part of capital prefigured similar developments inside the state. Canada's foreign policy management system was reorganized by adding international trade to the external affairs ministry and its renaming as the Department of Foreign Affairs and International Trade (DFAIT) (see Doern and Kirton, 1996: ch. 10). Although a traditional tenet of Canadian foreign policy, that for Canada to wield influence and authority, the most effective medium is a multilateral cooperative and rules-based system, continued to be influential, bilateral considerations tended to outweigh it in practice (Cutler and Zacher, 1992: 4; see also Cooper, 1997: ch. 2; Keenes, 1995). Canada's involvement in multilateral economic regimes increasingly became designed to support American preferences and policies – 'multilateralism was always first and foremost a product of American hegemony' (Black and Sjolander, 1996: 27). Thus in the 1980s the foreign and domestic policy response of the Mulroney government gave fresh impetus to the view that Canada was part of the American imperialist orbit (Nossal, 1997: 62). Nonetheless, it is clear that this relationship was was only partly a matter of necessity; it was also a matter of choice driven by the outcomes of domestic politics in Canada. The policy record of the Mulroney years – the Canada–US Free Trade Agreement, the pursuit of deregulation, the elimination of some of the key elements of the welfare state, and the embrace of a more hawkish foreign policy – were clear signs that Mulroney had 'closed down the Canadian dream' of autonomy and independence (Martin, 1993: 272).

The state has proved compliant with the pressures brought to bear by capital and has emerged as one of the most enthusiastic proponents of globalization which, for Canada, bears a strong continentalist imprint. Elite opinion has become solidified around neoliberal internationalism. There is little echo of former experiments, however limited, with economic nationalism. Negotiation of international economic agreements has served to condition Canadian policy in neoliberal market directions, apparently acting as an external constraint, but in reality one of domestic manufacture. Thus, Canada is in a sense an 'exporter' of neoliberal trade and investment rules.

In turn, such agreements are a major instrument of internalization of globalization. Any external constraint created by globalization is of domestic origin.

Further reading

Clarkson, S. (2002) *Uncle Sam and Us: Globalization, Neoconservatism, and the Canadian State*. Toronto: University of Toronto Press.
Drache, D. (2004) *Borders Matter: Homeland Security and the Search for North America*. Black Point, N.S.: Fernwood.
Howlett, M., A. Netherton and M. Ramesh (1999) *The Political Economy of Canada: An Introduction*. 2nd edn Toronto: Oxford University Press.
Nelles, H.V. (2004) *A Little History of Canada*. Toronto: Oxford University Press.

Useful websites

<http://www.policyalternatives.ca>   Canadian Centre for Policy Alternative

<http://www.cprn.com/en>   Canadian Policy Research Network

<http://canada.gc.ca/acanada/acPubHome.jsp?lang=eng>   Government of Canada: About Canada

<http://www.canadawebpages.com/default.asp>   Politics Canada

7
Capturing Benefits, Avoiding Losses: the United States, Japan and the Politics of Constraint

Philip G. Cerny

1. Financial systems and national models of capitalism

The United States and Japan represent polar types of so-called 'national models of capitalism'. For reasons unique to their respective histories, their industrial organizations, financial systems, labor market structures, and patterns of state intervention, have taken on contrasting forms. As the authors in this book argue, globalization and the complex processes that make it up involve the accumulation of a range of pressures – economic, political, and social – that present challenges to the way national models work. Some national political systems, especially those of the United States and the United Kingdom, are widely seen to be in the vanguard of such changes as the result of the relative correspondence of their internal economic and social institutions and practices with emerging international and transnational patterns. Other systems, that of Japan in particular, are seen to be less structurally congenial, characterized by embedded institutions and practices that sustain and reinforce resistance to those patterns. These differences are often summoned up in the distinction between the 'arm's-length' American model and the Japanese 'strategic' or 'developmental' state (Johnson, 1982; Zysman, 1983).

Over recent decades, however, both systems have witnessed an uneven process of convergence, varying over time and affecting different economic and political groups in contrasting ways. For the United States, the relative decline of the 1970s and the 1980s – especially that of the traditional 'Rust Belt' economy – gave way first of the euphoria of the 'new economy' of the 1990s and, after the turn of the century, to financial market collapse, the 'bursting of the dot.com bubble', the emergence of financial scandals reminiscent of the Great Depression, and the rapid return of serious national budget deficits. The current George W. Bush Administration is trying to deal with this crisis by resurrecting the combination of supply side economics and military supremacy of the 1980s. For Japan, the maturing of the postwar boom economy – and the promise of economic superpower status that the 1980s seemed to hold – gave way in 1990 to an earlier bursting of the financial bubble and then to over a decade of economic stagnation and, in recent years, deflation. Successive Japanese governments have been able neither to resist change effectively nor to restructure the underlying system coherently.

The overall challenge of globalization for political actors is, as always, to minimize or compensate for losses while seeking to capture whatever benefits such processes of change might hold for their actual or potential constituencies. What globalization does is to alter the field of constraints and opportunities, the structure of rewards and penalties that actors face. In pursuing these objectives, politicians and bureaucrats over time come to develop strategic and tactical courses of action that they think might help to manipulate and shape that field more broadly. Of course, the pattern of constraints and opportunities will vary significantly across different institutional and policy issue areas. As analysts have often pointed out, in those issue-areas where significant interest groupings and political publics are disproportionately affected by real or perceived gains or losses, policymakers will seek to balance – or, more accurately, to juggle and manipulate – those interests along lines that will enable them to engage not only in short term bargaining but also in medium term coalition-building and the long term reshaping of institutional structures.

In this context, much of the comparative study of national models in advanced industrial societies in recent years has looked to industrial organization – mainly rooted in the relationship between production systems and labor market organization – as the key independent variable that explains how those models work and how they maintain the divergences among contrasting 'varieties of capitalism' (Crouch and Streeck, 1997; Kitschelt *et al.*, 1999; Hall and Soskice, 2001). Industrial organization is likely to be deeply embedded in a combination of the structures of fixed industrial capital (factories, machinery, etc.), labor patterns and trade union organizations, and cross-class ('catch-all') political parties (Kirchheimer, 1966), thereby politically privileging groups that can link producer interests and political coalitions (Goldthorpe, 1984; Cawson, 1985; Scholten, 1987).

In this context, the American political-economic system – with its weak unions, fragmented domestic producer groups, internationally oriented multinational corporations, and relatively deconcentrated political structures – will systematically privilege policies that favor liberalization and transnational openness. In contrast, other industrial countries tend in different ways to privilege more domestically 'organized' policy approaches, whether through neocorporatist bargaining processes (Germany, Austria, Scandinavia) or bureaucratically led state-industrial complexes (France, Japan). Consequently, industrial organization approaches privilege embedded practices rooted in relatively immobile capital structures.

However, another crucial issue area in this process concerns the working of national financial systems. Indeed, John Zysman, in his groundbreaking book *Governments, Markets and Growth* (1983), identified financial systems as constituting the key independent variable at the core of national models. Financial systems shape the process of capital allocation – 'where the money is', as the mid-twentieth century American bank robber, Willie Sutton, so famously said – therefore setting the parameters of continuity and change in industrial organization itself. In approaching the impact of globalization on national models, the main difference between the financial system approach and the industrial organization approach – although they overlap in significant ways – lies in the character of international and transnational market structures.

As noted above, industrial organization approaches privilege relatively immobile capital. In contrast, the financial system approach privileges the most mobile form of capital, money and finance. Global finance is far more integrated across borders than industrial capital. International capital flows reached 40–100 times the volume of trade flows in recent decades and now significantly exceed those found in the last major globalization epoch, the late nineteenth century. Finance and money also move instantaneously, especially with the development of 'new economy' information and communications technology, giving it greater velocity and impact. Furthermore, the market structure of the financial services industry itself, led by international finance, has been mutating everywhere, increasingly dominated by securities markets of various kinds rather than by institutionalized, intermediated bank capital. Finally, finance is fungible, unlike industrial capital; in other words, it can be used for anything and is needed for everything. Thus the financial systems approach privileges quite rapidly evolving practices rooted in relatively mobile capital structures, that is, those most sensitive to and closely imbricated with globalization.

Some national economic systems are *a priori* more open and vulnerable to the 'imperatives' of financial globalization than others. On the one hand, those of the United States and the United Kingdom are *financial market economies* (Coudrat, 1986; Loriaux, 1991). In such systems, the key to money and finance lies in how 'negotiable' financial instruments known as 'securities', such as stocks, shares, bonds, and, more recently, a multiplicity of innovative instruments including 'derivatives', 'asset-backed securities', and so on, are traded among buyers and sellers. Governments in these systems – if they wish to promote the expansion of financial markets in the name of general economic growth and development and therefore if private market actors are effectively to provide capital to the economic system as a whole – must keep themselves at arm's length from the sacrosanct market relationship between buyers and sellers.

Financial globalization too is driven by just this sort of financial market trading. Governments, while they can and do regulate such markets, that is, set the rules of the game and shape basic aspects of market design, are far less able to shape and control the actual *outcomes* of market transactions. They instead attempt to make the system as a whole work more smoothly by providing nurturing environmental conditions such as 'sound' monetary and fiscal policy, an effective legal system to adjudicate disputes, a market-friendly set of regulatory institutions and processes, and so on. International finance is thus particularly able to escape the clutches of the state in significant ways – especially through 'regulatory arbitrage' or the playing off of different regulatory jurisdictions against each other to get the best, most international-finance-friendly, deal (Cerny, 1993b, ch. 3; Lütz, 2004).

In 'arm's-length' financial systems such as the US and the UK, then, globalization is in large measure an extension of such market-friendly national practices onto a wider playing field (and vice versa). Indeed, British finance capital was already globalized in the nineteenth century (Ingham, 1984) and American finance capital, internationalized to some extent prior to the Great Depression but then renationalized as autarchic policies spread throughout the world in the 1930s, became increasingly internationalized once again once America became financially hegemonic after the Second World War through the Bretton Woods dollar exchange standard. The result today is a quasi-Anglo-Americanization of international finance – even giving transnational finance, that is, private sector linkages across borders, an overall advantage in shaping and forcing the pace of that convergence (Cerny, 2002).

Many late nineteenth and twentieth century national financial systems such as that of Japan, however, were based on very different structures and practices. Several key nation-states were 'late industrializers', wishing not to see capital flowing freely across borders but to keep it and build it up at home. At the same time that they protected domestic infant industries from destructive foreign competition, such countries adopted *credit-based* financial systems (Zysman, 1983) – also called 'debt-based economies' (Renversez, 1986) or 'overdraft economies' (Loriaux, 1991). Such systems were aimed at (a) keeping capital at home in order to promote the development of the domestic economy and to escape the financial market dominance of London and (later) New York, and (b) ensuring that investment flowed to industries that would come to constitute an independent, even self-sufficient, economic base for rapid 'catch-up' with (i) earlier industralizers (i.e. Britain), and/or (ii) countries with large, practically self-sufficient domestic resources and large-scale domestic markets (mainly the United States). For these countries, competitiveness meant resisting internationalization in the name of 'picking winners' and seeking to protect and expand national market share – not rushing into an international marketplace already dominated by their 'first mover' rivals.

These late industrializing systems focused on what Hilferding and Lenin called 'finance capital' – close triangular relationships between heavy Second

Industrial Revolution industries, government bureaucratic agencies and large banks. In finance, as in other sectors of these economies, governments fostered the development of monopolistic or oligopolistic *cartels* – that is, they promoted systematic attempts to *prevent* competition among producers and traders in order to resist external domination and promote import substitution industrialization (ISI) (Kemp, 1969). Relations between firms were organized around not competition but market sharing and price fixing. In the late nineteenth century, Germany in particular, and France to some extent, attempted to resist the entrance of British products and investment capital – which were seen as stifling domestic attempts at industrialization and strangling them at birth – through conscious policies of cartellization. In Japan since that time, and in many developing countries in the twentieth century (Haggard, 1990; Kemp, 1983; Harris, 1986), elites have consciously adopted nationally specific versions of this development strategy.

This chapter therefore attempts to interweave two arguments. On the one hand, I suggest, not surprisingly, that the United States's embrace of globalization has been driven primarily by the position and structure of the financial services industry in the United States. Nevertheless, that process has not left the American financial system unscathed. It has led to a dramatic shakeout in the domestic structure of the system both in times of financial market expansion and in times of slump. The United States, having enjoyed a relatively insulated economy because of its size and resources, is now enmeshed in transnational financial webs, even if they are partly of its own making. This process is one not merely of *de*regulation, of course, but also of *re*-regulation – tweaking, streamlining and even reinforcing regulatory institutions to make them more effective in underpinning the stability and legitimacy of markets – ensuring their 'safety and soundness' and counteracting 'market failures' – while refraining as far as possible from intervening directly in market processes and outcomes. This broader approach is called 'liberalization', combining deregulation and re-regulation in order to refine and enforce market norms.

On the other hand, Japan has been an exemplar of resistance to change, despite the announcement of several programmes of financial regulatory reform and a structural crisis of the system. Nevertheless, political and economic pressures for structural change continue to mount and the accumulation of minor, partial reforms is accelerating. The financial systems of the United States and Japan may never look quite like each other, but actors in both systems are pushing opportunistically to find hybrid solutions to a range of growing problems in an era of financial market instability and price collapse (on 'hybridization', see Lütz, 2004). Thus the end of the new economy boom of the 1990s has seen not the demise of globalization but rather its intensification in a new phase of slump-driven financial market convergence.

2. Globalization and the American financial system: gridlock and flexibility

In order for people to behave as genuine 'economic' actors and to exchange the surpluses they produce (or own) in a systematic and efficient manner with a range of other specialized producers – producers too numerous to meet face-to-face – they need money. Throughout history, for money to be widely acceptable, usable and reliable, it has been provided and guaranteed by institutions and mechanisms, which can stand *above* market processes as such, that is, by governments. And herein lies the paradox. For markets to be 'efficient', classical economic theory requires the greatest possible decentralization of decision-making – the widest possible range of buyers and sellers exchanging price signals so that everything offered for sale is actually sold (the market 'clears'). But state provision of a functioning monetary system and a system of financial regulation to support it is normally the bottom line. Each such financial system – made up of a monetary system, a system of financial markets and institutions, and a system of financial regulation – constitutes a powerful framework of rules, rewards, and penalties shaping economic behavior. Different financial systems also interact with each other in the international financial and political arena.

Several factors, some of which are specifically characteristic of the American financial system, make that system both highly problematic and vulnerable, yet extremely flexible and resilient, in today's world. These factors include:

- a particularly American tradition of financial pluralism, which weakens markets and institutions in critical ways but strengthens them in others;
- the divided system of financial regulation in the US and the syndrome of 'entropy' or 'gridlock' found in American government in general, which block adaptation at one level but adapt pragmatically and flexibly to global imperatives at another; and
- the changing role of the US in a world which looked a few years ago to be beating America at its own game but is today adapting painfully to a more open and diversified international financial system.

The ideology that lay behind the American Revolution was one of resistance to centralized political and economic power. Nowhere has this suspicion been more deeply rooted than in attitudes toward the financial system. The early US was overwhelmingly rural, and internal development strengthened populist opposition to both political and economic centralization, with a mushrooming of local banks through the first half of the nineteenth century while political opposition and the constitutional weakness of the national government combined to ensure that no real central bank was set up and that the individual states were in control of banking regulation. Nevertheless, despite the seeming anarchy of the banking system, banks and other capital markets played an indispensable role in a rapidly growing economy. With the coming of the Civil War, the Federal Government took on a notably stronger role in the financial system, private financial institutions expanded at all levels, and the country embarked on a massive industrialization boom which propelled it to potential international leadership. The different levels of the system all expanded, especially during periods of economic boom. Not until the Great Crash of 1929 did a fully-fledged, system-wide shakeout occur.

Boom and slumps – especially the Panic of 1907 and the Great Crash of 1929 – gradually changed the face of the system. The Federal Government took greater control of the currency, reshaped the system of financial markets and institutions, and established a more complex regulatory system. National banks were not allowed to set up branches until 1922; many states further restricted intrastate branching too. The number of commercial banks peaked at almost 30 000 in 1921 before steadily declining in the 1920s and dramatically shrinking after the Great Crash. During the period of rapid industrial development in the later nineteenth century, the securities markets were mainly the exclusive sphere of the traders themselves and of the large investment banks and commercial banks which had grown up in the urban centers, especially around New York City's Wall Street. The investment banks, especially J.P. Morgan, in addition to trading government securities, were crucial middlemen in underwriting stocks and bonds for many of the huge new corporations or 'trusts', especially railroads and public utilities, and controlled the boards of key industries. As well as domestic investment, they channeled foreign investment both into the US and out and played a key role in controlling the rest of the financial system.

While the mixed financial system described here was extremely flexible and effective in financing economic development, its fragmentation made it vulnerable to economic slumps and financial panics. In 1907, only the active intervention of Morgan in providing liquidity to institutions in trouble prevented the crash from spreading. In December 1913 Congress passed the Federal Reserve Act, a compromise between those who feared too much Wall Street control and those who feared too much Federal Government control. Thus the US finally got itself a central bank, but one that had a semi-decentralized structure and was intended to support, rather than to run down, the plural financial system. Almost immediately afterwards, the First World War made America's international financial role central to the world economy. The US became the world's leading creditor. However, as well as having an economy centered in a huge, protected continental market – more isolated from external trade and payments than the developed European economies – the US also attempted to return to *political* isolationism after the war. The international financial system now had a quasi-suspended Gold Standard, no international lender of last resort, a reserve currency (sterling) whose role was greatly reduced, and a potentially stronger currency (the dollar) whose international role was circumscribed by American isolationism. With the Great Crash of 1929, huge cracks appeared in the financial system, leading to major reforms (Kindleberger, 1973).

The election of President Franklin D. Roosevelt in 1932 led to a far-reaching attempt at *compartmentalization* of the financial system, enforced through a new system of regulation brought in by the New Deal. This arrangement was intended to prevent the domino effect of market failure in one market or subsector of financial services from causing market failure in others. That pattern of compartmentalization was to dominate the system until the 1970s. Although the Great Depression had a variety of causes and effects, among the most visible was the virtual collapse of large swathes of the financial system up to 1934. Close to 10 000 banks failed from the beginning of 1930 to the end of 1933 (4000 in 1933 alone), a reduction from nearly 25 000 to around 15 000. The 'New Deal system' included a strengthened and more independent Federal Reserve with increased powers to control bank reserves, to lend to banks, and to engage in systematic open-market operations. At the same time, the US went off the Gold Standard, as did the other major industrial countries, and the President was given wide powers to undertake a range of actions in the monetary field without reference to Congress. The Federal Deposit Insurance Corporation (FDIC) was established, guaranteeing small deposits and undercutting the psychology of bank runs until the 1980s.

The most important reforms were contained in the Banking Act of 1933 and the Securities Exchange Act of 1934, expanded and extended in the Banking Act of 1935. The first contained (*inter alia*) provisions known as the Glass-Steagall Act. The Glass-Steagall Act prohibited commercial banks from engaging in the securities business. Commercial banks could no longer have investment affiliates, nor could investment banks take deposits. Restrictions were placed on interlocking directorates. In the Securities Exchange Act of 1934, the stock and bond markets were put under a new body, the Securities and Exchange Commission (SEC), which would regulate and supervise the activities of brokers and dealers, attempt to control conflicts of interest and require extensive disclosure of information about securities issues. This compartmentalized system worked with little in the way of negative repercussions for about three decades.

Stock markets themselves remained relatively moribund until the 1950s. Not only did government spending both state and federal pump money into the economy which previously would have come from private sources, but the financing of government itself, whether through taxes or borrowing, soaked up private funds. And after the Second World War, although a system of free trade and managed exchange rates (the Bretton Woods System) was set up, this went hand-in-hand with controls on international capital flows and US support for various systems of domestic economic management elsewhere, including Japan. However, to make this settlement viable, the compartmentalized financial system in the United States had to be protected from foreign financial competition – which might link financial market sectors across borders and in turn across compartmental boundaries at home. But as both domestic and international economic activity grew in the 1950s and 1960s, banks and financial markets looked for ways to get around compartmental barriers. The expansion of private sector economic activity also began to make the government's domestic economic policy instruments less effective at fine-tuning the economy. In boom conditions, spending and reflation, rather than kick-starting economic activity, became 'sticky'. Finally, international financial interpenetration grew dramatically from the 1960s onwards (Strange, 1986; Khoury, 1990).

Fundamental changes were therefore gathering momentum by the 1960s at the core of the US financial system itself – the major urban, internationally linked commercial banks, the investment banks, and the stock markets in particular, where exclusive, club-like arrangements inherited from the nineteenth century came under serious threat from outside competition. These changes stemmed from the interaction of two crucial trends, domestic and international. On the one hand, there was growing political and economic dissatisfaction with the Keynesian welfare state settlement on both the right and the left, with the growth of government spending and regulation in the name of poverty reduction and social justice under President John F. Kennedy's 'New Frontier' and President Lyndon B. Johnson's 'Great Society', and with an amalgam of both stagnation and inflation (labeled 'stagflation'). On the other hand, a profound transformation of world finance was taking place which could no longer be blunted by domestic economic policy. Financial globalization was only in its infancy at the end of the 1950s, but by the end of the 1960s it was an established fact. American influence in the postwar international monetary system became more and more fragmented, until the US opted out in 1971.

The dollar was the anchor currency of the Bretton Woods System, and its value was fixed to that of gold; other currencies, however, were merely fixed in terms of their dollar value. In effect, the US could continue to export dollars (the result of its growing current account deficit) without having to reduce the value of the currency itself. Other countries, particularly France, accused America of printing money but 'exporting inflation' to others, what President de Gaulle of France called the 'exorbitant privileges' of America's having the dollar both as its national currency and as the top international currency that had to be accepted everywhere else. The 'Euromarkets' – markets based in London where expatriate dollars were re-loaned without the sort of regulatory requirements applied to domestic currencies – rapidly developed to handle the new liquidity. European governments called for a devaluation of the dollar against gold, but the new Administration of President Richard M. Nixon, elected in 1968, argued that other currencies should themselves *revalue* against the dollar. Meanwhile, the strong dollar attracted more foreign imports and the current account (balance of payments) deficit turned into a chronic deficit on the balance of *trade* too. The Nixon Administration introduced import quotas and other protectionist measures. In August 1971, the US broke the official link between the dollar and gold, and soon the world went on to a system of floating exchange rates. In effect, the New Deal attempt to control finance in order to privilege productive capital was abandoned.

The bursting of the Bretton Woods dam resulted in the structure of the international economy being increasingly centered around rapidly globalizing financial markets and money flows. More and more money would be needed just to hedge against changes in exchange rates, interest rate differentials and divergent marginal returns between countries from different financial instruments (Strange, 1986). Furthermore, financial flows would penalize governments pursuing economic policies which reduced returns on financial instruments (for example, active fiscal policies, trade policies, social policies or industrial policies) and would undermine independent monetary policies too. Finally, globalization of financial markets made it more and more difficult for domestic financial markets to be effectively regulated and stabilized. After 1973 a new cycle of booms and slumps, inextricably intertwined with financial bubbles and panics, returned to the US and the world economy. Boundaries between financial institutions and markets were widely breached and severely eroded. This in turn set up pressures for regulatory change, usually referred to – imprecisely – as 'deregulation'. In addition, far-reaching changes in communications and information technology revolutionized both global and domestic financial market structures. Walls between international and domestic levels became more and more permeable, producing complex knock-on effects and chain reactions.

Larger financial institutions, the 'money center' banks that pioneered the globalization process from the 1960s onwards, increasingly pushed against the boundaries of the regulatory system. However, they found international competition increasingly tough going in the 1980s, putting new pressures on the regulatory system. Futhermore, new powerful institutions – pension funds and mutual funds – came to dominate crucial aspects of the financial system. Meanwhile, the center of gravity of international finance itself moved away from traditional banking to complex financial innovation, 'disintermediation' and 'securitization' (Cerny, 2000b; see below). Finally, increasingly intense price competition cut a swathe through small institutions – the community banks and Savings and Loans. The number of banks fell from about 14 500 in 1984 (its postwar high) to around 7 000 in the late 1990s, and the current merger process, mainly among regional groupings of medium-to-large sized banks, continues to gather pace. Nevertheless, as the US Treasury has stated: 'If the United States had the same ratio of banks to population [as Canada], it would have about seventy five banks, of which about fifty six would operate nationwide' (United States, 1991, pp. xvii–17).

However, *regulatory pluralism* – a range of different agencies supervising assorted activities and sectors within the financial services industry – has resisted consolidation and streamlining. Agencies have defended their own turf and pressure groups representing different industry sectors have put up fierce political resistance in Congress. During the 1990s the dramatic recovery of the American economy was fed by a more dynamic financial system, rapidly evolving to cope with the ultra-competitive global financial environment. New and volatile international circuits of capital reached deep inside the US financial system itself. It was American dollars, American banks, and American multinational firms that were the major players.

These internationalized markets were also the first to produce, out of competitive necessity, two more features which shaped structural change:

- complex types of *financial innovation* which went far beyond the traditional instruments of bank loans and fixed-rate bonds, including a range of currency hedges, variable-rate bonds, perpetual notes, interest rate swaps and other 'derivatives' and 'off-balance-sheet' instruments such as revolving credit faclities, special purpose entities and the like; and
- the introduction of *new technology* to process orders and trades (Cerny, 1997).

Although the larger institutions were the spearhead of the deregulation movement, it infected the smaller institutions too with the view that their only future was to be able to compete on price with the big boys for their specialized services.

The dynamic of change was further accelerated by the increasingly complex structure of interaction between the domestic and international levels. Federal budget deficits and a growing trade deficit led to a growing need to finance those 'twin deficits' – a need significantly greater than the capacity of American institutions to meet from domestic funds. Interest rates had to be raised to attract capital from abroad, mainly from Japan, to a lesser extent from Europe, but also from cuts in Third World loans after the debt crisis erupted in 1982. Other countries had to raise their own interest rates to compete for funds (and prevent capital outflows to the US) – bringing about a convergence of interest rates around the world. It also kept the dollar high despite the large trade deficit, worsening that deficit and undermining the international competitiveness of large sectors of American industry (the Rust Belt). It turned the US from a creditor nation into a net debtor by the mid-1980s.

Deregulation in the United States, still by far the world's largest economy, has forced other countries, big and small, to deregulate their own banks and securities markets in order to compete to attract mobile international financial capital (or at least to prevent capital flight). An international 'ratchet effect' was at work. The same process can be seen in the securitization and disintermediation of finance – the trend away from traditional bank loans (particular contracts between specific bankers and borrowers, based on the former's knowledge of the latter's creditworthiness) toward the selling of *negotiable* securities (which can be bought and sold by any 'bearer') that can later be traded in a secondary market, the most liquid of which are international markets. This process has also led to financial innovation, especially derivatives. Nevertheless, financial liberalization itself took place not through a strategic, proactive approach but through a series of reactive, sector-specific, pressure-group-driven, and often ad hoc decisions by often competing power centers within the American state. The creation of new regulatory bodies too has also occurred on an ad hoc basis at both federal and state levels, one agency at a time. American public bureaucracies, especially the independent regulatory agencies, are highly susceptible to capture by the very private interests which they are intended to regulate.

Broader proposals for regulatory reform have been examined several times since the mid-1980s (Cerny, 1994 and 2000b). The McFadden Act that prevented banks from opening branches outside their home states was finally repealed in 1994 and the National Securities Markets Improvement Act passed in 1996 brought many state and federal regulations into line. Glass-Steagall was finally repealed in 2000. However, the deregulatory rush has been brought to a halt by the subsequent financial market collapse. The bear market triggered off by the bursting of the 'dot.com bubble' has highlighted the underside of the boom. Deregulation and innovation have permitted the creation of financial pyramids that have been extremely vulnerable to short term as well as long term swings in market conditions, exemplified by the failure of the hedge fund Long-Term Capital Management in 1998 (bailed out by the Fed). Furthermore, as in any period of boom, individuals and companies have tested the edge of the envelope through abusive practices and fraud, often leading to spectacular bankruptcy as in the cases of Enron and WorldCom. Financial services firms have been in the line of fire at both federal and state level as the Sarbanes-Oxley Act of 2002 tightened up regulations on accountancy and auditing firms, establishing a new Public Company Accounting Oversight Board (if there's a problem, set up a new agency) and as the New York State Attorney General has fined several major financial services firms for using their supposedly independent research units as salesmen. In January 2003 the Securities and Exchange Commission adopted a new set of rules on corporate governance and accounting and is required to implement further measures mandated in the Sarbanes-Oxley Act, although key measures have been renegotiated and watered down because of resistance by sectors of the financial services industry both in the US and abroad.

The US is still the world's largest economy. Even its tradition of financial pluralism has important benefits in a global financial system. Federal Reserve Board Chairman Alan Greenspan has argued that the US financial system has helped the economy weather a series of both economic and political shocks, reinforced by similar changes in the international financial system that have allowed 'lenders to become more diversified and borrowers far less dependent on specific institutions or markets for financing' (paraphrased in the *International Herald Tribune*, 8–9 March 2003). US financial institutions have played a wide range of roles in the process of globalization *despite* gridlock in the political and regulatory system. Its various regulators are more and more closely connected with each other as well as with their respective counterparts abroad. However, whatever the competitive advantages and disadvantages of the American financial system, its success or failure will be increasingly determined by transnational conditions, not by conditions in some imaginary, insulated domestic market. As with the expansion of the 1990s, the debate over what to do in *global* terms to respond to what was until recently a global slump is only just beginning.

3. Globalization and the Japanese financial system: rigidity and deadlock

In the 1970s and 1980s, the Japanese model – or 'developmental state' (Johnson, 1982) – was thought not only to be a uniquely successful, exceptional approach to the problems of advanced capitalist society but also to embody a different potential approach for others to copy in the future, even the United States. Since that time, however, a combination of Japan's post-1989 crisis and the expansion of neoliberal, market-oriented economic globalization has undermined what is now seen as the myth of Japanese prowess and caused some key Japanese policymakers to attempt basic structural reforms. As has already been pointed out, today's international financial system involves the extension of more open market structures and market-like practices across borders. In this context, the Japanese financial system is becoming increasingly a 'price-taker' rather than a 'price-maker' in the global financial marketplace. The continued success of the postwar Japanese model up to the end of the 1980s rested on two conditions:

1. the ability of Japan to resist the kind of competitive marketization, globalization, and neoliberal *laissez faire* represented by Thatcherism and Reaganism; and
2. the ability of Japanese firms, backed up by the state, to *exploit* that very globalization and marketization to expand their world market shares and use others' openness to their own advantage by exporting or establishing overseas operations.

The Japanese financial system was based on collaborative relationships between government and industry embodied in state support for raising investment capital: whether directly by providing subsidies to firms;

indirectly through guarantees and the subsidization of interest rates and payback conditions for bank loans to industry; or even more indirectly through anti-competitive regulations and supportive practices which often permit or even encourage firms and cartels to manipulate financial markets themselves in order to ensure a substantial and liquid supply of capital at rigged prices (Morishima, 2000). The provision of such cheap, long-term capital (sometimes called 'patient capital'), especially in the context of Second Industrial Revolution-type development where extremely large investments were needed in order to achieve viable economies of scale and scope (Chandler, 1990), had enabled Germany, Japan, France, and some Asian economies to develop rapidly through most of the twentieth century (in peacetime). Japan's success at promoting leading edge export industries, especially in new fields like consumer electronics, made it a threat to American and European competitiveness. It also fostered the development of political coalitions, interest group collaboration and bureaucratic practices, which gave these governments at various times a potential strategic role in promoting development.

Successful control and promotion of investment demanded that intermediary institutions, whether dominated by private sector banks or by governments (but usually involving some synergy between the two), had to be able to provide investment capital that was both cheap and liquid. This is not to say that such systems did not possess capital markets, but that the *dominant* mode of capital provision and price-setting was through banks, especially those banks with close, entrenched linkages with particular firms and sectors – as well as with key government ministries and agencies. Financial markets as such played a secondary role, for example in Japan as a venue where established financial and industrial firms carried out deals among themselves in order to manipulate the supply and cost of capital through pre-arranged share transactions. But large investments required large institutions with deep pockets, whether private or public.

However, such institutions had also to be protected. Monopolistic and oligopolistic behavior was seen at worst as a necessary evil, at best a positive side effect of a solidaristic social hierarchy based on deference and trust, but most of all indispensable, not to line the pockets of investors (though it often did), but to benefit domestic industrialization and development in the national interest. Prior to the Second World War, such bank-led systems were often linked with authoritarian regimes; afterwards, they were sustained by a range of embedded bureaucratic practices and neocorporatist coalitions. Nowhere was the cartellized, intermediary-led model more fully imposed and entrenched than in Japan. In the nineteenth century, it was entrenched in the private sector through the big *zaibatsu* trading companies (the forerunners of today's *keiretsu*), it was forcibly imposed by the military regime prior to and during the Second World War, it survived the American Occupation, and it formed the basis of the Japanese developmental state model until recent years (Katz, 1998).

The postwar Japanese financial system was built upon several interlocking foundations.

1. *Insulation from outside capital.* Both the availability of foreign exchange and its use were closely regulated and rationed by the government, particularly by the Ministry of Finance. Dependence on domestic bank financing has been the major method by which public–private networks and influence relationships have been signed and sealed. These restrictions have been progressively lifted since the mid-1960s and change since 1990 has to a large extent been driven by a combination of a crisis of domestic institutions and an influx of foreign financial firms and investors, increasingly welcomed by sectors of the government and bureaucracy.

2. *Rationing of domestic capital* as well, through both direct and indirect control of the Ministry of Finance (MoF). Large loans, especially those above ceilings set by the MoF, had to be approved, and the MoF (and other ministries) kept a close watch on their uses to ensure that they went to the appropriate infant industries, especially the competitive and highly promoted export sector. Such loans were also usually at discounted, non-market rates in order to keep capital costs low and encourage investment, supplemented by public sector financing funded primarily by savings held in the postal savings system (*zaito* funds). However, from the 1970s onwards such low cost, long term loans went increasingly to the non-competitive, protected sector, as competitive firms found their own sources of capital from their export success; indeed, much of the 'bad loans crisis' of the late 1990s and early 2000s is said to result from banks having *too much* to lend in recent decades, leading to a sharp increase in non-performing loans.

3. *'Administrative guidance'*, that is, a mix of formal and informal practices whereby banks and other firms regularly consult with their supervising ministries – broadly speaking, the MoF for financial institutions, the Ministry of International Trade and Industry for the competitive exporting sector, the Ministry of Posts and Telecommunications for the telecoms sector, the Ministry of Construction for the construction sector, and so on – and are basically told how to run their businesses. Successful, profitable businesses have over time been able to make more independent decisions; other firms have been more constrained. Mikuni and Murphy (2002) argue that administrative guidance was never really just guidance but an authoritative command system that firms saw as crucial to their survival and success. It is often argued that the MoF today is divided on how far to change the system, with some younger cadres in particular concerned to promote practices compatible with competitiveness in a more open, globalizing context. In these circumstances, administrative guidance itself is a two-edged sword through which bureaucrats themselves can become agents of marketization.

4. *Institutionalized networks of interlocking personnel* among politicians, bureaucrats and business elites, cutting across public and private sectors. Although these networks operate at many levels, probably the best known has been the practice of *amakudari* or 'descent from heaven', that is, the practice of placing newly retired Japanese bureaucrats in senior positions – some more or less honorary, some very influential – in the very firms in the private or semi-public sectors they had previously been supervising. This phenomenon has been particularly notable in the financial sector – with former MoF officials heading the list. Some stronger institutions, such as former *zaibatsu* banks, have always rejected such parachuting, and in today's context when institutions increasingly want to be seen to be independent in a more open financial marketplace, *amakudari* seems to be losing some of its influence and legitimacy.

5. *The 'convoy system'.* Change in the financial system was only allowed to proceed at the speed of the slowest ship in the convoy, in order to protect the whole system from being undermined bit by bit. The convoy system led for many years, among other things, to government-managed mergers of unprofitable institutions with (usually) larger institutions with deeper pockets. Prior to the 1990s, MoF-sponsored merger activity often sought to maintain the size, market share, loan portfolio and sometimes even the distinct internal structures of the failing institutions, including jobs.

More recent intervention by the MoF and the newer agencies spun off from it such as the now defunct Financial Reconstruction Commission (FRC) and the ever more important Financial Services Agency (FSA – formerly the Financial Supervisory Agency, now an independent ministry), has at least ostensibly been predicated upon the condition that major restructuring *should* take place – whether in restructuring banks' loan portfolios or having government agencies take over such loans while seeking partners or selling them on (as with the US Savings and Loans crisis of the late 1980s). However, the big banks no longer have such deep pockets, being highly vulnerable themselves to the bad loans crisis, and have since the mid-1990s increasingly been forced into so-called 'megamergers', reducing the number of major commercial banks (called 'city banks') from 11 to four – and three in the near future. And firms outside the traditional banking sector are playing an increasing role, especially as the Big Bang reform process has made it possible for financial holding companies to be set up to cut across these boundaries.

However, the convoy approach, like much of the cartellized financial system (and other sectors of industry too), has also often been justified not only for its role in ensuring the safety and soundness of the banking system but also as a kind of social policy to protect jobs, both in the banks themselves and in the firms with which they are linked through their loan portfolios. It is this 'stakeholder' facet, which is most under threat from financial globalization, because international investors and foreign firms are interested primarily in 'shareholder value' (return on capital) and not in subsidizing loss-making activities. There is a growing level of public scrutiny both from the media and some more active shareholders that makes it more difficult to undertake restructurings if they are not justified by market criteria – in other words, if they do not involve real cost-cutting, structural streamlining, labor flexibilization, efficient investment and profit maximization.

6. *The* keiretsu *system*. Modelled on the big prewar *zaibatsu* trading houses which were partially dismantled by the postwar occupation authorities, the *keiretsu* are basically conglomerates made up of firms which are sometimes formally merged but more often held together by extensive cross-shareholdings. At the core of each of these conglomerate networks has been a main bank that has played various coordinating roles involving not only the supply of investment capital but also other cartel-like inter-firm arrangements on pricing, cross-subsidization of profitable and loss-making activities, arrangements with internal and external suppliers, wholesale and even retail distribution, the manipulation of share prices for cross-held shareholdings, etc. However, with opening up to international finance and the sort of liquidity, negotiability and transparency required in the global marketplace, *keiretsu* are directly in the line of fire. There are significant indicators today that *keiretsu* relationships are being partially unwound. However, the extent of the 'bad loans crisis' made such restructuring more difficult.

Thus the postwar governance system was kept together by a range of mutually reinforcing practices and financial linkages not only between the state (politicians as well as bureaucratic agencies) and firms but also among and within firms themselves. However, globalization not only threatens the very cohesion of the state–bank–industry nexus at the heart of its capacity to act as a cartel, but also provides a powerful, globally expanding alternative source of capital and transnational systemic organization. Those international financial firms and other economic actors, who seek outlets for their investment demand profitability, not market share, and managerial control, not the maintenance of cosy links with politicians, bureaucrats, and other cartel members. At the same time, with the bursting of the bubble, domestic networks become more fragile as entrepreneurial individuals look to find new niches and even reshape the system more widely. And finally, politicians and bureaucrats find it necessary at least to think more frequently about tinkering with the system itself in order to counteract stagnation, control spending and get out of the growing crisis – or at least to be seen to do so – and occasionally even to propose genuine reforms.

At one level, the challenge stems from the sheer *amount* of highly mobile international capital that is available today, dwarfing the capacities of bank-led systems in general to provide cheap, liquid capital for investment in general. At a time when the Japanese government is becoming more and more indebted – up to 150 per cent of GDP (by far the highest level among

developed countries), especially to Japanese banks – government debt, far
from being inflationary, is actually taking more out of the money supply
than it puts back in through new spending on politically opportunistic,
often localized projects with little multiplier impact on the economy. Banks
may try to continue lending to prop up the economy but these loans are less
and less likely to be repaid, undermining the banks themselves.

At a second level, however, the challenge comes from changes that are
required in the structure of the financial system itself – that is to say, the
process of marketization. For capital to be made available, both foreign market actors and internationally linked domestic market actors must be confident that their money will gain a market rate of return and that the financial
instruments they have bought can be sold again at market prices ('liquidity').
To tap these sources effectively, investment must be able to flow into uses
that are determined in the markets, not by state planners, 'relationship'
bankers or oligopolistic industrialists. This involves a redirection of investment away from older industries – even leading to what Joseph Schumpeter
called the 'creative destruction' of existing fixed capital – and toward newer,
more flexible, 'post-Fordist' industries.

Indeed, this is exactly what *was* happening, however unevenly and
sporadically, in Japan at the end of the twentieth century. Richard Katz
(1998) argued that Japan has developed a 'dual economy', that is, an economy fundamentally structurally divided between the internationally competitive export sector (the focus of the 'developmental state') and a
backward, protected sector which is dragging the economy and the state
down with its growing weight. *Financial Times* journalist Gillian Tett went
further, arguing that Japan now has what has called a 'split economy'
(10 February 2000 and 24 February 2000) between older sectors on the one
hand and new economy sectors on the other. I would suggest that it is in fact
a *three-way split or* 'triple economy'. The internationally competitive export
sector – the product of the era of intermediary led catch-up – is still crucial,
but, as Katz and many other authors have pointed out, is increasingly 'hollowing out'. International competitiveness has drawn many of these industries to produce in other parts of Asia and the world (including the United
States and Europe) rather than in Japan. At the same time, the protected
sector – including, today, many banks as well as agriculture, distribution,
construction and a range of other uncompetitive industries – is still being
protected, but is under increasing pressure to restructure, driven by the need
to seek capital from outside traditional channels as well as by growing
government deficits.

However, the third sector, the so-called 'new economy', while extremely
dynamic at the turn of the century, has suffered from a severe credit crunch.
Banks still do not lend sufficiently to smaller firms despite MoF and Bank of
Japan (BoJ) pressure to do so, venture capital has dried up, initial public offer-
ings (IPOs) are more and more difficult to arrange and there is a shrinking of

new financial markets originally set up to service this sector. In this sense, Japan's recent experience is not all that different from those of the United States or Germany. The internationally competitive export sector has for some years grown steadily more independent from its bureaucratic sponsors because it no longer needs their capital. Many firms in this sector also need to restructure, but that restructuring increasingly comes through international channels, as has been the case with Nissan since its effective takeover by Renault. Japan's trade surplus has remained surprisingly healthy, especially given the growth of exports to a rapidly expanding Chinese economy. The protected sector, meanwhile, has if anything become *more* dependent on traditional domestic channels of support. Restructuring of vast swathes of subsectors and firms would lead to extreme consequences for production and employment. Japan has already been going through a crisis of demand for some years, with consumption levels stagnating despite regular attempts by the government to reflate the economy; retrenchment in the protected sector would hit demand hard.

At the same time, the volatility of political coalitions in the 1990s made the predominant Liberal Democratic Party much more dependent on support from that sector, especially from agriculture, as its urban base has eroded (Pempel, 1998). The level of unemployment, having grown at the time of writing to around 5.8 per cent – less than in much of Europe, but similar to US levels – would be badly hit by closures in this sector, as it has already carried the burden over the past couple of decades for the hollowing out of the export sector. In this situation, governments around the turn of the century have relied on regular reflationary packages and a very loose monetary policy (including, at the time of writing, a zero-interest-rate policy). However, with the public debt burden far higher than in other industrialized countries, such an approach is unsustainable in the medium term.

The state is thus split between the political imperatives of maintaining the protected sector (both financial and industrial), on the one hand, and the imperatives – economic and political – of restructuring that sector and promoting the development of an internationally linked, marketized financial system. At the time of writing, evidence of schizophrenic reactions to this dilemma abound. The Big Bang program initiated by the Hashimoto Government in 1996 has for the most part been legislated for, but parts of it are variously accelerated and postponed depending on the balance of influence at different times among and within political coalitions and factions, bureaucratic agencies and competing private firms and sectoral interests (Honda, 2003). The high level of non-performing loans in the banking sector – mainly loans to chronically unprofitable firms (known as 'zombie companies') – means that banks are undermining their own performance by sustaining such firms. The reform plans of Prime Minister Koizumi and Finance Minister Takenaka have been watered down and resisted by politicians, bureaucrats and banks alike (Mulgan, 2002). Indeed, pressure for reform has,

If anything, been reduced partly by the success of banks in unwinding their bad loans, on the one hand, and a burst of export-led growth in late 2003–mid 2004, on the other – although that growth slowed significantly before picking up again in 2005.

The state, although having initiated the Big Bang program in order to try to *control* the process of financial liberalization (Vogel, 1996), is increasingly being whipsawed by accelerating trends in the financial markets. Indeed, this process has taken on significant new characteristics with financial globalization. Some of those trends have come from abroad, whether from what the Japanese call *gaiatsu* or external pressures – whether directly from the US government, which has been pressuring Japan for many years to liberalize and marketize its domestic economy – or from international investors who want to escape the constraints of the cartel system and realize a higher market return on their capital. However, many of the most important changes have actually come from internal pressures, what has sometimes been called *naiatsu* (in a *neologistic* response to *gaiatsu:* cf. Brown, 1994; Kusano, 1999).

At one level *naiatsu* comes from within the political system and the bureaucracy as the result of growing intergenerational differences between more internationalist and more domesticist bureaucrats, political calculations stemming from fear of missing the liberalization boat altogether as the post-bubble recession has dragged on (and which are continuing to dominate both the rapidly changing internal politics of the Liberal Democratic Party LDP and the fractious coalition politics of the Japanese party system more widely), and growing inter-agency and intra-agency disputes as regulatory functions have been spun off through organs such as the Financial Services Agency (FSA). Nevertheless, their work is increasingly in the media and political spotlight, comparisions are increasingly made with experiences and institutional structures in other countries, intra-agency struggles abound, and the outcomes they seek to impose and control are increasingly market-oriented and aimed at replacing stagnating institutions with more dynamic, profitable ones. Finally, there have been political pressures from new constituencies such as individual as well as institutional savers and lenders, urban voters and the like, said by analysts increasingly to resent the practice of government subsidies for protected sectors, especially agriculture, rural construction, and so on. The LDP, out of power for a while in the early 1990s and ruling in recent years through a volatile coalition, has been losing much of its already weak urban support and today is overwhelmingly a rural party.

Thus the main pressures for change have come not from government leadership but from the confluence of domestic and international trends that both challenge the practices at the heart of the Japanese model and comprise an alternative market structure template. This template is perceived by a growing range of actors as a potentially viable option for internalization into the Japanese system (as well as into domestic financial systems more widely). The key actors are:

1. foreign firms and investors seeking to enter or expand within the Japanese market;
2. domestic firms and investors seeking to get out of the vicious circle of the protected sector;
3. new entrepreneurs seeking to expand venture capital activities especially in new technology sectors such as the internet or to import practices such as hostile takeovers;
4. old firms restructuring and downsizing in the face of international competition whether in industrial sectors like the automobile industry (Nissan) or through bank megamergers;
5. young consumers turning to fashionable high-tech products such as tamagochi (electronic pets) and pokemon games that are poorly reflected in official statistics – which privilege traditional industries – and the like.

Although the most important financial innovations during the Second Financial Revolution of the 1980s and 1990s have been in the securities area, banks have sought to catch up and to compete with securities firms – with the former's greater capitalization and financial strength giving them a competitive edge despite the latter's innovative lead. It was not until the mid-1990s, especially with the Big Bang program, that significant progress began toward lowering compartmental barriers within Japan. As in the United States, a major means to this end has been to allow different firms to merge into federalized holding companies made up of partially or wholly owned subsidiaries operating in different market sectors. Holding companies were the basis of the pre-war *zaibatsu* and as such were prohibited after the war in order to prevent their renascence, although that prohibition was easily bypassed in various ways.

Today, holding companies have once again been legalized and indeed are the basis for much of the inter-firm restructuring taking place within the Japanese financial sector. In contrast to the *zaibatsu* model, however, in which holding companies could manipulate the relationships between their subsidiaries as they liked in terms of cross-subsidization, insider trading and the like, today in Japan as elsewhere such subsidiaries increasingly have to be characterized by certain levels of internal compartmentalization, what the British call 'Chinese walls', among different market sector activities as well as between financial service activities/institutions and non-financial firms which may become involved in cross-ownership relations with the former. The acceleration of changes to accounting rules and corporate governance rules, as with other issues, has created a public and media awareness of the problems and specific cases of conflict of interest, and so on, are being targeted. For example, combined with a range of changes in accounting practices – especially with firms being increasingly obliged to keep and publish consolidated accounts – the separation of banking and securities businesses is increasingly being cut across. Japanese financial services firms are currently in the throes of profound structural changes allowing them to engage in new forms of arbitrage fundamental to competitiveness.

With different markets opened up to arbitrage, the second key structural reform is to enable market actors to fully compete on price and quality of service across those markets. The first stage of this type of reform was to deregulate interest rates, beginning in the late 1970s, although a combination of administrative guidance and the convoy system ensured that Japanese banks basically charged the same interest rates until the mid-1990s. Indeed, the cultural inhibition against breaking ranks is still strong in traditional banking sectors. However, a combination of the bad loans crisis, financial innovation primarily in the securities field, the lack of compartmentalization in global financial markets, and the rapid pace of change in Japanese securities markets has put such traditional practices very much on the defensive. It is highly likely that they are on their way out except in certain kinds of financial institutions catering to special constituencies such as small regional banks, agricultural cooperatives, credit unions and the like. Even here changes are proceeding surprisingly rapidly because such institutions have also been severely affected by non-performing loans and lack of profitability. At the same time, the question of financing the public sector deficit and the limited scope of the Japanese government bond market may well be not only crowding out private sector spending and investment but also holding back change through deflation.

Perhaps the most important reform leading to extensive price competition across the entire system is the deregulation of brokerage commissions in securities markets, as in the United States, Britain, France, and other countries. The freedom of market actors to negotiate commissions is probably the principal means of undermining cartel-like price fixing in the financial services sector. After brokerage commissions were completely liberalized in October 1999 after having been progressively deregulated over the previous two years, Japanese financial markets were hit by a veritable avalanche of change. Much of it is still inchoate, but it bears a remarkable resemblance to wider trends in financial markets around the world and is increasingly subject to much the same structural tends and conjunctural fluctuations as those markets.

Probably the most striking manifestation of these changes at the time has been the increasingly visible entry of foreign financial firms into Japan. Although foreign investment firms, which had surged into the country in the late 1990s, increasingly withdrew between 2000 and 2002, they are currently returning, due to the liquidity crunch in the traditional financial sector and the restructuring strategies of Japanese firms as companies reshuffle their assets, the *keiretsu* system restructures, and the banking sector comes under increasing pressure. Japanese banks have traditionally held much of their capital in equities, but the collapsing stock market has dramatically undermined their value. Since 2003, government regulations on capital adequacy have forced banks to sell off much of their equity holdings, and in order to strengthen their capital adequacy ratios a range of major banks have made agreements with foreign firms such as Merrill Lynch, Goldman Sachs and the like to invest in their own stock. Foreign investors and firms are now welcomed by a growing range of market actors, the business media and workers in the financial services sector. Foreign firms are becoming very fashionable as employers of high-flying Japanese graduates, once the province of the bureaucracy or the top Japanese institutions.

In the 1990s, much of the attraction for foreign firms was not only the anticipation of structural market reforms but also the prospect of financing Japan's version of the new economy boom. Today, of course, that boom has stalled. Japanese firms, which for example once dominated new sectors of consumer electronics as they came along, are far less competitive than before. Their only technological edge seems to be in the booming domestic mobile phone industry, but the fact that Japanese technology is not fully compatible with systems in other countries has severely limited their penetration of export markets. Financial institutions are still preoccupied not with growing the Japanese economy, but with the troubles of the financial system itself. Nevertheless, there is some evidence that the bad loans crisis, so deeply embedded in the state-industry networks that had grown up to promote postwar development (Amyx, 2003), may be partly working itself out. Capital adequacy rules, new corporate governance rules, more aggressive bank inspections and the decisions of major banks to push ahead with restructuring despite their hesitations have once again raised the prospect of broader based reform.

In addition to the banks, brokerage firms have been badly hit by the stock market crash, with newer, smaller firms in the greatest trouble. Merger and acquisition activity, for example, which has been the source of much financial sector profitability in the United States and Britain, was more or less ruled out in the postwar Japanese system and its faint stirrings in the late 1990s proved to be stillborn. Attempts to create new equity markets for start-up companies, especially the Tokyo Stock Exchange-sponsored 'Mothers' market (Market for High Growth and Emerging Stocks) and Nasdaq Japan, have flopped – as such markets have tended to do in other countries too. These failures may be due less to system resistance in Japan than to the post-2000 international bear market, which has seriously affected liquidity everywhere, especially in marginal markets; the effects of the two variables are nonetheless closely intertwined. At the same time, however, adjustments in the governance structure of financial markets themselves is converging across borders as exchanges seek new capital in order to update their technological systems and the like, with mutual and partnership forms increasingly giving way to public companies.

Thus despite – perhaps even because of – stagnation and financial crisis, marketization of Japanese finance is still proceeding at a rapid if uneven pace. Despite a string of politically motivated delays, many of the Big Bang reforms promised and partially legislated for in 1996–98 are now finally coming on stream of their own accord. Furthermore, at the same time, Prime Minister Koizumi and Finance Minister Takenaka are apparently committed to further, ostensibly far-reaching measures. However, these measures are being unevenly implemented, and opposition, however entrenched, has not coalesced around an alternative. Sub rosa guerrilla political warfare has been the order of the day. Splits in the opposition parties have played into the hands of the resisters, but Koizumi has apparently maintained his commitment to reform despite frequent tacking. Public and media opinion, as well as pressures from modernizing sectors among some party politicians, bureaucrats and private sector groups has grown stronger in favor of continuing the reform process, and there seems to be a growing momentum for reform and anger at resisters.

4. Conclusions

The United States in recent decades has benefited from its large internal market, its ability to call on sources of external capital whether for industrial expansion in the nineteenth century or for financing the twin deficits of the late twentieth and early twenty-first, its deconcentrated political and regulatory structures, and its arm's-length pattern of state-economy interaction. Nevertheless, globalization creates losers as well as winners, and the financial slump of the first years of the twenty-first century is increasingly forcing the United States to increase the weight and scope of its regulatory apparatus as the 'irrational exuberance' of the 1990s in terms of over-optimism, naïveté, abuse and fraud shakes out. For Japan, the 'system that soured' (Katz, 1998) has managed to resist wholesale reform for well over a decade despite severe stagnation and deflation. Yet pressures for restructuring are continuing to grow and the financial system finally appears to be responding. Furthermore, given the deep embeddedness of the postwar Japanese model – suffering today from its own earlier success – the 'two steps forward, one step back' approach of successive governments has probably been crucial for developing social and political support for the ongoing process of restructuring.

The experiences of the United States and Japan suggest that despite the stark contrasts between the two national models, globalization is leading to an uneven convergence of the two financial systems and, through that, of the two models more generally. Even so, there is no isomorphism here. Not only do deeply entrenched institutions and practices lead to 'different roads to globalization', but the outcomes are not identical either. Nevertheless, all national models exhibit increased hybridization as they interact with each other and with mobile, fungible, abstract global finance. Rather than distinct national models of capitalism, we are once again in the presence of varieties of neoliberalism, with financial globalization providing a lever for both international trends – *gaiatsu* – and domestic pressures – *naiatsu* – to push in the same direction, that is, toward increasingly highly regulated but pro-market, arm's-length, liberalization. 'Path dependency' is a moving process – not merely the static reproduction of past patterns of behavior – and hybrid neoliberal paths are continually being negotiated and entrenched anew. In each case, new constraints and potential benefits create new political choices, patterns of coalition-building and strategies for institutional change. The United States and Japan, like other countries in a globalizing world, are just beginning what will very likely be a long and tortuous process of creative adjustment to a more open and volatile international financial environment.

Further reading

The best overall comparative political economy treatments of regulatory systems in general, and financial systems in particular, are John Zysman's classic *Governments, Markets, and Growth: Financial Systems and the Politics of Industrial Change* (Ithaca, New York: Cornell University Press, 1983); Steven K. Vogel's *Freer Markets, More Rules: Regulatory Reform in Advanced Industrial Countries* (Ithaca, New York: Cornell University Press, 1996); and Henry Laurence's *Money Rules: The New Politics of Finance in Britain and Japan* (Ithaca, New York: Cornell University Press, 2001). More recently, however, Susanne Lütz's comparative study of the United States, Britain, and Germany is the definitive comparative work (although it doesn't include Japan): 'Convergence Within National Diversity: The Regulatory State in Finance', *Journal of Public Policy* 24(2) (August 2004), 169–19.

On the United States, see the author's 'Money and Power: The American Financial System from Free Banking to Global Competition', in Grahame Thompson (ed.), *Markets*, vol. 2 of *The United States in the Twentieth Century* (London: Hodder and Stoughton for the Open University, 2nd edition, 2000) pp. 169–207, and Helen A. Garten, *US Financial Regulation and the Level Playing Field* (Basingstoke: Palgrave, 2001). On Japan, see the authoritative works of Richard Katz: *Japan, The System That Soured: The Rise and Fall of the Japanese Miracle* (Armonk, NY and London: M.E. Sharpe, 1998); and its sequel, *Japanese Phoenix: The Long Road to Economic Revival* (M.E. Sharpe, 2003), as well as the author's 'Governance, Globalization and the Japanese Financial System: Resistance or Restructuring?', in Glenn Hook (ed.), *Contested Governance in Japan* (London: Routledge, 2005).

Useful websites

<www.iif.com>   Institute of International Finance

<www.sec.gov>   United States Securities and Exchange Commission

<www.treas.gov>   United States Department of the Treasury

<www.federalreserve.gov>   Federal Reserve System

<www.fsa.go.jp>   Japan's Financial Services Agency

<www.mof.go.jp>   Ministry of Finance

<www.boj.or.jp/en>   Bank of Japan

Very expensive, but also very useful, is the monthly business publication *Financial Regulation International* (London: Informa Magazine Publishing). Indispensable news sources include, of course, the *Financial Times*, but also the English-language *Nikkei Weekly*.

8
The Evolution of the Swedish Model

Sven Steinmo

Sweden provides an excellent case to study the effects of globalization on advanced welfare states for several reasons. Indeed, this case study provides a particularly interesting example of how a specific country has coped, adapted to and internalized the pressures imposed by global competition in recent years (Chapter 1, this volume) precisely because it is *the* country that many analysts have predicted would be forced to succumb to the supposedly unrelenting global pressures for lower taxes and cut backs to the welfare state. As is well known, Sweden is the most heavily taxed country in the world. Its 'universalist' welfare state is one of the most generous and egalitarian in the modern world (Rothstein, 1998). In addition, this country has long had one of the world's most open economies (Cameron, 1984; Katzenstein, 1985). In short, if globalization were going to force a 'race to the bottom' anywhere, certainly Sweden would be its first target.

In this chapter, I examine the evolution of Swedish tax policy over the past several decades. Taxation is at the core of the 'globalization' argument. Proponents of this view argue that taxes drive up costs of labor and investment and concomitantly finance economically inefficient social policies. In this view, globalization will allow capital and high value labor to more easily exit high tax domains and thus will ultimately force competition between states for these resources. The inevitable result (or so the argument goes) is that vote-seeking politicians will understand this logic and cut both taxes and social spending (Lindbeck, 1997; McKenzie and Lee, 1991).

This case study confirms the broader analysis conducted by Swank and Steinmo (2002) showing that the link between international competition and tax policy is attenuated at best. I argue more directly here that the contention suggesting that globalization should lead toward an end of the state (Korten, 1995; Lash, 1985; Pontusson, 1992) is simply wrong. Instead the chapter demonstrates that while there have indeed been important transformations in both political institutions and economic structure in Sweden, these transformations *preceded* the era now widely understood to be the era of globalization from the mid-1980s onwards. Second, precisely as suggested in the opening chapter in this volume, this case study argues that while the Swedish Model – as it was once understood – has evolved over the past several decades, the choices available to Swedish policy-makers has been remarkably broad. We will see here a particularly clear example of how 'contemporary politics entails both a process of choosing between different versions of neoliberalism and the attempt to innovate creatively *within* the new neo-liberal playing field', as the editors write in the introduction. Thus, we shall see here a case where the Social Democrats have indeed adopted many aspects of neoliberal and market-based thinking, but perhaps surprisingly, the evidence does not support the proposition that Swedish Social Democrats have consequentially also had to abandon their redistributive ambitions.

The following analysis will instead demonstrate how Swedish political economy has changed quite dramatically since it was first heralded as 'the Middle Way'. I will specifically examine tax policy and show how it has adapted the new political economic realities facing this country at the end of the twentieth century and into the next. This case study evidence suggests neither 'An End to Redistribution' (Steinmo, 1994), nor that 'There Is No Alternative' (TINA), as Mrs Thatcher was fond of saying. Instead, it appears that the Swedes are continuing their historical pattern of manipulating some kind of middle ground between the rampant liberalism of free markets and controlled markets in the hands of a large and powerful state. Swedish tax policy is adapting to the realities of the New Political Economy, but it is not dying because of it.

1. The Swedish model

Sweden has long been held up to the world as a particular and unique political economy that has accomplished many of the kinds of redistributive and social policy ends that leftists in most other countries could scarcely dream of: not only has Sweden developed into one of the most egalitarian countries in the world, it has also become one of the richest. Sweden, it is widely agreed, has been able to achieve these remarkable results because of her unique political/economic system – generally referred to as the Swedish Model. There have been literally dozens of books written about this model (and now its death) over the past decades and, as a consequence, the very meaning of the term has become muddied. Today, when scholars and pundits refer to the Swedish Model they tend to imply anything from a general political culture of cooperation and compromise, to specific union wage strategies, to the fact that the Swedish public sector is the largest (as a percentage of GDP) of any country in the world. In this chapter, I refer to the Swedish Model as meaning the specific combination of political and economic institutions that were unique to Sweden. I specifically mean to separate these institutions from the large welfare state that was in many ways a product of these institutions – though, as we shall see, they also contributed to the model's demise. The Swedish Model has two basic components: first it is meant to describe a 'neo-corporatist' institutional structure (in which policy-making is dominated by huge, centralized employer and employee federations under the coordination of the Social Democratic Party elite). This political decision-making system facilitated the 'Politics of Compromise'. Secondly, the model consisted of a particular system of wage agreement in which the employer and employee federations set national wage policy with the explicit aim toward increasing wages of the lower income workers and holding back potential wage claims of workers in more economically advantaged sectors of the economy (Hancock, 1972; Heclo, 1974).

It is important to understand that this neocorporatist model depended rather fundamentally on two particular policies that are not often thought of in most other countries as being promoted by the left. Specifically, Sweden developed a somewhat unusual tax regime that, on the one hand, taxed personal income, consumption and wealth very heavily, but on the other, taxed capital and corporate income remarkably lightly (Steinmo, 1988). Secondly, this system explicitly exposed domestic producers to international competition to a greater extent than most other larger political economies (Katzenstein, 1984). These seemingly curious outcomes can be explained in two different ways. First, there was a specific historic compromise over tax policy between the Social Democrats and big employers over how far labor would press its anti-capitalist ambitions (Pontusson, 1987). Second, both capital and labor came to understand that international competition could act as a stimulus for innovation and could also provide necessary market discipline (Rothstein, 1988).

Though marginal tax rates were quite high, Swedish Ministry of Finance officials had become very accomplished in creating tax expenditures designed to direct investment to particular sectors of the economy, promote employment, and/or encourage investment (or build up stock reserves) during economic downturns (Hansen, 1969). The effects of these multiple and very deep tax incentives was that large Swedish corporations paid only nominal corporate profit taxes.[14]

While large corporations and big capitalists[15] paid very little in taxes as long as they kept their capital in productive assets in Sweden, smaller and privately held firms and ordinary workers paid extraordinarily heavy tax burdens. Though rarely publicly stated, the explicit corporate tax policy goal of the Social Democratic governments in the postwar years was to squeeze capital into the large, internationally competitive manufacturing industries. At the same time, Sweden maintained an open international trade policy, which was explicitly aimed at forcing Swedish firms to maintain international competitiveness. These firms were, of course, precisely the firms that were strongly represented within LO (Sweden's large centralized union organization), and were also the same firms that had by now developed a 'working relationship' with the Social Democrats in classic corporatist arrangements (Hancock, 1972).

The bottom line of this deal between labor, capital and the Social Democratic government was that capital would be not only be allowed to coexist even while Socialists were in power (Pontusson, 1986: 460), but the Socialists and their labor union allies would conduct wage strategies[16] and tax policies that would explicitly favor corporate capital. The other side of this corporatist 'deal' was that big unions and a big state would also be tolerated, employment would be held at very high levels[17], and when economic change was called for, the individual worker and his family would be fully compensated for economic costs of structural transformation.[18] Specific policies favoring unions were also introduced[19] and a wide variety of public insurance, education, and welfare programs was established and expanded (Rothstein, 1988).

It is essential to understand that this was a profoundly elite driven system. A key feature of this corporatist compromise, though rarely explicitly acknowledged, was the extent to which a quite small group of leaders from the major economic interests in society would sit together and haggle out the economic plan for the country. This often meant that unions would impose wage discipline and that the employer federation (SAF) would agree to national wage bargains that would explicitly undermine many of their constituent members. The Social Democratic government was held outside the specific annual wage negotiations, but quite clearly were there holding both carrots and sticks. In many cases, this explicitly meant tax carrots and tax sticks.

It should also be specifically noted – in the context of the current debate about the conflict between redistribution and 'globalization' – that this tax-high public spending system was self-consciously designed to equalize wealth and income in Sweden. Swedish economic elites believed that their system of active labor market policies and incentives favoring economic dynamism and flexibility in both the corporate sector and among workers overcame this conflict. Indeed, it was widely believed that it was *more efficient* to have a highly educated and well-paid workforce, which could facilitate international competition.

By virtually all accounts, the system worked. Sweden was widely known to have the most egalitarian society in the western world (Atkinson and Smeeding, 1995; Gottschalk and Joyce, 1995; Palme, 1993). Swedes were unmistakably proud of this fact and admired themselves for having achieved very high levels of economic growth *and* high levels of economic justice (Heclo and Madsen, 1987; Svallfors, 1989).

In sum, by many accounts Sweden had achieved the best of many worlds by the mid-1970s: this small country in the north of Europe had one of the most egalitarian systems in the world, had essentially eliminated poverty, and educated one of the most dynamic and flexible workforces found in any capitalist economy. At the same time the economy was quite productive, efficient and dynamic, and dominated by major internationally competitive firms such as Volvo, ASEA, and Ericsson. Finally, the government was democratic, highly stable, efficiently run by a well-trained and well-insulated, technocratically-oriented elite that possessed 'an arsenal' of policy devices designed to keep the Swedish economy open, competitive and dynamic. It was small wonder that a virtual army of academics, labor union officials and politicians from around the world flocked to Sweden to see exactly how this miracle had been constructed, and what could be learned from this country's obvious success (cf. Hancock, 1972; Rustow, 1955).

2. Cracks in the Swedish Model: is something rotten in Stockholm?

Perhaps all bubbles must deflate. In retrospect it seems that no sooner had Sweden become recognized as the premier example of 'the Middle Way' between the individuating and inegalitarian capitalism of the West and deadening and inefficient socialism of the East, than the 'system' began to leak.[20] There is insufficient space here to detail the evolution of the changes in the Swedish political economy from the 1970s through the 1980s but a few general points must be noted, so that we may better understand the new context in which tax policy began to turn in the 1980s and 1990s.

It is tempting today to argue that the fall of Swedish corporatism resulted from globalization and/or internationalization of the world economy. But closer look at the *timing* of the changes in Swedish political life draws pause. If, as many have argued (and as we have suggested above), the key component of the distinctive Swedish Model was effectively a class compromise between labor and large capital, then globalization can scarcely be the central explanatory variable: Put bluntly, by the time 'globalization' was even coined in the popular media, and before it became such a central concern for policy-makers, the Swedish Model was already quite ill.[21] Indeed, if we take the view that' 'globalization' is a much longer or deeper phenomenon that goes back several decades, one could instead argue that 'globalization' (i.e. stiff international competition for labor, capital, and technology) was in many ways *responsible for* the particular character of the Swedish Social Democratic Model. In short, the Social Democratic elite came to understand in the 1940s and 1950s that by exposing the Swedish economy to international competition they would force capital and labor to be more innovative and flexible and thereby productive (Bergstrom, 1982; Lindbeck, 1975; Steinmo, 1989; Swenson, 2002).

At any rate, there is widespread agreement today that the traditional neocorporatist model in Sweden began to break down in the 1970s. Certainly the watershed event was a massive wildcat strike beginning in the iron mines in the north of Sweden (Kiruna) in 1969. These strikes were exceptional because they were strikes from the heart of the working class *against the union organization and their political allies in Stockholm.* In economic terms the strike did little lasting damage to the Swedish economy, but it opened massive fissures and created enormous self-doubt among both the LO leadership as well as the left of the Social Democratic Party. In many ways, the strike could be understood as a strike against the Swedish Model itself. Of course there were many specific complaints, and demands, but the most critical complaint was that the unions and the SDP had lost touch with their own base. The accusation implied in these strikes was that the past several decades of cooperation with big capitalists had turned the working class leaders from 'socialists' into capitalist stooges. Though the strike itself was eventually settled in favor of many of the miners' demands, the more basic accusations implied in the strike left serious self-doubt in the minds of the leadership. What kind of union and what kind of Social Democracy is it that workers themselves feel they must strike against?

These doubts led to significant self-examination and rethinking both within the Party and inside the LO. The results were multiple: First, the unions became less quiescent and began to demand both higher wages from employers in their national wage negotiations *and* more public spending from the Social Democratic government and more explicitly redistributive (populist) tax measures. Secondly, the Social Democratic Party too (at least significant portions of the left within the Party) came to question its own legitimacy. Several substantial changes grew out of these self-examinations, including the 1974 constitutional change that was intended to make Swedish democracy more direct and more responsive to citizens.[22] Third, the LO began to make new political demands intended to restructure private ownership of Swedish capital.[23] Finally, citizen demands for increases in spending on popular public programs skyrocketed. It is very important to note that up to the early 1970s, Sweden did not have a particularly large public sector when compared with other rich industrialized European democracies. Indeed, contrary to the standard image, the Swedish model did not necessarily imply an especially large welfare state.

The politicization of the Swedish political economy had substantial consequences for the model itself. Most importantly, the SAF came to believe that the LO and the Social Democrats could no longer be trusted (Rothstein, 2000). Moreover, as Olof Ruin points out, 'At the parliamentary level the most important development in the 1970s, parallel to the new constitution, was the weakening of the executive'; as a result, he argues, the government was less able 'to take unpopular decisions', and to 'distance itself from special interests' (Ruin, 1981: 149–50). In sum, by the mid-1970s the 'Swedish Model', that is, a political economy of cooperation and mutual respect dominated by relatively benevolent, secure and highly technocratic elites, was not yet dead, but it was certainly quite ill.

3. Structural changes in the economy

Along with the politicization of Swedish democracy in the 1970s the Swedish economy was also in the process of important structural changes. Some of these changes were simply the products of the maturing of the Swedish industrial base. Ironically, however, some of these changes were also the direct consequence of the public policies introduced in the previous decade. Thus, for example, the increasing demand for public programs, expanded the number of public employees. These employees where not traditionally organized by LO unions (who generally represented classical 'workers') but were instead organized by either the TCO or by SACO unions. The significance of this change is that while Sweden – which had once been noted for its highly centralized wage negotiation system and unified and disciplined union structure – was now developing a fragmented union structure. Though unionization as a percentage of the workforce expanded in these years, the growth of the public sector meant that working class interests themselves began to diverge. It is far easier to find a common front between the interests of miners and auto workers, for example, than it is to find a common interest between medical doctors and day care employees. Ironically, then, a consequence of unionizing the entire society and building a big welfare state was to undermine worker solidarity in Sweden.

The fragmentation of union interests had direct consequences for both wage demands and public spending in Sweden. In the 'old' Swedish Model, union wage demands could be tempered by the economic realities of the international marketplace, and decisions once reached at the elite level could be implemented at the local shop-floor level owing to the high degree of power of the central union organization. But by the late 1970s and early 1980s the Swedish political economy was quite different. The SAF wished to abandon the commitment to national wage deals, in part so that its members could pay higher paid workers more and hold down wages of lower paid workers. Also, public employees (who have no international market discipline to temper their demands) were increasingly dominating the wage demand picture. Finally, the union organizations themselves were less able (and probably less willing) to hold wages back so that profits were maintained – or public spending could be held in check. Given these basic facts, Sweden quickly developed strong inflationary proclivities. The government, desperately trying to maintain Swedish international competitiveness, felt that its only alternative was to periodically devalue the Swedish kronor (Jonung, 1999).

The second structural change facing the Swedish economy was increasing competition in the traditional industries in which Sweden had so long been a leader. Mining, steel, shipbuilding and autos were each stung by growing competition from lower wage economies. It is of course extremely difficult to dis-aggregate the inflationary wage pressures specifically facing these industries in Sweden from the more general world-wide trend in these industries to lower wage economies. But it is certainly fair to say that the specific wage pressures in combination with the growing rigidity of the Swedish labor market resulting from the various Social Democratic policies introduced in the 1970s did not help. For example, it is also widely recognized that though the increasingly frequent (and sometimes quite dramatic) devaluations could temporarily improve Swedish industry's international price competitive position, these policies did little to nothing to increase the long-term competitiveness of the Swedish economy in anything like the way that the traditional Swedish model might have done.[24]

In sum, by the late 1970s and early 1980s, Sweden was in a process of undergoing substantial changes in both her political decision-making institutions and in her economic structure (upon which the political institutions in many ways depended). Neither of these changes were products of what is now referred to as 'globalization' – unless all we mean by this term is the long-term maturation and growth of advanced capitalism. Instead, the Swedish model was crumbling because of the increased politicization of the polity and the concomitant demands put on the economy by the growing public sector.

4. Adapting and evolving in a globalizing world

The political and structural changes discussed above had direct implications for the Swedish system. First, increasing demands for public programs and increasing wage demands from public employees directly led to the need for high taxes. Taxes eventually spiraled to over 60 per cent of GDP by 1990.[25] Secondly, the combination of this tax pressure and the inflationary tendencies in the Swedish economy meant that ever more Swedish citizens were being pushed up into personal income tax brackets which were originally intended to affect only the very richest taxpayers.[26] In the short run, of course, the Treasury needed this 'bracket creep'[27] because it 'automatically' increased revenues. In the longer run, these officials understood quite clearly that tax rates of this magnitude contributed directly to the inflationary cycle gripping Sweden in these years. In simple terms, workers and even, quite importantly, public sector workers discounted the extra costs of taxes into their wage demands.

The Swedish economics elite both within the Ministry of Finance and in the economics profession more generally saw these developments as a crisis. The crisis was both economic/fiscal and a crisis of confidence. Whereas in the past, these elites believed they could manage their economy quite effectively, now they were increasingly convinced that such management was no longer possible. What were once thought of as 'labor market partners' were now simply 'interest groups'. In addition, whereas the political system in the earlier era insulated the fiscal elite and gave them enormous policy autonomy, now political demands on both the tax and spending sides were increasingly difficult to shut out. In the words of one senior Ministry of Finance official:

> I was taught in college that we could manage the economy via fiscal manipulations. But now in Sweden, and other countries too, we have less faith in politicians. We now realize that political asymmetries are so large that you have to be careful about what you recommend. Politicians don't only do what their economic advisors recommend; they also have to listen to interest groups ... If economists think that political decisions are symmetric, then they use false assumptions. Politicians have short time horizons. (Interview with author, April 2000)

This sense of crisis was not widely shared by either politicians or average citizens in Sweden in the 1980s. To the extent that there were problems with the tax system, for example, it was generally believed that this was because it was not progressive enough (Hadenius, 1986; Svallfors, 1989). To the extent that there was a problem with Swedish democracy, it was that political elites were *not responsive enough*. As Table 8.1 shows, political trust substantially increased in this era of 'crisis'.

Most non-Swedes find it surprising that Swedes did not revolt against their tax burden long before it reached 60 per cent of GDP. Few Americans, in particular, can understand how and why a people could tolerate paying over half their income to the tax authorities. But what non-Swedes fail to understand is that most Swedes clearly believe they get a lot for the high taxes they pay. Survey after survey has shown that while Swedes (like virtually all citizens in modern welfare states) agree that 'taxes are too high', only a minority of citizens support tax cuts if they are forced to choose them in exchange for reductions in public spending. By the early 1990s at least 65 per cent of Swedes received a direct public subsidy from their government (Lindbeck, 1997).

Certainly as a consequence of this basic fact, Sweden seemed to defy Downs's (1960) prediction that government would be too small in a

Table 8.1 Declining faith in public institutions

Year	1968	1973	1976	1979	1982	1985	1988	1991	1994
Disagreeing with A	60	51	48	34	37	34	32	29	28
Disagreeing with B	51	44	39	34	36	31	32	27	25

Percent Population disagreeing with the following statements: (A) The Riksdag does not pay much attention to what ordinary citizens think. (B) Parties are interested in people's votes, not in their opinions.

Source: Holmberg, 1999, p. 107.

democracy.[28] In fact, Swedes clearly believed that they got much for their tax dollar and as a consequence there was very little public pressure to cut taxes even though tax burdens were so high (Edlund, 1999; Hadenius, 1986; Svallfors, 1989; Svallfors, 1997). Moreover, in most areas of public spending, strong majorities favor *increases* in spending – even if it may mean increases in their taxes (cf. Svallfors, 1997).

5. A 'neoliberal' turn by the 'socialists'?

Beginning in the late 1970s, Swedish economists as well as officials in the Ministry of Finance began seriously to question the long-term viability of the taxs system that was evolving. Again, there were several interrelated issues: most importantly, taxes were driving up wages and thus contributing to the inflationary pressures and economic imbalances. Secondly, these elites came to believe that tax rates were being pushed so high that even ordinary taxpayers were engaging in a variety of non-productive behaviors and/or working in the underground economy simply for the purposes of evading taxes (Agell *et al.*, 1995; Muten, 1988; Myrdal, 1982). The Ministry had a substantial problem, however: the majority of Social Democrats in the Riksdag (Parliament) as well as the leadership of the LO did not agree that these were the central issue. Quite to the contrary, these elites' preferences reflected the general perspective of Swedish citizens: the problem with the Swedish tax system, quite bluntly, was that the rich and the corporations paid too little in taxes, while the lower and middle classes paid too much (Edlund, 1999; Hadenius, 1986; Svallfors, 1989). The Minister and his men thus faced considerable obstacles in achieving their reform agenda.

In an interview Kjell Olaf Feldt, former Minister of Finance, recalled it as follows:

One of the most important issues I began to work on in the early 70s was to change the Social Democrats' perspective on how we get a just income distribution in society. The negative inheritance I received from my pre-decessor Gunnar Sträng [Minister of Finance 1955–76] was a strongly pro-gressive tax system with high marginal taxes. This was supposed to bring about a just and equal society. But I eventually came to the opinion that it simply didn't work out that way. These taxes created instead a society of wranglers, cheaters, peculiar manipulations, false ambitions and new injustices. It took me at least a decade to get a part of the party to see this. That was a big deal, to change the outlook that had been built up since the 1940s. That I burned for. (Sjöberg, 1999)

In pursuit of their ambitions to achieve tax reform, the Ministry of Finance began to commission a series of reports and analyses examining the effects of taxation on the economy, workers' willingness to work, leisure time, tax wedges, capital formation, and a wide variety of other economic effects. By the end of the decade the Socialists had passed a series of tax reforms, which simplified the tax code, increased consumption taxes and scaled back a series of tax expenditures. But it was not until 1991 (after they had been pushed out of office) that the government was able to pass the 'tax reform of the century'. Though finally introduced by a bourgeois coalition govern- ment in the 1991, tax reform represented the culmination of more than a decade's work on the part of Kjell Olof Feldt. The background research, justi- fication for the need for reform and econometric analysis of the economic and distributive effects of the reform, was for the most part completed in 1989. *It was the Social Democrats who had pushed for these apparently neoliberal tax policies.*[29] They pushed for these neoliberal policies not because they feared a political backlash, nor because they feared the flight of capital. Rather the keystone in their re-evaluation of their tax policy regime was the realization that the old system did not work the way they had once hoped it would. It was not so much the internationalization of capital that created this new reality but instead the increasing wealth of average Swedish work- ers and citizens. Steeply progressive taxes in Sweden were implemented in an era when the average citizen was quite poor. The late twentieth century real- ity was that these citizens were no longer poor. Now even average workers were paying very high marginal taxes. The result was that they began to cheat the system and attempt to find a myriad of ways to avoid paying their taxes. This new behavior, the Social Democratic elite feared, undermined confidence in the 'fairness' of the system *and* had significant economic disadvantages.

With this reform, Sweden took a huge step from a tax system that relied on very high marginal rates and then softened these rates with very deep tax loopholes, to a much broader-based tax system in which tax rates on all taxpayers were reduced and tax expenditures were radically scaled back. Not only was the top tax rate on income reduced from over 80 per cent to 50 per cent,[30] but the tax system was also simplified to the point where over 85 per cent of tax payers no longer submitted a tax return at all. After this reform, the tax code possessed so few tax write-offs that the government would simply send a letter to the taxpayer showing the amount of income they had earned in the year and asked the taxpayer to confirm that they had no extra (not already taxed) income. Since there were so few tax exemptions left in the system, the taxpayer could simply sign the slip and send it back to the authorities – no further taxes would be due, and usually no tax refund would be issued. Corporate and capital taxation was also radically reformed. Now all capital income faced a flat 30 per cent rate while deductions were substantially rolled back.[31] The Corporate Profits Tax was also scaled back and reformed. The marginal tax rate was reduced from 57 per cent to 30 per cent at the same time that many of the most generous tax expenditures available in the code were eliminated.

In sum, in this decade the Swedish tax system had been remarkably transformed. Whereas in the early 1980s the tax code relied on steeply progressive marginal tax rates and contained a large number of very deep loopholes which clearly shaped private economic activity in a wide variety of non-efficient and non-productive ways, the, new system was clearly less 'interventionist' and was now a virtually flat rate system (actually comprising two rates) with virtually no tax loopholes at all.[32]

6. Neo-liberalism on the ropes

When the Swedish tax reform of 1991 was finally introduced by the bourgeois coalition government, many analysts saw this as the beginning of the end of the Swedish Welfare State. Though tax levels were quite high certainly, gone was the public commitment to maintaining a progressive tax system. Moreover, since the tax reform was underfinanced,[33] many analysts assumed that the lost revenues would eventually have to be made up with increases in taxes on lower income earners, or cuts in benefits for lower income earners, or both. These predictions of course fit very well with the 'End of the Welfare State' analyses, which became so popular in the mid-1990s.

The tax reform also contributed to the massive economic crisis that struck Sweden in the early 1990s. It was once again the bourgeois coalition government's bad timing to come to office at the beginning of a recession just as they did in 1976, but there can be no gainsaying that the policies pursued by these governments, that is, each party trying to pay off its particular constituency, substantially worsened Sweden's economic situation. The tax reform, for example, was underfinanced, in no small part to make it easier for the coalition to pass it. At the same time the tax reform dramatically hastened a collapse in the real property market. Unemployment increased to double digits, whereas unemployment had never before in postwar history exceeded 4 per cent. Economic growth sank to *minus* 1.7 and 1.8 per cent in 1992 and 1993.

In the face of this economic disaster, the government found itself incapable of cutting housing support, child payments, social welfare payments, sickness benefits or any other major social program. In fact, these years actually witnessed an increase in public *spending* despite the fact that the bourgeois government was at the helm. The result was that the budget deficit increased to 13 per cent of GDP. At one point international confidence in the kronor sunk so low that the central bank was forced to increase the overnight lending rate to 500 per cent in a vain effort to protect the currency. Not only was the Swedish Model dying, it now appeared that the Swedish economy was lying on the deathbed next to it.

7. The 'socialists' return

Perhaps unsurprisingly, the direst predictions did not come to fruition (at least not yet). The Social Democratic Party (in coalition with the Left Party and the Green Party) returned to office in 1995. Sweden's unofficial 'Party of Government' quickly set about restabilizing Sweden's financial picture. At first it appeared that the socialists had accepted the basic TINA logic as they began cutting back several social welfare policies. But careful analysis of these policies suggests that rather than slash programs wholesale, most of these reductions were in fact designed to make them a bit more fiscally reasonable and remove some of the opportunities for abuse that had been created earlier by the stunning generosity of these policies.

But the new government did not appear to accept the idea that it must only cut welfare for the poor. Following earlier commitments to analyses of the redistributive effects of the tax reform, the government initiated several studies, which tried to examine the consequences of the reform after the behavioral changes it created had been considered. These studies revealed that the tax policy changes were indeed negatively redistributive. Armed with this evidence the government increased the top marginal rate of tax on very high income earners by 5 per cent and also reduced the Value Added Tax on food by 50 per cent. Since then the government has been trying to effectively 'hold the line' and re-establish fiscal balance. The results of their efforts have been very effective: tax revenues increased rather than declined, the Budget has been balanced and economic growth and productivity have rebounded.[34] Not only has financial balance been restored (indeed, just as in the United States after Clinton's increase in taxes on the very wealthy), but Sweden now appears to be benefiting from a substantial economic resurgence at the same time that it is generating quite substantial budget surpluses.

As Table 8.2 demonstrates, Sweden's economic and fiscal picture has improved markedly. Instead of using the budget surpluses to cut taxes on mobile capital as has been demanded by the right and by many business

Table 8.2 Output, employment and productivity: average annual percentage change, 1994–2002

	Sweden	United States	Germany	United Kingdom	OECD average
Average GDP growth	3.1	3.3	1.6	2.9	2.7
Productivity per worker	2.3	1.8	1.2	1.9	1.7
Employment	0.8	1.4	0.04	1.9	1.0
Productivity growth in manufacturing	6.5	4.0	2.8	1.7	NA

Source: Roseveare *et al.*, 2004: Table 3.

interests, the Finance Minister has chosen to *increase* public spending on child support yet again and to continue using the surplus for paying off Sweden's substantial public debt. Rather than dramatically scaling back public services, the government does not envision scaling back on the state anytime soon. Hans Karlsson, Minister for Employment in Sweden recently declared the following position: 'We – unlike our political opponents – are convinced that a high tax burden and good economic growth go together'. In short, rather than accept the neoliberal logic that argues that taxes and spending must be reduced, the Social Democrats have come to conclude, that 'a good, general welfare system, high taxes, strong collective agreements and labour laws are the *preconditions for growth*' (September 10, 2004) (emphasis added).

In sum, the Social Democrats have not given up their progressive ambitions. Contrary to many predictions on the left (and to the clear disappointment of others) the SAP has decided *not* to use the budget surplus, from which it now benefits in order to cut taxes on mobile capital. Instead, they have decided to use these revenues to add more aid to those at the bottom of the income scale. As is suggested in the introduction to this volume, the Social Democrats appear to be reaching for a new equilibrium within the logic of an increasingly competitive world. There is no *single equilibrium* necessary for economic success. Moreover, given the potent economic performance Sweden is now posting, combined with the daily discussions of the herds of new 'Internet' millionaires in Swedish media, there appears to be little political incentive to cut these people's taxes. Instead, the current debate appears to focus on how to use the new wealth to spread Internet access (broadband) to even the furthest reaches of the Swedish hinterland.

The Swedish model consisting of corporatist decision-making institutions, solidaristic wage policies, and the politics of compromise has clearly been transformed. But, the ambition and the political support for a largely egalitarian polity with a very large welfare state (and the taxes to support it) appear to live on quite healthily in Sweden today. The Swedish Model was undoubtedly a historically bounded institutional set-up that was in some sense bound to collapse. It did, however, enable the construction of a kind of social welfare state that now has its own political force. In short, though the model has certainly changed, adapted and evolved, its legacy is alive and quite well.

8. Rethinking the policy change in a globalizing world

In the crisis period of the 1930s and 1940s it was quite common to hear both pundits and scholars declare that capitalism had come to a crossroads: either economic change or political demands (or both) had brought about a transformation of capitalism as it had been known (Polanyi, 1944). Looking back, however, one could instead argue that it was the very policies developed in these decades that effectively 'saved' capitalism (Lindblom, 1973;

Schumpeter, 1947). Instead of destroying capitalism, the very welfare state that many believed would undermine its key mechanism, had the opposite effect: by redistributing wealth and dampening the vicious swings of the free market, state policy effectively increased aggregate demand and reduced uncertainty. The results were – contra the 'chicken little' hysterics – a virtuous cycle of growth, productivity, and increasing prosperity.[35]

Modern capitalism is currently undergoing transformations perhaps as dramatic as those witnessed earlier in the last century. Not only is capital and labor more internationally mobile than it has been at any time since the end of the First World War, but the new technologies of production are also increasingly pressuring capitalists and policy-makers alike towards more flexible regimes (Brooks, 2000; Drucker, 1986; *The Economist*, 10 February 2000). Equally, as Blyth (Blyth, 2002) and the authors in this volume have shown, a new economic hegemony appears to have emerged over the past several years. The case study here does appear to support the contention that Sweden has moved from 'embedded neoliberalism' to 'embedded neoliberalism' and this at the very least means that market mechanisms are viewed more favorably than traditional state regulatory mechanisms. But this case study should also give us pause before jumping to quick and easy explanations for this shift. In this case, at least, it appears that it was the Social Democratic elite of the left that initiated this ideational move *not* because they feared the wrath of the right or the exit of capital, *but rather* because many of the traditional policy tools initiated nearly 50 years earlier were no longer appropriate to the world the Swedes found themselves in at the century's end. In other words, in order to protect a successful and egalitarian social welfare state new ideas and new policies were called for. Instead of seeing the market as the enemy, even Social Democrats have come increasingly to believe that it can be their friend.

These changes, however, do not spell the end of the welfare state any more than changes earlier in the century spelled the end of capitalism. Instead, we are witnessing another 'Great Transformation' (Polanyi, 1944): one in which the specific relationship between public and private power is once again a subject of contestation. In short, the multiple equilibria observed in the latter part of the twentieth century have been upset. This does not suggest, however, that a new *single* equilibrium is imminent. Quite the contrary, institutional variation will once again structure how different nations respond to economic changes (cf. Steinmo, 1993) and, as a result, new yet still multiple, equilibria should continue to be the most likely result.

Further reading

Childs, Marquis (1974) *Sweden: The Middle Way*. New Haven: Yale University Press.
Rothstein, Bo (1988) 'State and Capital in Sweden: The Importance of Corporatist Arrangements', *Scandinavian Political Studies* 11 (3): 235–60.

Svallfors, Stefan and Peter Taylor Gooby (1999) *The End of the Welfare State?: Responses to State Retrenchment, [Routledge/Esa Studies in European Society 3]* London: Routledge.

Tilton, Timothy (1979) 'A Swedish Road to Socialism: Ernst Wigforss and the Ideological Foundations of Swedish Social Democracy', *American Political Science Review* 73 (2): 505–20.

Useful websites

<http://www.sweden.se>   Sweden SE, the official gateway website for Sweden

<http://www.cia.gov/cia/publications/factbook/geos/sw.html>   World Fact Book: Sweden

<http://www.const.sns.se/swedishpolitics>   SNS, Swedish Politics: Links and Resources

<http://www.scb.se/templates/tableorchart114967.asp>   Statistical Yearbook of Sweden. Lots of good data about Sweden in numbers

Part II

Developing and Transition Countries in Globalization

9
The Rise of Neoliberalism in Mexico: from a Developmental to a Competition State[36]

Susanne Soederberg

1. Introduction

One of the most predominant features of globalization, namely, the increasing mobility and power of global capital flows, has acted to constrain the scope of state intervention over the past two and a half decades, particularly in the area of economic policy formation. As we saw in the first part of this volume, within the context of the advanced industrialized countries (AICs), globalization has acted as the underlying impetus of the shift from various expressions of Keynesian demand management/welfare state to neoliberal forms of government intervention. The latter has been aptly captured by the term 'national competition states' (Cerny, 1993b, 1999; Hirsch, 1995). One of the main characteristics of competition states is that traditional policies aimed at achieving social justice through economic redistribution have been challenged and profoundly undermined by the marketization of the state's economic activities and its focus on attracting and retaining capital flows (Cerny, 1999: 3). This situation raises at least two interrelated questions. First, is it correct to assume these neoliberal forms of political regulation hold true for 'Third world' developmental states? And, second, if the states of emerging market economies have adopted the characteristics of a competition state, then to what degree, and with which political, social and economic consequences? In what follows I aim to provide answers to these questions by exploring key changes in the area of economic policy formation in Mexico from the 1982 debt crisis to the peso debacle in 1994/95.

The main argument I would like to put forward is that although the Mexican state has assumed the defining characteristics of an AIC competition state, this neoliberal form of state has succeeded neither in reducing the country's excessive vulnerability and dependence on external sources of capital, nor bringing about conditions for sustainable economic growth. As will become clearer below, neoliberal restructuring has resulted in tenuous forms of capital accumulation (i.e., the phenomenon of the *maquiladorization* of the economy) and increased the divide between rich and poor. The question that arises here is, why? I suggest that neoliberal restructuring is a complex and struggle-driven process involving tensions between domestic and international policy imperatives (cf. Underhill, 1997). While this contradiction is evident in AIC competition states, it is more pronounced in developing countries like Mexico. As I demonstrate below, this tension has resulted in a paradox: While neoliberal policies have led to deeper integration into the world economy, so as to draw in capital flows, these very policies have led to increased rates of poverty and higher levels of financial vulnerability. The latter forms of destabilization, according to the World Bank, entailed an increased possibility of further speculative attack against the peso at the end of 1994.

To understand better the strain between domestic and international forces of globalization and its role in shaping the Mexican state it is useful to look closely at the decline of the Mexican developmental state. I do this by first exploring the breakdown of the Bretton Woods system (1944–71) and, secondly, the emergence of what Philip Cerny refers to as 'embedded financial orthodoxy'.

2. The demise of the Bretton Woods system

The strength of the postwar, US-based world order was rooted in the strict control of international finance under the Bretton Woods system of fixed exchange rates that encouraged currency stabilization and liberalized international trade (Helleiner, 1994). In essence, the world order reflected what John Ruggie once referred to as an *embedded liberalism compromise*, a form of multilateralism that was not only predicated upon domestic intervention but also compatible with the requirements of domestic stability (1982). With regard to AICs, this durability corresponded to the congruence between national fordist forms of capital accumulation and Keynesian demand-management (Boyer and Drache, 1996; cf. Clarke, 1988; Hirsch, 1995). During the late 1960s, both capital accumulation patterns and corresponding state forms entered into crisis. The immediate expression assumed by this crisis has been the de-linking of the so-called real economy from finance. In effect, the predominance of money capital has had the effect of making the sphere of production more sensitive and vulnerable to the systemic volatility of the world economy caused by financial speculation (Soederberg, 2004).

Partly due to class-based struggles within the larger systemic crisis of capitalism, and partly authored through the so-called *non-decisions* of states to effectively regulate capital flows (Strange, 1998) international financial markets have obtained considerable power in the global political economy. To illustrate, '[t]he daily turnover in the foreign exchange market, which was about $15 billion in 1973 and about $60 billion in 1983 is now approximately $1.3 trillion, an amount perhaps sixty times the volume needed to finance trade, one that dwarfs the less than one trillion dollars available to the governments of advanced countries for exchange rate stabilization purposes' (Crotty and Epstein, 1996: 132). In contrast with the 1980s, the players in the international financial order are no longer transnational banks, but more mobile, less vulnerable insurance and pension fund managers and other portfolio investors (Strange, 1998). Although a large portion of financial flows remains firmly entrenched within AICs, and the 'triad' of the European Union, the US and Japan in particular (Hirst and Thompson, 1999; IMF, 2004a),[37] the shift from traditional banking activities to securitization have had serious implications for the South (World Bank, 2003: 36; Soederberg, 2004). As the Managing Director of the IMF, Michel Camdessus, put it, 'Not since the opening decades of the twentieth century have private portfolio capital inflows been such a significant source of financing for developing countries' (IMF, 1995: 2). Under these circumstances, national policy is largely formulated on the basis of perceived favorable investment environments for potential investors and creditors, such as low social overhead, minimal corporate taxation levels, and, more important, easy entry and exit requirements for foreign capital flows. Although 'sound fundamentals' are a key feature of a 'good business climate', given the speculative nature of today's capital markets, they far from guarantee stable financial inflows. As the Annual Report of the Bank for International Settlements makes clear, 'A striking feature of private sector capital flows in recent years has been the pace at which they surged into countries with significant structural or macroeconomic vulnerabilities – almost up to the eve of the financial crisis [in Thailand] – and their subsequent abrupt reversal' (1996: 37).

3. Embedded financial orthodoxy

In the current post-Bretton Woods era, the world economy is no longer characterized by the embedded liberalism compromise, but rather what Philip Cerny has dubbed the 'embedded financial orthodoxy' (1993a). This notion underscores that we are not experiencing a consolidated, post-fordist phase of capitalist development; but instead an extended phase of crisis. Embedded financial orthodoxy is marked by unstable cycles of boom and slump, and the preoccupation of states and capitals with the use of blunt instruments like interest rates (exchange rate manipulation such as devaluing a currency to boost exports) as opposed to fine-tuning, as well as the concern of financial stability, that is, a contagion-free environment of the so-called *infrastructure of the infrastructure* (Cerny, 1993a: 158, 2000b; Harvey, 1999).

State powers have also undergone changes in responding to this growing complexity within both the world economy and its borders. It is useful to underline that, as an integral moment of the wider social relations of capitalist production, the state remains a *capitalist* state regardless of its particular form. In this manner, the state (encompassing governmental, administrative and coercive apparatuses) is a material condensation of the specific configuration of class power within a particular mode of capital accumulation, such as ISI or EPI. The particular expression assumed by the state, such as a developmental or national competition state, derives from the power relations within the social forces of production (Soederberg, 2005). Policy formulation, therefore, is foremost shaped and constrained by the contradictory and dynamic qualities arising from the social relations of production (Poulantzas, 1978; Hirsch, 1995). Ensuring the continuation of the capital relation, and thereby the state's own existence, depends on ensuring domestic co-operation with its restructuring strategies as well as designing economic and social policy in such a manner as to attract and retain capital within its territory (Holloway, 1995: 127). Nevertheless, to guarantee the continuation of capital accumulation, the state must also attempt to disarticulate conflicts within the economic realm and thus appease and subdue these struggles. These tasks have become increasingly difficult within the pressures and constraints of embedded financial orthodoxy (see Cerny, 1993b, 2000b and c). In the case of Mexico, the attempts to commodify relations of production via deregulation, privatization, the shift from welfare to workfare principles, fiscal austerity, and so forth, has not only exposed the economy to more rigorous international competition but has also compromised the social reproduction of over half the population. The latter have found themselves falling through the extremely thin threads of a rapidly unraveling welfare net, resulting in a process that has seriously undermined the government's legitimacy required to maintain neoliberal policy continuity aimed at signaling a sound investment environment to financial markets. These conflicting domestic-international policy goals, which Geoffrey Underhill refers to as the key contradiction of the state as a 'schizoid institution' (1997), act as both hallmark and key impetus in bringing about new forms of state intervention.

4. Crisis of the Mexican developmental state

What distinguishes one state form from another – whether a developmental state or its AIC counterpart – is foremost the national specific form of capital accumulation and its corresponding political regime.[38] Mexico's ISI was characterized by capital-intensive production primarily for domestic consumption, high forms of protectionism, and heavily dependent on both foreign technology and investment. This accumulation pattern was accompanied by a developmental state, whose material and ideological bases rested upon the so-called 'Revolutionary Myth' aimed at the powerful labor sectors and national capitals. Mexico's Revolutionary Myth, or what Kevin Middlebrook refers to as 'revolutionary nationalism' (1995), was a fusion of nationalism and a commitment to socio-economic transformation that included some of the following features: the steady belief in the principle of the trickle-down theory; the acceptance of the cruel dilemma – that is, prioritizing industrialization/economic modernization before democracy; the belief that the Institutional Revolutionary Party (PRI) and government corporatist structures represented the interests of the average Mexicans (peasants and workers). In this light, the ISI model, which was based on capital as opposed to labor intensive production so as to reap higher and quicker profit margins, was legitimized by capitals by playing on the anti-imperialist sentiment of the Revolutionary Myth, with such rhetorical programs as the Mexicanization Policy, which requires that Mexican nationals hold majority ownership of enterprises in key sectors in the economy (Hellman, 1978: 61–2).

The form of state was characterized by an authoritarian regime based on a one-party control by the PRI, corporatism, high levels of state ownership in strategic activities in such areas as communications, petroleum and basic petrochemicals, railroad transportation, and banking. Taken together, these features allowed the government not only to act as regulator and employer, but also as direct investor. Cheap and abundant labor and credit, subsidized goods and services, lax taxation standards, and so forth, provided the developing industrial sectors with key inputs at low and stable prices. Owing to the highly exclusionary nature of capital-intensive industrialization, corporatism was an integral facet of the developmental state. As Diane Davis explains, through corporatist structures the PRI not only separated subordinate classes from each other, but also linked them to the state in ways that undermined their independent capacities for struggle against capitals or the state. Mexico's corporate political system helped to provide the institutional and ideological glue for pacts between the state, capital and workers (both urban and rural). This arrangement gave voice and power to national capital, as it brought national capital into the realm of the political sphere since it legitimized highly controlled subordinate class demands, thereby limiting interclass struggle (1993: 66).

In the mid-1970s, it had become increasingly apparent that Mexico's ISI model was only sustainable through frequent and large infusions of foreign credit largely from US-based banks. As the ISI entered further into crisis, so too did its vulnerability to external shocks, such as the Federal Reserve Bank's substantial interest rate hike from 1979 to 1981, which led to a mass exodus of capital from Mexico and whose apogee took the form of the 1982 balance-of-payments crisis, or more popularly referred to as the 1982 debt crisis. Parallel to this breakdown of the particular mode of capital accumulation in Mexico, the developmental state form also entered into crisis.

5. Toward a Mexican competition state

After the debt crisis, the Mexican state could no longer jump-start its economy by priming either public investment or current expenditures.

The penurious public piggy bank also precluded the use of incentive programs that necessitated government outlays (e.g., export or investment subsidies). This meant that capital investments and capital repatriation had to be stimulated by other means: luring capital inflows via the so-called demonstration effect. The latter refers to opening up the economy through a firm commitment to an EPI strategy. In what follows, I shall consider the changes of state interventionism in Mexico by leaning on Cerny's defining features of a competition state, that is, four interlocking policy changes that rose to the top of agenda-setting in the AIC states (Cerny and Evans, 2000a; Cerny, 1999: 10ff., see also Evans's Chapter 4 in this volume). Let us now turn to the first of the four features of the competition state.

6. Controlling inflation and neoliberal monetarism

The first policy modification of AIC states has been an emphasis on the control of inflation and general neoliberal monetarism (supply side economics) aimed at non-inflationary growth. This type of state interventionism is characterized by the reversal of the relative priorities of monetary and fiscal policy, that is, tighter monetary policy is pursued alongside looser fiscal policy through tax cuts (Cerny 1999). Although Mexico conforms to this first hallmark of a competition state, it is important to underline that this policy shift differs from the AIC model in that it was largely initiated by external political forces and geared primarily toward debt reduction.

In contrast with AICs, neoliberal monetarism was not a homegrown phenomenon that arose from an ideological backlash against Keynesianism. Additionally, unlike the AICs, who enjoyed relatively more policy leeway in dealing with the effects of the crisis, such as what some refer to as US President Reagan's Military Keynesianism, the economic circumstances in which the Mexican government found itself was presented in such a manner as to preclude any viable options other than to attempt to bring its runaway inflation rates under control via extremely high interest rates and fiscal austerity.[39] Moreover, in comparison with the method employed by the Group of Seven (G-7) countries during the late 1970s and early 1980s, the IMF argued that Mexico's exchange rate system was too volatile to use money targeting to influence prices and output (IMF, 1992). Instead the Fund reasoned that, in order to ensure required levels of new foreign investment, the Mexican government would have to allocate resources in accordance with global market signals such as prices, exchange rates and incomes. Washington's understanding of policy reform (see Williamson, 1990: 5ff., 1993: IMF, 1993: 2) was aimed primarily at increasing debt service capacities through export expansion and import compression, so that the overextended US-based banks could be repaid (Kapstein, 1994).

Striving to be a model debtor would prove to be politically difficult. Tight fiscal discipline, for example, weakened already thin social programs and reduced the resources for subsidies to favored groups, particularly in urban centers. Likewise the cozy relations between banks and businesses gave way to more market-dominated lending. Unsurprisingly, established interests in the state were quite reluctant to give way to neoliberal restructuring including, for example, the domestic financial oligopoly and indigenous agricultural and industrial capitals who produced for the domestic market.[40] Likewise, since the success of restructuring presupposed a huge amount of foreign capital investment to aid the transition to EPI, the state has held the door wide open to transnational capitals, especially from the US. The power of these groups has increased substantially within the Mexican social relations of production and state. At the same time, neoliberal policies were eroding the PRI's traditional bastions of support, such as state-subsidized unions, on whose support the PRI was particularly dependent in pushing through its neoliberal programs.

Seen from the above angle, President de la Madrid's post-crisis economic modernization program was an attempt to appeal to Mexico's international investors and creditors while practicing brokerage politics domestically (Story, 1986). Clearly such a program would be costly, both economically and politically. The government made up for lost sources of international revenue by increased domestic borrowing, primarily by issuing government treasury bonds, or CETES. Unsurprisingly this expansion of domestic debt helped fuel an annual inflation rate that by 1987 had reached 180 per cent. The high interest rates thus necessary to attract savings meant, in turn, higher payments on the government-issued, peso-denominated CETES and a resultant increase in the public deficit. From 1982 to 1988 total foreign debt amounted to an average of 61 percent of the GDP (IMF, 1992; Gurría and Fadl, 1995).

In 1986, the banks disciplined the government by refusing to become involved in the rollover of debt packages. The unregulated global financial markets meant that the banks were able to sell third-world debt in the secondary markets for a fraction of their face value to investors. The US government, under the auspices of the IMF, stepped in to cover the remaining bank loans. The result of this was that the Mexican government's financing requirements were to be derived from official lending and global security markets. This is evident by the fact that, the majority of capital inflows would arrive in the form of portfolio investment, mostly in the Mexican stock market. From 1990 to 1993 Mexico's stock market rose 436 per cent (Strange, 1998). To suck in financial flows, as well as to combat inflation (a key element in ensuring the former), the government set extremely high interest rates. From 1980 to 1989, the banking system modified weekly the interest rate, which rose steadily to the point of historical highs (Mendez, 1994: 247).

To demonstrate the government's commitment to the implementation of fiscal discipline, public investment was drastically cut. In 1988, for example, investment levels hit an all time post-Second World War nadir, which in turn greatly affected the maintenance and expansion of Mexico's infrastructure. Despite this, however, domestic debt was hovering at around 18.5 per cent of GDP in 1988 and it became necessary to signal creditworthiness by getting tougher on non-interest expenditures and government revenues. Owing to deteriorating state–labor relations, the government set out to devise several wage and price pacts in order to muster support for policies of fiscal restraint. During the late 1980s prices were regulated through a co-operation mechanism of a tripartite 'regulation-by-agreement' embedded in the Economic Solidarity Pact (PSE) and the subsequent Pact for Economic Stability and Growth (PECE), both of which were a kind of truce between labor and the government before the 1988 elections (Álvarez and Mendoza, 1993).

Due in part to its membership in GATT, and, in part, to paltry capital inflows, the government scrapped its policy of setting official prices (universal subsidization) at the beginning of 1987 in order to boost business confidence. In 1990 and again in 1991, the state lifted price controls on many products and made price setting more flexible. These steps resulted in a backlash from labor, especially considering the buying power of the minimum wage fell by some 40 per cent between 1980 and 1987. After numerous long and bitter strikes, the government eventually conceded to raising the minimum wage, albeit to only a fraction of what labor was demanding. Regardless of how unpopular these policies were, however, they seemed to be partly justified by their success: from 1987 to 1993, inflation tumbled and short-term economic growth had been achieved.

Given that the Washington Consensus held that competitive real exchange rate is the first essential element of an outward-oriented economic policy, in the late 1980s, Mexico wished to demonstrate its adherence to this goal by anchoring its exchange rate to the US dollar. This resulted in a strategy of overvalued real peso, the negative effects of which were made evident in Mexico's trade figures. Between 1987 and 1993, for instance, exports rose by a healthy 88 per cent but imports rose by an even larger 247 per cent, which translated into a trade deficit of approximately $13.5 billion by 1993 (Pastor, 1999: 212). To finance this trade imbalance, Mexico increased its dependency on foreign capital by converting much of its short-term peso-denominated CETES debt to dollar-denominated Tesobonos (Mexican government securities) in mid-1994. The latter constituted only 6 per cent of the total foreign holding of government securities in December 1993; only a year later these new financial instruments amounted to about half of Mexico's entire foreign debt (Pastor 1999; Strange 1998). However, when payments were due access to international capital markets dried up and the glass floor upon which the economy rested was shattered. By mid-1995, output was running 10 per cent *below* its level a year earlier, private capital spending had collapsed and employment had declined sharply. Clearly these economic circumstances did not signal a favorable business environment, given that many of

Mexico's multiple rolled-over bank loans were officially deemed non-viable (BIS 1996: 40ff.)

7. Shift from macroeconomic to microeconomic governance

The second characteristic of a neoliberal competition state is the shift from macroeconomic (e.g., objectives include full employment, economic growth and avoidance of inflation, balance-of-payments equilibrium, fiscal and monetary policy) to microeconomic interventionism as reflected not only in deregulation and industrial policy, but also in new social policy initiatives such as welfare-to-workfare schemes (Cerny, 1999). This policy shift was not evident in the Mexican case. Instead there has been a growing importance of micro-interventionism alongside sound macroeconomic policies. That is to say, owing to both the high conditionality tied to its loans from the IMF and Mexico's growing reliance on the secondary markets, the government continued to adhere to the emphasis placed on supplyside macroeconomic policy prescribed by Washington (Stiglitz, 2002). However, reflecting policy priorities in the US, Mexico was also encouraged to complement its macroeconomic policy with micro-interventionism targeted at the marketization of the social relations of production (such as deregulation and privatization) and the implementation of the larger continental rationalization strategy.

To attract foreign investment and reverse flight capital, the government undertook a series of deregulation and property reform measures that removed and simplified Mexico's plethora of bureaucratic regulations regarding business, particularly in the *maquiladora* sector. The state overhauled existing laws to allow majority foreign ownership in a number of sectors in the economy. Trade liberalization, which began in 1985, was the most far-reaching of all reforms undertaken by the Mexican state. President Salinas's National Development Plan (Poder Ejecutivo Federal, 1989) closely mirrored the Washington Consensus policies. After mid-1985, Mexico's industrial policy reflected the larger trade liberalization strategy as the government started dismantling its sector or firm-specific programs to promote industrial development, particularly in the auto parts industry, pharmaceutical industry and computer programs. Building on Mexico's membership of the GATT in 1986, the Plan called for trade liberalization as means for promoting specialization according to competitive advantage and combating inflation through international price competition. To overcome growing US protectionism and lowering levels of capital investment in the country, Mexico shifted its focus from a unilateral trade deregulation scheme to a trilateral free trade agreement with the US and later Canada in the form of NAFTA (Hart, 1990).

Financial liberalization, which began in 1988, included freeing interest rates, lifting credit controls and reserve requirements on private banks, shrinking the size of public development banks, and fully reprivatizing the commercial banks (Banco de México, 1990: 89–180). In 1990, supported by the interests of financiers and international manufacturers, President Salinas sent a constitutional amendment to Congress calling for the reprivatization of all banks. This move, premised on a commitment to low inflation rates, was part of a broad policy package designed to demonstrate the fact that Mexico was not only a safe investment site but also a preferred debtor nation. Of course, high interest rates had the effects of not only choking the economy but also inviting in speculative capital. Additionally, these reprivatization schemes, especially the establishment of a universal banking system, facilitated the integration of Mexico's financial system into the global political economy. By 2002 85 per cent of Mexico's banks were owned by foreigners from Canada, Spain, and the US – with the latter representing the largest takeover by US-based Citigroup ('Mexican Banks won't lend', *The Economist*, 10 October 2002).

By indicating that Mexico will not have to bear the burden of unexpected market shocks alone, the political strategy of economic integration *qua* external and internal deregulation added tremendous credibility to the new exchange rate regime. However, as Ilene Grabel (1999) astutely argues, the down-side of this new financial openness is the increased likelihood of a cross-border contagion, which is particularly disturbing in a country whose economy is marked by higher speculative capital formations than FDI and where the trend towards deteriorating current account deficits are prevalent (World Bank, 1998). Moreover, Grabel suggests that during panics, investors and lenders see emerging economies in an undifferentiated fashion, and thus Mexico is sentenced on the verdict of 'guilt by association' (1999).

Another pillar of microeconomic intervention was privatization. The largest and most politically significant privatizations occurred during the Salinas Administration, including banks and investment houses, telecommunications, air transportation, mining companies, steel producers, sugar mills, toll roads, and port facilities. From 1988 until 1994, for example, the number of state entities fell from 661 to 215. Despite the clear deterioration of Mexico's Revolutionary Myth, the government introduced an overhaul to Article 27 of the Constitution in 1992. This amendment privatized the preciously inalienable land grants enjoyed by the peasantry (*ejidos*) by permitting corporate and foreign ownership of former *ejido* agricultural lands, as well as joint ventures between *ejido* producers and business interests. The privatization of *ejidos* was undertaken to pander to the interests of the increasing presence of highly capitalized export agriculture sector, as opposed to the small peasant farmers who produce for the internal market. Apart from the goal of implementing more market-oriented forms of intervention, these policy changes represent a departure from agrarian policies originally designed either to pre-empt or control peasant insurgency within the corporatist structures of the state. The government strove to replace this traditional form of governance in the rural areas through the militarization of the public security system, which, in turn, did more harm than good to the state's ailing legitimation functions.

The agricultural sector was not the only sector affected by these reforms, for these privatization schemes also aggravated the relations with state-subsidized labor organizations, particularly the powerful CTM (industrial workers union). In several cases strikes have been used as the pretext to sell state enterprises and destroy unions simultaneously. The political ruling class remains dependent on labor's alliance in two key areas: (1) effective economic policy management whereby large, sustained cuts in real wages and fringe benefits were facilitated, and even partly legitimized, via the largely corrupt labor leadership's assistance in limiting rank-and-file demands; and (2) orderly presidential succession (Middlebrook, 1995: 300).

Despite these neoliberal strategies, overall medium-term economic growth was not achieved. Domestic debt was rapidly rising, and capital investment continued to contract (IMF, 1992). The policies of debt restructuring based on pro-market neoliberalism were not gaining consent from Mexicans, for high unemployment, falling real wages, and rising political conflict were far from the smooth equilibrium path of neoliberal tales (Pastor, 1999). The Mexican bourgeoisie was also distressed with the economic effects of modernization policies, particularly the increasing exposure to higher levels of international competition through trade liberalization without the security of government subsidization. The above-mentioned *pactos*, designed to bolster the cracking foundation of the corporatist compromise, failed to elicit the sought-after political support for the government's debt restructuring policies. This discontent was reflected in the federal elections in 1988 where many liberal middle-class voters, such as small and medium-sized business operators, shifted their support to the National Action Party (PAN), a right-wing, pro-business party, while a large number of working class Mexicans transferred their alliances to the then Democratic Front, which has now been renamed the Party of Democratic Revolution (PRD).

8. Transition from interventionism to strategic targeting

The third feature of an AIC competition state entails the transfer in focus of interventionism at the international level away from maintaining a range of strategic or basic economic activities aimed at retaining minimal economic self-sufficiency in key sectors, to a policy of flexible response to competitive conditions in a range of diversified and rapidly evolving international marketplaces (Cerny 1999). There is an observable shift from comparative advantage based on natural-resources endowments and factor proportions (i.e. capital–labor ratios) to competitive advantage based on so-called 'brain-power' industries, such as micro-electronics, biotechnology, the new materials industries, civilian aviation, telecommunications, and so forth (Thurow 1992: 45).

As I noted above, the Mexican state is moving towards retaining minimal economic self-sufficiency in key sectors. However, the very nature of NAFTA seems to preclude any move towards an economy based an indigenous form of flexible accumulation patterns. As the IMF itself notes, NAFTA is really about capital movements, transfer of technology, and location of production (1993: 18–19), which reproduces Mexico's technological dependence and reliance on large amounts of FDI. To date, Mexico's pro-competitive micro-industrial policy has simply meant further deregulation as opposed to any substantial investment in innovation-driven industry, which remains firmly rooted within the core countries such as the US. Thus, Mexico's comparative advantage continues to be its abundance of cheap and unskilled labor.

First, the nature of economic integration has been characterized by a *maquiladorization process*, or more plainly de-industrialization. As Kathryn Kopinak has suggested, the new industries in the *maquiladoras*, situated largely at the northern border, offer fewer jobs than the number lost from Mexican-owned industry and agriculture. Moreover, jobs in the *maquiladoras* are comparatively unskilled and poorly paid, which implies not only that workers have reduced purchasing power and thus increased economic inequality, but also that the internal domestic market has shrunk with the shift towards export production (1994: 150–1). Indeed, between the start of the peso crisis and July 1997, real wages in manufacturing fell by 39 per cent (Lustig, 1998: 210). What is more, the overlap in the US and Mexican export markets come with a built-in time bomb. As exports to the US have doubled, imports from the US have at least tripled, which predictably leads to more debt and current account problems, particularly since Mexico is using borrowed funds to pay for its imports. Further, the excessive net transfer of resources abroad made the economy extremely vulnerable to external shocks, particularly any deterioration in the terms of trade.

Second, to compete effectively against other emerging market economies, as well as AICs, for desperately needed capital inflows, the Mexican competition state must constantly seek to provide the most optimal credible investment environments for foreign investors and creditors, such as low taxation and social benefits, so as to retain and attract the highest amount of capital investment possible from the international financial markets (McConnel and MacPherson, 1994). The results of such competition have not been impressive. For one thing, capital investment remains inadequate vis-à-vis the existing public expenditure in the economy. For another, given the high interest rates and deregulated financial sector, capital flows are often speculative in nature to the detriment of Mexico's productive structure.

All this seems to imply that the short-term thinking of immediate financial gain takes precedence over the long-term thinking of industrial development. To illustrate, while FDI in actual production facilities increased by 57.6 per cent from 1989 to 1993, the more mobile portfolio investment rose by more than 8000 per cent, or 86.8 per cent of total foreign investment in Mexico (Pastor, 1999: 213). Speculative inflows render the economy vulnerable when these inflows suddenly reverse (as in the case of the 1994/95 peso crisis). More fundamentally, they increase the need of assigning high priority of the state to maintaining a favorable investment environment, particularly political stability, so that it may sustain its big current-account deficits. This situation becomes even more apparent when we consider that, within the framework of NAFTA, Mexico's trump card was its abundance of cheap and well-disciplined labor. Thus, containing heightening class conflicts was perceived as a linchpin in the overall strategy of attracting new foreign capital investment to maintain an overextended line of credit upon which the viability of neoliberal restructuring depended.

9. From welfarism to neoliberalism

The fourth and final characteristic of a neoliberal competition state refers to the shift in the focal point of party and governmental politics away from the general maximization of welfare within a nation (full-employment and the direct provision of public services) to the promotion of enterprises, innovation, and profitability in both private and public sectors (Cerny, 1999). How does the Mexican state correspond to this characteristic? From the perspective of the above mentioned policy constraints and pressures the Mexican state only conforms partly to its AIC counterpart. Concerning the move to promote private enterprises, the pressures of fiscal austerity forced a considerable decrease in public investment by between 53 and 87 per cent during the 1982–91 period (Lustig, 1998). Where government outlays were available, they were allocated towards providing the necessary infrastructure for transnational capitals involved in the significant 'inter-corporate' trade as opposed to the small and medium-size indigenous businesses. Given the capital-intensive nature of Mexico's productive structure, the country possesses a large reserve labor army and has never had comprehensive systems of unemployment insurance, or other forms of social overhead costs, which are repulsive to the potential investor. Despite growing levels of impoverishment in the 1980s and 1990s, the government did not implement sustained welfare programs. Such an endeavor would indeed involve an overhaul of the country's taxation system, increased debt, and would stand against the spirit of neoliberalism and the belief in the inherent justice of the market.

Although the government from 1988 began increasingly to champion social justice themes, President Salinas's reinvented notion of neoliberalism ('social liberalism') clearly broke from the revolutionary tradition as it did not reaffirm the legitimacy of *collective* social rights (Middlebrook, 1995: 304). The strategy of *social liberalism* was intended to give the appearance of a 'third-way' that aimed to avoid the failures of unfettered free-market capitalism and heavy-handed state intervention (cf. Giddens, 2001). In reality, the rhetoric of *social liberalism* was a form of social engineering designed to deflect the ongoing government involvement in the reorganizing social relations. This strategy was guided by the fatalistic assumption that globalization is both inevitable and unstoppable. In doing so, class-based choices inherent in neoliberal policy-making have become swept under the carpet. Moreover, with such slogans such as 'coming together' (*concertación*) of the Mexican people, as well as the common chant of AIC states, namely, 'globalization with a human face' (Cerny and Evans, 2000a) (or, in the Mexican case, *ajuste con rostro humano*), the government had hoped to portray itself not as a distributor of last resort; but rather, as a team leader who would guide Mexicans in the new competitive race. Moreover, the government sought to ensure political stability, which was a key prong in a credible investment environment, by implementing anti-poverty programs, such as the previously mentioned PRONASOL and, more recently (in mid-1997), the Program of Education, Health and Nutrition (PROGRESA). These programs were specifically aimed at appeasing and depoliticizing the increasing presence of resurgent popular movements, while generally acting as a bromide for the masses.

On the surface, through its promotion of innovation and efficiency, the government aimed to improve its bureaucratic decision-making via *technocratization* of the Mexican state. Neoliberal technocrats close to Salinas replaced more traditional *políticos* in the upper echelons of the government's bureaucracy and the locus of decision-making power shifted from more politically oriented institutions to the economic and financial entities of the government. The so-called *tecnócratas* are a managerial cadre class, whose common educational background, principally graduate training in economics in top US universities share a mutual conviction in the superiority of neoclassical economic instruments and belief in the market as a mechanism to allocate resources. Under the surface, and in light of the loss of majority of the PRI within Congress, this shift mirrored a Poulantzian 'refuge-centre' (1978) whereby the strategies of the top decision-makers could remain insulated from both other bureaucratic elements and societal interests. This has had the effect of making these policy decisions impersonal and above the reach of social forces.

Although in the later 1990s it became more difficult for the PRI to push through its neoliberal project, owing to its diminished power in the legislative arena and thus the increased presence of logrolling, the PRI was usually able to realize its policies through strong-arming and concessions. As Kenneth Shadlen (1999: 398) has demonstrated, from the late 1980s to the 1997 elections, debates over institutions and debates over policies displayed similar patterns: 'the president's original proposals are heavily criticized by the two main opposition parties [PAN and PRD] ... the opposition appears united in rejecting the president's proposals and on rough versions of counter-proposals; the president splits the opposition, negotiates directly with the PAN, and garners the necessary support to pass modified versions of the original proposals.'

However the reason for the above is not to be found in the usual explanations of Mexico's authoritarian regime; but instead in the historically determining and developing policy constraints associated with the wider debt restructuring strategies. At the heart of the relative power of the PRI within the legislative process lay the balance of class forces between transnational capital interests and the Bankers' Alliance, both of which stood firmly behind the PRI, and the weaker petty bourgeoisie who largely supported the PAN. Furthermore, both PRI and PAN shared the same policy-stance for upholding neoliberal values, with the PAN often characterized as more conservative than the PRI. Current President, Vicente Fox, the successful PAN candidate for the 2000 elections, has even been heralded as being more '*IMF than the IMF*'. With the PRD largely acknowledging basic tenets of the neocliberal approach, it appears that all major parties share the same commitment to providing the 'appropriate business climate' based on the prerogatives of embedded financial orthodoxy.

10. Conclusion

There is ample evidence to conclude that Mexico has adopted the broad characteristics of an AIC competition state. Even so, this neoliberal state form seems to rest upon wobbly footing, especially with respect to socioeconomic indicators and political legitimation factors. On the one hand, there exist relatively higher speculative, short-term portfolio investments than longer-term FDI in industrial production. On the other, real wages in Mexico are lower today than they were before the 1982 crisis, income inequality is higher, and although macro-economic recovery was impressive in 1996 the social effects of the 1995 experience were harrowing: mass underemployment is rampant, and stands alongside a reduction around 35–50 per cent of real value of wages and a deepening of poverty, which is estimated to affect 54 per cent of the population (Veltmeyer *et al.*, 1996: 139; Kopinak, 2004).

Mexico's general adherence through the 1980s and 1990s to the IMF structural adjustment policies, as well as its commitment to regulations and rules inscribed in the NAFTA, have resulted in a more international-oriented focus, particularly its growing dependence on the international financial markets. At the same time, this international focus restricts the government's scope in responding flexibly to domestic problems, particularly conflicting demands from labor and capitals. Although the neoliberal model has succeeded in strengthening transnational capitals at the expense of trade unions and other domestic interests, the inherent tension between domestic and international exigencies has led to a rather deep-seated paradox: on the one hand, the political ruling class and capitals in Mexico hoped to pursue the strategy of continental rationalization in order to overcome the barriers that emerge in capital accumulation, whose success depends on the attraction and retention of high levels of largely speculative capital inflows. On the other hand, the very nature of NAFTA, namely its tendency towards *maquiladorization* of the economy, exacerbates the already high levels of political instability and socioeconomic fragmentation, and thus perpetuates the threat of capital flight and investment strikes.

It is important to grasp that the 'accomplishments' of the neoliberal assault are class-based strategic reactions to the global financial markets, whose dominance was effectively augmented through state-led deregulatory measures. In short, the emergence of the competition state and its underlying impetus of embedded financial orthodoxy are not natural, logical occurrences; but rather human constructs that are neither automatic 'givens' nor irreversible. It appears that struggle is in the process of eroding the tenuous base of the neoliberal policy-transfer in Mexico. Although the neoliberal assault has been successful in repaying Mexico's international creditors and making those capitals involved in intercorporate production and trade within the NAFTA zone even more prosperous, it has been equally effective in weakening the thin wire of political legitimacy on which the state continually straddles the ever-widening and deepening divide of rich and poor in Mexico (Kopinak, 2004; Soederberg, 2004). Indeed, the shaky foundations of deteriorating forms of social justice and increased financial vulnerability, which underpin both an EPI mode of accumulation and competition state, translate into a bumpy and uncertain ride for the continuity of neoliberalism.

Further reading

Dominguez, J.I. and C. Lawson (eds) (2004) *Mexico's Pivotal Democratic Election*. San Diego, University of California: Centre for US–Mexican Studies.

Hellman, J.A. (1994) *Mexican Lives*. New York: New Press.

Middlebrook, K. and E. Zepeda (eds) *Confronting Development: Assessing Mexico's Economic and Social Policy Changes*. San Diego, University of California: Centre for US–Mexican Studies.

Otero, G. (ed.) (2004) *Mexico in Transition: Neoliberal Globalism, the State and Civil Society*. London: Zed Books.

Useful websites

<www.iabd.org>   Inter-American Development Bank

<www.mexonline.com>   Mexico Government & Politics

<www.maquilasolidarity.org>   Maquila Solidarity Network

<www.nafta-sec-alena.org>   NAFTA Secretariat

10
Globalization and the Internalization of Neoliberalism: the Genesis and Trajectory of Societal Restructuring in Chile

Marcus Taylor

1. Introduction

In approaching the debates over globalization, neoliberal hegemony and the 'competition state', the case of Chile is particularly instructive not least because far-reaching neoliberal reform long precedes the recent academic interest in globalization. Following the profound restructuring drive initiated under the dictatorial regime of Augusto Pinochet in the mid-1970s Chile has consistently been upheld as a pioneer in the application of neoliberal policies. The Chilean experience of neoliberalism, therefore, begins before the pivotal rise of Thatcherism and Reaganism in the centres of global capitalism, before the unrestrained global propagation of neoliberalism by international financial institutions, and before dramatic changes in the architecture of the international political economy that fashioned the extraordinary disciplinary power accredited to present-day transnational capitals. In other words, Chile began 'internalising neoliberalism' before globalization, as commonly applied, existed. This is not to suggest that the forces associated with globalization have not comprised increasingly pivotal moments in conditioning the actions of the Chilean state over the past two and a half decades. The global propagation of neoliberal policy ideals through various multilateral and national organizations alongside the coercion of economic relations imposed by relatively footloose transnational capitals are rightly understood to lie at the heart of the contemporary global political economy (see the introductory chapter to this volume for a systematic account of these debates). However, an analysis of the Chilean experience helps us understand that the process of 'internalizing globalization' is more complex than simply ascribing causation to a coercive external economic environment. In contrast, the rise of neoliberalism in Chile must be understood as an ongoing process of social transformation that has attempted to reshape the very fabric of Chilean society in order to re-establish the conditions for successful capital accumulation.

The genesis and trajectory of neoliberalism in Chile can be divided into three primary sub-periods, each of which is characterized by attempts to reformulate the relations between state and society and to redefine the manner of integration between the national economy and the world market. First the chapter examines the crisis tendencies associated with the stagnation of structuralist-inspired development strategy in the late 1960s and early 1970s. It highlights the growing tensions that led to the violent imposition of dictatorship and the first experiments with monetarism and neoliberal policy reform. Secondly, the chapter turns to the period of the debt crisis and a subsequent reorientation of the neoliberal trajectory in the mid- and late-1980s. Finally, examination of the period following the restoration of democratically elected governments in 1990 reveals a further modification of the neoliberal model labelled 'growth with equity'. Prior to these more empirically orientated sections, however, a brief synopsis of the analytical approach that informs this contribution is elaborated.

2. State, capital accumulation and crisis

With its complex position as both a subject and object of neoliberal restructuring, a concept of the state is pivotal for any analysis of 'internalizing globalization'. This is particularly evident in the Chilean case where the Pinochet regime was the predominant instigator of the restructuring process, much of which was directed against the historically developed institutional forms of the state. With this in mind, we need to be precise in our understanding of the state and its dynamics of action. As it appears, the state constitutes an ensemble of institutions and organizations within a geographically delineated area whose socially constituted function is 'to define and enforce collectively binding decisions on the members of a society in the name of their common interest or will' (Jessop, 1990: 341). In this institutional sense, the state is often referred to as a regime with an emphasis on the structures of political authority and the forms of mediation between these structures (e.g. the government/executive, judiciary, legislative, coercive apparatus, etc.). However, it is analytically important to retain a concept of the state-system as preceding the various individual moments of the state. As Peter Burnham suggests: 'It is the concept of the state-system as being prior to the government, the civil service, the military, judiciary, and other civil organisational forms taken by the state (even though the state has no existence independently of these forms) that makes it possible to understand the complexity and possible disjunctures which may arise between these forms' (Burnham, 1994: 6).

To posit a concept of the state-system as prior to the tangible institutional forms that it assumes is to problematize the form of the state in capitalist society (cf. Clarke, 1988). The modern state was historically constructed within and rests upon capitalist social relations, which can be characterized by the systematic need for those that own capital to expand its value through profit-making activities (capital accumulation). Within capitalist society the very reproduction of society – including the state-system itself – hinges on the relatively smooth continuance of this process. At a very basic level this entails that the state-system as a whole is subjected to considerable pressures to help secure the social conditions for capital accumulation. Nevertheless, far from being a smooth and harmonious process, the accumulation of capital necessarily produces notable social conflicts and strains. On the one hand, the pressures to maintain profits repeatedly generate conflicts between capital and labor within the production process. On the other hand, capitalist society suffers from an intrinsic tendency to subordinate social and environmental needs to the dictates of profit appropriation. These factors ensure that capital accumulation is not a harmonious process but instead gives rise to a range of social struggles including industrial strife, social movement activities and pressure group politics.

Tensions of this nature become most intense whenever the process of capital accumulation is hindered and a crisis period erupts. In such periods sluggish economic growth, the deterioration of the balance of payments, intense fiscal constraints, the threat of capital flight, and increased social unrest place severe strains on the state-system. State institutions are pressured to help resolve the crisis by securing the social conditions for the expanded accumulation of capital, while simultaneously attempting to manage the antagonisms inherent to this process. The latter task at times requires them to discipline particular social groups – such as workers, social movements but also occasionally particular businesses – to force them to restrain their actions within the limits of continued capital accumulation. The uneven nature of these pressures, however, can often prompt different responses from different aspects of the state system. Crisis thereby generates considerable strains within the state-system itself. Moreover, reasserting the conditions for capital accumulation can also prove a task that state managers do not effectively achieve, potentially leading to a generalized crisis of the state-system, such as occurred in Chile in 1973. This focus on crisis – and the manner by which state managers and institutions react to the inherent political, social and economic pressures – helps us to situate the rise of neoliberalism in Chile as a response to the dramatic crisis of the early 1970s, as well as to pinpoint the dynamics that lay behind its further evolution in the 1980s and 1990s.

3. Social crisis and the emergence of authoritarian neoliberalism

By the later 1960s signs of crisis within the Chilean political economy had become manifested through the relative stagnation of industries created under the structuralist development strategy of import substitution industrialization (ISI).[41] With copper providing almost 75 per cent of Chilean export-earnings in the postwar period, capital accumulation in Chile had been consistently vulnerable to the vicissitudes of world market prices for this commodity. In the mid-1960s the price of copper began a slow but steady descent. More immediate cause for concern, however, was to be found in a lack of dynamism in industrial sectors, particularly those orientated towards the domestic market operating under the protection of high tariff walls. Christian Democrat president Eduardo Frei's (1964–69) initial deepening of the structuralist development model through increased state credits to industry, infrastructural investments, agrarian reform and moderate social programmes designed to foment domestic demand did not fundamentally alleviate this stagnation. Moreover, the failure of the economy to respond to the new initiatives meant that the resources the state enjoyed were progressively more restricted precisely at a moment when escalating social mobilization was pressing for greater material compromises such as expanded social programmes. On the one hand, a multitude of independent labour and social movements augmented their pressure upon the regime for redistributive measures. On the other, support for the Socialist and Communist parties increased significantly until it reached one-third of the electorate (Roddick, 1989). The regime responded in 1968 with a shift to the right, cutting social expenditure and employing the security forces to crack down on the more explicit forms of popular mobilization (Stallings, 1978).

The dissolution of Frei's middle ground and the resulting polarization of Chilean society were sharply manifested in the general elections of 1970. Socialist candidate Salvador Allende won a narrow victory with 36.6 per cent of the vote, as compared to the Conservative candidate who received 35.2. Allende's programme of nationalization and increasing state intervention in distributional issues, however, was not able to overcome the growing crisis. Predicated upon price controls and general wage hikes, this demand-driven growth strategy initially served to increase production in domestic consumer industries. However, the inflation rate also began an ominous rise. Nationalization of key industries – particularly that of copper – at first provided the regime with a reasonably vibrant state sector. Nonetheless, the tendency to respond to growing industrial conflicts by nationalization brought many smaller and less profitable industries into the state's purview. Moreover, political uncertainty surrounding the regime and the trend towards nationalization made capitals located in the domestic consumption sector extremely reluctant to invest, even to cover the renewal of machinery necessary for the production process (Fortin, 1985).

In sum, while Allende's government acted under the banner of moving towards socialism, the restructuring served to deepen the state's economic role and expand redistribution within a capitalist framework. The upshot of these actions was an undermining of the basis for capital accumulation and the unleashing of even greater crisis tendencies. Although the Allende government prepared to moderate some of its reforms, other elements of the state-system (specifically the armed forces) began to mobilize in a contrary fashion. They sought to return the state to within the limits of renewed capital accumulation. With the crisis of accumulation deepening and the US government openly supporting the growing anti-Allende forces, the military emerged from the barracks on 11 September 1973 and unleashed a bloody yet successful coup. Through the overthrow of the Allende government, the violent repression of its actual and suspected supporters, and the banning of labour unions and opposition parties the authoritarian regime physically removed the immediate political dimension of the crisis. Nonetheless, the economic and social crisis remained and would elicit increasingly radical solutions from the new regime.

Despite the severity of the crisis the first year and a half of the military regime witnessed a relatively gradualist approach to macroeconomic management that sought to normalize – but not fundamentally change – Chilean economic structures. Under the banner of reasserting the primacy of the market, the new regime lowered price and wage controls from the Frei and Allende periods, and began to selectively reduce import tariffs. Social expenditure was also cut by over 20 per cent (Torche, 2000). Nonetheless, continued triple digit inflation and persistent economic stagnation pressed the military regime into adopting a more radical approach. Under the increasingly direct leadership of General Augusto Pinochet the military regime began to follow the prescription of a group of Chilean neoclassicist economists based at the Universidad Católica. These were the 'Chicago Boys', so-called owing to their training by Chicago-schooled monetarists such as Milton Freidman, who had gained some prestige by providing business interests and the Chilean right with an alternative economic and social platform during the Allende period. Their influence in the Universidad Catolica dated back to the mid-1950s and they enjoyed close connections with the major economic groups of the period. During the Pinochet period they would frequently switch between technocratic positions within the regime to posts within the conglomerates, therein providing a conduit for information exchange during a period when the regime was closed to formal dialogue even with business organizations.

The Chicago Boy orthodox neoliberal formula for societal transformation established a clear plan for setting Chilean capitalism back on its feet through a dramatic reversal of the state's role in society. The regime initially shied from implementing the full shock therapy called for by the monetarists, owing to the foreseeable social dislocation caused by the austerity element of this programme and the opposition of industrialists who were threatened by a dramatic reduction of tariffs and a collapse in domestic demand. However, the relentless nature of the crisis and the growing influence of several large conglomerates, whose position in international capital circuits and heavy concentration of liquid assets placed, them in a better position to survive or even profit from stabilization, paved the way for more radical methods. It is important to note that the internalization of neoliberal ideology by the military regime was not predicated solely on its supposed economic functionality. On the contrary, there existed considerable doubt that these throw-back ideas to an earlier stage of capitalism could be effective. At this historical juncture, long before neoliberalism had assumed the global hegemonic mantle that it presently enjoys, Keynesian assumptions regarding the necessity of state intervention to mitigate crisis were prevalent and the idea of a minimalist state seemed bizarre and suspect. Nevertheless, neoliberalism is not merely economic in nature, but rather envisages a wider societal transformation that necessarily comprises economic, social and political dimensions. This was specifically recognized by the Pinochet regime, which pronounced that it wanted to give Chile 'a new institutional basis ... to rebuild the country morally, institutionally and materially' (Taylor, 1998: 39). Rather than being a purely economic doctrine, Chilean neoliberalism emerged as a response to the *social* crisis that had reached a pinnacle in the Allende years. Withdrawing the state from historically developed roles – such as price controls, wage agreements, welfare policies, industrial policy – and reinserting the primacy of the market not only offered a possible solution to the economic manifestation of crisis, but also offered a manner of societal depoliticization by obliterating the circumstances in which the state had become the primary locus for political struggle.

In 1975 the full fury of an austerity programme was unleashed with remaining price controls abolished, wages left to deteriorate under hyperinflationary conditions, and a dramatic reduction in both tariffs and public expenditure. The result was a profound contraction of demand, spelling the demise of many small and medium firms, and a deep recession with per capita GDP contracting by a staggering 14.4 per cent. Unemployment climbed above 15 per cent and real wages collapsed, with the share of wages in the national product declining from 62.8 per cent in 1972 – one of the highest in Latin America – to 41.1 per cent in 1976 – one of the lowest (Petras and Leiva, 1994: 26). This dramatic increase in the rate of exploitation of labour was a fundamental pillar in the long-term recovery of Chilean capitalism (cf. Taylor, 2002). As such, although the austerity package did not restore an immediate macroeconomic equilibrium as intended (cf. Fortín, 1985), it nonetheless laid the basis for the greater transformation of Chilean society along the lines of the emerging neoliberal consensus within the military regime.

A central aspect of the neoliberal strategy was a profound alteration in the manner of articulation between domestic and global capital. The structural-ist doctrine of national-developmentalism, in its quest for domestic indus-trial expansion, sanctified a form of development in which the weaknesses of domestic production were to be overcome through state mechanisms. The latter sought to protect both domestically located productive capitals by means of tariff barriers and also to take a leading role in stimulating invest-ment through a variety of measures from tax relief to direct ownership. The neoliberal solution was more radical. The Chicago Boy analysis of the stag-nation and crisis of the Chilean economy centred on the rigidities that had developed within the economy owing to the limited mobility of capital. They related the latter to the stasis of capital in relatively ossified productive forms that entailed not only sizeable outlays on fixed capital but also an inflexible relation with the labour force governed by the historically devel-oped mediation of the state. Hence, the essence of the neoliberal solution was a shift in the state policy in order to prioritize capital as money rather than capital as production.[42]

A new dominance of capital in money-form was forged through the Pinochet regime's deregulation of both trade and finance. The implications were felt across Chilean society as liberalization in this manner went hand-in-hand with a profound reorganization of the Chilean productive structure. With respect to trade, by June 1979 the maximum tariff had been reduced to just 10 per cent. This soon prompted a reorientation of capital away from consumption good production for the domestic market and towards newly emergent export industries, particularly primary produce such as fruit, fish, wine, lumber and metals. Intrinsic to this process was a mass decomposition of the labour force, which was ejected from the crisis-stricken industrial and state sectors, and its partial recomposition as unemployed workers were absorbed into the informal sector, the export processing industries and service sector (Martínez and Díaz, 1996). Concurrently, a state-sponsored reversal of the land reform process served to transfer terrain away from the recipient peasantry toward large agro-capitalist enterprises.

In the financial sphere, alongside privatizing banks and freeing internal interest rates, the regime also opened the way for foreign capital to flow into domestic enterprise (see Table 10.1). From 1977 the regime enabled

Table 10.1   Distribution of payments to capital by main sectors (in %)

Years	Agriculture	Industry	Trade	Banking
1960–70	10.5	30.0	22.4	1.0
1981	7.3	20.9	27.8	18.0

Source: Fortín, 1985: 186.

domestic banks to borrow directly from international financial markets. One consequence was the newfound ability of domestic banks to borrow at international rates and re-lend domestically at hugely inflated levels, making incredible profits and therein helping consolidate the increasingly important position of the financial sector (Fortin, 1985; Soederberg, 2002).

Concurrently the few capitals that had access to international finance were also able to use this credit to buy up industries in the new export sectors and also to purchase state industries that the regime was privatizing at greatly subsidized prices. As such, this period witnessed the emergence of the 'grupos económicos', large conglomerates such as Luksic and Angelina, rooted in the financial sector and with vast yet constantly changing portfolios of investments (cf. Fazio, 2000). Alongside the re-entry of foreign firms into the mining sector, this concentration of capital led to the domination of all key sectors of the Chilean economy by a handful of domestic economic groups and multinationals (see Table 10.2).

The prioritization of finance, however, also proved to be a significant cause of the succeeding crisis. By the late 1970s inflation was reduced but not tamed, and GDP growth levels above eight per cent marked something of a recovery (although in 1979 GDP per capita remained only 95.5 per cent of that of 1971 (Fortín, 1985; 156)). Despite the proclamation of an 'economic miracle' by the advocates of neoliberalism, the largely illusionary joy was quickly dispelled. Much of the investment associated with this boom had been ploughed into unproductive and short-term ventures consistent with high-interest rates. Moreover, in order to compete against the free entry of foreign consumer goods, surviving domestic industries had borrowed heavily at high rates in an unsuccessful attempt to regain their market position by improving their methods of production. This even affected the new dynamic sectors as the sustained inflow of international capital caused an appreciation of the peso vis-à-vis the dollar that cut into the profits of

Table 10.2   Concentration in the export sector by 1988

Industry	Number of large firms	Industry share
Mining	7	97.1
Agriculture	8	80.6
Forest products	5	78.4
Fish products	6	51.1
Food	6	67.3
Wine and beverage	2	70.2
Wood	7	78.6
Paper, cellulose	2	90.0
Chemical products	2	71.4

Source: Petras and Leiva, 1994: 36.

export-orientated industries. Under these conditions, alongside a drop of commodity prices on the world market and a mammoth hike in international interest rates, the Chilean economy plunged into deep recession in 1982 and the debts of Chilean capitals soon became unmanageable.

4. From debt crisis to the second wave of neoliberalism

The military regime was in profound disarray when the full force of the debt crisis rocked Chile. State mangers based around the centralized authority of Pinochet quickly removed the original Chicago Boys from their positions and introduced a younger, more flexible, group of neoliberal technocrats. Production fell by 16.7 per cent, investment by over 40 per cent, official unemployment topped 26 per cent, and the economy was propped up only by sustained state intervention. Faced with a profound crisis of accumulation the regime was propelled into action in spite of the neoliberal rhetoric of state non-interventionism. Intervention took three immediate forms: the takeover of collapsing firms by the state, the socialization of the massive debts run up by Chilean capitals, and the introduction of large-scale emergency work programmes that offered less than subsistence wages to masses of unemployed workers. In desperation, the regime also signed a stand-by agreement with the IMF in 1983, a move that helped to stabilize the neoliberal orientation of the regime under conditions of crisis. In return for the influx of credit, the regime repledged its commitment to neoliberal orthodoxy, not only agreeing to uphold the foreign debts of all state companies and major domestic debtors but also to undo the emergency rise in tariffs implemented in 1982, cut state expenditure and initiate another wave of privatizations. Notably, this remanifestation of crisis provided the conditions under which real wages underwent a second drastic decline. When it came economic recovery was not translated into rising wages but, on the contrary, real wages continued to decline throughout the decade, and in 1987 remained at only 86 per cent of their 1970 level (Coloma and Rojas, 2000; Stallings, 2001).

Under the banner of 'pragmatic neoliberalism' the regime began to deepen many of the existing reforms through amplified forms of state intervention and, therein, enhance the neoliberal social transformation ongoing since 1975. By socializing the debts of the private sector, moderately augmenting its activities in financial regulation and increasing its infrastructural investment, the state took a greater role in providing the conditions for expanded accumulate after the debacle of the 1970s and early 1980s. This strategy has been hailed as a success by the promoters of neoliberalism on a global scale, and was behind the proclamation of a 'Chilean Model' worthy of emulation in the developing world (cf. Martínez and Díaz, 1996). Oblivious to the pronounced social polarization and deprivation of the period, such acclamation was largely based on rapid GDP growth, which averaged 6.7 per cent

annually over the 1985 to 1989 period. The latter is, in turn, largely attribut-
able to integration into international capital circuits, with a large expansion
of the quantity and value of raw material exports, particularly copper. It
should be noted, however, that when taking the 1982–89 period as a whole,
annual GDP expansion constituted a rather less miraculous 2.6 per cent,
slipping to 0.9 per cent when viewed in per capita terms (Stallings, 2001: 46).

Four main pillars of the deepened neoliberal model can be discerned. First,
restructuring sought to fortify Chile as a profitable site for global capital
investment by removing even more of the existing restraints on profitability.
These measures benefited both foreign capitals alongside the large domestic
groups and included the further abolition of taxes on wealth and capital
gains, and the withdrawal of restrictions on foreign profit remittances
(cf. Morguillansky, 2001: 180). Indeed, the passing of law DL 600 specifically
guaranteed the equal treatment of foreign and domestic capital. Foreign
direct investment flocked into the Chilean export sectors, particularly into
mining where foreign companies reclaimed a position unseen since the
early 1960s. That said, the regime wisely retained control of CODELCO, the
extremely profitable state-owned copper company that provided a major
source of revenue, half of which went directly to the armed forces.

Second, the reorientation of national production towards the world market
through a specialization in agricultural and raw material exports continued.
The majority of economic expansion occurring in the 1984–89 period was
precisely in these new 'dynamic poles' of Chilean production – minerals,
lumber, fishmeal and fruit exports all increased their role in export value
(CEPAL, 2001: 124). While in the 1960s the value of exports amounted to
13 per cent of GDP, this had risen to 20.7 per cent in the 1974–81 period and
underwent a further large jump to 29.6 per cent in the 1985–89 period
(Stallings, 2001). As indicated previously in Table 10.2, the bulk of this
expansion was performed under the aegis of the large economic groups who
continued to dominate the new-export sectors. Moreover, in many respects
the jobs created in the new export industries have proved the most under-
regulated and precarious. Specific examples are the fruit export sector and
the forestry sector. In the former labour contracts are overwhelmingly seasonal,
often with piece-rate wages, and there exists little employment protection or
rights (Gwynne and Kay, 1997). In the latter subcontracting processes maximize flexibility and profits for the large firms through a process of vertical
disintegration that passes down costs to workers through tenuous employment
under informalized labour conditions (Escobar and Lopez, 1996).

Third, the extraction of the state from previously established economic
and social activities continued with renewed large-scale privatization and
the re-imposition of strict fiscal discipline that incorporated a substantial.
reduction in state social expenditure (cf. Huber, 1996). The latter is particularly clear when examining state spending for several key areas of welfare
services. In education, for example, sharp budget cuts occurred immediately

after the imposition of dictatorship, with a 25 per cent cut between 1974 and 1976. Spending then rose again, approximating 90 per cent of the 1974 figure by 1979. However, after 1981 the decade was marked by a severe downward trend, with a cut of 25 per cent between 1982 and 1990 (Torche, 2000). This was directly reflected in the falling value of the per-student subsidy that the government transferred to educational institutions. Effects were felt across the education system, notably in the impoverishment of school resources and the decline of teacher wages (Raczynski, 1999). Similar cuts were experienced in the health system.[43] Moreover, concurrent to this retrenchment of state welfare, the 1980s witnessed the rapid expansion of private sector health and education activities utilized primarily by the top two quintiles of the population.

Fourth, the regime consolidated its violent repression of the labour movement with a rigid new labour code in 1980 that provided a resolutely pro-capital means of regulating labour relations and solving industrial conflict. Unions were once again allowed to form, but there could be no collective bargaining above the level of the individual firm. Striking was first prohibited and then limited, to 60 days, and employers were given the right to fire workers at will without giving reasons. In short, what emerged from the labour code was a repressive work environment that gave full reign to flexible conditions of exploitation, a situation that contributed greatly to the deterioration of real wages throughout the Pinochet period. Capital could downscale or rapidly switch from one productive investment to another without concern for the workers employed in the venture. Such flexibility was enhanced through privatization of the pension system that recast the old system of mutual contributions by state, firm and worker into an individual relation between worker and private pension company. One consequence has been the exclusion of over 40 per cent of the working population from any adequate pension (Taylor, 2003).

Unsurprisingly, neoliberal policies were not widely popular. The economic debacle of the early 1980s and the huge social costs involved – with levels of extreme poverty soaring from six per cent in 1969 to 30 per cent of the population in 1983 (Raczynski, 2000) – gave significant impetus to a growing protest movement. Popular protest was given direction by two political trends centred on a moderate and a more radical pole. The impact of growing social mobilization against the dictatorship was precisely to force the regime to attempt to further institutionalize its basis, thereby opening more room to the protest movement (cf. Fernández, 1993). One facet of this institutionalization was a constitution that provided for a referendum in 1988 offering a choice between a further eight years of Pinochet's 'protected democracy' or a return to civilian rule. The Pinochet regime greatly underestimated the level of opposition and, despite major advantages in terms of intimidation and media control, was shocked to find itself voted out of power by 54 to 46 per cent. Nevertheless, the regime was still able to exit on its own terms by setting up the institutional framework for a protected democracy. It negotiated the details of a constitutional transition with the more conservative wing of the opposition movement, leaving substantial institutional checks (so-called authoritarian enclaves) on the ability of post-authoritarian governments to promulgate any radical course of action. These barriers to democratic processes included the placement of designated senators-for-life in the senate (including Pinochet) and an electoral system that ensured a status quo between the parties of the right and the left in the Congress (cf. Taylor, 1998). In short, the authoritarian government sought to ensure that certain aspects of the state-system would remain faithful to the neoliberal project and limit the possible actions of the incoming democratic regime, known as the Concertación. The latter was formed from an alliance between the re-emergent Christian Democrat and Socialist parties.

5. The Concertación and 'growth with equity'

The Concertación coalition comfortably won the 1989 national elections and has proceeded to win both of the subsequent polls in 1994 and 2000. The three Concertación governments – Patricio Aylwin (1990–94), Eduardo Frei-Tagle (1994–99), and Ricardo Lagos (2000–06) – have all remained strictly within the bounds of the macro-level neoliberal policy framework. This gives a strong indication of the constraints on government action within the contemporary global political economy, but also the strength of Chilean social forces – including the large economic conglomerates and the parties of the right – committed to the neoliberal trajectory.

In terms of policies, the Concertación regime has played a strong role in abetting processes of integration into international capital circuits or, in other words, furthering the processes of transnationalization (see Chapter 1 in this volume). With respect to foreign trade, the governments have successively cut tariffs to below the minimal levels of the Pinochet regime, including the signing of several bilateral and multilateral trade agreements, therein making Chile the most open country in Latin America in terms of the movement of goods. Although differing in their precise terms, these agreements now cover trade with the NAFTA block, the MERCOSUR and the European Union; and both of the post-1994 governments have pushed for full entry into the NAFTA. Concurrent to this deepening of the free-trade policy, the Concertación has continued to court foreign capital by securing the conditions for profitable investment. In many respects, this wooing of foreign capital through providing optimum accumulation conditions reflects the tendencies noted in Cerny's a concept of 'the competition state' (Cerny and Evans, 2000a, see also the chapters by Cerny, Evans and Soederberg in this volume). Not only has governmental deregulation and privatization opened new areas for foreign investment – as in the newly privatized water treatment sector – but also traditional sectors have increasingly become sites for foreign investment. An exemplary example is the role of foreign capital in the construction sector. Transnational capital in this sector has grown from minimal levels at the end of the 1980s to a situation in which 50 per cent of investment is foreign and, moreover, where companies backed by foreign capitals take some 72 per cent of public works contracts (Fazio, 2000: 36).

Indeed, foreign direct investment has provided much of the lifeblood of the Chilean economy, particularly in the early and mid-1990s when large amounts of capital entered to partake in new initiatives with very attractive terms offered by the state. In the booming copper sector FDI investment was superior to all other sectors of the economy combined. This was partially determined by the high price of copper alongside significant tax breaks offered to transnational capital that placed the relative profitability of the state-owned copper sector at a serious disadvantage (Lagos and Franscico, 1999). As the same author notes, foreign firms have increasingly used the climate of deregulation to export unrefined copper in bulk to South East Asia to take advantage of cheaper processing. Such liberal exporting regulations play a major role in the unseemly trend of massively increased investment standing alongside an absolute reduction in the number of jobs in the Chilean copper industry from 104 000 to 92 000 over the decade (cf. Agacino *et al.*, 1998).

Faced with mounting inflows of foreign capital in the early 1990s, the Concertación government spurned neoclassical orthodoxy to levy a minor capital control that was intended to stabilize economic indicators. The latter was deemed necessary as the influx threatened to trigger a form of Dutch disease whereby capital inflows push up the value of the local currency thereby undermining the profitability of exports. Despite the contested effectiveness of the Chilean capital controls (cf. Soederberg, 2004, 2005), short-term portfolio capital nonetheless entered in large quantities, although below the level of FDI. This, of course, was not problematic during the boom years of the early and mid-1990s. However, when the shock waves of the Asian financial crisis hit Chile in 1998, $2.1 billion of capital flight plunged the economy into recession (IMF, 2000). Ironically, the government's response was to abandon the capital control and remaining impediments to the free movement of capital (i.e. its ability to exit under any future adverse circumstances) in order to try and encourage capital to return. Moreover, under the terms of a free trade agreement with the United States in the summer of 2003, the Chilean government pledged to refrain from any further restraints on capital movements.

Another essentially important aspect of the Concertación's attempt to secure the optimal conditions for capital accumulation has been the maintenance of the production relations established under the dictatorship. Although the labour movement had strong ties to the Concertación parties – both Christian Democrat and Socialist – they were to be profoundly disappointed with the lack of meaningful reform to the 1980 labour code.

While changes have been made during the 1990s, the new amendments are primarily of a defensive nature, operating on an individualistic and juridical framework rather than through the support and promotion of collective action. They offer better access to protective mechanisms when worker rights are abused but do not provide for organized labour to become a serious counterweight to the power of employers either at the level of the firm or in the national political ambit. Bargaining is still restricted to the individual firm and, while striking has been legalized once again, firms are permitted to hire replacement labour for the duration of industrial action. Under this system, national-level labour federations serve merely as political pressure groups that – with few tangible weapons that can pressure the government – are acknowledged to have relatively little weight.[44] By maintaining the extreme flexibility of Chilean labour and the suppressed role of the labour movement, the Concertación has responded to the demands of the business sector and played a role in keeping wage rises below productivity increases, thereby stunting the recovering trend in real wages (cf. Taylor, 2004; Fazio, 2001).

If continuity has overshadowed change for much of the Concertación's economic and labour policy orientations, the realm of social policy has proved something of an exception. In contrast to the neoliberal fundamentalist position of a strictly minimalist state, the Concertación has staked a significant portion of its political legitimacy upon a commitment to comprehensively increase social expenditure. Between 1989 and 2000 public social expenditure was almost doubled and the increases have been targeted in a fairly effective manner towards the lower-earning quintiles of the population. It should be noted, however, that these increases follow years of expenditure reduction by the military government and that public services in the late 1980s were generally recognized to be bordering on a state of crisis. Furthermore, although expenditures have been increased with positive ramifications throughout the social services, there remain acute structural problems owing to the internalized dual system of private and public service provision. In short, increasing expenditure within the social policy framework established in the authoritarian era has proved unable to overcome the failings of the latter, thereby curtailing the potency of sustained expenditure growth (cf. Taylor, 2003).

These sustained increases in social expenditure have been at the heart of what the Concertación has labelled 'growth with equity', a neoliberal development trajectory that gives consideration to social issues. Similar to the British Labour Party's 'Third Way' approach, a 'responsible' social strategy of this nature is contrasted to the older forms of Chilean populism as it rigidly grounds the expansion of social expenditure within the constraints of embedded neoliberal macroeconomic management. Increased social expenditure in this manner is often cited as an example of how the state retains considerable room for manoeuvre within the confines of globalization even in the realm of welfare provision, an area that is often presented as an anachronism in the era of heightened competitive pressures (cf. Teeple, 1995). Nonetheless, such optimism needs to be partially qualified by an understanding of the concrete conditions that allowed the aforementioned development. In this respect, the decade-long expenditure increases were greatly dependent on revenues drawn from an economic boom experienced in the early and mid-1990s. This period of expansion, predicated on the massive in flows of foreign capital and high prices for Chilean primary exports, gave rise to an average annual GDP growth rate of 8.3 per cent between 1991 and 1997. Concurrently, it must be noted that despite the positive effects of the boom in terms of social expenditure increases, rising real wages and the re-incorporation of the unemployed masses into the work force, the issue of equality remains at the forefront of the Chilean social panorama. Notwithstanding the Concertación's repeated claims of 'growth with equity', the outcome of the neoliberal development trajectory has been economic growth coupled to growing income inequality. The latter is testament to the pervasiveness of the polarizing form of social relations fashioned during the Pinochet period (see Table 10.3).

Finally, one further aspect of concern for Chilean policy-makers is the doubtful ability of Chilean capital accumulation to continue at the rates of the early and mid-1990s. Not only did the East Asian crisis provoke an immediate recession in 1998, but growth since that year has been relatively lacklustre. This is partly due to unfavourable global and regional conditions and partly to dramatic overproduction in key export industries. Dramatic increases in Chilean production of copper, lumber, salmon and fruit have contributed to a flooding of global markets and stagnant commodity prices, making Chile a partial victim of its own 'globalizing' success.[45] Additionally, the global spread of export-orientated strategies has also served to introduce

Table 10.3   Distribution of income, 1990–2000

Decile/Year	1990	1992	1994	1996	1998	2000
I	1.4	1.5	1.3	1.3	1.2	1.1
II	2.7	2.8	2.7	2.6	2.5	2.6
III	3.6	3.7	3.5	3.5	3.5	3.7
IV	4.5	4.6	4.6	4.5	4.5	4.5
V	5.4	5.6	5.5	5.4	5.3	5.7
VI	6.9	6.6	6.4	6.3	6.4	6.5
VII	7.8	8.1	8.1	8.2	8.3	7.9
VIII	10.3	10.4	10.6	11.1	11.0	10.5
IX	15.2	14.8	15.4	15.5	16.0	15.2
X	42.2	41.9	41.9	41.6	41.3	42.3

Source: MIDEPLAN, 2001: 18.

new competitors into these markets, thereby increasing both competition and saturation. While a Chilean financial crunch similar to that recently witnessed in other parts of the Southern Cone is unlikely, it is also doubtful that growth rates similar to those of the mid-1990s will be resumed. Consequently, this creeping exhaustion of the Chilean export model threatens to undermine the ability of the state to make the kinds of material compromises through the 'growth with equity' formula that formed the lynch pin of its political and social strategy in the 1990s. Indeed, facing mounting pressure in early 2002 to increase social expenditure to reduce the extreme polarities of the Chilean social structure, President Ricardo Lagos sided firmly with fiscal responsibility, announcing the fallacy of such proposed increases as a recipe for 'bread today, hunger tomorrow'.[46]

6. Conclusion

Processes of internalizing neoliberalism in Chile have fashioned a profound restructuring of the relationship between state and society alongside a pivotal shift in the relationship between the Chilean economy and the world market. As the case study demonstrates, it is important to avoid conceptualizing these processes as two isolated developments, each driven by their own dynamics and (il)logics. Rather, both have comprised different moments of a unitary and ongoing drive constantly to re-establish the conditions for the expanded accumulation of capital in Chile. The appeal of subordinating social phenomena to global market dynamics does not relate solely to an economic rationality, although imposing the discipline of capital upon the Chilean social formation certainly constituted a key factor in the primary exports boom of the 1990s. Internalizing neoliberalism through profound social restructuring offered a prospective solution to the social crisis of the pre-authoritarian period by fracturing the bases of social action and removing the state as a principal mediator of social relations. Nonetheless, creating a minimalist state could not be realized to the extent envisaged by the neoliberal ideologues of the late 1970s. Faced with economic and social collapse in the throws of the 1980s debt crisis, the Pinochet regime dramatically enhanced its forms of societal intervention in order to spur on the neoliberal revolution. Likewise, following the return of electoral politics in the 1990s the three successive Concertación governments have found themselves increasingly pressured to both satisfy the conditions for expanded accumulation through incorporating Chilean accumulation within global circuits of capital while concurrently mitigating the socially polarizing tendencies of the former. It is becoming clear that this latter challenge – of adhering to the discipline imposed by the mobility of capital in its money form while managing the social and political pressures inherent to the imposition of this discipline – is fast becoming the principal paradox for states of the Global South in the era of globalization (cf. Soederberg, 2004). The extent to which they can navigate this thorny terrain: will constitute the degree to which they have successfully 'internalized globalization'.

Further reading

Ffrench-Davis, Ricardo and Barbara Stallings (eds) (2001) *Reformas, Crecimiento y Políticas Sociales en Chile desde 1973*. Santiago: Ediciones LOM.
Oppenheim, Lois Hecht (1998) *Politics in Chile: Democracy, Authoritarianism, and the Search for Development, 2nd edition*. Boulder, CO: Westview Press.
Taylor, Marcus (forthcoming 2006) *From Pinochet to the Third Way? Neoliberalism and Social Transformation in Chile, 1973–2003*. London: Pluto Press.
Winn, Peter (ed.) (2004) *Victims of the Chilean Miracle: Workers and Neoliberalism in the Pinochet Era*. Durham, NC: Duke University Press.

Useful websites

<www.cepal.org>   United Nations Economic Commission on Latin America and the Caribbean

<www.mideplan.cl>   Government of Chile has a Ministry of Social Planning (in Spanish)

<www.worldbank.org>   World Bank Report and Statistics on Chile

<http://www.hrw.org/doc/?t=americas&c=chile>   Human Rights Watch

11
Neoliberalism under Crossfire in Peru: Implementing the Washington Consensus

Guillermo Ruiz Torres

1. Introduction

In 1990, the political elite in Peru were deeply split along two contradictory ideological lines regarding the implementation of a free market economy. One the one hand, the traditional ruling political-economic elite and most of civil society were against free market reforms. Specifically, this coalition, which supported an economic protectionist model in which the state played a central role, was comprised of entrepreneurial associations, trade unions, political parties of the left, centre and even factions of the right, as well as social movement groups (student organizations and peasant or neighborhood associations). On the other hand, an emerging political elite linked to international financial institutions (IFIs) and transnational corporations (TNCs), were stark proponents of a free market-oriented liberalization of the economy.

The confrontation among the various elite fractions was settled when Alberto Fujimori was elected President of Peru. Between 1990 and 2000 President Fujimori implemented an intense neoliberal policy affecting both the economy and the state. Considering the deep intensity of the conflict regarding the political and economic direction at the beginning of the 1990s, it is important to ask the following questions: how could the neoliberal model be implemented within this relative short time against the opposition of the majority of the population? And, relatedly, what role did the Peruvian state play with regard to the internalization of globalization?

This chapter aims to answer these questions. One of the main arguments to be presented here concerns two main factors that facilitated the implementation of a neoliberal economic model in Peru. First, owing to an economy with an accumulated inflation of 7000 per cent in the second half of the 1980s, economic stabilization – in one form or the other – was necessary. Second, two guerrilla organizations had formed to revolutionize Peruvian state and society, namely the *Partido Comunista del Perú* (PCP) [Communist Party of Peru], better known as the *Sendero Luminoso* [the Shining Path] and the *Movimiento Revolucionario Túpac Amaru* (MRTA) [Revolutionary Movement Túpac Amaru]. These two factors contributed decisively to the formation of a new consensus among the economic and political elite for the structural transformation process toward a free market economy in the era of global-ization. This consensus was seen as indispensable for both the redefinition of the guiding economic principles and also for the transformation of Peru's political institutions in order to implement these principles.

This chapter will also question the role of the Peruvian state during the implementation of the neoliberal economic model. Implementing the neolib-eral program and maintaining Fujimori's power became the state's most important aims during the 1990s. The state under Fujimori actively and forcefully assisted the transformation of its functions, by re-shaping its regu-lative goals and by ceasing to function as a traditional planning body for economic growth and development. In support of one of the main theses of this volume, the Peruvian case shows that the attraction of international capital and investment has become the central goal of the state, thus coin-ciding with Joachim Hirsch's description of the 'competition state' (Hirsch 1995; see also Soederberg in this volume).

2. The bumpy road to neoliberalism: social convulsion and authoritarian democracy

Neoliberal economic policy was not an entirely new phenomenon in Peru in the beginning of the 1990s. The military junta headed by Juan Velasco (1968–75) implemented an agrarian reform, expropriated oil and mining companies belonging to US-American corporations and implemented a model that attempted to substitute imports with Peruvian products. With this, Velasco aimed towards strengthening the national industry through self-supply. During this phase, the state became the most important political articulator because it organized large parts of Peruvian society through cor-porate associations as well as through the creation and control of trade unions, peasant movements and small business associations. The first mea-sures to liberalize the economy had already been undertaken during the sec-ond phase of the military junta under Francisco Morales Bermudez (1975–80). The first elected president after 12 years of military dictatorship, Fernando Belaunde (1980–85) from the rightist party *Acción Popular (AP)* [People's Action], also crafted a policy that promoted economic liberalization. In doing so, he did away with much of the instruments for a planned economy imposed by General Juan Velasco during the first phase of the military dic-tatorship (1968–75). Belaunde was not able, though, to intensify his policy, for he encountered strong opposition to his plans. This opposition came from entrepreneurs and business in sectors directly affected by his repeal of subsidies and tax relief. It also came from the majority of the population, since it was affected by the increase of unemployment and also the decrease of real wage levels brought about through Belaunde's reforms (Durand, 1999: 179).

The next president, Álan García Pérez (1985–90) from the center-rightist party *Alianza Popular Revolucionaria Americana – APRA* (American People's Revolutionary Alliance], reversed the path taken by Belaunde. (The model of the substitution of import was the dominating economic model in Latin America between the 1930s and the 1970s. It was aimed at promoting the development of national industries in order satisfy the domestic demand, promote the mass consumption and create jobs. This model was implemented in Peru under the military government headed by Juan Velasco (1968–75), rather later in comparison with other Latin-American countries such as Brazil and Argentina, and found its revival in a moderated version under García (1985–90)). García attempted to combat the economic crises in Peru through a protectionist policy that concentrated on national production and the renewal of industrialization measures aimed toward self-supply in lieu of imports. In doing so, García decided at the beginning of his term to limit the repayment of Peru's external debt to 10 per cent of the amount of foreign currency entering the country from export profits. As a result, the Peruvian state was declared insolvent by the International Monetary Found (IMF) and thus did not receive further approval for international loans (Durand, 1999: 182). Over time, the failure of García's policy became evident. The fiscal reserves were depleted, and the expected reactivation of the productive apparatus did not occur. Instead, capital was either transferred out of the country or invested in speculative businesses by large-scale entrepreneurs who were benefiting from the government's subsidies and tax relief policies (Manco, 1994: 30).

The ensuing economic crisis was also aggravated by massive social protests carried out by social movement organizations. These found their sharpest expression in the confrontation between the aforementioned guerrilla groups and the Peruvian state. The *MRTA*, for example, represented a threat for the capitalist elite of the Peruvian state, although not to the same extent as the Shining Path. The Shining Path, led by a professor of philosophy, Abimael Guzmán Reynoso, began its armed struggle in 1980 in Ayacucho, a southern province in the Peruvian Andes with the highest levels of poverty in Peru. The Shining Path aimed to take power in order to build a socialist state. In the course of the 1980s, it was able to count on the growing support among the population: especially poor peasants, but also workers, large segments of the unemployed urban population and students from public universities gave their support (Arce Borja, 1994).

In response, the systematic violation of human rights became a central pillar of the state's counter-insurgency strategy. Not long after the beginning of the armed confrontation, the military assumed control of the state's counter-insurgency policy and, in general, made a large impact on Peruvian society. During the 1980s and 1990s, a widely used practice against the guerrilla groups by the Peruvian state was to declare a state of emergency over vast regions of Peru and, at times, even over the entire country. The state of emergency policies suspended the once guaranteed civil rights resulting for the citizens of Peru in the loss of essential legal means to counter arbitrary practices (CNDDHH, 1998). These extraordinary powers allowed for conditions in which violations of human rights went unchallenged. In more than 20 years of repression and civil war, over 60 000 people lost their lives or disappeared.

Peru found itself in a state of crisis at the end of the 1980s. It was isolated from the international economic community, had an immense fiscal deficit and high rates of inflation and unemployment. Social protest was widespread and rumors of a military coup were making their rounds. The political parties and the representative system in general had lost their legitimacy for major segments of the population, which associated the system with corruption and mismanagement. Perhaps most importantly, the uprising led by the Shining Path, which had come to dominate extensive regions of Peru, intensified this crisis greatly, along with the militaristic, state-led backlash in response.

3. Neoliberalism and authoritarianism

In the context of the above crisis, Alberto Fujimori, a newcomer in the Peruvian political establishment was elected to the presidency in 1990. He brought with him an ideological mixture of neoliberalism (see Chapter 1 of this volume) and authoritarianism – a form of government utilized by a dominating power group to control the state's apparatus for its own interests almost without limit. (This power group monopolizes the decision-making process, and civil rights are not adequately guaranteed in order to protect the citizens from both the state itself. In most cases, human rights violations are authoritarian means to counter civil protest and resistance.) In lieu of a parliamentary majority and even the lack of a political party guaranteeing him a strong social basis, Fujimori found allies elsewhere, namely in the military, among owners of large businesses set to profit from the implementation of the IMF's reform catalogue and, above all, from IFIs, primarily the IMF itself, the World Bank, the Inter-American Development Bank (IDB) and the Club of Paris (see Chapter 1 in this volume).

The conditions placed upon loans from the IMF, the IDB and the World Bank included the implementation of structural adjustment programs (SAP) based on the Consensus of Washington (Gonzales, 1998: 22). This synthesized a set of recommendations formulated by IFIs for Latin American countries. This includes fiscal discipline, tax reform, the liberalization of interest rates, a competitive exchange rate, trade liberalization, the liberalization of policy regarding the inflow of foreign direct investment, privatization, deregulation, the strengthening of property rights and the redirection of public expenditure priorities towards fields offering both high economic returns and also the potential to improve income distribution, such as primary health care, primary education and infrastructure (Williamson, 2000: 252). Soon after assuming the presidency, Fujimori implemented the promised SAP and, in doing so, the IFIs became a main backer of Fujimori's internal policy. This was furthered by the support for the reintegration of the Peruvian state into the international financial system displayed by parts of the political elite, large-scale entrepreneurs and military circles, all of whom associated the deep economic crisis at the end of the 1980s with the lack of accessibility to new international loans (Cotler, 1994: 200).

Lacking a majority in parliament, however, Fujimori was forced continually to negotiate his policies with parliament. Beginning in 1991, a number of issues caused conflict between Fujimori and the opposition parties, especially the *APRA* and the leftist party *Izquierda Unida* (IU) [United Left]. These issues included the legislatively-driven widening of the neoliberal reforms, the extension of the powers of the *Servicio de Inteligencia Nacional* (SIN) (National Intelligence Service), a petition regarding the investigation of human rights violations and incidents of corruption (McClintock, 1999: 71). More and more, these parliamentary challenges represented an obstacle for Fujimori's reform process and for the authoritarian expansion of his power. On 5 April 1992 personal ambition and the will to stay in power led Fujimori, aided by his closest adviser, Vladimiro Montesinos, to enact the *autogolpe* (or, the 'self-perpetrated coup d'etat') (Cotler, 1994: 206). Assisted by the military, and arguing that the counter-insurgency policy was being boycotted, Fujimori closed down parliament, suspended the autonomy of several governmental institutions, among them the judiciary, the central bank and the *Contraloría General* [Comptroller General]. He also dissolved the *Consejo National de la Magistratura* [National Magistrate Council] and the regional governments.

The military supported the *autogolpe* because Fujimori intended to expand the scope of the counter-insurgency, to block investigations on human rights violations and to hinder judicial proceedings against such violations. Fujimori also counted on the support of the *Confederatión Institutional de Empresarios Privados* (CONFIEP) [Institutional Confederation of Private Entrepreneurs] and other associations representing large business, such as the *Asociación de Exportadores* (ADEX) [Exporters Association] and the *Sociedad National de Industrias* (SNI) [National Society of Industrialists]. These employers' associations tolerated Fujimori's authoritarian measures not only because they were interested in expanding the scope of the counter-insurgency, but also because they intended to profit from the further implementation of Fujimori's neoliberal model (Durand, 1999: 191).

It should be noted that Fujimori's coup d'etat was tolerated by the US, the Organization of American States (OAS) and the IFIs. There was no serious talk about sanctions, nor were there demands for a re-establishment of the overthrown institutions. Nor did the OAS commute Peru's membership according to its statutes. The latter state that only democratic and representative governments can be members of the organization (Wiener, 1998: 91). Without this pressure, Fujimori was able to draft a plan to re-establish the state's institutions according to his own power interests. As part of this process, elections for a constituent assembly were held in 1993, through which a new constitution was written. Fujimori's *Cambio 90* [Change 90] party won both the elections for the constituent assembly as well as the subsequent presidential elections in 1995. This success was guaranteed through Fujimori's clever use of state resources for the benefit of his election campaign, along with electoral fraud and the incapacity of the opposition to articulate an alternative political project (Beaumont, 1996; Schmidt, 1999: 102).

Thanks to a new constitution and to his majority in parliament, Fujimori was able to concentrate power in the executive. In this way, not only was he able to implement his policy with few obstacles, but he also gained control of the legislative and judicial branches, the *Jurado Nacional de Elecciones* (National Jury for Elections), through his ability to designate their highest representatives. Fujimori utilized his usurped power to obtain favorable judicial rulings, to manipulate electoral processes, to exert pressure on the mass media and those segments of business that were opposed to his positions as well as to extort wide segments of the impoverished population, mainly poor peasants and inhabitants of slums. The latter was accomplished mainly through his social policy (Planas, 1999: 226–7; Arce, 1996: 106). During electoral campaigns, persons from impoverished neighborhoods dependent on social programs were forced to assist Fujimori. In many cases, peasant communities were threatened with the loss of communal development funding if they did not vote for Fujimori. Government officials and members of the military also participated in Fujimori's electoral campaigns through mobilization or propaganda efforts. Fujimori's authoritarian control over the state apparatus allowed him to defeat any opposition that dared to criticize his policy of economic liberalization, the rampant human rights violations or his plan to perpetuate his power.

4. The restructuring of the state

Through his authoritarian power over the political decision-making process in Peru, Fujimori was able to carry out extensive restructuring of the state. Defined as a social relation between individuals, groups and classes, a state assumes a concrete form through a system of political institutions, bureaucratic structures and political mechanisms. The state forms and stabilizes social power relations through this concrete structure (Hirsch, 1995: 23). In Peru, this structure includes the executive, legislative and judicial branches, the National Jury for Elections, a central bank, municipal and regional governments as well as subaltern economic and political institutions. With a monopoly on the political decision-making process, Fujimori successfully attempted to gain control of and restructure the state apparatus in its entirety. The political framework for this restructuring was given to him by the constitution of 1993, which reduced the parliament to merely a house of representatives and empowered the president with vast executive and legislative competence. According to the new constitution, the president can enact 'decrees of urgency' without parliamentary involvement, which then can be authorized by parliament as 'laws of exception'. Most of the laws passed during the Fujimori government were created through such decrees of urgency or laws of exception. The state's apparatus was also centralized, mainly through the dissolution of the regional governments and the disempowering of the municipalities (Chirinos, 1999).

Fujimori's restructuring of the state also included the transformation of the state's function as an economic agent. In this process, the state was stripped of its function as a so-called motor of the economy and as an important investor in, and promoter of, strategic economic sectors. The Peruvian state reduced its contribution to the gross domestic product and abandoned its regulative function. This economic restructuring was accompanied by the promotion of policy framework conditions that were perceived to be necessary to attract foreign capital, such as the flexibilization of the labor market and favorable tax regimes. Additionally, Fujimori's determination to settle Peru's international debts greatly reduced the Peruvian state's distributive function. The state renounced its aims to create sustainable development and to take redistributive aspects into consideration. It also ceased its attempt to secure for the impoverished population access to the economic and social systems, for example, through promoting employment in selected productive sectors through providing agriculture subsidies or through the increase of consumption levels.

In this process, Fujimori's government also implemented social policy changes. This new orientation in the state's social policies was coupled with the political instrumentalization of the state's resources for Fujimori's power interests. Social expenditures were also not allowed to endanger the fiscal discipline, nor were they allowed to be utilized by political actors other than the central government (Beaumont, 1996: 47). To this end, Fujimori centralized the state's social programs, most importantly the *Fondo Nacional de Cooperación y Desarrollo* (FONCODES) [National Funds for Cooperation and Development]. Under the direct control of the executive branch, the administration of these funds was transformed into an instrument for extorting support for the government among the impoverished segments of the population, mainly peasant and slum communities (Arce, 1996: 105). *FONCODES* was not only instrumentalized, but it also came to represent a new social policy concept, through which the social programs began to be more effective through the incorporation of target stakeholders in the selection, design and implementation of social projects, although the participation of the stakeholders in the projects was reduced to a subaltern role. They received no repayment for their services and did not have any influence on decisive aspects of the social programs, that is, the scope, budget and controlling thereof. In general, a new economic and ideological connotation set the character and model of neoliberal Peru, in which the state both saved on expenditures and also forced many societal responsibilities into stakeholders that had previously been state responsibilities (Ruiz, forthcoming).

5. The authoritarian character of the neoliberal project in Peru

The fact that the neoliberal project was implemented in Peru at a time when the authoritarian character of the state was strong raises the question of whether the stark neoliberal model could have been established outside of this authoritarian framework. In order to appreciate the connection between both processes, we should consider that the ongoing civil war and the social protest movements hindered the realization of economic stabilization programs. Moreover, the guerrilla and the social protests were unfavorable when attracting investors. Fujimori's authoritarian policy aimed at undermining this opposition and creating a favorable climate for foreign investment. In the process Fujimori also extended his own control over the Peruvian state and society (Ruiz, forthcoming). Whether Fujimori promoted the state authoritarianism primarily in order to implement a neoliberal model or to extend his own power remains a question that is difficult to answer. At any rate, they seemed to be complementary processes.

For example, the implementation of measures that were perceived to be absolutely necessary for the reintegration of the Peruvian state into the international financial system received support from all parties, as did most of his counter-insurgency activities. Nonetheless, the left and center-right parties in parliament, the *IU* and the *APRA*, remained in most instances in opposition to Fujimori, in that they neither accepted a widening of the neoliberal model, nor the expansion of the President's powers.

A number of variables determined the hegemonic mixture of neoliberalism and authoritarianism imposed on Peruvian society under Fujimori. According to Gramsci's definition of hegemony, power is not only exercised through violence, but also through consensus achieved in the arena of the civil society. The consent of the people to accept the state's authority is, in this sense, achieved through influencing civil society institutions, such as educational, media, civic and cultural associations. One prominent economic variable serves as a good example: the economic stabilization and reintegration into the international financial system after the economic crisis of the 1980s had absolute priority for the Peruvian state. A consensus to this end existed among not only all political parties in parliament, but also under the entrepreneurs' associations and in extended segments of population (Iguíñez, 1999: 22). Accordingly, Fujimori was able to advance the liberalization of the economy under both hegemonic conditions and also under the pretext of fulfilling the obligations imposed by the international financial institutions.

It is necessary to consider the role of large business in this process, even though it is not a purely economic variable. Its support for Fujimori's neoliberal model was based on three general reasons: on the government's successes in the fight against the guerrilla, on its ability to transfer investments to new profitable segments or merge with international companies and on the government's liberalization of labour market legislation. In this context, it should be noted that the *APEX* and *SNI* supported Fujimori's economic stabilization efforts, but that they were opposed to a radicalization of the neoliberal reforms (Reyna and Toche, 1999: 61). This, though, did not necessarily represent an obstacle for Fujimori since, as a newcomer, he was not dependent on these groups. Moreover, they did not have a strong lobby, nor were they able to articulate common actions in order to pressure the government (Gonzales, 1998: 66).

The implementation of the neoliberal and authoritarian model in Peru can also be attributed to a number of political variables. One can be found in the deep crisis of Peru's party system at the end of the 1980s. This crisis was caused by a number of factors, among them the history of military intervention into civil affairs, the economic difficulties, the armed resistance and the general loss of face for parliament and its political parties. This crisis is perhaps most aptly expressed in Fujimori's triumph in 1990 – without the political backing by much of the established political elite (Lynch, 1996: 85). Owing to the absence of support for mainstream political parties, it became increasingly difficult for civic protest to be articulated against Fujimori's model. The traditional political parties *AP*, *PPC*, *APRA* and the leftist coalition *UI* received in 1980 92.7 per cent of the vote in the presidential elections. In 1985 they received 97.0 per cent and in 1990 68.0 per cent. In the elections for the constituent assembly in 1993 they received only 15.3 per cent of the vote, and in the presidential elections in 1995 a mere 6.3 per cent (Tanaka, 1998: 55).

Fujimori's centralization of state resources and functions should also be analysed as a further political variable aiding the implementation of his neoliberal and authoritarian model. The centralization process was geared towards dissolving institutions and mechanisms that could have provided a platform for opposition to his policies. This is most clearly the case regarding the dissolution of the regional governments and the reduction of the municipalities' powers. The strong opposition on the part of regional movements against privatization measures indicates the strategic importance of this centralization policy, curtailing opportunities for political articulation from local communities (Chirinos, 1999: 107).

The exhaustion of the Peruvian model of social articulation ought to be mentioned as one of the social variables that aided Fujimori's restructuring of the state. The increase of unemployment and underemployment and the development of the informal sector – results of the previous failed economic policies – caused unions and interest groups to lose their importance as political mediators (Tanaka, 1998: 174). Moreover, their demands increasingly failed to correspond with the interests and needs of the large and growing impoverished segments of the population who demanded access to basic needs, such as water and electricity, adequate schools and food assistance programs.

Over the course of the years, leftist groups also experienced a similar decline in influence. The economic crisis made the search for individual survival strategies necessary, rather than collective action aimed at achieving social objectives (Cameron, 1994: 126). This tendency was aggravated by the increased influence of the Shining Path among the impoverished (Roberts, 1998: 259). The Shining Path had, however, no interest in bringing about a movement against the neoliberal program, but rather worked toward taking over state power through a socialist revolution (Arce Borja, 1994).

The internal persecution and repression of the oppositional civil society is a further important variable when analysing the weak political response against Fujimori's neoliberal and authoritarian model. Social movement organizations, trade unions, peasant associations and students groups were widely persecuted.

Two socio-economic factors played a fundamental role in the failure to find an adequate answer to the neoliberal project. First, the growing participation of the population in the informal sector played an important role (Durand, 1999: 186). The stabilization of prices as a result of the reduction of inflation opened new perspective for these sectors, due to the fact that they were not directly affected by the freezing of wages. The second factor concerns the dependency of large sectors of the population on government grants in order to satisfy their basic needs. As already noted, Fujimori's social policy extorted support among the impoverished for his regime (Wiener, 1998: 131).

Cultural variables must also be taken into account in order to explain the changes that enabled the neoliberal discourse to assume hegemonic status in Peruvian society. The failure of the García government at the end of the 1980s, and the failure of the leftist projects to present a viable alternative, influenced the implementation of the neoliberal model, as did the relative political and economic stability obtained by Fujimori through his authoritarian government. The extensive militarization of the country also implied the defeat of the Shining Path and, consequently, the success of the neoliberal model. In this process, this model found greater ideological value and more appeal among wider sections of the population (Ruiz, forthcoming).

Finally, Fujimori's neoliberal project could not impose itself into the social imagination without a discursive offensive. With a discourse that can be characterized as neo-populist, Fujimori emphasized individual initiative and effort, pragmatism, the inefficiency of the 'polity' compared to the effectiveness of a 'technical' solution as well as the 'inevitable' process of the globalization. This offensive, which hindered the development of alternative mindsets, was, of course, not a one-man project. Numerous intellectuals, politicians and the mass media participated in it, thus helping to consolidate the hegemonic dominance of the neoliberal and authoritarian model. In this sense, it should also be stressed that Fujimori controlled vast segments of the mass media. His control over the mass media was based on the loyalty of the owners and of television, radio and press enterprises. Additionally, this control was supported by journalists and others in the mass media sector. Loyalty was also gained in part through political and economic pressure. Indeed, Fujimori's strategy of censorship, persecution and even the murder of journalists greatly helped to ensure his control.

6. Economic liberalization and privatization: fragile pillars of growth

The first step towards the redefinition of the state's role and economic stabilization was the implementation of a SAP. Its measures included the abolishing of all state subsidies for both producers and consumers. This led to a stark increase in the price index. For example, the price of fuel increased 3000 per cent, electricity 5270 per cent and telephone services 1300 per cent. At the same time, real wage levels decreased. The SAP's short-term goals included the lowering of inflation and the fiscal deficit as well as economic stabilization through strict monetary control (Gonzales, 1998: 47). These measures resulted in an increase of fiscal revenues and an influx of foreign currency into the state's reserves.

The SAP also included the opening of Peru's commerce to the world market. All import and non-tariff restrictions were eliminated, the tariff structure was reformed and tariffs themselves were reduced and standardized. The average tariff level fell from 66 per cent in 1989 to 16.1 per cent in 1992 and 13 per cent in 1997 (Abugattas, 1999: 120). However, this opening took place under unfavorable conditions for the national industry, which had been already experiencing economic crisis in the 1970s and had collapsed by the end of the 1980s (Abugattas, 1999: 123). Moreover, the economic growth of the early 1990s was in no sense stimulated through industrial production. Instead, investments were channeled toward the stock market and the construction sector as well as toward export-oriented industries dealing in raw materials, such as the mining, agriculture and fishing industries. This signified a return to the primary export model of the 1950s, and resulted in a general increase of unemployment. Around 250 000 jobs were lost between 1990 and 1997 in the industrial sector alone (Abugattas, 1999: 129).

A fundamental aspect of Fujimori's program was his policy of privatization. In 1991, a law providing the legal framework for the privatization process and promoting private investment was enacted (Decree Law No. 674, 27/09/1991; Ley de Promotión de la Inversión Privada en Empresas del Estado). Over the course of the next year, further laws were passed in order to promote private investment. These laws focused on attracting foreign capital to Peru. The state was authorized to provide limitless guarantees on the protection of investments (Decree Law No. 25575, 22/06/1992), tax regulations for foreign investors were created (Decree Law No. 25681, 23/08/1992), and the repayment of debt incurred by state-owned enterprises active in the investment process was suspended (Decree Law No. 25685, 21/08/1992) (Ruiz, 2002: 23). However, according to the constitution of 1993, the state was forced to assume a subaltern role to private entrepreneurial activities (Constitutión Política del Perú, 1993). In lieu of possibilities to directly influence the economy of Peru, the promotion of private investment became the highest priority of this 'competitive state'.

In 1991, public enterprises produced 15 per cent of the gross domestic product and provided 114 000 jobs. 28 per cent of exports and 26 per cent of imports were concentrated in these enterprises as well. Between 1991 and 1997, 132 of the 186 public enterprises were privatized, thus reducing the state's capital by 11.8 per cent (Gonzales, 1998: 55). In total, to companies with a value of 9.25 billion dollars were sold during the 10 years of Fujimori. Most of the generated income was used to settle the state's debt, rather than to generate new jobs or to reduce poverty levels. After 10 years of privatization a mere 223 million dollars remained in the State Treasury (CIDEF, 2002). In spite of this, the foreign debt increased from almost 20 billion dollars in 1990 to around 31 billion dollars in 2000.

Clearly the capitalist sector was the winner of the economic liberalization process. It increased its share of the total generated profit in Peru from 64.4 per cent in 1989 to 77.8 per cent in 1994, whereas the workers' share in this profit decreased from 34.4 per cent to 21.2 per cent (Gonzales, 1998: 115). From another perspective, TNCs benefited most from this process. Seventy-five per cent of the capital flows emerging from privatization came from these corporations (Ruiz, 2002: 46). Peruvian entrepreneurial groups, such as the *Banco de Crédito, Grupo Romero, Grupo Graña y Montero* profited from privatization as well (Ruiz, 2002: 30; Manco, 1994: 36).

According to Fujimori's government and the defenders of the neoliberal program, privatization should have eliminated a major source of the fiscal deficit. It should have also helped to lower the cost of – as well as improve – the services provided by the former public enterprises. In fact, public companies were sold undervalued, such as the public power company EDELNOR, which was privatized for 176 million dollars. (Between 1995 and 1997, the newly-privatized enterprise produced a profit of 120 million dollars. Within three years, 68 per cent of the buying price returned to the pockets of its new shareholders (Ruiz, 2002: 58)). Those companies that were profitable were sold off and the costs for services did not decrease, but rather increased after privatization. The state petroleum company PETROPERU generated over 1.3 billion dollars of profits between 1992 and 1998. This is twice the amount that the state received for the sale of parts of the company, which also means that PETROPERU generated these profits despite its reduced capacities. It would have made more significant gains without the privatization process (Ruiz, 2002: 69). State monopolies were also partly replaced by private monopolies. Because of deregulation, these private monopolies increased their rates as well: in 1994 the public telecommunications company *Empresa National de Telecomunicaciones del Peru (ENTEL-Peru)* was bought by *Telefónica-Spain. Telefónica-Spain* obtained with its purchase a monopoly in the telecommunication sector for nine years. With price deregulation, it could determine the market prices almost without any control. Additionally, over 120 000 jobs were lost through the privatization of public enterprises, and only 30 per cent of these were subsequently absorbed by the privatized companies (Ruiz, 2002: 48).

It should also be stressed that the state under Fujimori used around one-third of the capital flows gained from privatization for debt repayment. A further one-third was used for defence and internal security expenditures, thus leaving the last one-third for state and social expenditures (Ruiz, 2002: 48). Evident here are the new priorities of the Peruvian state at the time, namely guaranteeing the framework conditions for the accumulation of capital through ensuring internal security and implementing social policy change. The latter two expenditures were used to counter the negative consequences of the neoliberal program, namely the impoverishment of the population and the emergence and strengthening of political and social protest.

7. The social consequences of the free market politics

The flexibilization of labour market regulations was part of Fujimori's neoliberal model as well. These included the abolition of protective mechanisms for workers, the loss of social benefits, and the reduction of standards geared toward creating acceptable working conditions. The legal directives on wage agreements were modified, making collective bargaining difficult and more atomistic, thus placing the worker into an even inferior position vis-à-vis his employer. Fujimori's state also participated in collective negotiations in support of the employers associations. The rights of trade unions, for example, the right to strike or to organize, were also seriously limited (Mujica, 1999).

At the end of the 1990s, after 10 years of neoliberal policy, Peru registered higher indices of unemployment and poverty than before Fujimori came to power. Considering a total population of around 28 million inhabitants, unemployment had reached 10 per cent, and six million persons were unemployed or underemployed. 13 million lived in poverty, of whom four million were forced into extreme poverty. Although 41.6 per cent of the population lived in poverty in 1985, 55 per cent did so in 2000. Six million persons did not have access to health services, and 30 per cent of the children between three and four years of age suffered from chronic undernourishment. Illiteracy rose to 18 per cent (Haya de la Torre, 1999/2000).

8. External and internal pressure and the 'peripheral' competition state

External pressures in favor of the implementation of a neoliberal model cannot be denied in the case of Peru. In light of the deep economic crisis of the late 1980s, the IFIs and donor countries – most importantly the US – demanded that Fujimori carry out the aforementioned SAP as a condition for granting new loans. However, the Fujimori state implemented the neoliberal project with significantly more enthusiasm than was expected by the IFIs and donor countries. (Armeane Chosky, Vice-President of Human Sources and Operations Politics of the World Bank, pointed out in an interview that the liberalization of the economy was carried out more quickly and thoroughly in Peru than in Chile or Mexico (interview in *Gestión* 09/02/93, cit. Manco, 1994: 29)). For example, the demands did not include aggressive privatization, which in many instances brought net loss for the state. Nor did it include the creation of private monopolies, the elimination of price subsidies or the removal of most non-tariff import regulations. Quite simply, Fujimori's government not only fulfilled the demands of the IFIs and the donor countries, but also willingly radicalized the reforms according to their own neoliberal postulates. In this sense, the Peruvian example contradicts allegations that the state's role in economic governance automatically diminishes when faced with the constraints of globalization.

A more detailed empirical evaluation would be required to fully answer why the Peruvian state implemented the neoliberal model in such radical form. The following factors, though, may provide a cursory explanation. First, an alternative development model was lacking articulation. The Peruvian political elite were folly concentrated on the strict implementation of the neoliberal model, and it opposed any tendencies that could have interfered with the liberalization process (Gonzales, 1998: 49). Second, Fujimori's regime desperately wanted to satisfy the demands of the IFIs in order to get access to new loans. Through this, President Fujimori was interested in retaining his neoliberal public image and in acquiring new capital to finance his social policies and the counter-insurgency. Third, the policy of Fujimori's government was designed by technocrats in the Ministry of Economics and Finance, and it was influenced by the most orthodox principles of free market economy and by the lobbying of the IFIs. These technocrats strengthened the ideological character of the neoliberal project and made long-term decisions regarding Peru's economy. Fourth, some of these officials also had investments that benefited from liberalization. For example, when the law that allowed the investment in pension funds was enacted, the first to invest was a corporation connected with Fujimori's Minister of Economy, Carlos Boloña (Durand, 1999: 193). Fifth, after the fall of Fujimori's administration, it was revealed that large-scale corruption had occurred under Fujimori, in which large corporations, financial groups and parts of the mass media were involved. The role of corruption in the implementation of the neoliberal model, not in its individualized but in its structural form, is often disregarded in analyses of such transformation processes (Ruiz, 2002: 49; CIDEF, 2002).

As already discussed, the attraction of international investments was a central aspect within a neoliberal logic oriented towards the repayment of debt. This aspect corresponds with Hirsch's concept of the competition state. Accordingly, states strive to create conditions favorable for attracting and retaining foreign investments, thus making efforts to improve their position in the international economic standing (Hirsch, 1995; Cerny, 1999; see Chapter 1 in this volume). Unlike countries with high levels of development, in the Peruvian case – a peripheral, one could even say precarious, country – this re-orientation to a competitive state took place void of both infrastructure and human capital improvement program. Instead, the measures were oriented towards attracting international investment including labor market de-regulation, tax relief for international investors and privatization of public corporations below their real cost. Given that the state mainly tried to attract investments for the primary sector, it seems as if Fujimori was attempting to renew the production guidelines of the 1950s, which forced the country to base its economy on the export of raw materials, while also being dependent on foreign investors. When looking at the material, therefore, it is appropriate to speak of Peru as a 'peripheral competition stated', in which the state had ceased all attempt to guarantee a stable economic model and sustainable development, as well as taking aspects of social distribution into consideration.

9. The Toledo era: Fujimorism without Fujimori?

In September 2000, when a corruption affair involving Montesinos came to light, Fujimori announced his resignation from the presidency. Today, he lives in Japan as a Japanese citizen, safe from an extradition order by the Peruvian state. Montesinos is serving a prison sentence. Both are accused of numerous crimes. After Fujimori's fall, Valentin Paniagua from the *AP* led the transition government (2000–01). Thanks to having led the opposition movement against Fujimori, Alejandro Toledo was elected president in July of 2001.

Toledo's economic course has not differed from Fujimori's. It seems to have been reduced to the postulates of the Washington Consensus. The performance of the economy under Toledo confirms this assumption.

Between 2001 and 2004, economic growth was around 4.5 per cent per annum. However, this figure is strongly related to the increased productivity of the profitable mining sector, which is also benefiting from high prices on the international market (Azpur et al., 2004). Furthermore, Toledo announced at the beginning of his administration that privatization – especially in the energy sector – would be promoted in order to reactivate the economy and to reduce the fiscal deficit (Humala, 2002). This has proven to be politically unworkable in cases of the power companies EGASA and EGESUR in Arequipa in the south of Peru. Here, Toledo's plans encountered massive opposition from a regional movement that protested against the loss of jobs, the probable subsequent increase of electricity rates and the privatization of two profitable companies (Ruiz, 2002: 41).

The economic stability and growth in Peru is a disproportional source of profit for the financial markets in comparison to wage increases over the last years. Indeed, wages have increased five per cent since 2001, but this is not significant when one looks at the profit gained on the stock market in Lima, for example, an increase of 49 per cent in 2003 alone (Azpur et al., 2004). Additionally, Toledo's government has not fulfilled a number of societal demands. These include the creation of jobs, wage increases, the increase of subsidies in the agriculture sector, the fight against corruption and the decentralization of the state. In turning a blind eye to these demands, Toledo has sparked the emergence and spread of social protest headed by social movement organizations (trade unions, peasants' associations, regional movements etc.) (Ballón, 2002; Pizarro et al., 2004).

Following existing patterns when countering social conflicts, Toledo's government has implemented measures reinforcing the authoritarian tendencies of the Peruvian state. Since 2002, the executive has presented parliament with draft laws regarding the intensification of repression against social mobilization. For example, in February 2002, the executive unsuccessfully asked the parliament to pass a law making the blocking of streets during political demonstrations punishable with up to eight years in prison. In the following years similar drafts were presented to, but rejected by, the parliament (Pizarro et al., 2004). Leaders heading such popular protests have been persecuted, criminalized or thrown in prison. Additionally, a state of emergency and the suspension of many civil rights were also temporarily established to counter demonstrations. Even today, strong tendencies exist in the Peruvian state to maintain its authoritarian path.

Even though it seems exaggerated to describe Toledo's government as 'Fujimorism without Fujimori', it is evident that parallels do exist. As was the case during the government of Fujimori, Toledo's priorities lie in satisfying the financial demands of the donor countries, IFIs and TNCs, and not in satisfying the needs of the majority of the population. Perspectives for real change do not exist. Both the Toledo government and the political opposition are not interested in implementing structural changes aimed at a democratization of political decision-making or at a more equable distribution of resources in the society. For these, it would be essential to abandon the neoliberal model. The capacity of the social protest movements to articulate themselves and to translate social mobilization into political programs, though, remains underdeveloped. Let us hope that this will change over time.

10. Conclusion

The analysis of the Peruvian case shows that the implementation of the neoliberal model has been a lengthy process. It has also been rife with conflict. The deep crisis of governability at the end of the 1980s, as a result of the failure of the economic programs and the expansion of the guerrilla organizations, created the favorable conditions that were necessary to generate a consensus among the political elite concerning economic liberalization in the 1990s. Nevertheless, social protest has threatened this consensus. It has caused crises in governability and has also – at times – prevented the radical implementation of neoliberal measures. To counter this, authoritarianism was utilized as an instrument for this implementation. In this sense, the radical implementation of the neoliberal model served as a motor for the authoritarian transformation of the political system, which abolished mechanisms of representative democracy and excluded the non-governing elite from the processes of political negotiation. Because of profound social inequalities and social protest, it was also quite simply not possible to radically implement the neoliberal model in Peru without the aid of its authoritarian crutch.

The internalization of globalization was also made possible by a series of economic, political, social and cultural variables. Both the profound economic crisis and the fact that a subsidized and non-competitive economy could not guarantee economic development were determinant in the opening of Peru's economy to the world market. Likewise, this opening was made possible by the lack of legitimacy, articulation and mobilization of political parties, unions, social movements and the industrial and export-oriented entrepreneurs' associations in opposition to the neoliberal model. Socioeconomically, this model indirectly received support from the segments of the impoverished population that, submersed in unemployment or the informal economy, were not affected by the decrease of the real wage level as a consequence of the SAPs. Culturally, the neoliberal project was established in the Peruvian society by an aggressive public discourse, coordinated by the state by means of mass media, which emphasized the idea of individual effort as the only prerequisite for success.

The radicalization of the model in Peru even surpassed the demands of the IFIs and donor countries. The fact that the internal pressure to transform the economy was more intense than the external pressure had to do with the perceived lack of an alternative, coupled with the will to completely satisfy the expectations of the credit institutions and with the ideological direction of the technocrats in charge of formulating Fujimori's economic policy.

The state was the principal engine of this process, creating the conditions necessary to internalize the principles of globalization in Peru. However, it is not possible to completely identify the Peruvian state with Hirsch's notion of the 'competition state'. The Peruvian state was not oriented towards improving the productive infrastructure and towards promoting human capital, but rather tried to attract investments through the liberalization of labor market regulations, though privatization and through tariff exemptions. In the case of Peru, therefore, it would be more accurate to speak of a 'peripheral competition state', or a state wishing to attract investment without establishing a model that would guarantee sustainable economic development. Instead, its main premise lies in the payment of the state's international debt and reduces the country to an exporter of raw materials.

In the post-Fujimori era, the same economic policy applied in the 1990s is being furthered under the present government. The neoliberal model has demonstrated for more than 10 years that it reinforces social inequality, that it does not promote distributive economic growth and that it does not satisfy the basic demands of the population (see chapters by Soederberg and Taylor in this volume).

During the present government it is becoming increasingly clear that only civic mobilization can reign in the further liberalization of the economy. Unfortunately, the social movements are presently lacking organizational qualities as much as they are lacking the programmatic capacity to formulate and articulate an alternative project. Thus, the state continues to be structured on the basis of instruments oriented towards excluding the majority of the population from the political decision-making process. It also continues to resort to the criminalization of protest movements. Even though the perspectives are not the best, it is encouraging to see that the current movements against neoliberalism seem to be expanding into wider segments of Peruvian society, and in doing so, they are aiding the current attempts to break from neoliberal hegemony.

Further reading

Alexander, Kate S. (2003) 'Poverty and Politics in Peru', *Latin American Perspectives*, 30: 102–33.

Stern, Steve J. (ed.) (1998) *Shining and Other Paths: War and Society in Peru, 1980–1995*, Durham, NC: Duke University Press.

Teivainen, Teivo (2002) *Enter Economism, Exit Politics*, London: Zed Books.

Useful websites

<http://lcweb2.loc.gov/frd/cs/petoc.html>   A Country Study: Peru

<www.worldbank.org/pe>   World Bank's Country Profile – Peru

<www.desco.org.pe>   Centro de Estudios y Promoción del Desarrollo

<http://sisbib.unmsm.edu.pe/BibVirtual/bibvirtual.asp>   Universidad Nacional Mayor de San Marcos (virtual library)

12
Embedding Neoliberalism Through Statecraft: the Case of Market Reform in Vietnam

Mark Evans and Bui Duc Hai

1. Introduction: statecraft and market reform

In 1986 the Vietnamese government initiated a broad range of what it termed 'socialist oriented, mixed economy market reforms' in which the equitization or *co phan hoa* of state-owned enterprises (SOEs) was to play a central role. The process began slowly, but has increased in pace in the last few years as a consequence of external pressures from the IMF, the World Bank, and its most influential donors; positive lesson-drawing from China's 'reform and open door' policy; negative lesson-drawing from Russian 'shock therapy'; and, the acceptance by Vietnam's governing elite of the need to create the conditions for the establishment of a new development trajectory that combines elements of both the developmental state and competition state models of economic development (see Soederberg in this volume). Furthermore, improving relations within the United States created an international political climate conducive to increasing the scope and intensity of domestic neoliberal policy change.

This chapter presents a case study of economic reform with a particular emphasis on the equitization process and its social impact in order to illustrate the methods by which Vietnam's governing elite has sought to embed neoliberalism and reconcile the contradictory aims of market reform and market socialism. Equitization differs from privatization in the sense that the former involves the creation of joint stock companies in which the state retains a significant share of the enterprise and workers are provided with the opportunity to purchase shares in the enterprise. In contrast, privatization involves the transfer of state assets into private ownership. Until March 2004 it was illegal even to discuss the equitization process in the same context as privatization and the Vietnamese government was very quick to emphasize that equitization was not the same as privatization but formed an important part of the government's socialist-oriented, mixed economic plan.

Vietnam's Prime Minister, Phan Van Khai declared that 'the two fundamental aims of equitization are to mobilize capital and to ensure worker control post-equitization' (Government of Vietnam, 2000). For Van Khai, at least in public, 'this lay at the heart of Vietnam's national development strategy' and would be fostered through special codes of equitization which would be designed to protect workers during the process of market reform, create favourable conditions for worker shareholding and ensure 'worker mastery of the new economy'. In reality, however, Van Khai's sentiments are at best rhetorical and at worse deliberately misleading. While certain equited enterprises became joint stock companies, an increasing number are privately owned and run. Moreover, while the aims of mobilizing capital and ensuring worker control were probably always impossible to achieve, the government has made little attempt to implement the codes of equitization and thus realize its utopian ambitions. In stark contrast, the findings of our fieldwork reveal the emergence of profound gaps in the implementation of equitization. Redundancies have increased throughout the period of equitization, especially among middle-aged women working in low-skilled occupations in light industries, and the deliberate absence of an adequate social safety net for workers in the informal sector is resulting in misery for thousands of workers in former SOEs.

It is therefore our contention that socialist market-oriented reform will be short-lived in Vietnam. Equitization is a staging post to neoliberalism and the establishment of purer forms of privatization and can be understood within the context of a process of statecraft through which Vietnam's governing elite has sought to mediate the pressures of globalization and balance the interests of US governing elites, key donors (particularly the US and Japan), global financial institutions and conservative hardliners, while maintaining as much domestic harmony as possible. The concept of statecraft is used in this chapter to describe why, how and in whose interest governing elites adopt new development strategies as well as reshaping older development strategies in order to meet the real and perceived needs of globalization. The approach centers on the study of the Vietnamese governing elite and the politics of coping, adapting and internalizing globalization.

The data for this chapter was generated from two quantitative surveys conducted in equitized SOEs, together with insights from a range of qualitative elite interviews with members of the People's Committee of Hochiminh City; the Department of Labor; the Confederation of Labor in Hochiminh City; the Government's Advisor on Equitization; and, Directors of Equitized Companies in Hochiminh City.

The chapter is organized into three parts. It begins in section 2 with a brief account of the impact the US War had on social and economic postwar reconstruction in Vietnam. Section 3 provides an overview of the incremental process of market reform or *Doi Moi* in Vietnam from 1992–2004 and identifies the emergence of a developmental elite committed at first to a developmental state approach to national economic development but latterly increasingly to the aims of a neoliberal competition state. The chapter then presents a detailed examination of equitization (*co phan hoa*) as a way of illustrating this development trajectory and the way it has been mediated through a process of statecraft before proceeding to an assessment of its social impact.

2. Postwar reconstruction and development

There is not the space here to provide a detailed assessment of the impact of the US War on Vietnamese development. Suffice to say the consequences of the war live on and continue to impact on every aspect of social, economic and political life in the region. While the peasant guerrillas defeated the US armed forces militarily, US governmental elites continued to wage war on the peasants economically. In 1973 the US signed a peace agreement in Paris in which it promised to withdraw troops and pay $5 billion in compensation, but the money was never paid. Militarily the US armed Vietnam's enemies including the Khmer Rouge in Cambodia and although the tactic failed the economic war waged by the US against Vietnam was a success. From 1979 the US War moved into a different phase, a US trade embargo ensured that Vietnam remained one of the poorest countries in the world despite its reservoirs of crude oil, its status as the second largest rice producer in the region and its remarkable feats of postwar reconstruction (see Brown 1996).

There were at least three main obstacles to postwar reconstruction in Vietnam that created the space for the emergence of a neoliberal discourse by the mid-1980s. The first was the damaging impact of the US embargo on the Vietnam economy that led to a collapse in foreign investment, stagnant levels of trade, and slow growth in government revenue. The second was the adoption of an inappropriate postwar development strategy. Pham Van Dong, the Premier of Vietnam from 1976 to 1986, convinced the Vietnamese Communist Party (VCP) to slow down the collectivization of agriculture on the basis that it was impossible to change the mentality and working habits of the peasantry (Marr and White, 1988: 137). Hence, from 1975 to 1986, despite strong opposition from certain quarters of the VCP leadership, Vietnam adopted a Stalinist course of industrial economic development. This even ran counter to advice from Soviet policy-makers themselves who urged the VCP to develop the agricultural sector. On 28 March 1982, Mikhail Gorbachev, the future Soviet Premier, stated at the Vietnamese Fifth Party Congress, that 'it is important that Vietnam concentrates its efforts on developing the potential of its agriculture' (Sam, Hai and Khue, 2003: 13).

By the Sixth Party Congress, popularly considered to be the most important in party history, party leaders had become convinced that they had chosen the wrong development model and decided on a radically different course. From this moment a war of ideas emerged within the party between conservative hardliners such as party fixer Le Due Tho, former Vice Premier To Huu and the editor of the party newspaper, Nhan Dan and pragmatists such as the present Premier Phan Van Khai and former party leader Truong Chinh, who was now convinced that mixed economy market solutions were the only way to redress Vietnam's economic difficulties (see Moghadam, 2000).

However, two external events proved critical in informing Vietnam's incremental approach to market reform. The first was the collapse of the Soviet Union and resultant cut backs in aid and trade, which severely damaged Vietnam's economy. This included significant reductions in exports of oil and petroleum-based products such as fertilizer. The second was the success of China's incremental approach to market reform as a counterpoint to the horror stories accompanying the practice of shock therapy in the former Soviets and Eastern Europe (see: Bova, 1991 and Andriff, 1993).

In sum then, Vietnam's current development strategy has to be understood within the context of its recovery from the US War, the loss of financial, technical and structural support from the former Soviet Union, and the government's incremental strategy to escape from the constraints of a centrally planned, command economy.

3. *Doi Moi* and the rise of a developmental elite

The adoption of *Doi Moi* at the Sixth Party Congress signified the beginning of a major transformation in the social, economic, and political structures of Vietnamese society both as a response to economic crisis and as a product of the influence of a new party elite committed to a transition to a market economy. This initially included the Secretary General, Nguyen Van Linh, who had been pushing for radical market reforms in the south as far back as the early 1980s, and Vo Chi Chong, the Head of State. There have been five main features of *Doi Moi* since 1986: the introduction of a stabilization programme with monetary and fiscal policy reforms to control the money supply and prevent inflationary pressures: rural reforms to dismantle the system of collective farming and return agriculture to family farming (the 1993 Land Law formally gave land use rights to peasant households); price liberalization, devaluation, and financial sector reforms to introduce private commercial banks and higher interest rates; state enterprise reforms to end budgetary subsidies with one-third of the 2.4 million employees in the state enterprise sector moving to the private sector, the reduction of the number of state firms from 12 000 to 7000 through liquidation (2000) and the merger of failing firms into profitable ones (3000); and, the promotion of the private sector through openness to direct foreign investment, and, the liberalization of foreign trade (see: De Vylder and Fforde, 1988; Irvin, 1995).

Doi Moi was underpinned by a process of constitutional reform which was established through the creation of the 1992 Constitution. The most important institutions within the constitutional republic of Vietnam are the executive agencies. These include: the presidential and prime ministerial offices presently headed by President Tran Duc Luong (since 24 September 1997) and Prime Minister Phan Van Khai (since 25 September 1997); a cabinet headed by the Prime Minister and composed of the First Deputy Prime Minister, Nguyen Tan Dung (since 29 September 1997) and the Deputy Prime Ministers Vu Khoan (since 8 August 2002) and Pham Gia Khiem (since 29 September 1997), together with the heads of 31 ministries and commissions.

The 1992 Constitution also established a National Assembly elected by universal suffrage, as 'the highest representative body of the people and the only organization with legislative powers'. Elections to the assembly are held every five years. However, although it has become more assertive in recent times, particularly in relation to issues emerging from the process of market reform, it remains subject to party control. Approximately 80 per cent of National Assembly deputies are party members. The real power centre in Vietnamese politics, however, lies in the 15-member Politburo, last elected in April 2001 and headed by the General Secretary of the Communist Party, Nong Due Manh. It is the Politburo that largely determines government policy and its secretariat oversees the implementation of the national development plan.

As the following excerpts from recent speeches demonstrate, Vietnam's developmental elite is comprised of pragmatic rather than ideologically-driven neoliberals:

> Globalization inevitably means opening ourselves up to the rest of the world and making new friends with old enemies. This is the only way we can make our country prosperous and provide hope for future generations. (President, Nguyen Van An, Government of Vietnam, 2001a)

> The Government is deeply committed to facilitating private enterprise in Vietnam as this is the only way that we can maintain current levels of economic growth and achieve our socialist goals. (Deputy Prime Minister, Nguyen Tan Dung, speech to the National Assembly, 22 May 2003, reported in *Viet Nam News*, 23 May 2003)

> Old style socialism was too inward looking and made the mistake of ignoring the importance of the global economy; we can't make the same mistake. (Deputy Prime Minister, Pham Gia Khiem, speech to the National Assembly, 22 May 2003, reported in *Viet Nam News*, 23 May 2003)

The core members of the governing elite were all educated at Soviet universities and are long-time members of the Communist Party. Prime Minister, Phan Van Khai, for instance, studied at the National Economics University in Moscow. Even the more liberal members of the National Assembly such as its President, Nguyen Van An, studied at Donetsk University in the Ukraine, and Nguyen Ai Quec at the Communist Party School.

But what does this national development strategy consist of and who and what inspired it? The key features of Vietnam's structural adjustment to the global economy has emerged from consultative meetings with the World Bank, the IMF and its main donors, particularly Japan and, more recently, the US. It has four key dimensions, three of which represent neoliberal policies (World Bank, 2002d). The first dimension aims at 'gradual' integration with the global economy. Vietnam is committed under the Asian Free Trade Area (AFTA) and the 2001 Bilateral Trade Agreement with the United States to liberalize its trade and investment rules, abolish restrictions on all but five items, lower tariffs and gradually develop a transparent rules-based trading and investment system that will be required later for entry into the World Trade Organization (WTO).

The second dimension involves improving the climate for enterprise with the ambition of doubling domestic private investment over the coming decade through expanding the number of small and medium-sized enterprises.

The third dimension centres on strengthening the banking system to ensure efficient intermediation between domestic savings and investment. The objective of the banking reform programme in the short term is to ensure the stability of the banking system and in the medium to long term to promote better mobilization of domestic resources by improving allocation of those resources to commercially viable activities, and expanding banking services to encompass the whole of Vietnam. Finally, the final dimension focuses on the reform of state-owned enterprises 'to achieve a dynamic private sector, create more jobs and free up resources for poverty reduction programmes'. It is evident from this reform programme that Vietnam's governing elite has drawn positive lessons from China's incremental approach to market reform. As Prime Minister, Phan Van Khai, commented after a state visit to China in 2002, 'despite our historical differences, China's developmental success cannot be ignored and must serve as a model for Vietnam's approach to market reform' (Thoburn *et al.*, 2002: 14).

China's developmental successes have been the product of a considered, incremental development strategy that has rested on three main assumptions about transition planning and programming. First, that national economic transition plans should focus on the reconstruction of public infrastructure and economic management and developing the human resources, appropriate institutions of governance and forms of public management to deliver on development goals. The second assumption was that the civil service must be the prime mover in the process of economic transition. Consequently, successful transition requires the establishment of a strong, efficient and effective central administrative system. This normally involves restructuring through administrative reform aimed at improving efficiency, effectiveness and responsiveness. As Turner and Hulme (1997: 1) observe, 'it seems that all are agreed on the proposition that the nature and performance of public sector organizations are critical elements in determining developmental success'. Indeed countries that have experienced the most rapid and sustained development such as South Korea, Taiwan, Singapore, Thailand and Malaysia, all have highly effective public sector organizations, strong centres, entrepreneurial elites, relatively autonomous states, effective economic planning ministries, certain aspects of governance, and have engaged in civil service reform (see Leftwich, 2001). Thirdly, that successful economic transition requires engaging in progressive lesson learning from international experience but that ultimately indigenous solutions must be found to indigenous problems. Public administrators must engage in rational policy transfer and draw on the best overseas expertise that fits their own circumstances.

The close adherence to these three assumptions, allied to an incremental approach to market transition, has enabled China to avoid the catastrophe that has beset economy and society in most former Eastern bloc countries as a consequence of shock therapy. While China has consistently made the development of its economy its highest priority, it has recognized the importance of restructuring the institutional superstructure in order to deliver on its broader economic development goals (Xia, 1998: 412). This has led to a dramatic period of institutional reinvention to underpin the incremental process of market reform (Chen, 1998: 229). Vietnam's elite has closely followed China's 'reform and open door' policy, particularly the adherence to an incremental approach to market reform as a coping mechanism for maintaining social harmony, rebuilding domestic coalitions and encouraging increasing interdependence.

However, there are two glaring differences between the two countries' developmental strategies. The first is the absence of root and branch civil service reform in Vietnam, although the government has succeeded in professionalizing the upper echelons of the bureaucracy and developing an entrepreneurial central government cadre. The second is the relative failure to attract foreign investment and facilitate the creation of new private enterprises. However, both countries have neglected the importance of a balanced social dimension to market reform to offset the structural inequalities that emerge from market reform.

Nonetheless, substantial progress was achieved from 1986 to 1997 with Vietnam becoming one of the fastest growing economies in the world, although it did advance from an extremely low base-line with growth in GDP averaging around 9 per cent per year from 1993 to 1997. Indeed, Vietnam's developmental success by the mid-1990s led many commentators to characterize Vietnam as a developmental state (see: Leftwich, 2001, Quang, 2000). Although the economic progress of many developing countries in the 1980s and 1990s was slow, some achieved spectacular levels of growth and other forms of developmental success. These countries included South Korea, Taiwan, Botswana, Malaysia, Thailand and Mauritius. The character, capacity and role of the state are at the heart of their success. The concept of the developmental state has its lineage in

Friedrich List's (1885/1966: 175) argument in critique of Adam Smith about the need for developing states to use 'artificial means' (e.g. the state) to catch up with advanced nations.

It is a concept that has historically been used to describe the development successes of Imperial Germany, Meiji Japan, Tsarist Russia (which enjoyed remarkably high rates of industrial growth in the period before the First World War), and in some spheres where the state uses its power to promote and foster the industrialization process, in a fashion which the traditional teachings of market liberalism would have ruled out. In the aftermath of the Second World War it has been used to explain the achievement of remarkable rates of development through regulatory developmental intervention to promote the competitiveness of the nation in the world economy. The prime example of a developmental state was Japan. We say 'was' because Japan is now a developed state more akin to the competition state model in which liberalization has become the cornerstone of national economic planning. By the early 1950s, when Japan emerged from military defeat and occupation, she already possessed: a long tradition of public–private collaboration in the interests of economic development; highly-trained bureaucratic and managerial cadres, many of them graduates from the same elite schools sharing common belief systems, what Chalmers Johnson (1982) called 'the economic general staff'; and, a range of institutions with the capacity and will to bend to market forces in the pursuit of national goals.

Subsequently, the most successful developmental states of the 1990s such as South Korea, Singapore and latterly China are said to be characterized by four key features: a tight-knit relationship between the state and the private sector and the forging of a developmental elite; the existence of a powerful, expert, respected, continuous and autonomous elite bureaucracy; nationalism with a common view on national development goals; and, a weak civil society with poor human rights records. In all of these cases the developmental state does not dictate to the market but steers the efforts of market actors whom it can influence but not command through a process of statecraft. As Adrian Leftwich (2001: 15) notes:

> The distinguishing characteristic of developmental states is that their political purpose and institutional structures (especially their bureaucracies) have been developmentally driven, while their developmental objectives have been politically driven.

Vietnam certainly shares all of the core characteristics of a developmental state with one key sin of omission in the run-up to the Asian Crisis – the absence of a tight-knit relationship between the state and the private sector. Rather than prompting further reform, however, the Asian crisis reaffirmed the government's belief that shifting too quickly towards a neoliberal market-oriented economy would lead to disaster and growth in GDP of 8.5 per cent in 1997 fell to 6 per cent in 1998 and 5 per cent in 1999 (see Table 12.1).

4. Toward a competition state project?

Vietnam's failure to maintain rates of economic growth gave the developmental elite more autonomy to move more decisively towards the neoliberal competition state model. The government implemented the structural reforms needed to modernize the economy and to produce more competitive, export-driven industries and shifted its macro-level strategy from economic stability to growth. Subsequently, growth in GDP has risen from 6 to 7 per cent from 2000 to 2002 despite the onset of global recession. Vietnam's inflation rate, which stood at an annual rate of 300 per cent in 1987, has been below 4 per cent since 1997 with the exception of 1998 when it rose to 9.2 per cent. Since 2001 domestic investment has increased threefold, domestic savings fivefold, agricultural production has doubled and Vietnam has become the world's second largest exporter of rice (see Table 12.1).

However, these impressive figures conceal some major difficulties in economic performance. Many domestic industries, including coal, cement, steel, and paper, have reported large stockpiles of inventory and tough competition from more efficient foreign producers. Attempts to control balance-of-payments problems have not been successful and Vietnam's external debt accounted for 38.3 per cent of GDP in 2002 (see Table 12.1). Moreover, urban unemployment has increased and rural unemployment is estimated at between 25 and 35 per cent during non-harvest periods. Moreover, the state continues to exercise too much control over key areas of the economy such as the banking system and state-owned enterprises.

It is also important to note that Vietnam's improved economic performance in this period has been greatly helped by the normalization of its trading relationship with the US. Despite Vietnam's adoption of a socialist-oriented market economy in 1986, relations with the US did not start to improve until 1995 when the government initiated a more aggressive programme of market reform. President Clinton removed the trade embargo on Vietnam in 1994 following Vietnamese co-operation on the provision of information on prisoners of war and soldiers missing in action, and in 1998 granted a Jackson-Vanik waiver to Vietnam, which grants Vietnam normal trading rights subject to annual congressional renewal. The US–Vietnam Bilateral Trade Agreement, which came into force in 2001, significantly increased Vietnam's exports to the US in the short term but it came to an end in 2004. Nonetheless, this agreement has proved a critical juncture for both Vietnam's economy and for the normalization of US–Vietnam relations, although it

228   *Internalizing Globalization*

Table 12.1   Vietnam's economy and economic performance*

Character of economy

Gross domestic product	$39 billion
Real growth rate	7.24%
Per capita income	$483
Inflation rate	3%
External debt (2002)	38.3% of GDP, $13.1 billion
Natural resources	coal, crude oil, zinc, copper, silver, gold, manganese, iron

Sectoral performance

Agriculture and forestry (principally rice, maize, sweet potato, peanut, soya bean, cotton, coffee, cashews)	21.8% of GDP
Industry and construction (principally mining and quarrying, electricity, gas, water supply, cement, phosphate and steel)	40% of GDP
Services (principally wholesale and retail, vehicle repair, hotel and restaurants, telecommunications, tourism)	38.2% of GDP

Trading performance

Exports (principally garments/textiles, crude oil, footwear, rice, sea products, coffee, rubber, handicrafts)	$19.88 billion
Major export partners	Australia, US, EU, Japan, China, Singapore, Taiwan, South Korea, Hong Kong and Thailand
Imports (principally machinery, oil and gas, garment material, iron and steel)	$24,995 billion
Major import partners	Japan, China, Singapore, Taiwan, South Korea, Hong Kong and Thailand
Exports to the US (2003)	$4.55 billion
Imports from the US (2003)	$1.32 billion

Note: * Figures all 2003 unless otherwise stated.

would be wrong to exaggerate the social impact of the latter development. Anti-US sentiment remains socially embedded, although the increasing popularity and influence of US popular culture has mellowed the attitudes of younger generations.

5. Equitization and its social impact

It was argued earlier that equitization is a staging post to neoliberalism and the establishment of purer forms of privatization and can be understood within the context of a process of statecraft through which Vietnam's governing elite has sought to mediate the pressures of globalization and balance the interests of US governing elites, key donors such as the US and Japan, global financial institutions and conservative hardliners, while maintaining as much domestic harmony as possible. Equitization aims at bolstering the state economy in which public enterprises still play a leading role and attempting to ensure that all economic sectors are equal under the law and can develop through co-operation and healthy competition through enhancing the operational efficiency of SOEs. According to Decree 44-CP issued in June 1998, there are four types of equitized enterprises currently operating in Vietnam:

- SOEs that maintain the existing state capital value and issue shares to attract more capital for the development of the enterprise;
- SOEs that sell part of the existing state capital value of the enterprise;
- SOEs that equitize only part of the enterprise; and,
- SOEs that sell the entire existing state capital value of an enterprise.

It is worth elaborating here on some of the key articles of the Decree 44/1998/ND-CP that established the goal of equitization in Vietnam. Article 2 identifies these goals as, 'to mobilize the capital of the entire society, including individuals, economic and social organizations in and outside the country ... to create favourable conditions for workers to become shareholders and real owners' (Government of Vietnam, 1998: 3).

Article 9 of the codes of equitization deals with the issue of how the government will redeploy the finance generated from equitization. It identifies four legitimate uses: training and retraining to generate new jobs for workers; social assistance for redundant workers; increasing capital for priority SOEs and investing in high-quality equitized SOEs. In item 5 of Article 5, equitized SOEs are permitted to distribute part of the reward budget and the welfare budget to workers (without having to pay income tax) to buy their own shares, and to maintain and develop their welfare budgets through the formation of clubs and health clinics. However, the main purpose of the article was to ensure that these new company assets would belong to workers and be managed by the equitized company with the participation of the relevant local trade union.

In addition, Article 14 of the codes of equitization provides details of workers rights in equitized SOEs. These include: the right to buy priority shares at a 30 per cent discount for a maximum of 10 shares at $70, for every year they have spent with the company. Poor workers with an average income of $10 per month who are unable to make immediate payment for shares are also allowed to defer payment for five to 10 years without interest be charged.

In theory then, equitization has two main aims – to mobilize capital and to ensure workers control post-equitization through the creation of joint stock companies. The process of equitization thus constituted a radical change both to the mode and to the relations of production. Indeed, the transformation from state ownership to individual or collective ownership through shareholding is one of the most significant political and economic changes in Vietnam's postwar history and it has had a dramatic range of social implications. These will now be considered through an analysis of the process of equitization which will be divided into two main phases: the first phase of SOE reform from 1992 to 1998 and the second phase of SOE reform from 2000 to 2005.

The two periods are distinguished by an upsurge of external pressures and consequent interventions in Vietnam's economic development by international donors and global financial institutions that have featured heavily in the latter period of reform and have led towards the adoption of a competition state strategy.

6. The reform of state-owned enterprises, 1992–98

The Vietnamese government began to consider SOE reform in 1989. At that time Vietnam was almost totally isolated from the international community with only one donor, Sweden, contributing overseas development aid. Moreover, neither the World Bank nor the IMF had a presence in Vietnam. The problem of a loss making SOE sector prompted the leadership to turn towards privatization, but the collapse of the Soviet Union and the ensuing political, economic and social chaos caused by shock therapy led to a rethink. The concept of privatization was discarded and the government chose to use the more politically sensitive term 'equitization' to appease the party cadres.

The first phase of SOE reform was initiated through Decision 176/HNBT issued in 1992. This involved a range of management reforms to improve effectiveness and productivity with 720 000 workers moving out of the state sector compensated to the tune of $US 60 million. According to data provided by the Vietnamese General Statistics Office, in 1990 there were 12 084 SOEs operating in Vietnam, and this declined to 7060 in 1993 and then to 5300 in 2000. This represents a reduction in the SOE work force of just under one million workers; from 2.5 to 1.6 million. The first phase in the reform of SOEs was very slow, comprised mainly of pilot projects and resulted in only 116 enterprises being equitized between 1992 and 1998. In the policy review document 'Partnership for Development to 2010', the World Bank reported that over 'the last ten years, the number of SOEs has fallen to around 12 000 in 1990 and to around 5300 in 2000. Most of this reduction took place by 1994, but around 450 enterprises were equitized during the period 1992–2000' (see also World Bank, 2002b and 2002c).

However, the Vietnamese government did not possess the political will or even the desire to implement the reforms effectively and this has been reflected in the emergence of five profound gaps in the implementation of equitization. First, equitization currently means different things to different people. For example, the World Bank views the concept as interchangeable with privatization, while trade unions view it as a policy instrument for ensuring workers' control. At the same time the government is deliberately caught in two minds between the need to mobilize capital and the aspiration of workers' ownership and control. The outcome of this absence of effective policy steering manifests itself in the paucity of social policy and the social impact of equitization has almost been completely ignored.

Secondly, the Labour Code is far too expensive particularly with regard to pension rights. But instead of coming up with a viable policy alternative, the government has simply failed to implement the code. It is evident that the decrees of equitization are limited in terms of safeguarding the compensation rights of workers through penalty clauses and imposing time limits on the selling of shares. Moreover, the government has failed to respond to the problem of transferring pension rights from the public to private sector. This presents a significant obstacle in encouraging workers to move into the private sector.

Thirdly, significant governance or 'steering' problems have emerged in the process of policy implementation. The state needs to accept that it will always be held responsible by workers for failing to ensure that adequate compensation levels are paid to retrenched workers. However, it is equally evident that while the accountability route in this issue leads directly to government, the system of governance required to deliver a national policy of this magnitude requires the effective participation of trade unions and governmental organizations at the centre, in localities, and regions, together with international donors and non-governmental organizations. The national policy should be based on the principle of subsidiarity (that decisions should be made at the lowest level compatible with efficiency) but should be placed within a bargained national framework to ensure effective implementation. Successful market reform can only be achieved through effective, inclusive governance.

Fourthly, the government has failed to provide adequate public education about the process of market reform in order to empower workers to adapt their behaviour to the new realism and thus effect the behavioural changes necessary for it to succeed. It is evidently not in the interests of workers to become shareholders in companies that may prove to be uncompetitive in global markets. This is a high-risk strategy that could also prove to be divisive. Those working in competitive companies will enjoy greater privileges than those working in less competitive ones. It is illogical that all companies will do well as there are always winners and losers in a market economy. The early signs are that we are witnessing the emergence of dual labour markets and increased wage differentials between workers.

Fifthly, as Joseph Stiglitz observed in a seminar in Hanoi on 21 March 2002:

> Quick privatization is pushed by the Washington Consensus. These international organisations come to developing countries with large state sectors and say that one of the priorities is to privatize as quickly as possible. In practice this is the wrong policy. To develop your economy you can't do everything at the same time. You should focus on the priority of creating new enterprises. The development of new enterprises is more important than the privatization of old enterprises because it creates more wealth, jobs and national development. (Government of Vietnam Seminar on Market Reform, Hanoi, 21 March 2001)

The lessons from the former Soviet Union are quite clear; the rapid privatization of the state sector is not the key to development. It is much more important to ensure the conditions for the development of new enterprises. The capacity for the private sector to absorb large-scale redundant SOE labour is limited without further institutional change to promote SMEs in the private corporate sector. Indeed the social costs of privatization are often so great that development can be retarded for many generations to come.

7. The reform of state-owned enterprises, 1998–2005

The intention to accelerate the speed of equitization was announced by the government's Decree 44/1998/ND-CP issued on the 29 June 1998. Vietnam plans to reduce the number of SOEs to 2000 by 2005. Most of these SOEs are in the public sector and are corporate and strategic enterprises. In Vietnam's *Interim Poverty Reduction Strategy Paper* (IPRSP) for 2001–03, submitted to the World Bank in March 2001, the government announced its intention to 'implement a three year SOE reform program during the 2001–2003 period with annual targets to improve efficiency and to curtail losses in this sector ... the government of Vietnam will strive to effect equitization, divesture, sale, lease and liquidation of around 1800 SOEs' (Government of Vietnam, 2001b: 8). Between 60 and 65 per cent of these SOEs will be equitized, 350 SOEs each year from 2001 to 2003. This is in striking contrast to the 450 SOEs equitized between 1992 and 1998.

There are two main reasons why the speed of equitization has quickened. First, international donors increased their investment in structural reform and the conditions of loans and aid have added to the pressure on Vietnamese policy makers to increase the pace of reform. The World Bank and the IMF persuaded the Vietnamese governing elite of the merits of increasing the speed of equitization. The decision to accelerate the speed of equitization was largely a response to the World Bank's assessment of Vietnam's Development Report in 2002 in which it stated that 'implementation of the programme of reform actions supported by the IMF and the World Bank has been good, except for the SOE reform component which has slipped substantially'. In return for accelerating the speed of equitization, Vietnam has become a donor favourite with overseas development aid increasing from $200 million in 1993 to $2 billion. Indeed, Vietnam is now the fifth largest recipient of overseas development aid in the world. Moreover, over the next few years Vietnam is committed under AFTA and the 2001 Bilateral Trade Agreement with the United States to liberalize its trade and investment rules, lower tariffs and gradually develop transparency trading and investment rules to allow it to join the WTO (World Bank, 2000).

Secondly, the Vietnamese government has learnt enough lessons from the first phase of reform to justify further equitization and to push for the adoption of privatization. In spring 2004, the Vietnamese government convened a national conference on the restructuring of SOEs in Hanoi at which government officials criticized the equitization process for being nothing more than 'insider privatization'. This term was lifted straight from the World Bank's 2004 Poverty Report and represents a qualitative change in the political discourse underpinning market reform. Privatization is now an acceptable term and can be openly discussed. This also demonstrates that the governing elite has achieved the relative autonomy from domestic constraints that it requires in order to restructure domestic political institutions and practices around some of the core neoliberal propositions of the competition state model.

8. The impact of equitization on working conditions

Our survey of 100 equitized SOEs reveals that the majority of workers in equitized enterprises do not understand the conditions of their new employment. Prior to equitization workers enjoyed a range of social subsidies and health care benefits. Post equitization wages are higher but so is the cost of living. Moreover, the new workers do not understand the nature of shareholding, the operation of financial markets and the responsibilities of shareholders. The survey identified several interesting trends.

First, the number of retrenched workers is on the increase and this is in line with the World Bank's prediction that a further 400 000 workers will be made redundant from the process of SOE reform by 2005. Indeed, the Central Enterprise Management Reform Board (CEMRB) has estimated that 75 356 workers will be retrenched purely from liquidated and bankrupt SOEs (see Belser and Rama, 2001).

Secondly, the majority of these workers are unskilled women with low levels of education with the largest number being in the clothing industry

(53.16 per cent). Indeed women constitute 75 per cent of the total number of retrenched workers. Twenty-five per cent of these women have to rely on the assistance of their family, as there is no formal social safety net and hence their family's living standards decline dramatically as a consequence. In addition, the survey revealed that the compensation legally stipulated for retrenched workers through the Labour Code is often not provided. More than 50 per cent of all retrenched workers have been given only half the compensation due to them. Remarkably, however, 73 per cent have either found employment or become self-employed, albeit in very low paid work.

The survey also revealed a range of new trends in the working conditions of employees in newly equitized industries. These include:

- a decline in the number of workers with permanent contracts;
- an increase to the working day of up to one hour;
- fluctuating dividend income from shares;
- the erosion of social welfare entitlements in equitized SOEs (e.g. bonuses); and,
- poor vocational training for workers.

Some 29.5 per cent have been trained and retrained, but on average they receive only two months training during which workers have to accept only 28 per cent of their salary. This also runs contrary to the Labour Code which stipulates that they should receive 70 per cent of their salary.

Trade unions are presently playing an important role in articulating public concerns about the social costs of equitization. As the Deputy Chair of the Confederation of Labor in Hochiminh City observes:

> Post-equitization the role of trade unions is unclear. The owners of production are now the controllers of production and workers are wage laborers. It is now much more difficult to mobilize the workers as controllers as they don't own that many shares. Labor relations have now changed; there are owners and workers. (Author interview, 18 March 2002)

It is evident that the rights of Vietnamese workers have largely been ignored during the process of equitization. As the Deputy Chair of the Confederation of Labor observes, 'it was agreed at the outset that compensation should be paid but appropriate compensation has not been paid and an adequate social safety net has not been put in place' (*ibid.*). In former SOEs income levels have increased but not in absolute terms. Moreover, workers in SOEs have many forms of social entitlement established and delivered through labour codes that are not afforded to workers in equitized companies. In short, salaries may have increased in the private sector but welfare entitlements have decreased. Thus the challenge for trade unions is highlighted, 'we need to ensure a balance between the availability of jobs, levels of income and social entitlements for all workers' (*ibid.*). It is evident that the Vietnamese public is becoming increasingly concerned about the social costs of equitization. This has been reflected both in heated debate within an increasingly vocal National Assembly and the mounting of a concerted media campaign aimed at exposing corrupt practices during the equitization process. It is noteworthy that 85 per cent of our respondents viewed equitization as a corrupt practice (see *Vietnam News* and *Nguoi lao dong* since 2001).

Workers also have a range of misgivings about the government's expectation that they become shareholders. As one interviewee argues, 'The policy is fair but unrealistic and unattractive to workers because almost all employees are poor and cannot afford to purchase shares, no matter how much of a discount is given'. Workers are also concerned with the increase in the pace of equitization as it has become increasingly evident that the regulations governing the process are being ritually broken. Decree 44 issued by the government in 1998 abandoned the compulsory requirement of an independent auditor to value the total asset of SOEs. Subsequently the assets of SOEs might be over or undervalued and this has led to many instances of corruption.

9. Conclusion: embedding neoliberalism through statecraft

The concept of statecraft has been used in this chapter to describe why, how and in whose interest governing elites adopt new development strategies as well as reshaping older development strategies in order to meet the real and perceived needs of globalization. Our approach has centred on the study of the Vietnamese governing elite and the politics of coping, adapting and internalizing globalization. How has statecraft been used to manage the process of market reform? There are four main conclusions which can be drawn from this study.

First, in the early 1990s we observed the emergence of a pragmatic developmental elite committed to economic growth and the achievement of national development goals through the 'incremental' implementation of a neoliberal project. The political formula for achieving the aims of this project was derived from the developmental state model and involved: an unsuccessful attempt to forge a tight-knit relationship between the state and the private sector and a relatively successful attempt to establish a developmental elite; the creation of a powerful, expert, and increasingly respected elite bureaucracy; and, the attempt to develop a nationalist project through the achievement of a cohesive 'elite' view on national development goals.

The project initially proved successful in galvanizing the Vietnamese economy and led to remarkable rates of growth. However, this concealed certain vulnerabilities in the Vietnamese economy that reflected the inability of the governing elite to break free from the yoke of older development strategies and achieve relative autonomy from domestic forces in opposition to the neoliberal project. This was reflected in the failure of the state to implement key aspects of structural reform, mobilize private capital through equitization and create a vibrant private sector. It was also reflected in the absence of banking reform.

Secondly, Vietnam's failure to maintain rates of economic growth in the mid-1990s through to the Asian Crisis in 1997 gave the developmental elite more autonomy to move more decisively towards a competition state model of development. This decision was exacerbated by external pressures from the IMF, the World Bank and its most influential donors; particularly Japan and the United States. Indeed the normalization of relations within the US created an international political climate conducive to increasing the scope and intensity of domestic neoliberal policy change.

This shift in the development strategy has been founded on the recognition of Vietnam's governing elite that the market is the core institution of modern capitalist societies and that domestic politics should primarily be concerned with making markets work well. This has led to an attempt to restructure domestic political institutions and practices around some of the core propositions of the competition state model. Hence, although neoliberal practices are far from achieving hegemony in Vietnam they appear to represent the beginning of a new development trajectory that combines elements of the developmental state model with elements of the competition state model. The main constraint to the full-hearted adoption of this road to globalization remains the old party cadres and this has been reflected in the way that the state continues to exercise too much control over key areas of the economy, such as the banking system and state-owned enterprises.

Thirdly, the US War provides the crucial context for understanding the incremental approach to market reform in Vietnam. The Vietnamese people, particularly in the North, strongly associate market reform with the discourse of Americanization. Hence, the process of structural adjustment needed to be managed carefully, ensuring that an image of governing competence and relative autonomy from international forces is constantly portrayed. When viewed from this context the very use of the concept of 'equalization' by the Vietnamese government is symbolic of the impact of economic globalization. Indeed this case study represents a striking example of the problems of attempting to embed neoliberalism in a transition state.

Fourthly, the incremental approach to market reform has provided the best conditions for effective statecraft in the sense that it has allowed the governing elite to mobilize gradually a domestic coalition in support of restructuring while maintaining the support of the World Bank, the IMF, Japan and the US. In short, the incremental development strategy has proved to be the governing elite's key coping strategy for adapting and mobilizing globalization. The Vietnamese governing elite has clearly followed the advice Joseph Stiglitz gave at a Hanoi seminar in 2001:

> You will receive a great deal of advice to quicken liberalisation, privatisation and so on – you should do this, you should do that. Most of these are not real objectives. They are just means to an end. The objectives, in my view, are raising the living standards and social welfare of the Vietnamese people. (Government of Vietnam Seminar on Market Reform, Hanoi, 21 March 2001)

It would therefore be wrong to argue that Vietnam's transitional trajectory from a developmental to a competition state is due to exogenous forces alone. Indeed, as Huntington (1991) has observed of the current wave of democratic transitions, the incremental nature of this process has reflected just how important the effective management of domestic constraints has been for the governing elite. The Vietnamese government has sought to achieve effective statecraft through a Janus-faced strategy of simultaneously appeasing both domestic and international interests. This is reflected in the two paradoxical aims of equitization – to mobilize capital and to ensure workers' control post-equitization. In short then, statecraft is about the politics of coping, adapting and internalizing globalization. It involves short-term tactical manoeuvring – qualities that are essential to every successful market reform strategy and its ultimate success rests on winning the war of political ideas.

Further reading

Duiker, W. (1995) *Vietnam: Revolution in Transition*. Boulder, Co: Westview.
Fforde, A. and Vylder. S. (1996) *From Plan to Market: The Economic Transition in Vietnam*. Boulder: Westview Press.
Marr, D. (1995) *Vietnam 1945: The Quest for Power*. Berkeley and Los Angeles: University of California Press.
Marr, D. (1995) *Vietnam Strives to Catch Up*. New York: Asia Society, Asian Updates.

Useful websites

<http://www.gksoft.com/govt/en/vn.html>   About Vietnam's government and politics

<http://servercc.oakton.edu/~wittman/discuss.htm>   E Journals and Discussion Lists on Vietnam

<http://www.yale.edu/seas/bibliography>   Vietnam Virtual Library

<http://www.refstar.com/vietnam/onlinestudy.html>   Studying the Vietnam War

13
Globalization and Post-Soviet Capitalism: Internalizing Neoliberalism in Russia

Anastasia Nesvetailova

1. Introduction

Since its re-emergence as a sovereign state in 1991, Russia has been pursuing economic and political restructuring strategies. These processes have been strongly intertwined with changes at the global level. Like in many other countries across the globe, the ideology of market-driven globalization and a minimalist state predetermined Russia's choice of a reform path. This chapter examines the role of such a decision for Russia's attempts to build capitalism. It aims to provide an explanation for some of the key problems encountered by the country in the process of economic liberalization and reforming the state, and to outline a transformation of Russia's neoliberal project. Specifically, this chapter suggests that the numerous crises during the 1990s have discredited the model of disembedded laissez-faire liberalism adopted by the Yeltsin regime. The early years of the millennium have witnessed a reformulation of the neoliberal agenda in Russia. Under Putin, the Russian state is seeking to re-establish its centrality in setting the trajectory of the country's neoliberal agenda. One of the greatest challenges to this process is the political legacy of oligarchic groupings and the deeply entrenched social polarization brought about by the Yeltsin era of laissez-faire restructuring.

2. Theoretical perspectives

Scholars from different schools of international political economy (IPE) and other disciplines in the Social Sciences have analysed various aspects of Russia's political and socioeconomic restructuring. Mainstream IPE analyses stress the importance of national interests in the post-Cold war world order, and shed light on the enduring conflict of interests between post-Soviet Russia and the West. Although limited to realist readings of economic and political change, mainstream IPE accounts help explain the lack of international effort to support economic reform in Russia by pointing to lasting Western doubts about the future of Russia as a democratic state (Kissinger, 1994, 2000; Trenin, 2002). Studies within neo-Gramscian and Marxian political economy have challenged the narrowness of realist and geopolitical explanations of Russian crisis. Instead, they point out the importance of transnational class allianes and networks in setting the agenda and course of Russian neoliberalism (Bedirhanoglu, 2004; Clarke, 2003; Cox, 1999; Radice, 2000; Shields, 2003; van der Pijl, 1998, 2001a and b). Institutional and critical political economy provide informed accounts of the interrelations between economic, political and societal changes in Russia during transition (Hausner *et al.*, 1995; Lane, 2000; Pickles and Smith, 1998; Sokol, 2001; Solnik, 1998; Woodruff 2000). Finally, scholars in human geography, history, sociology and anthropology strive to see Russian transformations within a regional context, stressing important spatial, social, and cultural aspects that set Russia aside from the experiences of Central and Eastern European countries (Hann, 2002; Hedlund, 1999; Kideckel, 2002; Lynch, 2002; Reddaway and Glinski, 2001). Considering the complexity of factors shaping Russian capitalism, as well as the changing global context of this process, it is vital not to be overly deterministic in finding a theoretical framework that explains successes and failures of neoliberalism in Russia. This chapter therefore contends that it is important to remain critical and open-minded in analysing the structure and agency of Russian transformation in the age of global neoliberalism.

3. Shock therapy and disembedded liberalism

The collapse of the USSR in 1991 presented Russia with an urgent need to adapt its economy, the political regime and societal institutions to the laws of an open economy and new principles of international integration. The foundations of Marxism–Leninism, the official doctrine of the Soviet Union, were now bankrupt. In their search for an alternative program of economic development that would overcome the deficiencies of socialism, Russian policymakers strived to emulate the experience of advanced capitalist countries, namely the US and the UK. The success of the Anglo-American model in overcoming a deep structural recession and inflation during the 1980s seemed pertinent to the challenges facing the new Russian government in 1991–92.

As Chapter 1 of this volume maintains, all national neoliberal programs aimed at adjusting the economy to the imperatives of the globalizing market were founded on the aspiration to free the economy and society from the rigidities of the welfare state. In Russia, importantly, the newly exposed failures of the communist state and command administration implied that reforms based on a 'softer' version of neoliberal state strategy – that would have accommodated a compromise between the effects of marketization and social needs – were rejected outright as 'remnants of the past system', and thus as 'hostile' to the aspirations of new Russian democracy (Reddaway and Glinski, 2001; Tsygankov and Tsygankov, 2004). Russia's radical reform program was formulated by three powerful groups of intellectuals. One group consisted of Western economists, including J. Sachs, S. Fisher, L. Summers and D. Lipton. Another group included leading Russian economists, most notably Egor Gaidar. The third group comprised the IFIs, primarily the IMF and the World Bank, closely connected to the US government, particularly during the Clinton presidency (Aslund, 2002: 76).

Like elsewhere in the global political economy, Russia's reform project was founded on three crucial components. First was the idea that in order to transform itself into an efficient and prosperous capitalist country, Russia should make the market mechanism the core of its domestic political and socioeconomic structures, as well as the basis of international integration. Second, it was necessary to overcome the prevalence of the state in all major areas of life, and to eliminate the path-dependence of most economic, social and political institutions on centralized state command, provision and ideological guidance. Third, building capitalism in Russia required a creation of a new middle class, a layer of new property owners and entrepreneurs that would recognize the material benefits of marketization and thus would constitute the social base of neoliberal reforms.[47] In the economic sphere, price and trade liberalization, financial deregulation and privatization became the central components of Russian neoliberal project (Aslund, 2002: 77–8). This package of measures was not only an elegant theoretical model, it constituted the core of the paradigm of the Washington Consensus that had been implemented in several Latin American countries. The experience of Poland after 1989 also implied that formerly planned economies would respond well to rapid marketization (Aslund, 2002: 405; Gustafson, 1999: 12).

4. Economic openness and price liberalization

Liberalization, privatization and macroeconomic stabilization were key to the success of reform strategies, and the government's priority was to allow the free price mechanism to mend the distortions of central planning. In January 1992 the Gaidar government liberalized the majority of prices practically overnight; later during that year, foreign trade and financial markets were freed from state control. This sequence of liberalization was a crucial policy mistake since other facets of the economic system, such as domestic prices for raw materials, the rigid industrial complex inherited from the command economy, as well as the labor market, were left far behind the rapid changes in the sphere of consumption, external trade and finance. Price deregulation immediately led to hyperinflation: in 1992 annual inflation reached 2500 per cent. Moreover, financial liberalization prioritizes speed at the expense of institutional and structural balance. Trade and price liberalization thus unleashed a gulf between the real economy and the financial sector. In the absence of tangible productivity increases in the real sector, as well as of an efficient regulatory oversight, price and financial liberalization created an environment particularly conducive to financial speculation. In 1992, when the state price of oil in Russia was only 1 per cent of the world market price, domestic prices of other commodities were about 10 per cent of world prices. Managers of state companies bought oil, metals, and other commodities from the state enterprises they controlled, acquired export licenses and quotas from corrupt officials, arranged political protection for themselves, and then sold the commodities abroad at world prices (see Stiglitz, 2002).

Here it is important to note that although the opportunities for capital accumulation were vast in the early 1990s, survival of new firms was far more uncertain. This was due both to the ambiguity in the course of reforms,[48] and to the hardened economic conditions at the time. Following external trade liberalization, cheap imports flooded Russian markets, and domestic producers could not compete with imported goods. Soviet-time inter-enterprise links had broken down and this disruption in networks was paralleled by rapidly rising prices for inputs and supplies. While industrial producers struggled to survive, consumers could not afford to buy final goods at market prices since increases in real wages lagged drastically behind inflation. Russia's shock therapy aggravated the economic crisis of the late Soviet period and transformed it into a profound economic depression. In 1992, in the wake of first deregulation measures, Russia's GDP contracted by almost 15 per cent from its 1989 level. It was only in 1999 that the country's GDP reached a 1.5 per cent increase over its 1989 level. The overall recession of the Russian economy and contraction of output continued for eight years and was one of the deepest in Eastern Europe (Kolodko, 2001).

In the financial sector, liberalization created serious systemic risk. In 1991–93 capital requirements for a banking license were extremely low, while monitoring and supervision were at best formal. As a result, in the early 1990s, the number of Russian banks went from fewer than 10 to over 2500 (Perotti, 2001: 6). Around 80 per cent of banks conducted business with dangerously low funding capital: in 1998 the overall volume of banking capital was around $10 billion, which was less than a capital base of a single large American bank (Ershov, 2000). An efficient network of institutional control was absent and the newly formed commercial banks tried to survive by buying up strategic shares and establishing exclusive, long-term business relations (Mennicken, 2000: 46). While the financial sector grew exponentially throughout the 1990s the real economy suffered a severe contraction. While employment in the banking and financial sector increased by 80 per cent, employment in industry fell by 40 per cent, construction by 44 per cent and science by 54 per cent. Total employment fell during the 1990s by over 20 per cent (Clarke, 2003).

During the 1990s, new banks gained profits mostly by speculating on the rouble: in the climate of high inflation, banks could hold on to transfer payments for clients while earning the float. The inflationary period of 1992–95 also saw the emergence of many non-bank financial institutions, such as investment or insurance funds, that were designed as pure Ponzi pyramids[49] (Radaev, 2000). New 'hedge' and 'investment' funds launched an attack on the unprepared Russian public, luring people into buying the 'shares' of an investment fund for 100 roubles today and selling them for 200 roubles tomorrow. The most infamous of such pyramids was the so-called MMM Fund that collapsed scandalously in 1994, fleecing its 'shareholders' of millions of roubles.

5. Global financial orthodoxy and socioeconomic costs of Russian laissez-faire

In accordance with the IMF stabilization packages of the early 1990s, the Russian central bank had to cut back on monetary emission and raise interest rates. Following the radical monetary tightening of 1993–95, the money supply shrank to as low as 15 per cent of Russia's GDP[50] (Commander and Mummsen, 2000: 116). From mid-1993, the credit environment tightened and 'many Russian firms found that they had run up debts to suppliers that they were unable to repay ... They started to rely on barter and various kinds of IOUs to maintain production networks. As the barter trade expanded, so too did debts for taxes. Local governments, faced with the revenue shortage, developed mechanisms for in-kind taxation. As the vast fiscal implications of barter became clear, the federal government too found itself forced to concede to the use of alternative means of payment of taxes, which it began to do from the fall of 1994. By 1996–97, non-cash tax collections accounted for around 40 per cent of federal revenues and over 50 per cent of provincial budgets' (Woodruff, 2000: 461–2). The share of barter in total transactions reached its peak of 54 per cent in August 1998. The rate of demonetization in local and regional budgets was even higher. Demonetization of the economy had not only economic, but social costs. As long as industrial enterprises were kept at the margins of bankruptcy the workers were not laid off, but they were not paid either. As of January 1998 the average industrial worker was owed nearly two months of back wages, and in agriculture the average delay was more than four months (Aslund, 2002; Bedirhanoglu, 2004: 31; Ershov, 2000).

In the context of a deep economic recession, rising unemployment and prices, unpaid wages and pensions, the social costs of Russia's neoliberal transition became the most traumatic outcomes of the laissez-faire reforms. Comparisons with the late Soviet years, when the effects of a deep structural crisis had already been apparent, are staggering. In the last years of the USSR its GDP per capita was ranked as number 43 in the world. In 2000 Russia was ranked at number 135. Between 1989 and 1999, Russian GDP per capita halved: from $2554 to $1249. In 1989, around 11.5 per cent of the population lived below poverty line; in 1999, the figure rose to more than 35 per cent (Buiter, 2000: 61–11; World Bank, 2002d: 8–9).

6. Washington Consensus and Russian laissez-faire

In February 1992 Russia became a member of the IMF. After that date the reform measures implemented by the government were conducted in close consultation with the IMF staff and, crucially, with dependence on the signals given by the IMF to other international fora namely, the World Bank, London and Paris Clubs, international credit rating agencies and private investors (Bedirhanoglu 2004: 23). Between 1992 and 1999 the IMF disbursed $22.1 billion in loans to Russia. The most substantial amounts of money came in at most uncertain times of the Yeltsin presidency: the presidential campaign of 1995–96 ($5.5, $3.8 billion, respectively); and in 1998 ($6.2 billion) (Smee, 2004: 19). On the one hand, the monetarist drive of the IMF programs helped Russia stabilize its economy and in particular to tame high inflation in 1992–94. On the other hand however, much of the IFIs' guidance, technical advice and financial assistance has been counterproductive and politically biased: 'western decision not to support Russian reforms in early 1992 doomed the whole of the CIS to hyperinflation, delayed stabilization and perverted later reforms' (Aslund, 2002: 406–11). Stiglitz (2002) charges the Bretton Woods institutions with pushing Russia to privatize too rapidly, to open up external trade and capital account, and thus, effectively, with creating the chaotic environment conducive to 'asset stripping' and kleptocracy in Russia.

Most crucially for the socioeconomic climate in Russia, throughout the 1990s, the attention of the IMF was focused on macroeconomic indicators. Although the IMF provided technical assistance on ways of targeting safety nets, little practical effort was made to reform the social expenditures from general fiscal tightness. Having registered a dramatic increase in poverty levels in Russia, the CIS, Central and Southern Europe and the Baltics (CSB), the World Bank commented:

> positive developments largely explain the rise in inequality in CSB: rising returns on education, decompressing wages, and emerging returns to risk-taking and entrepreneurship. These forces are welcome despite the increase in inequality, because they signal that the market is now rewarding skills and effort, as in more mature market economies. (World Bank, 2002d: xiv)

The IMF, in turn, despite its concerns about the situation, did not push hard for higher social expenditures or a reform of the social safety net. 'In general, the IMF felt that it could not, against a background of weak revenues, insist on achieving both a satisfactory overall fiscal balance and the protection of social expenditures' (Smee, 2004). Conversely, the Fund's demands on Russia to maintain the schedule of debt repayments severely constrained the resources of the national budget available for social and welfare needs. Indeed, in 1997, Russia spent only 52 billion roubles on education, health and social policy combined, while 118 billion roubles went on external and domestic debt repayments. In 1999 these figures stood at 88 and 288 billion roubles, respectively (IMF, 2004b: Table 15).

7. 'Capitalists without capitalism': privatizing the state

Privatization was the third pillar of the Russian neoliberal program: it was supposed to ensure a smooth transfer of assets from the state to the private sector. However, the first two pillars of reforms – trade and price liberalization – put obstacles in the way of such a transfer. The high inflation of 1992–95 had wiped out the savings of most ordinary Russians so there were not enough people in the country who had the money to buy the enterprises being privatized (Stiglitz, 2002: 143). At the same time, the nascent layer of new Russian capitalists – company managers and directors who had access to export markets – accumulated total export rents of no less than $24 billion in the peak year of 1992, or 30 per cent of GDP. In the environment of high inflation private revenues from trade speculation were not accumulated in Russia but were invested abroad in hard currency, leading to massive capital flight. Throughout the 1990s annual capital flight out of Russia averaged $25–26 billion per year, while foreign direct investment in the Russian economy averaged $4–6 billion per year (Aslund and Dmitriev, 1999; World Bank, 2002d: 7). Effectively, the country's wealth was redistributed from the majority of Russian population to company directors and managers (World Bank, 2002d: 76).

There were two key groups of actors driving this process of 'stealing the state', who later became Russia's most powerful businessmen and billionaires with a global reach. The first group, particularly prominent in banking, included young men who established commercial banks with the help of *Komsomol*[51] assets in the late 1980s. In the uncontrolled economic climate of 1986–87, local *Komsomol* agents rushed to appropriate those party assets over which their committee could assert control. The second large group was those industrial managers who led the nomenklatura privatization and asset stripping. The prominence of these actors derives from their success at securing control over the assets they managed at the expense of central state administrators (Solnik 1998: 124, 251). Thus Russian mass privatization of 1992–94 turned out to be a device to transform the political authority of the former nomenklatura into its economic power. Hyperinflation conditions of the time reinforced this process, crowding small entrepreneurs out of the market. For although mass privatization enabled the workers and managers to become major stakeholders in about 70 per cent of the privatized enterprises, given their inherited ability to control the labor collective, the managers became de facto owners of the enterprises without any formal responsibility (Bedirhanoglu, 2004: 24–5, Gray, 1998)

8. The rise of the Russian oligarchy

Against the backdrop of the devastating socioeconomic crises of the early 1990s, Yeltsin and his government became deeply unpopular; his chances of being re-elected in 1996 for the second term were slim. Opinion polls reflected Russians' consistent preference for a political force that would reverse the destruction and redress social justice: in January 1995 Yeltsin had only 8 per cent of the votes, while the leader of the Communist party, Zyuganov, got more than 20 per cent (VCIOM, 1995). The government urgently needed finance to cover the growing budget deficit and ensure voters' support. Despite explicit corruption, undemocratic actions and feeble progress of economic reform, the West was ready to support Yeltsin in his presidential bid. In 1995–96 the IMF disbursed its largest loans to Russia, totaling \$5.5 and \$3.8 billion, respectively (Smee, 2004). In addition, American political consultants were brought in 'to save the world for capitalism'. For instance,

> [c]onsultants for Republican governor Pete Wilson and close associates of Clinton advisor Dick Morris, together with a TV advertising production company, Video International, all worked under cloaked arrangements in Yeltsin's camp, passing on to their Russian counterparts the art of spin doctoring. They boasted of saving Yeltsin from certain defeat and Russia from a return to the Cold War, and admitted to using a host of dirty tricks in their advertising strategy to sow fear among Russians. Their political ads, mostly aired over state-run television and radio stations, warned that a Zyuganov victory would bring back a command economy and a climate of terror. Ignored were the out-of-control economy, Yeltsin's own predilections for autocratic control, and his broad use of repressive tactics while serving as an unelected head of state. (Sussman and Galizio, 2003: 326–7)

Besides help from the West however, it was crucial for Yeltsin to ensure a solid domestic support from the influential elites. He turned to a selected group of Russian bankers, who had capitalized on voucher privatization and market opportunities of 1992–95 and thus controlled substantial financial assets. Suggested by the bankers themselves, a mechanism called 'loans for shares' was launched. The logic of the scheme was quite straightforward: financiers would provide the government with the much needed funds to cover the budget deficit. In return for the 'loans' to the state the banks acquired managing control over various state enterprises, mainly in oil and other natural resource industries, for a temporary period. The tricky condition was that if the state could not repay the loans back the banks would have the right to sell their shares in auctions and get their money back. Yet when this happened systematically at the end of the set dates the 'loans-for-shares' mechanism became a de facto privatization of large-scale state companies. The amounts paid in return for the world's leading natural resource companies were nowhere near real values; the enterprises were practically given away for free (Bedirhanoglu, 2004: 32–3). The resulting extreme concentrations of wealth gave rise to the term 'oligarch' in Russia (Buiter, 2000: 606, Freeland, 2000). Yeltsin was re-elected in 1996, and his government, now headed by a new generation of neoliberal reformers and closely linked to the oligarchs, proceeded with economic restructuring.

By the late 1990s, oligarchic groups represented a firmly established form of structuration in the Russian political economy. Yavlinsky (2003) estimates that three or four groups control no less than 70 per cent of the economy. According to Forbes the assets of the 36 richest Russians amount to $110 billion – 24 per cent of the country's economic output. Because of their closeness to the government, Russian oligarchic groups are sometimes compared with Japanese *keiretsu* or South Korea's *chaebol*: they leveraged their political connections, so that powerful 'clans' have emerged both in the centre and the regions (Gustafson, 1999; Sakwa, 2000: 200). Yet, unlike Japan or South Korea, Russian oligarchs have never formed an organized political force that would fulfill the function of big corporations in Asian capitalism (see Cerny in this volume). On the contrary, Russian oligarchy on the whole is quite fragmented: the tycoons are often at war with one another and their influence on politics is mostly achieved via aggressive competition in lobbying the Duma or via direct services they provide to members of the government (Pappe, 2000). According to the number of super-rich, Russia is currently ranked at number four in the world; according to GDP per capita indicators however, Russia is 78th in the world (Sakwa, 2004: 214, IMF 2004b).[52] By 1998, the effects of social polarization, the finance-driven mode of international integration, the ideological bias of foreign advice and misguided policy actions by the government had become unsustainable.

9. The end of Russian laissez-faire: the financial crisis of 1998

By 1997 the Russian economy seemed to have overcome the macroeconomic instability of the early 1990s. After five years of high inflation Russian authorities succeeded in stabilizing the price level and the rouble. The IMF, having registered a firm drop in inflation, praised the government's policies:

> Inflation has declined – from nearly 50 per cent in 1996 to about 15 per cent in 1997; the exchange rate has stayed within its predetermined band, and the balance of payments has remained broadly favorable. And last

year the Russian economy grew for the first time since the breakup of the former Soviet Union – if only by a modest 0.5 per cent of GDP. (Camdessus, 1998)

Despite such praise from the IMF chief, in the first quarter of 1998 the federal budget was still running a deficit 6.1 per cent of GDP. Faced with a choice between monetary emission and debt financing of the budget deficit, Russia opted for the latter: borrowing extensively, both at home and abroad. Continual issuing of high-yield government short-term bonds (GKOs) and long-term bonds (OFZs) became the major source of earnings for the Ministry of Finance (Glaziev, 1998). A chronic federal budget deficit has fuelled the supply of government debt paper, and high yields in 1995–96 have attracted both resident and non-resident buyers, especially after Russia received credit ratings in the autumn of 1996. In June 1997 the stock of GKOs and OFZs surpassed 100 per cent of the federal revenue. In reaction to market turbulence, and especially following the collapse of the Asian economies in late 1997, the government shifted its borrowing abroad to push domestic yields lower and opened the GKO market to non-residential participants (Sutela, 1998: 110). Russian banks also joined in the GKO boom: from mid-1990s, commercial banks and investment companies switched to GKO–OFZ trade as a major source of profits (Ershov, 2000).

By mid-1998 the GKO market turnover yielded over 300 billion roubles; while the existing money mass M2 was only 370 billion roubles. If in 1994 the internal sources represented 90 per cent of the federal budget deficit financing, in 1998 the internal debt was financed almost entirely from external borrowings. The bias toward external financing channels started to distress both individual banks' portfolios, and the country's levels of indebtedness as a whole (Erickson, 1999; Ershov, 2000: 289; Federal Council, 1999). In July 1998, when the fragility of Russian finance became clear, the IMF intervened with a support loan of $22.6 billion.[53] The IMF rescue package did not work. Once the foreign exchange reserves used by the central bank to finance the outstanding government's obligations had been exhausted, Moscow had to devalue the rouble and ultimately declare default (Buchs, 1999). By January 1999, the rouble's value dropped fourfold.

Moreover, there are speculations that part of the IMF July loan itself ended up in the foreign bank accounts of members of the Russian government. Since 1998, the 'vanishing billions' of the IMF credits have been the subject of investigations by the FBI and Swiss officials linked to the even larger Bank of New York scandal involving the alleged laundering of up to $10 billion in dirty Russian money (Whittle, 2000). Investigators suspect that elaborate schemes for money laundering, involving foreign bank and offshore accounts, were constructed with the assistance of Russian oligarchic structures, such as Menatep and Yukos[54] (World Bank, 1999).

10. Lessons from the crisis: Washington Consensus undermined

The August crisis came as enormous international shock. Michel Camdessus, overwhelmed with the results of Russia's reforms, confessed: 'not many had anticipated how difficult and protracted the process of the transformation of the state would be after some 70 years of the Soviet regime, and how dependent the economic transformation would be on the renewal of the state' (Camdessus, 1997). The Russian financial crisis of 1998 invited a critical reflection of the role the West played in Russian transformation during the 1990s. As a senior IMF official recognized, the Fund made two crucial mistakes in handling Russian reform. The first was the abolition of oil export duty, which the IMF instigated against the advice of the Russian authorities in May 1996. 'Given the importance of collecting as much revenue as possible in the 1996–98 period, it would have been better to have postponed the abolition of export duty on oil until the excise tax collection system and the government's authority were stronger' (Smee, 2004: 33). Second, the IMF supported the government's wish to liberalize access to the GKO market by foreign investors in 1996 (Smee, 2004: 33). As documented above, liberalizing the fragile financial market in Russia and thus exposing it to international financial contagion and speculative runs by foreign investors was a central factor in the collapse of the governmental debt pyramid. Moreover, the IMF policies worsened the 1998 crisis: 'by inducing greater foreign borrowing, by making Russia's position once it devalued so much less tenable, the IMF was partly culpable for the eventual suspension of payments by Russia on its debts' (Stiglitz, 2002: 147).

The August financial crisis exposed the disembedded nature of Russia's neoliberal project of the 1990s. Throughout the decade Russia's reformist governments quite naively understood 'neoliberalism' as a package of economic liberalization, privatization, and stern restriction of the aggregate demand. Such vision led to the emergence of a mutant, quasi-market type of political economy. While the central elements of neoliberalism – private property, liberalization and a minimalist state – have been imported into Russia, they did not facilitate a comprehensive transition from planned to market economy. Neither did they induce Russia's transformation into a modern 'competition' state. Not only was the actual implementation of neoliberal restructuring hampered by Russia's structural and political crises; the perils of building capitalism were aggravated by institutional failures, power conflicts and global economic volatility. The 1998 crisis became a watershed in Russia's neoliberal project. The devaluation of the rouble and bankruptcies of many commercial banks destroyed the fortunes of the nascent middle class, shrinking real incomes of the population fourfold. The crisis erased the country's fragile financial system, pushed foreign investors to turn away from Russia, amplified social polarization and precipitated the end of

Yeltsin's political reign.[55] Along with the Asian financial crisis of 1997–98, Russian default launched a backlash against the principles of the Washington Consensus in emerging markets, and pushed the Bretton Woods institutions to recognize the limitations of the 'one-size fits all' reform programs (Florio, 2002).

11. Re-embedding the state: Putin's neoliberal agenda

Faced with deep unpopularity with the Russian people, economic and political crisis, Yeltsin resigned from the office in December 1999, six months before the end of his presidential term. After his successor, Vladimir Putin, came to power in 2000 many observers concluded that democracy and liberalism had no future in Putin's Russia. A former KGB officer, Putin prioritized the idea of a strong, effective state. He initiated a series of reforms to re-establish the centrality of the federal government in the Russian political system, and launched an attack on some of the most conspicuous oligarchs. To many advocates of neoliberalism, both in Russia and in the West, Putin's policies stand in stark contrast to Yeltsin's explicit emphasis on liberalization and deregulation, both in the economic and politic realms. As Soros put it, Putin's state 'is unlikely to be built on the principles of an open society. It is more likely to be based on demoralization, humiliation and frustration of the Russian people' (*The Guardian*, 17 April 2000).

Yet throughout his presidency, Putin has enjoyed an extraordinary popularity with the Russians.[56] During his five years in office, he has been striving to transform Yeltsin's legacy of the privatized fragments of the totalitarian economic apparatus into a modern state based on the rule of law and efficient functioning of the market economy (Fruchtmann, 2001). His political program can be seen as an attempt to secure political legitimacy and a social base for Russian market economy: 'We need a consolidated and effective state power system in order to act on urgent social and economic problems and security issues' (Putin, 2001). Market economy, Putin argues, should be founded on the central role of the state in negotiating private and public interests, on the rule of law, on developed civil society and, crucially, on social stability and high living standards (Putin, 2004).

To these ends, the government launched a comprehensive program of socioeconomic reform, aimed at completing economic restructuring. The major issues on the reform agenda include fiscal reform, structural economic reform, and changes in labor and pensions codes (Nicholson, 2001: 881). Together, these shifts are aimed at enhancing the efficiency of the welfare system and are founded on the idea of a constructive partnership between the public and the private sector, and the prioritization of Russia's internal economic needs (Putin, 2004). To date, the most notable progress on the reform agenda has been achieved in the area of taxation and fiscal reform. Russian income tax has been lowered to a uniform rate of 12 per cent and is one of the lowest in the world. In 2005 the base rate for the unified social tax (ESN) will decrease from 35.6 to 26 per cent. Reform of the pension and medical insurance systems are under way, as are changes in Russian social benefits law.[57]

Have these efforts been successful? According to most statistical accounts, the current economic revival of Russia is spectacular. In 1998, real GDP growth contracted by 5.3 per cent from its 1997 level. Since 1999, the GDP has been growing and steadily reached 6.7 per cent in 2004. Employment and real wages have also been increasing steadily. Supported by the rouble devaluation, Russia's current account has been in surplus since 1999; the central bank's foreign reserves have been growing since 1999 and are the sixth highest in the world. Since 2000 the federal budget has been kept in surplus, allowing the government not only to keep its obligations on domestic and foreign debt repayments, but also increase its expenditures on social policy, education and health care.[58] Russia's fiscal health is among the best in the world: foreign debt is less than 20 per cent of GDP, compared with 78 per cent in 1999 (Weafer, 2004).

12. Putin and the West

Although his endeavours to enhance the role of the state in Russia are increasing compared to Soviet-style methods of autocracy and isolationism (Shevtsova, 2004), Putin himself recognizes the inevitably of global competitive context for Russia's political, economic and social transformation:

> Russia is being actively integrated into the international community. And despite the harsh competition ... it is particularly important for our country to find allies and itself to be a reliable ally for others. We are building constructive, normal relations with all the world's nations ... However, I want to note something else: the norm in the international community, in the world today, is also harsh competition – for markets, for investment, for political and economic influence. And in this fight, Russia needs to be strong and competitive. (Putin 2002)

The global context of Russia's neoliberal transformation has been supportive of Putin's endeavors.[59] Since 1998, there has been a paradigm shift in Western attitudes towards Russian economic reform. As Chapter 1 of this volume reflects, the Washington Consensus, while still intact, is less confident that liberalization can work quickly in all countries. Yet, despite a heavy critique of the IMF policies during the 1990s, the Fund keeps advocating further liberalization of the economy. While Russia has not approached the IMF for new loans since 1998, the Fund remains a close adviser and assessor of the country's economic policies. This time it puts a more pronounced emphasis on transparency, institution-building and broadening the tax base.[60]

However, despite the benign external economic and political conditions, and despite the recorded domestic macroeconomic achievements, critics contend that the agenda of urgent structural reform in Russia remains unfulfilled, partly because the leverage of the international community over the country's leadership is now much weaker than in the Yeltsin era (Shevtsova, 2004). Skeptics also argue that the post-1998 revival is a temporary phenomenon, attributed to devaluation and high world oil prices, neither of which will be sustained in the long run (Rutland, 2002). Moreover, in early 2005, some of the social and welfare reforms of the Putin administration unleashed an unprecedented wave of social discontent of Russia's pensioners and other groups marginalized by the reforms.[61] On the political centralization front observers note that Putin has hot managed to abolish the system of vested interests of major power clans.[62] As a result, 'crony capitalism' of the 1990s is thriving under the patronage of the president (Medvedev, 2003).

13. Toward a petro-state or competition state?

It remains to be seen whether Russia's current economic upsurge is entirely dependent on oil revenues or whether it is a reflection of real enhancement of the reforms' efficiency.[63] Yet there is no doubt that the current fiscal strength can be used to push economic restructuring, if the political will is there to actually support the reform program and to use fiscal resources to fund the mechanisms required for real and sustainable change in the economy (Weafer, 2004).

In this regard, Putin and his government are in a good position to use the financial cushion provided by high world oil prices to try and compensate for the drastic discrepancies in the social distribution of the country's economic product that occurred during the Yeltsin period. One of the most notable efforts to alleviate such polarization is the long-awaited law on the natural resource (hydrocarbon production) rent. According to the proposed drafts of the bill Russian raw materials companies will have to pay a differentiated tax on the right to extract oil and other resources on Russian territory. The new tax would add around 3 billion roubles to federal budget revenues, but increase the tax burden of oil firms and hence compromise the privileged position the Russian oligarchy has enjoyed since 1995. There is little doubt that Russia's private raw materials exporters have long benefited from low tax rates and their privileged access to the Kremlin. At present the Russian government receives somewhat less than half the world price from oil exports, while some European governments (Great Britain, Norway) receive about 70 per cent of the world price. Some estimates show that the oil sector benefits from a theoretical rent of $30 billion a year, yet pays only about $11 billion in taxes.[64] Unsurprisingly, the Russian oil lobby, most notably the Yukos company, aggressively lobbied the Duma against the adoption of the new law (Glaziev, 2003). Putin, however, supported the idea of a new tax by saying that 'the current payment system in this area does not provide for the recovery of fair and economically justified amounts of natural rent' (in *Kommersant Daily*, 22 March 2004). With Khodorkovsky imprisoned for nine years on various changes of fraud and tax evasion, the draft law is expected to be put before the Russian Duma in 2005.[65]

While politically Putin is often heavily criticized for his authoritarian tendencies, the advocates of the minimalist state, who regarded the (post-Soviet) Russian state as an adversary of democracy and civil society, overlook an important fact of Russian society today. As the devastating outcomes of laissez-faire restructuring showed, the paradox of the Russian state is that despite its endemic deficiencies there is still no substitute to state power. Even pro-Western liberals in Russia today admit that stateless capitalism is not an option for the society whose historical and current environment lacks viable alternative instruments of political, economic and societal governance. The experience of the neoliberal idea in Russia during the 1990s showed that although the state, by suppressing the economy, polity and civil society, poses the greatest problem of transformation, the very same state is also the main guarantor of reform (Medvedev, 2003; Reddaway and Glinski, 2001: 630; Sakwa, 2000: 200–8; Shlapentokh, 2003a, b).

At the same time, it is clear that Russia has not rejected the ideas of neoliberalism. What has been rejected, rather, is a deterministic, narrowly-set economic liberalism of the Yeltsin period, which prioritized marketization and liberalization at all costs, but was disembedded from the institutional dynamics within the Russian society and polity. Putin, in contrast, is promoting a more measured strategy of politico-economic transformation. Aiming to establish a constructive relationship between the state, business sector, and the public, Putin is searching for political and social legitimacy for Russia's neoliberal project. The implementation of this objective is likely to be marked by a complex set of Russia's internal socioeconomic and political dynamics. It will also proceed in close correlation with the evolution of the neoliberal consensus at the global level. Together, the complexity of global and national transformations over the past two decades suggests that while economic imperatives constitute the core of any version of neoliberalism, economic changes are inevitably mediated by a host of other forces, such as history, global geopolitics, national governmental policies, transnational class alliances and national economic and social institutions.

14. Conclusion

Russia's journey to capitalism has been a protracted one. The implementation of the neoliberal project in Russia has been intertwined with wider processes of globalization from the very start. In this complex symbiosis, the devastating costs of reforms of the 1990s, as well as the changed vector of global neoliberal consensus, have facilitated a reorientation of Yeltsin-style *disembedded neoliberalism* of the 1990s into Putin's *neoliberal compromise* of the 2000s. While politically Putin is criticized for undemocratic methods it is evident that an enhanced role of the Russian state in regulating the process of liberalization and economic restructuring can help to mend at least some of the devastating social costs unleashed by the crude version of Yeltsin's laissez-faire reforms.

As this chapter aimed to show, at least two groups of factors help explain this change of political discourse and it is important not to isolate their roles. First, domestically, the social discontent that followed the introduction of shock therapy in the 1990s delegitimated Yeltsin's chosen path of disembedded marketization and laissez-faire restructuring. Poverty, social polarization, unemployment, crime, corruption and disease have become tantamount to the efforts to build capitalism in Russia, and the future of Russian neoliberalism required a reformulation of the reform strategy. Second, world financial instability of the late 1990s was an important factor driving the change within the neoliberal elite at the global level. In particular, the failure of the IMF and the World Bank to prevent, diagnose and manage crises in East Asia and Russia in 1997–98 has exposed profound deficiencies and ideological bias of the paradigm of the Washington Consensus, and pushed global institutions to adopt a more explicit social focus in globalization promotion (see Chapter 1 of this volume).

Therefore, the trajectory of Putin's neoliberal project is being shaped by strategies and actions of various political agents, both in Russia and globally. His biggest and yet unsolved challenge in this process is the astounding degree of social polarization produced by the decade of laissez-faire experiments. His biggest obstacle in addressing this problem is the ambitions of the Russian oligarchy, institutionalized in the economic, political and even civil society structures. While the Yukos case may suggest that Putin's state is able to re-capture its autonomy vis-à-vis the oligarchy, other developments noted above indicate that the transformation of a consolidated private wealth into a leading political force in today's Russia, supported by global economic openness and transnational capital structures, has far outpaced the attempts to awaken the Russian state. In order to re-establish its social legitimacy in the long run, the Russian state will have to abandon its traditional political arsenal of rule by confrontation and oppression, and instead find a more constructive way of reconciling the ambitions of private business with the socio-economic needs of a large majority of the population.

Further reading

Clarke, S. (1992) 'Privatisation and the Transition to Capitalism in Russia', *New Left Review*, 196, November/December, 3–28.
Derluguian, G. (2001) 'Recasting Russia', *New Left Review*, No.2, November/December, 23–42.

Job, S. (2001) 'Globalising Russia? The neoliberal/nationalist two-step and the Russification of the West', *Third World Quarterly*, 22(6), 139–54.

Robinson, N. (1998) 'The global economy, reform and crisis in Russia', *Review of International Political Economy*, 6(4), 198–219.

Useful websites

<www.worldbank.org.ru>   The World Bank Russia Country Office

<http://www.cdi.org/russia/johnson/>   Johnson's Russia List

<http://www.polity.ru/engl/polity.htm>   The Polity Foundation

<www.gateway2russia.com>   Gateway to Russia

Notes

1 *The Economist* deemed New Zealand 'an international model for economic reform' (1993) and was impressed by its 'exhilarating dash for economic freedom' (1985).

2 These tables are compiled by the author from several issues of the OECD, *Economic Survey: New Zealand* and Massey, 1995, Dalziel and Lattimore, 1996, Bollard, 1988.

3 *Economic Management* was authored by a team of treasury officials known as 'Economics II'. It consisted of Graham Scott, Bryce Wilkinson, Rob Cameron, and Roger Kerr. The study foreshadowed devaluation, abolition of interest and exchange controls, the floating of the dollar, Family Care, the General Tax on Goods and Services, the fringe benefits tax, and the ending of assistance to industry and agriculture (Jesson, 1987, 124).

4 For a good overview of the Chicago School see Reder, 1982. Chicago School economist Milton Friedman strongly criticizes government's asserted tendency to curtail the freedom of the individual. He postulates a minimalist role for the state. Only the unregulated market will provide for the most efficient setting of prices, send out the 'right' signals, and thereby foster and encourage the activities of the utility-maximizing individual. Consequently, Friedman rallied against the welfare state and state intervention (Friedman, 1962).

5 Friedrich Hayek, epitomizing the Austrian School, portrayed state interventionism into the economy as both dangerous and self-perpetuating. The state is portrayed as an inevitably power-maximizing leviathan, eager to maximize its own power at the expense of the liberties of individual citizens, thereby commencing a journey down a 'road to serfdom' (Hayek, 1944).

6 Public Choice, originating at the Universities of Chicago and Virginia, is commonly associated with James Buchanan, but can trace its roots back to Joseph Schumpeter's writings (a critical assessment is Self, 1987). It is argued that bureaucracies are self-perpetuating, ever-expanding, and keen on inflating their size and budget. Bureaucrats, far from being benevolent individuals working in the interest of the greater public good, are really just utility-maximizing actors. Thus, they attempt to maximize their department's budget, size and scope and disregard the common good. By implication, certain economic activities are better turned over to the much more efficiency-oriented private sector where such malicious tendencies will presumably be kept in check through competition.

7 In 1986, Manning, Treasury Official Rob Cameron and Alan Gibbs and David Emanuel went on to found the New Zealand Branch of the Australian New Right think tank 'Centre for Independent Studies' (Jesson, 1987, 120). This center and its publications in turn served as a sustaining intellectual force, after the initial economic results of the reforms proved less than satisfying.

8 Financial assistance of the Social Sciences Research Council of Canada, through the MCRI grant, The Globalism Project (Principal Investigator: Gordon Laxer) is gratefully acknowledged.

9 The term 'national policy' has been variously defined as 'conscious nation-building policies of successive federal governments' (Eden and Molot, 1993: 232) and 'overarching federal development strategies for achieving economic growth and social cohesion within the Canadian political community' (Bradford, 1998:3).

10 Of course, Canadian statism is remarkable only in comparison to its southern neighbour. By European standards the Canadian state has played a relatively unobtrusive role whether considered in economic or social terms. One explanation for this is the weakness of the subordinate classes and the corresponding relative strength of capital.

11 This does not mean, of course, that the other forms of sovereignty existed in pure form prior to the current round of international agreements, only that they have been diminished by them.

12 Krasner notes that invitational infringements of Westphalian sovereignty have received less attention than infringements through intervention. Clearly, domestic capacity can be reduced as a result of such invitations. Reasons advanced for such voluntary reductions of capacity by 'rulers' include: 'tying the hands of their successors, securing external financial resources, and strengthening domestic support for values that they, themselves embrace' (Krasner, 1999: 22).

13 Texts of all WTO agreements can be found in World Trade Organisation, 1999c.

14 It was widely understood that companies had many more tax write-offs available to them than they took advantage of generally.

15 Sweden has long been dominated by a relatively small number of very powerful capitalists. Some of these, like the Wallenberg family, are well known even internationally. The degree of concentration of economic power in the hands of a self-conscious 'Power Elite' would have awed C. Wright Mills.

16 This was called the 'Solidaristic Wage Policy' in which LO unions would hold down wages in the most productive/profitable sectors (large firms, manufacturing, mining etc.) and push up relative wages in the less productive/profitable sectors (textiles, farming, small firms). The idea was to encourage structural modernization and change in the economy by literally increasing profits in some sectors while driving other companies and sectors out of business.

17 Unemployment was never allowed to exceed 3 per cent until the 1980s.

18 This was called Active Labor Market Policy, which would pay workers to be retrained or relocated without suffering personal economic costs.

19 Most importantly, the Ghent unemployment insurance was established which effectively gave the unions control over unemployment insurance (cf. *Rothstein*, 1992). But other 'pro-union' public policies were also set up and certainly the 'anti-union' incentives common throughout the capitalist world were eliminated.

20 It should be noted that few observers (especially academics) saw these strains at the time. It is only now, retrospectively, that we are able to see the origins of what began to pull the model apart.

21 For similar arguments see Rothstein, 2000.

22 Several changes were introduced in the new Constitution. The most significant, however, was the elimination of the upper house of the Riksdag (Parliament) (Sydow and Riksbankens jubileumsfond, 1997). This reform transformed Swedish governance in that now a relatively small change in election outcomes could actually change who held the reigns of government. Indeed, the Social Democrats lost power in 1976.

23 'Wage Earner Funds' were to be created though both increased profits taxes and increases in wage taxes. Though never fully implemented the idea behind this policy was to create a huge public fund, which would essentially 'buy out' Swedish capital and thereby realize the socialist ideal of workers owning the means of production (Åsard, 1984).

24 For a good representation of the views commonly held by economists in Sweden at the time see Lindbeck, 1983.

25 These taxes, moreover, were widely spread across the various revenue categories: The majority of income earners paid marginal income tax rates *over* 50 per cent, social insurance charges (employers paid) reached over 35 per cent, and the Value Added Tax was quite broadly distributed at a flat rate of 25 per cent on most goods and services. The curious result was a tax system that produced enormous revenues, but was not in itself particularly progressive (Steinmo, 1993).

26 Moreover, these high tax rates had been used by finance officials in their micro management objectives. It was widely understood that in all but a few isolated cases (i.e. tennis stars and movie directors) the very rich very rarely paid these super high marginal rates. The tax expenditure system had been designed to allow the 'big capitalists' to retain their wealth holdings as long as they left them in the corporate sector inside Sweden. By the mid-1980s, however, average industrial workers were paying marginal tax rates in excess of 50 per cent of income.

27 'Bracket creep' refers to the process by which revenues grow as taxpayers are pushed into high tax brackets by inflation.

28 Downs's logic was quite simple: because people would not see the benefits of public spending as easily or directly as they see the costs of taxes, they would favor tax cuts (or restraint) over spending.

29 See (SOU, 1987, 1989a, 1989b, 1989c).

30 Essentially, a two-tier personal income tax system was created. All taxpayers paid flat rate local income tax (30 per cent in most districts). Income over 74 824 kronor (approximately $9500) per year was also subject to the flat rate national income tax of 20 per cent.

31 There were a large number of income tax base broadening measures, certainly the most important of these was to eliminate the deductibility of all interest payments from personal income tax. Before the reform, this write-off was so tax favorable that a large number of Swedes borrowed money for investment (particularly in real estate) and then deducted the interest. Given that almost all Swedes at that time had marginal income tax rates between 50 and 80 per cent, this meant that the government effectively paid at least half of the cost of the investment. This 'cash machine' resulted in a *net loss* in capital income tax revenue to the government (Agell *et al.*, 1995).

32 The corporate tax system was similarly reformed, though the elimination of 'loopholes' was less complete – in no small measure because the distinction between a loophole and business expense is more difficult to discern.

33 Sweden was in the midst of the most serious recession in postwar history at the time. Thus it is difficult to specifically evaluate the exact costs of the tax reform. Subsequent analyses, however, suggest that the reform cost the Treasury approximately 3 per cent of GDP (Agell, 1996).

34 Indeed, Sweden has received high marks from a variety of often surprising sources; see the International Monetary Fund's recent analysis (Thakur *et al.*, 2003).

35 Certainly these policies also contributed to inflation, but few, we suspect, would have traded the inflation of the 1970s for the economic downswings of the 1890s or 1930s.

36 An earlier version of this chapter appeared in *Competition & Change*, 2001 (5), 135–63. Copyright permission from Routledge/Taylor & Francis Group is gratefully acknowledged.

37 There are about 10 countries in the South that receive the lion's share of foreign direct investment '(in descending order) – China, Brazil, Mexico, Argentina, Poland, and the Czech Republic, Chile, the Republica de Bolivariana de Venezuela,

Thailand, and India. These countries account for about 69 per cent of total FDI flows to the developing countries in 2003' (IMF, 2004a: 95).

38 John Zysman (1983) defines AICs *developmental* states as non-Anglo-Saxon state regulations, strong-state technocratic *dirigisme*, corporatist structures (such as France and Japan).

39 There were, of course, alternatives available to the Mexican state – one of which was to reject a repayment schedule that would harm the social infrastructure of the country. The Argentine state's refusal to follow a repayment plan suggested by the IMF as well as its private creditors (e.g. bondholders) after its default in 2001 is a case in point (for further reading on transitional debt architecture, see Soederberg, 2006).

40 It was not until after 1988 that the so-called Bankers' Alliance acquiesced to the government's neoliberal strategy (Veltmeyer *et al.*, 1996: 140ff.; Maxfield, 1990).

41 Structuralist theories of development suggested that developing countries would not be able to recreate the modernizing trajectory of the already developed countries without significant intervention by the state. State intervention, they argued, was necessary in order to correct widespread market failures in developing societies (such as poor information for economic agents, insufficient demand for products, etc) and also to promote the growth of domestic industries by providing cheap credit to firms and by sheltering them from international competition through tariffs and other protectionist measures. This development strategy was often termed 'import substitution industrialization' (ISI) owing to its aim of replacing imports with domestically manufactured goods. For an excellent account of structuralist thought in Latin America see Kay, 1989, and also see the chapters in this volume by Soederberg and Ruiz for analysis of the breakdown of ISI in Mexico and Peru respectively.

42 For a wider discussion cf. Clarke, 1988; Gamble, 2001.

43 For a more detailed examination of post-1973 social policy reforms in Chile, see Taylor, 2003.

44 At the turn of the millennium, the organized labour movement began to assume a more directly confrontational role. The post-1998 economic downturn coincided with the growing frustrations over the Concertación's failure to make substantial changes to the labour code and, in 2003, this culminated in the first national strike since the Allende period, cf. Taylor, 2004.

45 *La Otra Económia*, Santiago de Chile, April 2002.

46 *El Mostrador*, Santiago de Chile, 15 April 2002.

47 Since the political, ideological and economic machine of the Soviet system had spent 70 years denouncing the concept of private property and individual freedom of entrepreneurship, capitalist transformation in Russia required instilling a new culture of individualistic, market-orientated behavior. For decades, generations of Russians were accustomed to state provision of de facto lifetime employment, reasonable wages, free education and health care, as well as various other welfare benefits. In the new market system, such dependency on the state was considered counter-productive: individuals themselves were expected to rely on market mechanisms to be able to afford goods and services.

48 Yeltsin was permanently at war with the Duma, the Russian parliament, over the course of the economic reform. Politically, Yeltsin's policies of reforming the state steered toward Western democracy and values. The Duma, dominated by left-wing parties, regarded this stance as a betrayal of patriotism; economically, many draft bills were rejected by the Duma and often had to be reinforced by presidential decrees. Most conspicuously, in October 1993, Yeltsin commanded a storm of the Duma building where leading pro-left parliamentarians were besieged; some of

them were later imprisoned. Notably, the West chose to ignore the undemocratic attack on the parliament, and continued to support Yeltsin throughout the 1990s.

49   The name of the scheme derives from a famous speculator, Charles Ponzi, who operated in the 1920s in the US. A Ponzi scheme entices initial investors, after they have made a lot of money, to tell their success stories to another round of investors, who then invest even more in the scheme, allowing the hoaxer to pay off the second round of investors, whose success story entices an even larger round of investors, and so on. The scheme must collapse eventually, since the supply and trust of investors cannot increase forever (Shiller, 2001: 64).

50   In advanced countries this figure is usually within 60–100 per cent, and in other transition economies 25–30 per cent.

51   The youth branch of the Communist Party.

52   By March 2003, Russia could boast 17 billionaires, while the average monthly income was 3868 roubles ($110). In 2003 more than 22 per cent survived on less than minimum living wage of just 2000 roubles (Sakwa 2004: 214; IMF 2004b).

53   The Fund provided $11.2 billion of the sum, the World Bank contributed $6 billion; the rest was supplied by the Japanese government. The bailout money was supposed to support the currency, which Stiglitz (2002) argues made little sense. The rouble had been overvalued since 1994 hurting Russian exports, exacerbating structural discrepancies in the economy, and ultimately was one of the factors in the 1998 crisis. Maintaining the currency at a higher rate, as the IMF envisaged, was a serious miscalculation and would have been detrimental to the recovery.

54   Yukos denies that it has been involved in transfer pricing schemes, but oil industry analysts calculate that its subsidiaries effectively lost hundreds of millions in revenue in 1998 by selling its oil to the holding company at bargain rates. Yukos, like all petroleum companies hit by low world oil prices in 1998, reported a $79 million loss for 1998.

55   When asked about the failures of the 1990s, Russians placed the Chechen war first (18 per cent), followed by the collapse of the USSR (15 per cent), privatization and inflation (10 per cent and 12 per cent), the August 1998 default (6 per cent), Yeltsin's coming to power (6 per cent), 7 per cent of respondents linked the drop in living standards to economic troubles. When asked what role Yeltsin played in Russian history, 67 per cent believed he had a negative influence on Russia, while only 19 per cent thought positively of him (FOM, 2000, various poll data).

56   On the eve of the presidential elections in May 2004, Putin's approval ratings firmly stood at 82 per cent. In the latest parliamentary elections in 2003 more than 70 per cent of Russians voted for his party, United Russia (FOM, 2004, various data). However, Putin's rating plunged to an all-time low of around 40 per cent in early 2005, following the introduction of the Law on the Monetization of Social Benefits.

57   It is notable that the biggest political contrast with the Yeltsin era lies in Putin's relationship with the parliament. While Yeltsin was at odds with the Duma throughout his presidency, Putin is fortunate to have control of the Duma de facto through his own party, United Russia (Nicholson, 2001).

58   In 2003, 10 per cent of total budget revenues went on debt repayments, while 13.4 per cent were dedicated to education, health and social policy program (IMF 2004b).

59   In particular, changes in the Russia–US relations have provided Putin with considerable discretion in his domestic policies. The Clinton administration shaped its foreign policy around the promotion of democracy and market reform, with Russia being the prime pupil. This provided strong political and hence financial incentives for the adoption of reform by the Yeltsin government.

After August 1998, US enthusiasm for this policy sharply eroded, and dropped completely with the arrival of George W. Bush (Rutland, 2002).

60   The Fund's recommendations center on developing the oil sector and Russia's external debt repayments. Although in 2000–04 Russia was already repaying its debt to the IMF ahead of schedule, the IMF is pushing Russia to use the advantage of high exports revenues and repay its debt to the IMF before the deadline: 'repaying the external debt ahead of schedule is a good opportunity to save on interest charges; and generally it is a very good strategy' (*Nezavisimaja Gazeta*, 17 November 2004). Most recently, under the Fund's pressure, Russia conceded to writing off 90 per cent of its Iraqi debt.

61   In the first few months of 2005, a wave of anti-Putin and anti-government protests and demonstrations, mainly organized by pensioners, veterans of war, students, single mothers and military personnel, engulfed Russia. The protests followed government-induced changes to Russian social benefits law. The new law means that social benefits and provisions, such as subsidies, free health care and travel for people not in full-time employment (until 2005 provided 'in kind') will now be priced and 'monetized', and transferred from federal to regional budgets. Given vast economic disparities between Russia's regions, this change has exacerbated the bias between economic support to pensioners in richer and poorer regions. For more details, see <http://www.wsws.org/articles/2005/jan2005/russ-j27.shtml>.

62   Apart from the show trials of Berezovsky, Gusinsky and Khodorkovsky, Putin did not try to unravel the network of clans and cliques. Rather, he incorporated them into the power vertical of the state, curtailing the political ambitions of big business and appointing loyal chekists as curators of major companies like Gazprom (Medvedev, 2003).

63   High oil revenues, so necessary to pull Russia out of the 1998 crisis, can threaten the broader economic goals. High oil profits keep the rouble too strong and encourage domestic inflation at a higher level than the official statistics show. Rising liquidity of export companies may also create a speculative bubble, for instance in real estate, which eventually led to the Asian crisis of 1997.

64   A World Bank analysis based on recalculating trade figures suggests that 'transfer pricing' schemes alone allowed Russian oil groups to avoid paying about $10 billion a year in tax (*Financial Times*, 10 December 2003).

65   The law on natural rent tax has been a highly controversial issue of Russian politics since 2000. Apart from political conflicts between the parties around its validity and essentially 'statist' orientation, the prolonged period of decision-making is also associated with the complex methodology of calculating the amount of tax on oil and other hydrocarbon exports. As this chapter goes to press there are no clear signs that Russian parliamentarians are any closer to resolving their disagreements. President Putin in turn has publicly stated that there will be no re-consideration of the results of most of the privatization deals of the early 1990s.

Bibliography

Abugattas, L. (1999) *Estabilización, reforma estructural y desempeño industrial*, in J. Crabtree and J. Thomas (eds) *El Perú de Fujimori 1990–1999*, Lima: Universidad del Pacífico/Instituto de Estudios Peruanos.

Agacino, R., C. González and J. Rojas (1996) *Capital Transnacional y Trabajo: El Desarollo Minero en Chile*, Santiago: Ediciones LOM.

Agacino, R., C. González and J. Rojas (1998) *Capital Transnacional y Trabajo: El Desarollo Minero en Chile*, Santiago: Ediciones LOM.

Agell, J. (1996) 'Why Sweden's Welfare State Needed Reform', *Economic Journal* 106 (November): 1760–71.

Agell, J., L. Berg and P.-A. Edin (1995) 'Tax Reform, Consumption and Asset Structure', in *Tax Reform Evaluation Report 16*. Stockholm: National Institute of Economic Research.

Ahijado, M., J. Begg and D. Mayes (1993) 'The Competitiveness of Spanish Industry', *National Institute Economic Review*, November, 90–104.

Alan, J. (1986) *Sovereign Statehood: The Basis of International Society*, London: HarperCollins.

Albert, M. (1991) *Capitalisme contre capitalism*, Paris: Le Seuil.

Albert, M. (1993) *Capitalism Against Capitalism*, London: Whurr.

Altvater, E. and B. Mahnkopf (1996) *Grenzen der Globalisierung. Ökonomie. Ökologie und Politik in der Weltgesellschaft*, Münster: Westphälisches Dampfboot.

Álvarez, A.B. and G. Mendoza (1993) 'Mexico 1988–1991: A Successful Economic Adjustment Program?', *Latin American Perspective*, 78(20): 32–45.

Alza, A. (2000) 'Adolfo Suarez's Stewardship of the Transition – a Memoir', in M. Threlfall (ed.) *Consensus Politics in Spain: Insider Perspectives*, London and Berkeley: University of California Press.

American Enterprise Institute (1987) *The New Consensus on Family and Welfare*, Washington, DC: AEI.

Amyx, J.A. (2003) 'The Banking Crisis in Japan: Policy Paralysis in the Network State', paper presented at the annual convention of the International Studies Association, Portland, Oregon, 24 February–1 March.

Andriff, W. (1993) 'The Double Transition from Underdevelopment and from Socialism in Vietnam', *Journal of Contemporary Asia*, 23(4): 515–31.

Anglade, C. and C. Fortín (eds) (1985) *The State and Capital Accumulation in Latin America: Volume 1*, London: Macmillan.

Apeldoorn van, B. (1999) 'Transnationalisation and the Restructuring of Europe's Socio-Economic Order: Social Forces in the Construction of "Embedded Neoliberalism" ', *International Journal of Political Economy*, 28(1): 12–53.

Aragón, J. (1990) 'El cambio tecnológico en el desarollo del capitalismo español', in E. Criada, A. Durán, J. Aragón *et al.*, *Ciencia y cambio tecnológico en España*, Madrid: Fundación Primer de Mayo, 43–103.

Arce Borja, L. (ed.) (1994) *Guerra Popular en el Perú. El Pensamiento Gonzalo*, Frankfurt am Main: Zambon Verlag.

Arce, M. (1996) 'Qué tan eficiente es la política social del FONCODES', *Pretextos*, 9: 95–113.

Armijo, L.E. (ed.) (2001) *Debating the Global Financial Architecture*, Binghampton, NY: State University of New York Press.

Åsard, E. (1984) 'Industrial and Economic Democracy in Sweden: From Consensus to Confrontation', Paper presented at ECPR, 12th Joint Session, 13–18 April, at Salzburg, Austria.

Aslund, A. (2002) *Building Capitalism*, Cambridge: Cambridge University Press.

Aslund, A. and Dmitriev, M. (1999) 'Economic Reform Versus Rent Seeking', in A. Aslund and M. Olcott (eds) *Russia After Communism*, Washington, DC: Carnegie Endowment for International Peace.

Atkinson, A. and T. Smeeding (1995) 'Income Distribution in OECD Countries', Paris: Organization for Economic Cooperation and Development.

Azpur, J., R. Pizarro, E. Toche, L. Trelles and C. Zavalla (2004) *Perú Hoy. Los Mil Días de Toledo*, Lima: Desco.

Balassa, B. (1981) *The Newly Industrializing Countries in the World Economy*, New York and Oxford: Pergamon Press.

Ballón Echegaray, E. (2002) 'El Toledismo y el Movimiento Social', in *Perú Hoy. Toledo: A un año de Gobierno*, Lima: Venica.

Banco de México (1990) *Informe Anual 1990*, México: Banco de México.

Bank for International Settlements (1996) *66th Annual Report*, Basle: Bank for International Settlements.

Banting, K. (1987) *The Welfare State and Canadian Federalism*, second edn, Kingston and Montreal: McGill-Queen's University Press.

Bauman, Z. (1998) *Globalization: The Human Consequences*, Cambridge: Polity.

Beaumont, M. (1996) 'Reforma del Estado y Política Social como reconstituyentes de la Trama Social', *Pretextos*, 9: 41–51.

Beck, U. (2000) *What Is Globalization?* Cambridge: Polity.

Bedirhanoglu, P. (2004) 'The Nomenklatura's Passive Revolution in Russia in the Neoliberal Era', in L. McCann (ed.) *Russian Transformations: Challenging the Global Narrative*, London and New York: RoutledgeCurzon.

Béjar, H. (1999) *Situación y perspectivas de la política social*, in H. Béjar (ed.) *El Perú realmente existente*, Lima: Centro de Estudios para el Desarollo y la Participación.

Belser, P. and M. Rama (2001) *State Ownership and Labor Redundancy: Estimates Based on Enterprise-Level Data from Vietnam*, World Bank Policy Research Working Paper No. 2599, Washington, DC: World Bank.

Berger, S. and R.P. Dore (eds) (1996) *National Diversity and Global Capitalism*, Ithaca, NY: Cornell University Press.

Bergstrom, V. (1982) *Studies in Swedish Post-War Industrial Investments*. Uppsala: Almquist and Wiksell.

Berliner Zeitung (15 July 1996) 'Strukturreform zu lange verschoben' [Structural reform put off for too long – Interview with head of BDI Henkel].

Berliner Zeitung (15 April 1997) 'Industrie hält Standort für Mittelmaß' [Major business considers business environment to be mediocre].

Berliner Zeitung (20 September 1997) 'BDI-Chef attackiert SPD-Vorstand' [BDI Head attacks SPD leadership].

Berliner Zeitung (30 May 2003) 'Wirtschaft: Agenda 2010 ist das Minimum' [Agenda 2010 is the minimum demand].

Berliner Zeitung (2 June 2003a) 'Lob für den Kanzler' [Encouragement for the Chancellor].

Berliner Zeitung (2 June 2003b) 'Schröder zwingt SPD auf Kurs' [Schröder forces SPD to follow his course].

Bertelsmann Stiftung (2002) *Internationales Beschäftigungs-Ranking*, Gütersloh.
Beuter, R. (1994) 'Germany and the Ratification of the Maastricht Treaty', in F. Laursen and S. Vanhoonacker (eds) *The Ratification of the Maastricht Treaty: Issues, Debates and Future Implications*, Dordrecht: Martinus Nijhoff Publishers, 87–112.
Bilbao Ubillos, J. (1995) 'Privatizaciones y política financiera del sector público', *Hacienda Pública Española*, 132: 49–61.
Black, D. and C.T. Sjolander (1996) 'Multilateralism Reconstituted and the Discourse of Canadian Foreign Policy', *Studies in Political Economy*, 4: 120–45.
Blyth, M. (2002) *Great Transformations: Economic Ideas and Institutional Change in the Twentieth Century*, New York: Cambridge University Press.
Bollard, A. (ed.) (1988) *The Influence of United States Economics on New Zealand: The Fulbright Anniversary Seminars*, Wellington: New Zealand Institute of Economic Research, Research Monograph 42.
Bollard, A., B. Silverstone and R. Lattimore (1996) *A Study of Economic Reform: The Case of New Zealand*, Amsterdam: North Holland.
Boston, J. (1987) 'Thatcherism and Rogernomics: Changing the Rules of the Game – Comparisons and Contrasts', *Political Science*, 39(2): 129–52.
Boston, J. (1989) 'The Treasury and the Organisation of Economic Advice: Some International Comparisons', in B. Easton (ed.) *The Making of Rogernomics*, Auckland: Auckland University Press.
Boston, J. (1991) 'The Theoretical Underpinnings of Public Sector Restructuring in New Zealand', in J. Boston *et al. Reshaping the State: New Zealand's Bureaucratic Revolution*, Auckland: Oxford University Press.
Bova, R. (1991) 'Political Dynamics of the Post-Communist Transition: A Comparative Perspective', *World Politics*, 44: 113–38.
Boyer, R. and D. Drache (1996) (eds) *States Against Markets*, New York: Routledge.
Bradford, N. (1998) *Commissioning Ideas*, Toronto: Oxford University Press.
Brodie, J. and J. Jenson (1988) *Crisis, Challenge and Change: Party and Class in Canada Revisited*, Ottawa: Carleton University Press.
Brodie, Janine (1990) *The Political Economy of Canadian Regionalism*, Toronto: Harcourt Brace Jovanovich.
Brooks, S. (2000) 'Understanding the Recent Change in the Structure of Global Production', Ph.D. dissertation in Political Science, Yale University, Princeton.
Brown, D.M. (1991) 'The Evolving Role of the Provinces in Canadian Trade Policy', in D.M. Brown and G. Smith (eds) *Canadian Federalism: Meeting Global Challenges?*, Kingston: Queen's University Institute of Intergovernmental Relations.
Brown, F. (1996) 'Vietnam's Tentative Transformation', *Journal of Democracy*, 7(4): 73–87.
Brown Jr, J.R. (1994) *Opening Japan's Financial Markets*, London: Routledge.
Buchs, T. (1999) 'Financial Crisis in the Russian Federation', *Economics of Transition*, 7(3): 687–715.
Buesa, M. (1994) 'La política tecnológica en España: Una evaluación en la perspectiva del sistema productive El caso de la industría electrónica española durante los años 80', *Información Comercial Española*, 726: 161–82.
Buesa, M. and J. Molero (1987) 'La intervención estatal en la remodelación delsistema productivo – el caso de la industría española durante los años 80', *Estudios de Economía* (7): 271–95.
Buiter, W. (2000) 'From Predation to Accumulation? The Second Transition Decade in Russia', *Economics of Transition*, 8(3): 603–22.
Burnham, P. (1994) 'The Organisational View of the State', *Politics*, 2: 67–81.

Business Council on National Issues (1985) *Canadian Trade, Competitiveness and Sovereignty: The Prospect of New Trade Agreements with the United States*, Ottawa: BCNI Canada.

Callinicos, A. (2001) *Against the Third Way*, Cambridge: Polity.

Calmfors, L. and J. Driffill (1988) 'Centralization of Wage Bargaining', *Economic Policy*, 6: 13–61.

Camdessus, M. (1997) 'Crisis of the State', Address at the Moscow Institute of International Affairs, Moscow, 2 April, Washington, DC: IMF.

Camdessus, M. (1998) 'Russia and the IMF', Address at the US–Russian Business Council, July, Washington, DC: IMF.

Cameron, David (1984) 'Social Democracy, Corporatism, and Labour Quiescence, and the Representation of Economic Interests in Advanced Capitalist Society', in J. Goldthorpe (ed.) *Order and Conflict*, Oxford: Oxford University Press.

Cameron, M.A. (1994) *Democracy and Authoritarism in Peru. Political Coalitions and Social Change*, New York: St Martin's Press.

Canada (1985) Report: Royal Commission on the Economic Union and Development Prospects for Canada, 3 vols., Ottawa: Ministry of Supply and Services.

Carillo, S. (2000) 'The Consensus Building Role of the Spanish Communist Party', in M. Threlfall (ed.) *Consensus Politics in Spain: Insider Perspectives*, Bristol: Intellect.

Carroll, W.K. (1986) *Corporate Power and Canadian Capitalism*, Vancouver: University of British Columbia Press.

Castells, M. *et al.* (l986) *El desafío tecnológico: España y las nuevas tecnologias*, Madrid: Alianza Editorial.

Cawson, A. (ed.) (1985) *Organized Interests and the State: Studies in Meso-Corporatism*, London: Sage.

CEPAL (Comisión Económico de América Latina y el Caribe) (2001) *Anuario estadistico de América Latina y el Caribe 2000*, Santiago: CEPAL.

Cerny, P.G. (1990) *The Changing Architecture of Politics: Structure, Agency, and the Future of the State*, London and Thousand Oaks, CA: Sage.

Cerny, P.G. (1991) 'The Limits of Deregulation: Transnational Interpenetration and Policy Change,' *European Journal of Political Research*, 19 (1/2): 218–41.

Cerny, P.G. (1993a) 'American Decline and the Emergence of Embedded Financial Orthodoxy', in Philip G. Cerny (ed.) *Finance and World Politics: Markets, Regimes and States in the Post-hegemonic Era*, Cheltenham, UK: Edward Elgar.

Cerny, P.G. (ed.) (1993b) *Finance and World Politics: Markets, Regimes and States in the Post-Hegemonic Era*, Cheltenham, UK and Brookfield, VT: Edward Elgar.

Cerny, P.G. (1994) 'The Dynamics of Financial Globalization', *Policy Sciences*, 27(4): 319–42.

Cerny, P.G. (1997) 'The Search for a Paperless World: Technology, Financial Globalisation and Policy Response', in M. Talalay, C. Farrands and R. Tooze (eds) *Technology, Culture and Competitiveness: Change and the World Political Economy*, London and New York: Routledge.

Cerny, P.G. (1999) 'Reconstructing the Political in a Globalizing World: States, Institutions, Actors and Governance', Paper presented to the Workshop 'National Models and Transnational Structures', Joint Meetings of Workshops, European Consortium for Political Research, Mannheim, Germany, 26–31 March, mimeo.

Cerny, P.G. and M. Evans (2000a) 'New Labour, Globalisation and the Competition State', *Harvard Papers* 70, Centre for European Studies, Harvard University.

Cerny, P.G. (2000b) 'Embedding Global Financial Markets: Securitization and the Emerging Web of Governance', in K. Ronit and V. Schneider (eds) *Private Organizations in Global Politics*, London: Routledge.

Cerny, P.G. (2000c) 'Money and Power: The American Financial System from Free Banking to Global Competition', in G. Thompson (ed.) *Markets*, vol. 2 of *The United States in the Twentieth Century*, London: Hodder and Stoughton for the Open University.

Cerny, P.G. (2000d) 'The New Security Dilemma: Divisibility, Defection and Disorder in the Global Era', *Review of International Studies*, 26(4): 623–46.

Cerny, P.G. (2000e) 'Globalization and the Restructuring of the Political Arena: Paradoxes of the Competition State', in R. Germain (ed.) *Globalization and Its Critics*, London: Macmillan, 117–38.

Cerny, P.G. (2002) 'Webs of Governance: National Authorities and Transnational Markets', in D.M. Andrews, C.R. Henning and L.W. Pauly (eds) *Governing the World's Money*, Ithaca, NY: Cornell University Press.

Cerny, P.G. (2003). 'Globalization as Politics', in J. Busumtwi-Sam and L. Dobuzinskis (eds) *Turbulence and New Directions in the Global Political Economy*, Basingstoke: Palgrave Macmillan, 1–32.

Cerny, P.G. and S. Endo (2004) 'Reluctant Leadership: Dilemmas of Operationalizing Hegemony', Paper presented at the annual convention of the International Studies Association, Montreal, Quebec, Canada, 17–20 March.

Cerny, P.G. (2005a) 'Terrorism and the New Security Dilemma', *Naval War College Review*, LVIII [58](1) (Winter): 11–33.

Cerny, P.G. (2005b) 'Governance, Globalization and the Japanese Financial System: Resistance or Restructuring?', in G. Hook (ed.) *Contested Governance in Japan*, London: Routledge.

Chandler Jr, A.D. (1990) *Scale and Scope: The Dynamics of Industrial Capitalism*, Cambridge, MA: Harvard University Press.

Chen, R. (1998) *Experiences and Problems in the Current Administrative Reform in China*, Guangdong: Guangdong Higher Education Press.

Clayton, R. and J. Pontusson (1998) 'Welfare-State Retrenchment Revisited – Entitlement Cuts, Public Sector Restructuring, and Inegalitarian Trends in Advanced Capitalist Societies', *World Politics*, 51 (1).

Clarke, S. (1988) *Keynesianism, Monetarism and the Crisis of the State*, Aldershot, UK: Edward Elgar.

Clarke, S. (2003) 'Globalisation and the Development of Russian Capitalism', Paper presented to the international conference 'Marx and the challenges of the 21st century', Havana, 5–8 May, available at: <http://www.nodo50.org/cubasigloXXI/congreso/clarke_10abr03.pdf>.

Clarkson, S. (1985) *Canada and the Reagan Challenge*, Toronto: James Lorimer and Company.

Clarkson, Stephen D. Drache and M.S. Gertler (eds) (1991) 'Disjunctions: Free Trade and the Paradox of Canadian Development', in *The New Era of Global Competition: State Policy and Market Power*, Montreal: McGill-Queens University Press.

Clarkson, Stephen (1993) 'Constitutionalizing the Canadian–American Relationship', in D. Cameron and M. Watkins (eds) *Canada Under Free Trade*, Toronto: James Lorimer.

Coates, David (2000) *Models of Capitalism: Growth and Stagnation in the Modern Era*, Cambridge, UK: Polity.

Cohen, M.G. (2001) 'From Public Good to Private Exploitation: GATS and the Restructuring of Canadian Electrical Utilities', *Canadian–American Public Policy*, 48: 130–45.

Coloma, F. and P. Rojas (2000) 'Evolución del Mercado Laboral en Chile: Reformas y Resultados', in F. Larrain and R. Vergara (eds) *La Transfomación Economica en Chile*, Santiago: Centro de Estudios Públicos.

Commander, S. and C. Mummsen (2000) 'The Growth of Non-monetary Transactions in Russia: Causes and Effects', in P. Seabright (ed.) *The Vanishing Rouble*, Cambridge: Cambridge University Press.

Comisión Investigadora de los Delitos Económicos y Financieros cometidos entre 1990–2001 – CIDEF (2002), *Informe Final de Investigación*, Lima: Congreso de la República del Perú.

Cooper, A.F. (1997) *Canadian Foreign Policy*, Scarborough, Ont.: Prentice-Hall.

Coordinadora Nacional de Derechos Humanos (CNDDHH) (1998) *Informe 1998*, available at: <www.cnddhh.org.pe>.

Cotler, J. (1994) *Política y Sociedad en el Perú. Cambios y continuidades*, Lima: Instituto de Estudios Peruanos.

Coudrat, C. (1986) 'États-Unis: une économie de marchés financiers', in F. Renversez (ed.) *Les systèmes financiers*, Les Cahiers Français 224 (January–February), Paris: La Documentation Française.

Cox, R. (1987) *Production, Power and World Order: Social Forces in the Making of History*, New York and Guildford, Surrey: Columbia University Press.

Cox, R. (1993) 'Gramsci, Hegemony, and International Relations: An Essay in Method', in S. Gill (ed.) *Gramsci, Historical Materialism and International Relations*, Cambridge: Cambridge University Press.

Cox, R. (1999) 'Civil Society at the Turn of the Millennium: Prospects for an Alternative World Order', *Review of International Studies*, 25(1): 17–29.

Chirinos Segura, L. (1999) *La Actual Coyuntura de la Descentralización: Regiones y Gobiernos Locales en Perspectiva*, in H. Béjar (ed.) *El Perú realmente existente*, Lima: Centro de Estudios para el Desarollo y la Participación.

Criado, E. (1990) 'El sistema científico-técnico en España', in E. Criada, A. Durán and J. Aragón *et al. Ciencia y cambio tecnológico en España*, Madrid: Fundación Primer de Mayo, 107–52.

Crotty, J. and G. Epstein (1996) 'In Defence of Capital Controls', in L. Panitch (ed.) *Socialist Register*, London: Merlin Press, 23–41.

Crouch, C. and W. Streeck (eds) (1997) *Political Economy of Modern Capitalism: Mapping Convergence and Diversity*, London: Sage.

Cutler, A.C. and M.W. Zacher (1992) 'Introduction' in A.C. Cutler and M.W. Zacher (eds) *Canadian Foreign Policy and International Economic Regimes*, Vancouver: UBC Press.

Czada, R. (1998) 'Vereinigungskrise und Standortdebatte. Der Beitrag der Wiedervereinigung zur Krise des westdeutschen Modells', *Leviathan*: 24–59.

Dalziel, P. and R. Lattimore (1996) *The New Zealand Macroeconomy – A Briefing on the Reforms*, Auckland: Oxford University Press.

Das, B.L. (1998) *An Introduction to the WTO Agreements*, Penang: Third World Network.

Davis, D.E. (1993) 'The Dialectic of Autonomy: State, Class, and Economic Crisis in Mexico, 1958–1982', *Latin American Perspectives*, 78(3): 46–75.

Deacon, A. (2000) 'Learning from the US? The Influence of American Ideas Upon "New Labour" Thinking on Welfare Reform', *Policy and Politics*, 28(1): 5–18.

Destatis (2005) [German Federal Office for Statistics] 'Arbeitsmarkt', Available at: <www.destatis.de>.

Deyo, F. (1987) *The Political Economy of the New Asian Industrialism*. New York: Cornell University Press.

DIW [Deutsches Institut für Wirtschaftsforschung] Berlin, in cooperation with Institut für Weltwirtschaft an der Universität Kiel and Institut für Wirtschaftsforschung Halle (1999), *Gesamtwirtschaftliche und unternehmerische Anpassungsfortschritte in*

Ostdeutschland, available at: <http://www.diw.de/deutsch/publikationen/wochenberichte/docs/99-23-1.html#FN11>.

Doern, G.B. and B.W. Tomlin (1992) *Faith and Fear: The Free Trade Story*, Toronto: Stoddart.

Doern, G.B. and J. Kirton (1996) 'Foreign Policy' in G.B. Doern, L.A. Pal and B.W. Tomlin (eds) *Border Crossings: The Internationalization of Canadian Public Policy*, Toronto: Oxford University Press.

Dolowitz, D. (2000) 'Policy Transfer and British Social Policy: Learning from the USA?', Buckingham, UK: Open University Press.

Douglas, R. and L. Callen (1987) *Toward Prosperity*, Auckland: Bateman.

Douglas, R. (1993) *Unfinished Business*, Auckland: Random House.

Dornbusch, R. (1993) 'The End of the German Miracle', *Journal of Economic Literature*, 31(3): 881–5.

Downs, A. (1960) 'Why Government's Budget is too Small in a Democracy', *World Politics*, 12: 541–63.

Drucker, P.F. (1986) 'The Changed World Economy', *Foreign Affairs*, 64(4): 768–91.

Dunleavy, P.J. (1994) 'The Globalization of Public Services Production: Can Government Be "Best in World"?', *Public Policy and Administration*, 9(2): 36–64.

Durán López, F. *et al.* (1994) *La Formación Professional Continua en España*, Madrid: MTSS/MTAS.

Durand, F. (1999) *La Democracia, los Empresarios y Fujimori*, in T. Soldevilla Fernando (ed.) *El Juego Politico. Fujimori, la oposición y las reglas*, Lima: Friedrich Ebert Stiftung.

Dyck, R. (1996) *Canadian Politics*, Toronto: Nelson.

Easton, B. (1988) 'From Reagonomics to Rogernomics', in A. Bollard (ed.) *The Influence of United States Economics on New Zealand: The Fulbright Anniversary Seminar*, Wellington: New Zealand Institute of Economic Research, Research Monograph (42).

Easton, B. (1989) (ed.) *The Making of Rogernomics*, Auckland: Auckland. University Press.

Easton, B. (1994) 'How did the Health Reforms Blitzkrieg Fail?' *Political Science*, 4(2): 205–25.

Easton, B. (1997) *The Commercialisation of New Zealand*, Auckland: Auckland University Press.

Easton, B. and R. Gerritsen (1995) 'Economic Reform: Parallels and Divergences', in F. Castles *et al.* (eds) *The Great Experiment: Labour Parties and Public Policy Transformation in Australia and New Zealand*, Auckland: Auckland University Press.

The Economist (1985) 1 June: 19.

The Economist (1991) 'The long, long J-curve', 15 June.

The Economist (1993) 13 November: 155.

The Economist (1996) 'Economic freedom', 13 January: 21.

The Economist (2000) 'Have factory will travel', 10 February: 65–6.

The Economist (2004) 'The second transition', 24 June: 10.

Eden, L. and M.A. Molot (1993) 'Canada's National Policies: reflections on 125 Years', *Canadian Public* Policy, 19(3): 232–51.

Edlund, J. (1999) *Citizens and Taxation: Sweden in Comparative Perspective, Doctoral Theses at the Department of Sociology, Umeå University*, Umeå: Umeå University Press.

Ehrenreich, B. (2002) *Nickel and Dimed: On (Not) Getting By in America*, New York: Owl Books.

Erickson, R. (1999) 'Comment on an Accounting Model of Russia's virtual economy', *Post-Soviet Geography and Economics*, 40(2): 18–32.

Ershov, M. (2000) *Valytno-Finansovye Mekhanismy v Sovremennom Mire*, Moscow: Ekonomika.

Escobar, S. and F. Diego Lopez (1996) *El Sector Forestal en Chile: Crecimiento y Precarización del Empleo*, Santiago: Ediciones Tierra Mia / PET.

Evans, M. (2003) *Constitution-Making and the Labour Party*, Basingstoke: Palgrave Macmillan.

Evans, M. (ed.) (2004) *Policy Transfer in Global Perspective*, London: Ashgate.

Evans, M. and P.G. Cerny (2003), 'Globalization and Social Policy', in N. Ellison and C. Pierson (eds), *Developments in Social Policy 2*, Basingstoke: Palgrave Macmillan, 19–40.

Fajertag, G. and P. Pochet (eds) (1997) *Social Pacts in Europe*, Bruxelles: ETUC.

Fazio, H. (2000) *La transnacionalización de la economía chilena: Mapa de la Extrema Riqueza al año 2000*, Santiago: LOM.

Fazio, H. (2001) *Crece La Desigualidad*, Santiago: LOM.

Federal Council (1999) 'Zaklychenie vremennoi komissii Soveta Federacii po rassledovaniy prichin, obstojatelstv I posedstvii prinjatija reshenii pravitelstva Rossii i centralnogo banka Rossiiskoi Federacii to 17 avgusta 1998 goda', *Sovet Federacii Rossii*, Moscow.

Fernández Jilberto, A. (1993) 'Chile: The Laboratory Experiment of International Neoliberalism', in H. Overbeek (ed.) *Restructuring Hegemony in the Global Political Economy*, London: Routledge.

Financial Times Deutschland (2002) 'Was die Parteien gegen die Arbeitslosigkeit tun wollen', 29 May.

Fine, B. *et al.* (2001) *Development Policy in the Twenty-First Century: Beyond the Post-Washington Consensus*, London: Routledge.

Florio, M. (2002) 'Economists, Privatization in Russia and the Waning of the "Washington Consensus" ', *Review of International Political Economy*, 9(2): 359–400.

FOM (various issues) Moscow: The Public Opinion Foundation, available at: http://bd.english.fom.ru/

Fortín, C. (1985) 'The Political Economy of Repressive Monetarism: the State and Capital Accumulation in Post-1973 Chile', in C. Anglade and C. Fortín (eds) *The State and Capital Accumulation in Latin America: Volume 1*, London: Macmillan.

Fowke, Vernon (1952) 'The National Policy – Old and New', *Canadian Journal of Economics and Political Science*, (18): 271–86.

Frankfurter Rundschau (2002) 'Bis ins letzte Wohnzimmer', 13 July.

Frankfurter Rundschau (2002) 'Rot-Grün: Episode oder Epoche? Teil I: Gerechtigkeit', 25 June.

Frankfurter Rundschau (2002) 'Rot-Grün: Episode oder Epoche? Teil II: Arbeit', 27 June.

Freeland, C. (2000) *The Sale of the Century*, London: Little, Brown and Co.

Friedman, M. (1962) *Capitalism and Freedom*, Chicago: University of Chicago.

Fruchtmann, J. (2001) 'Putin's Approach to Economic Policy-Changes in Style and Content', Paper given at the BASEES Annual Conference, 6–9 April, Cambridge, UK.

Funk, L. (2001) 'The German Alliance for Jobs: Dead End or Miracle Cure?', *German Politics*, 10(1): 217–24.

Gamble, A. (2001) 'Neoliberalism', *Capital & Class*, 75: 90–112.

Garcia-Díaz, J.A. (2000) 'Tackling the Economic Crisis: The Government's Consensual Strategy', Chapter 4 in M. Threlfall (ed.) *Consensus Politics in Spain: Insider Perspectives*, Bristol: Intellect.

Gardner, Lloyd C. (1964) *Economic Aspects of New Deal Diplomacy*, Boston: Beacon Press.

Garrett, G. (1998) *Partisan Politics in the Global Economy*, Cambridge: Cambridge University Press.

Giddens, A. (1998) *The Third Way: The Renewal of Social Democracy*, Cambridge, UK: Polity.

Giddens, A. (2000) *The Third Way and Its Critics*, Cambridge: Polity.

Giddens, A. (ed.) (2001) *The Global Third Way Debate*, London: Polity.

Giddens, A. (2002) *Where Now for New Labour?*, Cambridge, UK: Polity.

Gilbert, C. and D. Vines (2003) *The International Monetary Fund and its Critics*, Cambridge, UK: Cambridge University Press.

Gill, S. (1990) *American Hegemony and the Trilateral Commission*, Cambridge: Cambridge University Press.

Gill, S. (1995) 'Globalisation, Market Civilisation and Disciplinary Neo-liberalism', *Journal of International Studies*, 24(3): 399–423.

Gillespie, R. (1990) 'The Break-up of the Socialist Family: Party-Union Relations in Spain 1982–89', *West European Politics*, 13(1): 47–62.

Glaziev S. (1998) *Genocid*, Moscow: Terra.

Glaziev, S. (2003) *Blagosostojanie I Spravedlivost. Kak Pobedit Bednost V Rossii*, Moscow: BSG Press.

Goldfinch, S. (1997) 'Treasury and Public Policy Formation', in C. Rudd and B. Roper (eds) *The Political Economy of New Zealand*, Auckland: Oxford University Press, 60–76.

Goldfinch, S. and B. Roper (1993) 'Treasury's Role in State Policy Formulation during the Post-war Era', in B. Roper and C. Rudd (eds) *State and Economy in New Zealand*, Auckland: Oxford University Press, 56–68.

Goldschmitt, W. (1996) 'Ein Musterland am Ende der Welt' [A Model Country at the End of the World], *Die Welt*, 2 April.

Goldstein, J. and R. Keohane (eds) (1993) *Ideas and Foreign Policy: Beliefs, Institutions, and Political Change*, Ithaca, NY: Cornell University Press.

Goldthorpe, J.H. (1984) *Order and Conflict in Contemporary Capitalism*, Oxford, UK: Clarendon Press.

Gonzales de Olarte, E. (1998) *El Neoliberalismo a la Peruana. Economía política del ajuste estructural, 1990–1997*, Lima: Instituto de Estudios Peruanos/Consorcio de Investigación Económica.

González Romero, A. and R. Myro Sánchez (1989) 'La recuperación de la inversión industrial en España, 1985–88: sus objectivos y factos determinantes', *Moneda y Crédito* (188): 17–55.

Gottschalk, P. and M. Joyce (1995) 'The Impact of Technological Change, Deindustrialization, and Internationalization of Trade on Earnings Inequality: An International Perspective', in K. McFate, R. Lawson and W.J. Wilson (eds) *Poverty, Inequality, and the Future of Social Policy: Western States in the New World Order*, New York: Russell Sage.

Gough, I. (1996) 'Social Assistance in Southern Europe', *Southern European Society and Politics*, 1(1): 1–23.

Gould, Ellen (2002) *The European Commission's GATS Position: A Bad Bargain for Canada*, available at: <http:www.Canadians.org/publications/analysis-gats-request.pdf>, last accessed 11 May 2003.

Gould, J. (1985) *The Muldoon Years*, Auckland: Hodder and Stoughton.

Government of Vietnam (1998) *Official Gazette*, No. 30 (GoV: Hanoi).

Government of Vietnam (2000) Partnership for Development, consultative group meeting for Vietnam, 14–15 December (GoV: Hanoi).

Government of Vietnam (2001a) *The Vietnam Government's Socioeconomic Development Strategy, 2001–2010* (GoV: Hanoi).

Government of Vietnam (2001b) *Vietnam Interim Poverty Reduction Strategy Paper for 2001–2003*, submitted to the World Bank on 5 March 2001 (GoV: Hanoi).

Gowa, Joanne S. (1983) *Closing the Gold Window: Domestic Politics and the End of Bretton Woods*, Ithaca, NY: Cornell University Press.

Gowan, P. (1999) *The Global Gamble: Washington's Faustian Bid for World Dominance*, London: Verso.

Grabel, I. (1999) 'Mexico Redux? Making Sense of the Financial Crisis of 1997–98', *Journal of Economic Issues*, XXXIII (2): 375–81.

Grahl, J. (2001) 'Social Europe and the Governance of Labour Relations', in G. Thompson (ed.) *Governing the European Economy*, London: Sage, 133–64.

Gramsci, A. (1971) 'Problems of Marxism', in *Selections from the Prison Notebooks*, edited and translated by Q. Hoare and G. Nowell Smith, New York: International Publishers.

Gramsci, A. (1992) *Selections from the Prison Notebooks*, updated edn, transl. Q. Hoare and G. Nowell Smith, New York: International Publishers.

Gray, A. (1998) 'New Labour – New Labour Discipline', *Capital and Class*, 65: 1–8.

Gray, J. (1999) *False Dawn: The Delusions of Global Capitalism* [revised edn] London: Granta.

Grinspun, R. and R. Kreklewich (1994) 'Consolidating the Neoliberal State: Free Trade as a Conditioning Framework', *Studies in Political Economy*, 43, Spring: 33–61.

Gunther, R., G. Sani and G. Shabad (1986) *Spain After Franco: The Making of a Competitive Party System*, Berkeley, London: University of California Press.

Gurría, J.A. and S. Fadl (1995) 'Mexico's Strategy for Reducing Financial Transfers Abroad', in R. Grosse (ed.) *Government Responses to the Latin American Debt Problem*, Miami: North-South Center Press, 121–49.

Gustafson, B. (1997) *New Zealand Politics 1945–1984*, in R. Miller (ed.) *New Zealand Politics in Transition*, Auckland: Oxford University Press, 3–13.

Gustafson, T. (1999) *Capitalism Russian-Style*, Cambridge: Cambridge University Press.

Gwynne, R. and C. Kay (1997) 'Agrarian Change and the Democratic Transition in Chile: An Introduction', *Bulletin of Latin American Research*, 16(1): 3–10.

Haas, P.M. (1992) 'Introduction: Epistemic Communities and International Policy Coordination', *International Organization*, 46(1): 187–224.

Hadenius, A. (1986) *A Crisis of the Welfare State? Opinions About Taxes and Public Expenditure in Sweden*, Stockholm: MiniMedia AB.

Haggard, S. (1990) *Pathways from the Periphery: The Politics of Growth in the Newly Industrializing Countries*, Ithaca, NY: Cornell University Press.

Halimi, S. (1997) 'La Nouvelle-Zelande: éprouvette du capitalisme totale' [New Zealand: test tube of total capitalism] *Le monde diplomatique*, 10–11 April.

Hall, Peter A. (1986) *Governing the Economy: The Politics of State Intervention in Britain and France*, Oxford/New York: Oxford University Press.

Hall, Peter A. (ed.) (1989) *The Political Power of Economic Ideas: Keynesianism Across Nations*, Princeton: Princeton University Press.

Hall, Peter A. and David Soskice (eds) (2001) *Varieties of Capitalism: The Institutional Foundations of Comparative Advantage*, Oxford, UK: Oxford University Press.

Hancock, Donald (1972) *Sweden: The Politics of Post-Industrial Change*, Hindsale, Illinois: Dryden Press.

Hann, C. (2002) 'Farewell to the Socialist "Other" ', in C. Hann (ed.) *Postsocialism. Ideas, Ideologies and Practices in Eurasia*, London, New York: Routledge.

Hansen, B. (1969) *Fiscal Policies in Seven Countries*, Paris: OECD.

Hanson, B. (1998) 'Whatever Happened To "Fortress Europe": External Trade Liberalisation in the EU', *International Organisation*, 1 (Winter): 55–85.

Harding, R. and W.E. Paterson (eds) (2000) *The Future of the German Economy: An End to the Miracle?*, Manchester: Manchester University Press.

Harris, N. (1986). *The End of the Third World*, Harmondsworth, Middx: Penguin.

Harrison, J. (1978) *An Economic History of Modern Spain*, Manchester: Manchester University Press.

Harrison, J. (1985) *The Spanish Economy in the Twentieth Century*, London and New York: Routledge.

Hart, J. (1992) *Rival Capitalists: International Competitiveness in the United States, Japan and Western Europe*, Ithaca, New York: Cornell University Press.

Hart, M. (1990) *A North American Free Trade Agreement: The Strategic Implications for Canada*, Halifax: Institute for Research on Public Policy.

Harvey, D. (1999) *The Limits to Capital*, London: Verso.

Hassel, A. (1999) 'The Erosion of the German System of Industrial Relations', *British Journal of Industrial Relations*, 37(3): 484–505.

Hassel, A. and W. Streeck (2004) 'The Crumbling Pillars of Social Partnership', in H. Kitschelt and W. Streeck (eds) 'Germany Beyond the Stable State', *Special Issue of West European Politics*, 26(4): 101–24.

Hausner, J., B. Jessop and K. Nielsen (eds) (1995) *Strategic Choice and Path-Dependency in Post-Socialism*, Aldershot, UK: Edward Elgar.

Haya de la Torre, A. (1999/2000) 'Las consecuencias sociales del modelo', *Cuadernos*, (37): 50–5.

Hayek, F. (1944) *The Road to Serfdom*, Chicago: University of Chicago Press.

Heclo, Hugh (1974) *Modern Social Politics in Britain and Sweden*, New Haven: Yale University Press.

Heclo, Hugh and Henrik Madsen (1987) *Policy and Politics in Sweden*, Philadelphia: Temple University Press.

Hedlund, S. (1999) *Russia's 'Market' Economy. A Bad Case of Predatory Capitalism*, London: UCL Press.

Held, D. and M. Koenig-Archibugi (2003) *Taming Globalization: Frontiers of Governance*, Cambridge: Polity.

Helleiner, E. (1994) *States and the Reemergence of Global Finance: From Bretton Woods to the 1990s*, Ithaca: Cornell University Press.

Hellman, J.A. (1978) *Mexico in Crisis*, New York: Holmes & Meier Publishers.

Henderson, J. (1993) 'The Role of the State in the Economic Transformation of East Asia', in C. Dixon and F. Drakakis-Smith (eds) *Economic and Social Development in Pacific Asia*, London: Routledge.

Heritier, A., D. Kerwer, C. Knill, D. Lehmkuhl, M. Teutsch and A.-C. Douillet (2000) *Differential Europe: The European Union Impact on National Policymaking*, London: Rowman and Littlefield.

Heywood, P. (ed.) (1999) *Politics and Policy in Democratic Spain: No Longer Different?*, London: Frank Cass.

Hilferding, R. (1981) *Finance Capital: A Study of the Last Phase of Capitalist Development*, London: Routledge.

Hirsch, J. (1995) *Der nationale Wettbewerbsstaat. Staat, Demokratie und Politik im globalen Kapitalismus*, Berlin: VSA Verlag.

Hirsch, Joachim (1998) *Vom Sicherheitsstaat zum nationalen Wettbewerbsstaat*, Berlin: ID-Verlag.

Hirst, P. and G. Thompson (1999) *Globalization in Question: The International Economy and the Possibilities of Governance*, Cambridge: Polity.

Hobbes, T. (1998[1668]) *Leviathan*, Oxford: Oxford University Press.

Hobsbawm, E. (2000) *On the Edge of the New Century*, New York: New Press.

Holden, C. (1999), 'Globalisation, Social Exclusion and Labour's New Work Ethic', *Critical Social Policy*, 19 (4): 529–38.

Holloway, J. (1995) 'Global Capital and the National State', in W. Bonefeld and J. Holloway (eds) *Global Capital, National State and the Politics of Money*, New York: St Martin's Press.

Holman, O. (1996) *Integrating Southern Europe: EC Expansion and the Transnationalisation of Spain*, London: Routledge.

Holmberg, S. (1999) 'Down and Down We Go: Political Trust in Sweden', in P. Norris (ed.) *Critical Citizens. Global Support for Democratic Governance*, Oxford: Oxford University Press, pp. 103–22.

Honda, E. (2003). 'Financial Deregulation in Japan', *Japan and the World Economy*, 15: 135–40.

Houle, F. (1990) 'Economic Renewal and Social Policy', in A.-G. Gagnon and J.P. Bickerton (eds) *Canadian Politics: An Introduction to the Discipline*, Peterborough, Ont.: Broadview.

House of Commons, Social Security Committee (1998) *Social Security Reforms: Lessons from the United States of America*, HC 82, London: HMSO.

Howse, R. (1990) 'The Labour Conventions Doctrine in an Era of Global Interdependence: Rethinking the Constitutional Dimensions of Canada's External Economic Relations', *Canadian Business Law Journal*, 16(3): 45–78.

Huber, E. (1996) 'Options for Social Policy in Latin America: Neoliberal versus Social Democratic Models', in G. Esping-Andersen (ed.), *Welfare States in Transition*, London: Sage.

Huelsemeyer, Axel (ed.) (2003) *Globalization in the Twenty-First Century: Convergence or Divergence?*, Basingstoke: Palgrave Macmillan.

Humala, U. (2002) 'Globalizando el Perú', in *Perú Hoy. Toledo: A un año de Gobierno*, Lima: Umbechto.

Huntington, S. (1991) *The Third Wave*, Norman, OK: University of Oklahoma Press.

Hutton, W. (1995) *The State We're In*, London: Jonathan Cape.

Iguíñiz, J. (1999) 'La estrategia económica del gobierno de Fujimori: una visión global', in J. Crabtree and J. Thomas (eds) *El Perú de Fujimori 1990–1998*, Lima: Umbechto.

IMF (1992) *Mexico: The Strategy to Achieve Sustained Economic Growth*, Occasional Paper (99). Washington DC: IMF.

IMF (1993) *IMF Survey*: 25 January, Washington, DC: IMF.

IMF (1995) *The IMF and the Challenges of Globalization – The Fund's Evolving Approach to its Constant Mission: The Case of Mexico*, Address by Michel Camdessus, Managing Director of the International Monetary Fund at the Zurich Economics Society, Zurich, Switzerland on 14 November 1995, available at: <http://www.imf.org/external/np/sec/mds/1995/MDS9517.htm>.

IMF (2000) *Chile: Selected Issues*, Staff Country Report No. 00/104. Washington DC: IMF.

IMF (2004a) *Global Development Finance: Harnessing Cyclical Gains for Development*, Washington, DC: IMF.

IMF (2004b) *The Russian Federation. Statistical Appendix*, Country Statistics, Washington DC: IMF.

Ingham, G. (1984) *Capitalism Divided? The City and Industry in British Social Development*, London: Macmillan.

Instituto Nacional Estadistica (1977) *Anuario*, Madrid: INE.

Irvin, G. (1995) 'Vietnam: Assessing the Achievements of Doi Moi', *Journal of Development Studies*, 31(5): 725–50.

James, A. (1986) *Sovereign Statehood: Basis of International Society*, London: HarperCollins.

Jesson, B. (1987) *Behind the Mirror Glass*, Auckland: Penguin Books.

Jessop, B. (1990) *State Theory, Putting Capitalist States in their Place*, Cambridge: Polity.

Jessop, B. (1994) 'From the Keynesian Welfare to the Schumpeterian Workfare State', in R. Burrows and B. Loader (eds), *Towards a Post-Fordist Welfare State?*, London, Routledge: 13–37.

Johnson, C. (1982) *MITI and the Japanese Miracle: The Growth of Industrial Policy 1925–75*, Stanford, California: Stanford University Press.

Johnson, J.R. (2002) 'How Will International Trade Agreements Affect Canadian Health Care?', Discussion Paper 22, Ottawa: Commission on the Future of Health Care in Canada.

Jonung, L. (1999) *Med Backspegeln Som Kompass: Om Stabiliseringspolitiken Som Läroprocess: Rapport Till Eso – Expertgruppen För Studier I Offentlig Ekonomi. [With the Rearview Mirror as a Compass: On Stabilization Policy as a Learning Process: Report to the Eso Expert Group for the Study of the Official Economy]*, Ds: Departementsserien 1999: 9, Stockholm: Fakta info direkt.

Joseph, K. (1972) 'The Cycle of Deprivation', Speech to Conference of Pre-School Playgroups Association, 29 June.

Joseph, K. (1974), 'Britain: a Decadent New Utopia', Speech delivered in Birmingham on 19 October 1974, reprinted in the *Guardian*, 21 October.

Kapstein, E. (1994) *Governing the Global Economy: International Finance and the State*, Cambridge: Harvard University Press.

Katz, R. (1998) *Japan, The System That Soured: The Rise and Fall of the Japanese Miracle*, Armonk, NY and London: ME Sharpe.

Katzenstein, P. (1985) *Small States in World Markets: Industrial Policy in Europe*, Ithaca, NY: Cornell University Press.

Katzenstein, P.J. (1996) *The Culture of National Security: Norms and Identity in World Politicsm*, New York: Columbia University Press.

Kavanagh, D. (1990) *Thatcherism and British Politics*, Oxford: Oxford University Press.

Kay, C. (1989) *Latin American Theories of Development and Underdevelopment*, London: Routledge.

Keenes, E. (1995) 'The Myth of Multilateralism: Exception, Exemption and Bilateralism in Canadian International Economic Relations', *International Journal*, 50(4): Fall.

Keohane, R.O. (1984) *After Hegemony: Cooperation and Discord in the World Economy*, Princeton: Princeton University Press.

Keohane, R.O. and J.S. Nye (1977) *Power and Interdependence: World Politics in Transition*, Boston: Little, Brown.

Kelsey, J. (1997) *The New Zealand Experiment – A World Model for Structural Adjustment?*, Auckland: Auckland University Press.

Kemp, T. (1969) *Industrialization in Nineteenth Century Europe*, London: Longman.

Kemp, T. (1983) *Industrialization in the Non-Western World*, London: Longman.

Khoury, S.J. (1990) *The Deregulation of the World Financial Markets: Myths, Realities, and Impact*, London: Pinter.

Kideckel, D. (2002) 'The Unmaking of an East-Central European Working Class', in C. Hann (ed.) *Postsocialism: Ideas, Ideologies and Practices in Eurasia*, London: Routledge.

Kindleberger, C.P. (1973) *The World in Depression 1929–1939*, London: Allen Lane the Penguin Press.

Kirchheimer, O. (1966) 'The Transformation of the Western European Party Systems', in J. LaPalombara and M. Weiner (eds) *Political Parties and Political Development*, Princeton, NJ: Princeton University Press, 177–200.

Kissinger, H. (1994) *Diplomacy*, New York: Simon and Schuster.

Kissinger, H. (2000) 'Mission to Moscow', *Washington Post*, 15 May, A15.

Kitschelt, H., P. Lange, G. Marks and J.D. Stephens (1999) 'Convergence and Divergence in Advanced Capitalist Democracies', in Kitschelt, Lange, Marks and Stephens (eds) *Continuity and Change in Contemporary Capitalism*, Cambridge: Cambridge University Press.

Klein, N. (2000) *No Logo: Solutions for a Sold Planet*, London: Flamingo.

Kolodko, G. (2001) 'Globalization and Catching-up: from Recession to Growth in Transition Economies', *Communist and Post-Communist Studies*, 34: 279–322.

Kopinak, K. (1994) 'The Maquiladorization of the Mexican Economy', in R. Grinspun and M.A. Cameron (eds) *The Political Economy of North American Free Trade*, New York: St Martin's Press.

Kopinak, K. (ed.) (2004) *Social Costs of Industrial Growth*, San Diego, University of California: Center for US–Mexican Studies.

Korten, D. (1995) *When Corporations Rule the World*, West Hartford: Kamarian Press.

Krasner, S.D. (1999) *Sovereignty: Organized Hypocrisy*, Princeton: Princeton University Press.

Kroeger, A. (1996) 'Changing Course: The Federal Government's Program Review of 1994–95', in A. Armit and J. Bourgault (eds) *Hard Choices or No Choices: Assessing Program Review*, Toronto: Institute of Public Administration of Canada.

Krugman, P. (2001) 'Enron Goes Overboard', *New York Times* (17 August).

Kusano, A. (1999) 'A Deregulation in Japan and the Role of *Naiatsu* (Domestic Pressure)', *Social Science Journal Japan*, 2(1): 65–84.

Lagos L. and J. Francisco (1999) 'Chile exportador de cobre en bruto: una involución en la composicion de las exportaciones de su principal riqueza mineral', *Revista de Economia & Trabajo*, 9: 45–63.

Laird, S. (1999) 'The WTO's Trade Policy Review Mechanism – From Through the Looking Glass', *World Economy*, 22(6): 90–212.

Lane, D. (2000) 'What Kind of Capitalism for Russia?', *Communist and Post-Communist Studies*, 33: 485–504.

Langille, David (1987) 'The Business Council on National Issues and the Canadian State', *Studies in Political Economy*, 24: 41–85.

Lash, S. (1985) 'The End of Neo-Corporatism? The Breakdown of Centralized Bargaining in Sweden', *British Journal of Industrial Relations*, 23: 215–39.

Lattimore, R. (1987) 'Economic Adjustment in New Zealand: A Developed Country Case Study of Policies and Problems', in F. Holmes (ed.) *Economic Adjustment: Policies and Problems*, Washington, DC: IMF.

Laxer, J. (1983) *Oil and Gas: Ottawa, the Provinces and the Petroleum Industry*, Toronto: Lorimer.

Layard, R. (1997) *What Labour Can Do*, London: Warner.

Layton, J. (1976) 'Nationalism and the Canadian Bourgeoisie: Contradictions of Dependence', *Canadian Review of Studies in Nationalism*, 3(2): 84–100.

Leadbeater, C. (2000) *Living On Thin Air*, London: Faber.

Leftwich, A. (2001) *States of Development*, Cambridge: Polity.

Lemieux, D. and A. Stuhec (1999) *Review of Administrative Action under NAFTA*, Scarborough, Ont.: Carswell.

Leslie, Peter (1987) *Federal State, National Economy*, Toronto: University of Toronto Press.

Liberal Party (1993) *Creating Opportunity: The Liberal Plan for Canada*, Ottawa: Liberal Party of Canada.

Lieber, R.J. and D.S. Rothchild (1979) *Engle Entangled: U.S. Foreign Policy in a Complex World*, New York and London: Longman.

Lieberman, S. (1982) *The Contemporary Spanish Economy: A Historical Perspective*, London: Routledge.

Lieberman, S. (1993) *Growth and Crisis in the Spanish Economy*, London: Routledge.

Lijphart, A. (1984) *Democracies: Patterns of Majoritarian and Consensus Democracies in 21 Countries*, New Haven, CT: Yale University Press.

Lindbeck, A. (1975) *Svensk Ekonomisk Politik [Swedish Economic Policy]*, Stockholm: Aldus/Bonniers.

Lindbeck, A. (1983) 'The Political Economy of Redistribution and the Expansion of the Public Sector', Stockholm.

Lindbeck, A. (1997) *The Swedish Experiment*, Stockholm: Studieförbundet Näringsliv och samhälle.

Lindblom, C. (1973) *Politics and Markets*, New York: Basic Books.

Lindblom, C.E. (1977) *Politics and Markets: The World's Political-Economic Systems*, New York: Basic Books.

List, F. (1885/1966) *The National System of Political Economy*, New York, AM. Kelley.

Loriaux, M. (1991) *France After Hegemony: International Change and Financial Reform*, Ithaca, NY: Cornell University Press.

Lustig, N. (1998) *Mexico: The Remaking of an Economy*, Washington, DC: Brookings Institute Press.

Lütz, S. (2000) 'From Managed to Market Capitalism? German Finance in Transition', *German Politics*, 9: 149–70.

Lütz, S. (2004) 'Convergence Within National Diversity: The Regulatory State in Finance', *Journal of Public Policy*, 24(2) (August): 169–97.

Luz, M.A. (2001–02) 'NAFTA, Investment and the Constitution of Canada: Will the Watertight Compartments Spring a Leak?', *Ottawa Law Review*, 32(3): 23–44.

Lynch, A. (2002) 'Roots of Russia's Economic Dilemmas: Liberal Economics and Illiberal Geography', *Europe-Asia Studies*, 54 (1): 36–7.

Lynch, N. (1996) *Crisis y Perspectivas de los Partidos Políticos en el Perú*, in *Argumentos. Estudios críticos de la sociedad* (December 1996): 81–93.

Macdonald, D.S. (1998) 'Chapter 11 of NAFTA: What are the Implications for Sovereignty?', *Canada–United States Law Journal*, 3(4): 34–55.

Manco, M. (1994) *Privatización en el Perú. Aproximación a un Balance Crítico*, Lima: Universidad Nacional Mayor de San Marcos, available at: <http://sisbib.unmsm. edu.pe/bibvirtualdata/libros/CSociales/capl.pdf>.

Marr, D. and C. White (eds) (1988) *Post-war Vietnam*, Ithaca, New York: Cornell University Press.

Martin, L. (1993) *Pledge of Allegiance: The Americanization of Canada in the Mulroney Years*, Toronto: McClelland and Stewart.

Martínez, J. and A. Diaz (1996) *Chile The Great Transformation*, Washington, DC: Brookings Institute.

Martínez-Lucio, M. (1992) 'Spain: Constructing Institutions and Actors in a Context of Change', in A. Ferner and R. Hyman (eds) *Industrial Relations in the New Europe*, Oxford: Basil Blackwell.

Massey, P. (1995) *New Zealand – Market Liberalization in a Developed Economy*, New York: St Martin's Press.

Maxfield, S. (1990) *Governing Capital: International Finance and Mexican Politics*, Ithaca: Cornell University Press.

McBride, S. (1983) 'Public Policy as a Determinant of Interest Group Behaviour: The Canadian Labour Congress, Corporatist Initiative, 1975–78', *Canadian Journal of Political Science*, 2(2): 501–17.

McBride, S. (1992) *Not Working: State, Unemployment and Neoconservatism in Canada*, Toronto: University of Toronto Press.

McBride, S. (2001) *Paradigm Shift: Globalisation and the Canadian State*, Halifax: Fernwood Books.

McBride, Stephen (2003) 'Quiet Constitutionalism in Canada: The International Political Economy of Domestic Institutional Change', *Canadian Journal of Political Science*, 36(2): 257–73.

McBride, Stephen and John Shields (1997) (2nd edn) *Dismantling a Nation: Canada and the New World Order*, Halifax, N.S.: Fernwood Books.

McBride, S. and K. McNutt (2004) 'Outpost of Empire: American Social Policy Triumphalism on the Canadian Periphery?', 7th GASSP Seminar, 'The Rise and Fall(?) of the International Influence of American Social Policy', Hamilton, Ont. September.

McClintock, C. (1999) 'Es autoritario el gobierno de Fujimori?', in T. Soldevila Fernando (ed.) *El Juego Político. Fujimori, la oposición y las reglas*, Lima: Belini.

McConnel J. and A. MacPherson (1994) 'The North American Free Trade Area: an Overview of Issues and Prospects', in R. Gibb and W. Michalak (eds) *Continental Trading Blocs: The Growth of Regionalism in the World Economy*, Chichester: John Wiley & Sons.

McKenzie, R.B. and D. Lee (1991) *Quicksilver Capital: How the Rapid Movement of Wealth Has Changed the World*, New York: Free Press.

McQuaig, L. (1992) *The Quick and the Dead: Brian Mulroney, Big Business and the Seduction of Canada*, Toronto: Penguin.

Medvedev, S. (2003) *Russia 2010: Mid-term Scenarios*, Marshall Center, October.

Meidner, R. (1992) 'The Rise and Fall of the Swedish Model', *Studies in Political Economy*, 39: 159–71.

Méndez, J. Silvestre M. (1994) *Problemas Económicos de México*, México: McGraw-Hill.

Mennicken, A. (2000) 'Figuring Trust: The Social Organisation of Credit Relations', *Ökonomie und Geselllschaft*, Jahrbuch 16, Marburg: Metropolis Verlag.

Menz, G. (1999) *A Model Strategy for Small States to Cope with and Survive in a Globalized World Economy? Analyzing Model New Zealand*, Paper presented at the European Consortium for Political Research Joint Session of Workshops, March 1999, Mannheim, Germany, available at: <http://www.essex.ac.uk/ecpr>.

Menz, G. (2005a) *Varieties of Capitalism and Europeanization: National Response Strategies to the Single European Market*, Oxford: Oxford University Press.

Menz, G. (2005b) 'Old Bottles – New Wine: The New Dynamics of Industrial Relations', *German Politics*, 14(2) June: 1–12.

Merrett, C.D. (1996) *Free Trade: Neither Free Nor About Trade*, Montreal: Black Rose Books.

MICYT (1992) *Plan de Apoyo a la Internacionalizacion de la Empresa Espanola*, Madrid: MICYT.

Middlebrook, K. J. (1995) *The Paradox of Revolution: Labor, The State and Authoritarianism in Mexico*, Baltimore: Johns Hopkins University Press.

MIDEPLAN (2001) *Impacto Distributivo de Gasto Social 2000*, Santiago: Mideplan.

Mikuni, A. and R.T. Murphy (2002) *Japan's Policy Trap: Dollars, Deflation, and the Crisis of Japanese Finance*, Washington, DC: Brookings Institution Press.

Minaeva, T. (2003) 'Prirodnaja Renta', available at: <http://nakanune.ru/articles/jekonomika/prirodnaja_renta_panaceja_mif>.

MINER (1989) *La Política Industrial en el Horizonte 1992*, Madrid: MINER.

MINER (1995) *Una política industrial para España: una propuesta para debate*, Madrid: MINER.

MINER (various years) *Informe anual sobre la industria española*, Madrid: MINER.

Ministerio de Economía y Hacienda (1993) *El Plan de convergencia a largo plazo*, Madrid: Ministerio de Economía y Hacienda.

Moghadam, V. (2000) 'Social Development, State Capacity and Economic Reform: the Experience of Vietnam', in D. Ghai (ed.) *Social Development and Public Policy*, London: Macmillan/URISD.

Moran, M. (2003) *The British Regulatory State: High Modernism and Hyper-Innovation*, Oxford: Oxford University Press.

Morguillansky, G. (2001) 'Privatizaciones y su impacto en la inversion', in R. Ffrench-Davis and B. Stallings (eds) *Reformas, Crecimiento y Políticas Sociales en Chile desde 1973*, Santiago: LOM.

Morishima, M. (2000) *Japan at a Deadlock*, London and New York: Macmillan and St Martin's Press.

Motamen-Scobie, H. (1998) *The Spanish Economy in the 1990s*, London: Routledge.

MTAS (various years) *La Política de Empleo en España*, available at: <www.mtas.es/empleo>.

Mujica Petit, J. (1999) 'Libertades sindicales en el Perú', in H. Béjar (ed.) *El Perú realmente existente*, Lima: Indicos.

Mulgan, A.G. (2002). *Japan's Failed Revolution: Koizumi and the Politics of Economic Reform*, Canberra: Asia Pacific Press.

Muten, L. (1988) 'Tax Reform – an International Perspective', in *Vårt Economiska Läge [Our Economic Situation]*, Stockholm.

Myrdal, G. (1982) 'Dags För Ett Bättre Skattesystem [Time for a Better Tax System]', in *Skatter [Taxes]*, edited by L. Jonung. Malmo: Liberforlag.

Myro Sánchez, R. and J. Martínez Serrano (1992) 'La penetración del capital extranjero en la industría española', *Moneda y Crédito* (194): 149–87.

Myro Sánchez, R. (1993) 'Las empresas públicas', Chapter 12 in J.L. García Delgado (ed.) *España economía*, Madrid: Espasa Calpe.

Nagel, J. (1998) 'Social Choice in a Pluralitarian Democracy: The Politics of Market Liberalization in New Zealand', *British Journal of Political Science*, 28: 232–57.

Narr, W.D. and A. Schubert (1994) *Weltökonomie. Die Misere der Politik*, Frankfurt am Main: Suhrkamp.

Navarro, M. (1990) *La política de reconversión: balance critico*, Madrid: Eudema Actualidad.

Nesvetailova, A. (2002) 'Asian Tigers, Russian Bear and International Vets? An Excursion in the 1997–98 Financial Crises', *Competition and Change*, 6(3): 251–68.

New Zealand Treasury (1984) 'Economic Management', Wellington: NZ Treasury.

New Zealand Treasury (1987) 'Government Management', Wellington, NZ Treasury.

Nicholson, M. (2001) 'Putin's Russia: Slowing the Pendulum Without Stopping the Clock', *International Affairs*, 77(3): 867–84.

Niosi, Jorge (1985) *Canadian Multinationals*, Toronto: Garamond Press.

Nossal, K.R. (1997) *The Politics of Canadian Foreign Policy*, Scarborough, Ont.: Prentice-Hall.

Oakeshott, M. (1976) 'On Misunderstanding Human Conduct: A Reply to my Critics', *Political Theory*, 4(3): 353–67.

O'Connor, James R. (1973) *The Fiscal Crisis of the State*, New York: St Martin's Press.

OECD, *Economic Surveys: New Zealand*, Paris: OECD, various issues.

OECD, *Economic Surveys: Spain*, Paris: OECD, various issues.

Ohmae, K. (1990) *The Borderless World: Power and Strategy in the Interlinked Economy*, London: HarperCollins.

Ornstein, M. (1985) 'Canadian Capital and the Canadian State: Ideology in an Era of Crisis', in R.J. Brym (ed.) *The Structure of the Canadian Capitalist Class*, Toronto: Garamond Press.

Osborne, D. and T. Gaebler (1992) *Reinventing Government: How the Entrepreneurial Spirit is Transforming the Public Sector, From Schoolhouse to Statehouse, City Hall to the Pentagon*, Reading, MA: Addison-Wesley.

Ouellet, R. (2002) *The Effects of International Trade Agreements on Canadian Health Measures: Options for Canada with a View to the Upcoming Trade Negotiations*, Discussion Paper 32, Ottawa: Commission on the Future of Health Care in Canada.

Oye, K.A. and D. Rothchild (eds) (1979) *Eagle Entangled: United States Foreign Policy in a Complex World*, Boston: Little Brown.

Palme, M. (1993) *Five Empirical Studies on Income Distribution in Sweden*, Stockholm.

Panitch, L. (ed.) (1977) *The Canadian State: Political Economy and Political Power*, Toronto: University of Toronto Press.

Panitch, L. and C. Leys (1997) *The End of Parliamentary Socialism. From New Left to New Labour*, London: Verso.

Pappe, Y. (2000) 'Oligarchi bez oligarchi', *Expert*, 13(3): 45–61.

Pastor Jr, M. (1999) 'Globalization, sovereignty, and policy choice: Lessons from the Mexican peso crisis', in D.A. Smith, D.J. Solinger and S.C. Topik (eds) *States and Sovereignty in the Global Economy*, London: Routledge.

Pempel, T.J. (1998) *Regime Shift: Comparative Dynamics of the Japanese Political Economy*, Ithaca: Cornell University Press.

Penrose, E.F. (1953) *Economic Planning for the Peace*, Princeton: Princeton University Press.

Perotti, E. (2001) 'Lessons from the Russian meltdown: the economics of soft legal Constraints', Working Paper no. 379, Amsterdam: University of Amsterdam.

Petitbò, A. (1993) 'Globalización, política industrial y competencia', *Economía Industrial*, 292: 15–30.

Petras, J. and F.I. Leiva (1994) *Democracy and Poverty in Chile: The Limits to Electoral Politics*, Boulder, CO: Westview Press.

Phillips, S. (2000) 'The Demise of Universality: The Politics of Federal Income Security in Canada, 1978–1993', Paper presented at the annual meeting of the British Columbia Political Studies Association, Victoria (May).

Philpott, D. (2001) *Revolutions in Sovereignty: How Ideas Shaped Modern International Relations*, Princeton: Princeton University Press.

Pickles J. and A. Smith (eds) (1998) *Theorising Transition: The Political Economy of Post Communist Transformations*, London: Routledge.

Pincus, J.R. and J.A. Winters (2002) *Reinventing the World Bank*, Ithaca: Cornell University Press.

Pizarro, R.L. Trelles and E. Toche (2004) *La Protesta Social Durante el Toledismo*, in J. Azpur *et al. Perú Hoy. Los Mil Días de Toledo*, Lima: Desco.

Planas Silva, P. (1999) *El Fujimorato. Estudio Político-Constitucional*, Lima: Desco.

Poder Ejecutivo Federal (1989) *Plan Nacional de Desarrollo, 1989–1994*, Mexico City: Presidencia de la República.

Polanyi, K. (1944) *The Great Transformation*, New York and Toronto: Farrar & Rinehart.

Polanyi, K. (1957) *The Great Transformation*, Boston: Beacon Press.

Pontusson, J. (1986) 'Labor Reformism and the Politics of Capital Formation in Sweden', Ph.D. dissertation, Department of Political Science, UC Berkeley, Berkeley, CA.

Pontusson, J. (1987) 'Radicalisation and Retreat in Swedish Social Democracy', *New Left Review*, 165: 79–92.

Pontusson, J. (1992) *The Limits of Social Democracy: Investment Politics in Sweden*, Ithaca: Cornell University Press.

Poulantzas, N. (1978) *State, Power, Socialism*, London: New Left Books.

Power, M. (1997) *The Audit Society: Rituals of Verification*, Oxford: Oxford University Press.

Pratt, Larry (1982) 'Energy: The Roots of National Policy', *Studies in Political Economy* 7 (Winter): 27–59.

Putin, V. (2001) Annual Address to the Federal Assembly, Moscow: The Kremlin.

Putin, V. (2002) Annual Address to the Federal Assembly, Moscow: The Kremlin.

Putin, V. (2004) Annual Address to the Federal Assembly, Moscow: The Kremlin.

Quang, T. (2000) *Vietnam's Challenges on the Path to Development*, Department for International Development, Hanoi.

Raczynski, D. (1999) 'Políticas socials en los años noventa en Chile. Balance y desafios', in P. Drake and I. Jaksic (eds) *El Modelo Chileno: Democracia y desarrollo en los noventa*, Santiago: LOM.

Raczynski, D. (2000) 'Overcoming Poverty in Chile', in J.S. Tulchin and A.M. Garland (eds) *Social Development in Latin America: The Politics of Reform*, Boulder: Lynne Rienner Press.

Radice, H. (2000) 'Globalization and National Capitalisms: Theorizing Convergence and Differentiation', *Review of International Political Economy*, 7(4): 719–42.

Radaev, V. (2000) 'Return of the crowds and rationality of action a history of Russian "financial bubbles" in the mid-1990s', *European Societies*, 2(3): 271–94.

Reddaway, P. and D. Glinski (2001) *The Tragedy of Russia's Reforms. Market Bolshevism Against Democracy*, Washington: US Institute for Peace.

Reder, M. (1982) 'Chicago Economics: Permanence and Change', *Journal of Economic Literature*, 20: 1–38.

Regini, M. (1999) *Between De-regulation and Social Pacts: The Responses of European Economies to Globalization*, Working Paper 1999/133, Madrid: Instituto Juan March.

Reich, R. (1991) *The Work of Nations: Preparing Ourselves for 21st Century Capitalism*, New York: Knopf.

Renversez, F. (1986), 'France: une économie d'endettement', in F. Renversez (ed.) *Les systèmes financiers*, Les Cahiers Français 224 (January–February) Paris: La Documentation Française: 3–25.

Reyna, C.E. and Toche (1999) *Perú Hoy. El Gobierno y las Instituciones en 1999*, Lima: Desco.

Rhodes, M. (1996) 'Southern European Welfare States: Identity, Problems and Prospects', *South European Society and Politics*, 1(3): 1–22.

Rhodes, R.A.W. (1994), 'The Hollowing-out of the State: the Changing Nature of the Public Service in Britain', *Political Quarterly*, 65(2): 138–51.

Rhodes, R.A.W. (1996), 'The New Governance: Governing without Government', *Political Studies*, XLIV(4): 652–67.

Rhodes, R.A.W. (1997), *Understanding Governance*, Milton Keynes: Open University Press.

Richards, R.G. (1991) 'The Canadian Constitution and International Economic Relations', in B.D.M. Brown and G. Smith (eds) *Canadian Federalism: Meeting Global Challenges?*, Kingston, Ont.: Queen's University Institute of Intergovernmental, Relations.

Richardson, J. (1992) 'Free Trade: Why Did it Happen?', *Canadian Review of Sociology and Anthropology*, 5(9): 307–27.

Riddell, P. (1983) *The Thatcher Government*, Oxford: Robertson.

Risse, T. (2002) 'National and Collective Identities: Europe Versus the Nation State', Chapter 4 in P. Heywood, E. Jones and M. Rhodes (eds) *Developments in West European Politics 2*, Basingstoke: Palgrave, 77–93.

Roberts, K.M. (1998) *Deepening Democracy? The Modern Left and Social Movements in Chile and Peru*, Stanford, California: Stanford University Press.

Robertson, R. (1992) *Globalization: Social Theory and Global Culture*, London: Sage Publications.

Roddick, J. (1989) 'The State, Industrial Relations and the Labour Movement in Chile', in H. Carrière and J. Roddick (eds) *The State, Industrial Relations and the Labour Movement in Latin America: Vol 1*, London: Macmillan Press.

Rodrik, D. (1997) *Has Globalization Gone Too Far?*, Washington, DC: Institute for International Economics.

Roper, B. (1977) 'New Zealand's Postwar Economic History', in C. Rudd and B. Roper (eds) *The Political Economy of New Zealand*, Auckland: Oxford University Press.

Roper, B. and C. Rudd (eds) (1993) *State and Economy in New Zealand*, Auckland: Oxford University Press.

Roseveare, D., M. Jørgensen and L. Goranson (2004) 'Product Market Competition and Economic Performance in Sweden', in *Economic Department Working Papers*, Paris: OECD.

Rothstein, B. (1988) 'State and Capital in Sweden: The Importance of Corporatist Arrangements', *Scandinavian Political Studies*, 11(3): 235–60.

Rothstein, B. (1998) *Just Institutions Matter: The Moral and Political Logic of the Universal Welfare State*, New York: Cambridge University Press.

Rothstein, B. (2000) 'Trust, Social Dilemmas, and Collective Memories', Goteborg, Sweden: Department of Political Science, mimeo.

Royo, S. (2000) *From Social Democracy To Neo-liberalism: The Consequences of Party Hegemony*, Basingstoke: Macmillan.

Ruggie, J.G. (1982) 'International Regimes, Transactions and Change: Embedded Liberalism in the Postwar Economic Order', in S.D. Krasner (ed.) *International Regimes*, Ithaca: Cornell University Press.

Ruin, O. (1981) 'Sweden in the 1970s: Police-Making [sic] Becomes More Difficult', in J. Richardson (ed.) *Policy Styles in Western Europe*, London: George Allen and Unwin.

Ruiz Caro, A. (2002) *El Proceso de Privatizaciones en el Perú durante el período 1991–2002*, Serie Gestión Pública (No. 22), Instituto Latinoamericano y del Caribe de Planificación Económica y Social – ILPES, Santiago de Chile: Naciones Unidas.

Ruiz Torres, G. (forthcoming) *Demokratie und Autoritarismus im Peru der 90er Jahre*, Frankfurt am Main: Zambon Verlag.

Rustow, D. (1955) *The Politics of Compromise*, Princeton: Princeton University Press.

Rupert, M. (2001) *Ideologies of Globalization*, London and New York: Routledge.

Rutland, P. (2002) 'The Politics of Regulatory Reforms in a Petro-state', Paper to the fifth annual conference 'Public Sector transition' 24–25 May, available at: <http://ourworld.compuserve.com/homepages/paulgor/screen_r.htm>.

Sabatier, P. (1988) 'An Advocacy-Coalition Model of Policy Change and the Role of Policy-Oriented Learning therein', *Policy Sciences*, 21: 129–68.

Sakwa, R. (2000) 'State and Society in Post-Communist Russia', in N. Robinson (ed.) *Institutions and Political Change in Russia*, London: Macmillan.

Sakwa, R. (2004) 'Russia and globalisation', in L. McCann (ed.) *Russian Transformations. Challenging the Global Narrative*, London and New York: RoutledgeCurzon.

Salmon, K. (1995) *The Modern Spanish Economy: Transformation and Integration into Europe* (2nd edn), London: Pinter.

Sam, T., B. Hai and T. Khue (2003) *Evaluating the Social Impact of Equitization in Vietnam*, Hochiminh City: ISSHO.

Sassen S. (1996) *Losing Control: The Decline of Sovereignty in a Age of Globalization*, New York: Columbia University Press.

Savoie, Donald J. (1999) *Governing from the Centre: The Concentration of Power in Canadian Politics*, Toronto: University of Toronto Press.

Scharpf, F.W. (1991) *Crisis and Choice in European Social Democracy*, Ithaca, NY: Cornell University Press.

Scharpf, F.W. and V.A. Schmidt (eds) (2000) *Welfare and Work in the Open Economy: Diverse Responses to Common Challenges*, Oxford: Oxford University Press.

Schellenberger, R. (1998) 'Neuseelands neues Wahlsystem gerät unter Druck [New Zealand's new electoral system under pressure]', *Berliner Zeitung*, 5 October.

Scholte, J.A. (2000) *Globalization: A Critical Introduction*, Basingstoke: Palgrave.

Slaughter, A.-M. (2004) *A New World Order*, Princeton, NJ: Princeton University Press.

Schmidt, G.D. (1999) 'Crónica de una Reelección', in F. Tuesta Soldevilla (ed.) *El Juego Político. Fujimori, la oposición y las reglas*, Lima: Friedrich Ebert Stiftung.

Schmidt, V.A. (2000) 'Values and Discourses in the Politics of Adjustment', in F.W. Scharpf and V.A. Schmidt (eds) *Welfare and Work in the Open Economy: From Vulnerability to Competitiveness*, Oxford: Oxford University Press.

Schmidt, V.A. (2002) *The Futures of European Capitalism*, Oxford: Oxford University Press.

Schneiderman, D. (1996) 'NAFTA's Takings Rule: American Constitutionalism Comes to Canada', *University of Toronto Law Journal*, 1(46): 90–118.

Schneiderman, D. (2000) 'Investment Rules and the New Constitutionalism', *Law and Social Inquiry*, 3(25): 14–35.

Scholten, I. (ed.) (1987) *Political Stability and Neo-Corporatism: Corporatist Integration and Societal Cleavages in Western Europe*, London: Sage.

Schröder/Blair (1999) 'Der Weg nach vome für Europas Sozialdemokraten', *Blätter für deutsche und internationale Politik*' 7/1999, 76–84.

Schumpeter, J.A. (1947) *Capitalism, Socialism, and Democracy* (2nd edn), New York/ London: Harper and Borthers.

Schwartz, H. (1991) 'Can Orthodox Stabilization and Adjustment Work? Lessons from New Zealand, 1984–1990', *International Organization*, 45(2): 221–56.

Segura, J. *et al.* (1989) *La industria española en la crisis 1978–84*, Madrid: Alianza Economía y Finanzas.

Serf, P. (1987) *Government by the Market? The Politics of Public Choice*, Basingstoke, UK: Macmillan.

Shadlen, K.C. (1999) 'Continuity amid Change: Democratization, Party Strategies and Economic Policy-Making in Mexico', *Government and Opposition*, 34(3): 397–419.

Share, D. (1989) *Dilemmas of Social Democracy – The Spanish Socialist Workers Party in the 1980s*, New York: Greenwood.

Sharp, A. (ed.) (1994) *Leap into the Dark: The Changing Role of the State in New Zealand since 1984*, Auckland: Auckland University Press.

Shevtsova, L. (2004) 'The Limits of Bureaucratic Authoritarianism', *Journal of Democracy*, 15(3): 67–77.

Shields, S. (2003) 'The "Charge of the Right Brigade": Transnational Social Forces in the Neo-liberal Configuration of Poland's Transition', *New Political Economy*, 8: 2.

Shiller, R. (2001) *Irrational Exuberance*, Princeton, NJ: Princeton University Press.

Shlapentokh, V. (2003) 'Russia's Acquiescence to Corruption Makes the State Machine Inept', *Communist and Post-Communist Studies*, 36: 19–31.

Shonfield, A. (1969) *Modern Capitalism*, New York: Oxford University Press.

Siebert, H. (1997) 'Labor Market Rigidities: At the Root of Unemployment in Europe", *Journal of Economic Perspectives*, 11 (Summer): 37–54.

Siebert, H. (1999) 'How can Europe Solve its Unemployment Problem?', Kiel, Germany: Kiel Institute Discussion Paper No. 342.

Simeon, R. (1987) 'Inside the Macdonald Commission', *Studies in Political Economy*, 2 (44): 167–79.

Sjöberg, T. (1999) 'Intervjun: Kjell-Olof Feldt [Interview: Kjell-Olof Feldt]', *Playboy Skandinavia*, 5: 37–44.

Smee, J. (2004) 'The IMF and Russia in the 1990s', Working Paper WP/04/155, Washington DC: International Monetary Fund.

Smiley, D. (1967) *The Canadian Political Nationality*, Toronto: Methuen.

Soederberg, S. (2002) 'An Historical Materialist Account of the Chilean Capital Control: Prototype Policy for Whom?', *Review of International Political Economy*, 9(3): 56–79.

soederberg, S. (2004) *The Politics of the New International Financial Architecture: Reimposing Neoliberal Domination in the Global South*, London: Zed Books / New York: Palgrave.

Soederberg, S. (2006) *Global Governance in Question: Empire, Class, and the New Common Sense in Managing North–South Relations*, London: Pluto Press / Ann Arbor: University of Michigan Press, forthcoming.

Sokol, M. (2001) 'Central and Eastern Europe a Decade After the Fall of State-socialism', *Regional Studies*, 35(7): 64–55.

Solnik, S. (1998) *Stealing the State: Control and Collapse in Soviet Institutions*, Cambridge, MA and London: Harvard University Press.

Soria, C. (2002) *Los Cuatro Suyos no termina en Arequipa. Las razones de una crisis y sus posibles salidas*, in *Perú Hoy. Toledo: A un año de Gobierno*, Lima: Desco.

Soskice, D. (1999) 'Divergent Production Regimes: Coordinated and Uncoordinated Market Economies in the 1980s and 1990s', in H. Kitschelt, P. Lange, G. Marks and J.D. Stephens (eds) *Continuity and Change in Contemporary Capitalism*, Cambridge, UK: Cambridge University Press, 101–35.

SOU (1987) *Utredning Om Reformerad Inkomst Beskattning [Proposition to Reform Income Taxation]*, Stockholm.

SOU (1989a) *Reformerad Företagsbeskattning [Reformed Corporate Taxation]*, Vol. 34. Stockholm: SOU.

SOU (1989b) *Reformerad Inkomstbeskattning [Reformed Income Taxation]*, Vol. 33. Stockholm: SOU.

SOU (1989c) *Reformerad Mervärdesskatte [Reformed Vat]*, Vol. 35. Stockholm: SOU.

Stallings, B. (1978) *Class Conflict and Economic Development in Chile, 1958–1973*, Stanford, CA: Stanford University Press.

Stallings, B. (2001) 'Las Reformas Estructurales y el Desempeño Socioeconomico', in R. Ffrench-Davis and B. Stallings (eds) *Reformas, Crecimiento y Políticas Sociales en Chile desde 1973*, Santiago: Eddiciones LOM.

Steinmo, S. (1988) 'Socialism vs. Social Democracy', *Politics & Society*, 9(4): 34–51.

Steinmo, S. (1989) 'Political Institutions and Tax Policy in the United States, Sweden and Britain', *World Politics*, XLI (4): 500–35.

Steinmo, S. (1993) *Taxation and Democracy: Swedish, British and American Approaches to Financing the Modern State*, New Haven: Yale University Press.

Steinmo, S. (1994) 'An End to Redistribution? Tax Reform and the Globalization of the World Economy', *Challenge* (Nov./Dec.): 1–9.

Steinmo, S. (2002) 'Globalization and Taxation: Challenges to the Swedish Welfare State', *Comparative Political Studies*, 35(7): 839–62.

Stiglitz, J. (2002) *Globalization and its Discontents*, New York: Norton & Norton.

Stone, D. (1996) *Capturing the Political Imagination: Think Tanks and the Policy Process*, London: Frank Cass.

Story, D. (1986) *The Mexican Ruling Party: Stability and Authority*, New York: Praeger Publishers.

Strange, S. (1986) *Casino Capitalism*, Oxford: Blackwell.

Strange, S. (1996) *The Retreat of the State: Diffusion of Power in the World Economy*, Cambridge: Cambridge University Press.

Strange, S. (1998) 'The New World Order of Debt', *New Left Review*, 1(230): 91–114.

Streeck, W. (1993) 'The Rise and Decline of Neo-corporatism', in U. Lloyd, B. Eichengreen and W. Dickens (eds) *Labor and an Integrating Europe*, Washington, DC: 80–99.

Streeck, W. (1996) 'Le Capitalisme Allemande: Existe-t-il? Peut-il Survivre?', in C. Crouch and W. Streeck (eds) *Les capitalismes en Europe*, Paris: La Découverte, 33–55.

Streeck, W. (1998) 'The Internationalization of Industrial Relations in Europe: Prospects and Problems', MPIfG Discussion Paper 98/2, Köln: MPIfG.

Streeck, W. and K. Yamamura (2002) *The Origins of Nonliberal Capitalism: Germany and Japan in Comparison*, Ithaca, NY: Cornell University Press.

Sutela, P. (1998) 'The Role of Banks in Financing Russian Economic Growth', *Post-Soviet Geography and Economics*, 39(2): 96–124.

Sussman, G. and L. Galizio (2003) 'The Global Reproduction of American Politics', *Political Communication* 20: 309–28.

Svallfors, S. (1989) *Vem Älskar Välfärdsstaten?: Attityder, Organiserade Intressen Och Svensk Välfärdspolitik [Who Loves the Welfare State? Attitudes, Organized Interests and Swedish Welfare Policy]*, Arkiv Avhandlingsserie 30, Lund: Arkiv.

Svallfors, S. (1997) *The Middle Class and Welfare State Retrenchment: Attitudes toward Swedish Welfare Policies*, Paper presented at Third Conference of the European Sociological Association, at the University of Essex, August 27–30, 1997.

Swank, D. and S. Steinmo (2002), 'The New Political Economy of Taxation in Advanced Capitalist Democracies', *American Journal of Political Science*, 46(3): 477–89.

Swenson, P.A. (2002) *Capitalists against Markets: The Making of Labor Markets and Welfare States in the United States and Sweden*, Oxford/New York: Oxford University Press.

von Sydow, B. and Riksbankens jubileumsfond (1997) *Parlamentarismen I Sverige: Utveckling Och Utformning Till 1945*, Hedemora: Gidlund i samarbete med Riksbankens jubileumsfond.

Tanaka, M. (1998) *Los Espejismos de la Democracia. El colapso del sistema de partidos en el Perú, 1980–1995, en perspectiva comparada*, Lima: Indico.

Taylor, L. (1998) *Citizenship, Participation and Democracy: Changing Dynamics in Chile and Argentina*, London: Macmillan Press.

Taylor, M. (2002) 'An Historical Materialist Critique of Neoliberalism in Chile', *Historical Materialism*, 10(2): 45–67.

Taylor, M. (2003) 'The Reformulation of Social Policy in Chile, 1973–2001: Questioning a Neoliberal Model', *Global Social Policy*, 3(1): 24–46.

Taylor, M. (2004) 'Labour Reform and the Contradiction of the "Growth with Equity" in Chile, 1990–2001', *Latin American Perspectives*, 34(4): 76–93.

Teeple, G. (1995) *Globalisation and the Decline of Social Reform*, Toronto: Garamond Press.

Thakur, S., M. Keen, B. Hovath and V. Cerra (2003), *Sweden's Welfare State: Can the Bumblebee Keep Flying?*, New York: International Monetary Fund.

Thelen, K. (2001) 'Varieties of Labor Politics in the Developed Democracies', in P.A. Hall and D. Soskice (eds) *Varieties of Capitalism: The Institutional Foundations of Comparative Advantage*, Oxford: Oxford University Press.

Thoburn, J., Nguyen Thi Thanh Ha and Nguyen Thi Hoa (2002) *Globalization and the Textile Industry of Vietnam: Impacts on Firms and Workers*, Unpublished manuscript, Department for International Development, Hanoi.

Threlfall, M. (2000) 'Introduction: the Challenge of Consensus Politics in Spain', in M. Threlfall (ed.) *Consensus Politics in Spain: Insider Perspectives*, Intellect: Bristol.

Thurow, L. (1992) *Head to Head: The Coming Economic Battle Among Japan, Europe and America*, New York: William Morrow and Company.

Torche, A. (2000) 'Pobreza, Necesidades Básicas y Desigualidad: Tres Objetivos Par una Sola Política Social', in F. Larraín and R. Vergara (eds) *La Transformación Económica de Chile*, Santiago: Centro de Estudios Públicos.

Trebilcock, Michael J. (2001) 'The Supreme Court and Strengthening the Conditions for Effective Competition in the Canadian Economy', *Canadian Bar Review*, 80: 542–604.

Trenin, D. (2002) *The End of Eurasia*, Washington, DC and Moscow: Carnegie Endowment for International Peace.

Turner, M. and Hulme D. (1997) *Governance, Administration and Development: Making the State Work*, Basingstoke: Macmillan.

Tsygankov, P. and A. Tsygankov (2004) 'Dilemmas and Promises of Russian Liberalism', *Communist and Post-Communist Studies*, 37(1): 53–70.

Underhill, G.R.D. (1997) 'Private Markets and Public Responsibility in a Global System: Conflict and Co-operation in Transnational Banking and Securities Regulation', in Geoffrey R.D. Underhill (ed.) *The New World Order in International Finance*, New York: St Martin's Press.

United States, Department of the Treasury (1991) *Modernizing the Financial System: Recommendations for Safer, More Competitive Banks*, Washington, DC: United States Government Printing Office.

United States Senate Hearings (19 April 1994) *New Zealand's Economy*.

Valdes, J. (1995) *Pinochet's Economists: The Chicago School in Chile*, Cambridge: Cambridge University Press.

Van der Pijl, K. (1998) *Transnational Classes and International Relations*, London: Routledge.

Van der Pijl, K. (2001a) 'From Gorbachev to Kosovo. Atlantic rivalries and the re-incorporation of eastern Europe', *Review of International Political Economy*, 8(2): 275–310.

Van der Pijl, K. (2001b) 'International Relations and Capitalist Discipline', in R. Albritton, M. Itoh, R. Westra and A. Zuege (eds) *Phases of Capitalist Development*, Basingstoke: Palgrave.

de Vylder, S. and A. Fforde (1988) *Vietnam: An Economy in Transition*, Stockholm: Swedish International Development Authority.

VCIOM 1995, Presidential Ratings. Downloaded on 4 November 2004, available at: <http://www.cs.indiana.edu/~dmiguse/Russian/polls.html>.

Vegh, G. (1996) 'The Characterization of Barriers to Interprovincial Trade Under the Canadian Constitution', *Osgoode Hall Law Journal*, 34: 359–75.

Veltmeyer, H., J. Petras and S. Vieux (1996) *Neoliberalism and Class Conflict in Latin America: A Comparative Perspective on the Political Economy of Structural Adjustment*, London: Macmillan.

Viñals, J. *et al.* (1990) 'Spain and the "EEC cum 1992" Shock', in C. Bliss and J. de Maceda (eds) *Unity with Diversity in the European Economy*, Cambridge: Cambridge University Press.

Vogel, S. (1996) *Freer Markets, More Rules: Regulatory Reform in Advanced Industrial Countries*, Ithaca, NY: Cornell University Press.

Vreeland, J.R. (2003) *The IMF and Economic Development*, Cambridge, UK: Cambridge University Press.

Wade, R. (1990) *Governing the Market: Economic Theory and the Role of Government in East Asian Industrialisation*, Princeton, NJ: Princeton University Press.

Walker, R. (1998) 'The Americanisation of British Welfare: a Case Study of Policy Transfer', *Focus*, 19(3): 32–40.

Weafer, C. (2004) 'Economic Reforms: With Actions or Slogans?' *Russian Investment Review*, 1 November.

Wendt, A. (1999) *Social Theory of International Politics*, Cambridge: Cambridge University Press.

Whittle, G. (2000) 'Russian Leader Faces £3bn Questions', *The Times*, 25 July.

Wiener, F.R.A. (1998) *El Reeleccionista*, Lima: Indicos.

Williamson, J. (ed.) (1990) *Latin American Adjustment: How much has Happened?*, Washington, DC: Institute for International Economics.

Williamson, J. (1993) 'Democracy and the "Washington Consensus"', *World Development*, 21(8): 1329–36.

Williamson, J. (2000) 'What Should the World Bank Think about the Washington Consensus?', *World Bank Research Observer*, 15(2) (August): 251–64.

Wolf, M. (2004) 'False Rumours of a Death in the South', *Financial Times*, 16 November.

Wolfe, R. (1996) 'Global Trade as a Single Undertaking: the Role of Ministers in the WTO', *International Journal*, 4(44): 99–120.

Woodruff, D. (2000) 'Rules for Followers: Institutional Theory and the New Politics of Economic Backwards in Russia', *Politics and Society*, 28(4): 89–101.

World Bank (1998) *Financial Vulnerability, Spillover Effects, and Contagion: Lessons from the Asian Crises for Latin America-World Bank Latin American and Caribbean Studies: Viewpoints*, Washington, DC: World Bank.

World Bank (1999) Transition Newsletter, July/August.

World Bank (2000) *Vietnam 2010: Entering the 21st Century*, Joint Report of World Bank, Asian Development Bank and United Nations Development Program, Washington DC: World Bank.

World Bank (2002a) *Transition: Ten Years*, Washington DC: World Bank.

World Bank (2002b) *Partnership for Development to 2010*, Washington DC: World Bank.

World Bank (2002c) *Modernizing the Management of Public Debt and SOE Fiscal Risks: Assessment for Technical Assistance and System Needs*, unpublished manuscript.

World Bank (2002d) *Vietnam Development Report*, Washington DC: World Bank.

World Bank (2003) *Global Development Finance: Striving for Stability in Development Finance*, Washington, DC: World Bank.

World Trade Organisation (1999a) *An Introduction to the GATS*, Geneva: World Trade Organisation.

World Trade Organisation (1999b) *The GATS: Objectives, Coverage and Disciplines*, Geneva: World Trade Organisation.

World Trade Organisation (1999c) *The Legal Texts: The Results of the Uruguay Round of Multilateral Trade Negotiations*, Cambridge: Cambridge University Press.

Wright, A. (1977) *The Spanish Economy 1959–76*, London: Macmillan.

Xia, S.Z. (1998) *Administration*, Zhongshan: Zhongshan University Press.

Yavlinsky, G. (1998) 'Russia's Phoney Capitalism', *Foreign Affairs*, 77(3): 67–79.

Zohnlhoefer, R. (2001) 'Rückzug des Staates auf den Kern seiner Aufgaben? Eine Analyse der Wirtschaftspolitik in der Bundesrepublik Deutschland seit 1982', in M.G. Schmidt (ed.) *Wohlfahrtsstaatliche Politik: Institutionen, Politischer Prozess und Leistungsprofil*, Opladen: Leske + Budrich: 227–61.

Zysman, J. (1983) *Governments, Markets, and Growth: Financial Systems and the Politics of Industrial Change*, Ithaca: Cornell University Press.

Index